ENGLISH G

access 1

FÖRDERN & FORDERN

Kopiervorlagen auf 3 Levels
mit Lösungen und Lernlandkarten

mit **Audio-CD**

Cornelsen

Vorwort

Liebe Lehrerinnen und Lehrer,

die Schullandschaft in Deutschland ist seit einigen Jahren geprägt von weitreichenden Veränderungen. Neue Schulformen sind entstanden, Lehrpläne wurden methodisch-didaktisch weiterentwickelt, in der Lehrerschaft hat sich ein Bewusstsein entwickelt, dass es Heterogenität in jeder Lerngruppe gibt, unabhängig davon, um welche Schulform es sich handelt.

Auch für Sie als Lehrerin oder Lehrer am Gymnasium bedeutet dies, dass Ihre Schülerinnen und Schüler mit unterschiedlichen Voraussetzungen von den Grundschulen auf die weiterführende Schule kommen. Auch am Gymnasium gibt es Schülerinnen und Schüler mit unterschiedlichen Begabungsprofilen in einer Klasse. Um Schülerinnen und Schüler mit weniger Vorwissen zu fördern und lernschnellere Schülerinnen und Schüler gleichzeitig zu fordern, ist neben gezielter Unterstützung und Hilfe vonseiten der Lehrkräfte auch ein differenzierteres Aufgaben- und Übungsangebot gefragt. Nur so können Lernerfolgserlebnisse erzielt werden, die motivieren.

Das neue Englischlehrwerk *English G Access* reagiert auf diese Situation am Gymnasium mit neuen differenzierenden Lernangeboten und führt diese Innovation auch in Begleitmedien fort.

Mit dem neuen *Fördern & Fordern*-Ordner möchten wir Sie dabei unterstützen, die individuellen Lernprozesse Ihrer Schülerinnen und Schüler zu begleiten. Hier finden Sie zu allen zentralen Lernfeldern des Schülerbuchs eine Fülle an Kopiervorlagen mit passgenauem Übungsmaterial auf drei verschiedenen Anforderungsniveaus, die Sie sowohl im binnendifferenzierenden (Förder-)Unterricht als auch zur Vor- bzw. Nachbereitung von Klassenarbeiten einsetzen können.

Was zeichnet das Übungsmaterial in *Fördern & Fordern* aus?

Das Novum des *Fördern & Fordern*-Ordners ist seine enge Verzahnung mit dem Schülerbuch (ISBN: 978-3-06-032543-6) und weiteren zentralen Begleitmedien wie der Lehrerfassung Schülerbuch (ISBN: 978-3-06-033070-6), den Handreichungen für den Unterricht (ISBN: 978-3-06-033048-5) und den Vorschlägen für die Leistungsmessung (ISBN: 978-3-06-033050-8).
Dieser Ansatz erleichtert Ihnen die Unterrichtsvorbereitung und ermöglicht eine optimale Begleitung Ihrer Schülerinnen und Schüler, sei es durch die Auswahl von differenzierendem Übungsmaterial im (Förder-)Unterricht oder bei der Vor- und/oder Nachbereitung von Klassenarbeiten.

Sie finden Verweise zu ***Fördern & Fordern***

- in den Handreichungen für den Unterricht in der Randspalte (Verweise zu Einsatzszenarien zur Binnendifferenzierung).
- in der Lehrerfassung des SB oben in der Kopfzeile, abgekürzt durch „FöFo".
- in den Vorschlägen zur Leistungsmessung. Hier erhalten Sie zu jeder Aufgabe einen Verweis, welches Material aus *Fördern & Fordern* begleitend eingesetzt werden kann. Die Verschränkung der Vorschläge zur Leistungsmessung mit Fördern & Fordern ermöglicht damit eine optimale Vor- und/oder Nachbereitung von Klassenarbeiten.
- Darüber hinaus enthält das Inhaltsverzeichnis dieses Ordners Seitenangaben, die auf das SB zurückverweisen.

Was beinhaltet der Ordner?

Um den Umgang mit *Fördern & Fordern* für Sie leicht handhabbar zu gestalten, ist das Material als Ordner mit Inhaltsverzeichnis und Register ausgestattet. Damit ist der schnelle Zugriff auf das jeweils relevante Übungsmaterial möglich. Eine Übersicht über alle Lernfelder pro SB-Unit, dem eigentlichen Übungspool vorangestellt, ermöglicht eine schnelle Orientierung.

Das vorliegende Material selbst umfasst vier Bestandteile:

1. Den Kern dieses Ordners bilden 300 Seiten Arbeitsblätter auf drei unterschiedlichen Anforderungsniveaus mit passgenauen Übungen zu allen Lernfeldern der Units unter Berücksichtigung aller Kompetenzen.
   An passenden Stellen finden sich Arbeitsblätter mit selbstdifferenzierenden Aufgabenstellungen und Arbeitsblätter, die die Durchführung kooperativer Lernformen ermöglichen.
2. Die in die Lernfelder der Units einführenden **Lernlandkarten** ermöglichen die Selbsteinschätzung für Schülerinnen und Schüler.
3. Der Ordner enthält zudem eine eingeklebte **Audio-CD** zu Aufgaben, mit denen Kompetenzen im Bereich Hörverstehen trainiert werden können. Die Tondateien werden zusätzlich für die S online als MP3-Files angeboten.
4. Der Lösungsanhang enthält die **Lösungen** und **Hörtext-Transkripte** der *Fördern & Fordern*-Tonaufnahmen sowie methodisch-didaktische Hinweise zu Materialien, die methodisch besonders innovativ konzipiert wurden.

Fördern & Fordern elektronisch

Neben diesem Ordner bieten die Cornelsen Schulverlage *Fördern & Fordern* auch als digitale Fassung im Unterrichtsmanager zu *English G Access Band 1* an (ISBN Basispaket (Download): 978-3-06-033529-9; Premiumpaket (Download): 978-3-06-033624-1; Premiumpaket (DVD) 978-3-06-033625-8). Sämtliche Kopiervorlagen, Lösungen und Transkripte sind dort als editierbare Word-Dokumente enthalten, damit sie individuell an die Bedürfnisse der Schülerinnen und Schüler anzupassen sind. Natürlich beinhaltet die digitale Variante ebenfalls die Tondateien.

Wie Sie das Material aus Fördern & Fordern einsetzen können:

Pro Unit finden Sie, dem Aufgabenpool von *Fördern & Fordern* vorangestellt, eine übersichtliche Lernlandkarte, die die jeweiligen Lernfelder der Unit vorstellt. Neben der inhaltlichen Orientierung für Sie und Ihre Schülerinnen und Schüler dient die Lernlandkarte in Ihren Lerngruppen zugleich auch als Selbsteinschätzungsinstrument. Die Schülerinnen und Schüler nehmen auf dieser Lernlandkarte die individuelle Einschätzung ihres Kompetenzstandes in den zentralen Lernfeldern vor. Der Umgang mit den Lernlandkarten soll die Lernenden damit auch für die eigene Vorbereitung sensibilisieren.
Ausgehend von dieser Einschätzung, nach Bedarf auch in Absprache mit Ihnen als Lehrkraft, können Ihre Schülerinnen und Schüler anschließend passgenaue Arbeitsblätter auf verschiedenen Anforderungsniveaus zu den einzelnen Themen bearbeiten. Leistungsschwächere Schülerinnen und Schüler erhalten die Möglichkeit zur Aufarbeitung individueller Schwächen und beugen damit rechtzeitig der Entstehung von größeren Wissensdefiziten vor. Leistungsstärkere Schülerinnen und Schüler können Sie mit motivierenden lernzielgleichen Aufgaben auf anspruchsvollerem Niveau fordern.

Die Aufgaben im Übungspool decken sämtliche kommunikative, methodische und sprachliche Kompetenzen ab, die in English G Access, Band 1 eingeführt werden: *Listening*, *Speaking*, *Reading*, *Writing* und *Mediation* sowie *Language* (*Grammar*, *Words* und *Pronunciation*). Die aus dem Schülerbuch bekannten Formen der Binnendifferenzierung (Differenzierung nach Leistung, nach Neigung, nach Methode, nach Lerntempo) finden hier Berücksichtigung und unterstützen Sie als Lehrerin oder Lehrer dabei, die Lernwege Ihrer Schülerinnen und Schüler unter Berücksichtigung zielgleicher Ergebnisse individuell zu begleiten.

Die Englischredaktion und die Autorinnen und Autoren von *Fördern & Fordern* wünschen Ihnen viel Freude und Erfolg beim Einsatz der Materialien!

Track	Unit	Titel	Einzellaufzeit
1		Copyright Cornelsen Schulverlage GmbH Berlin	0.49
2	HWG	Meet my friend Philip	0.50
3	HWG	Where to go on a sunny day in Plymouth	1.16
4	HWG	Philip and Mia at the zoo	2.20
5	HWG	Poppy packs her bag	1.14
6	Unit 1	A workshop	2.12
7	Unit 1	At what time?	2.29
8	Unit 1	In the new class	0.56
9	Unit 1	In the new class	1.30
10	Unit 1	Feelings	2.01
11	Unit 1	At the airport	1.10
12	Unit 2	Would you like some tea?	2.53
13	Unit 2	Silky the seal	0.56
14	Unit 2	Who is this?	0.51
15	Unit 2	The odd one out	1.29
16	Unit 2	The Bakers' crazy house	1.33
17	Unit 3	Join my club	2.32
18	Unit 3	On air – part 1	1.30
19	Unit 3	On air – part 2	1.01
20	Unit 3	On air – part 3	1.44
21	Unit 4	Different weekends	1.31
22	Unit 4	Tony the traveller	2.58
23	Unit 5	At Cawsand Beach	4.23
24	Unit 5	In Plymouth Harbour	2.13
25	Unit 5	At Dartmoor Zoo	5.07

Gesamtlaufzeit der CD: 47'31''

English G Access I Band 1

Fördern & Fordern

Im Auftrag des Verlages herausgegeben von
Jörg Rademacher, Mannheim

Erarbeitet von
Dr. Claudia Börger, Stuhr
Michael Dills, Berlin
Senta Friedrich, Tamm
Timo Keller, Kornwestheim
Anne Tebben, Mannheim

In Zusammenarbeit mit der Englischredaktion
Dr. Christiane Kallenbach (Projektleitung),
Ulrike Berendt, Christiane Bonk, Gwendolyn Düwel

Beratende Mitwirkung
Dr. Claudia Börger, Stuhr (Konzeption)
Birgit Trefz, Backnang (Material)

Illustrationen
Christian Bartz, Berlin; Roland Beier, Berlin;
Judy Brown, Sutton; Tobias Dahmen, Utrecht/NL;
Elke Hanisch, Köln; Jane Smith, London

Tonaufnahmen
Clarity Studio Berlin

Umschlaggestaltung
kleiner & bold, Berlin

Layout und technische Umsetzung
zweiband.media, Berlin

www.cornelsen.de
www.englishg.de/access

1. Auflage, 1. Druck 2014

Druck: Salzland Druck, Staßfurt

ISBN 978-3-06-033045-4

Inhalt gedruckt auf säurefreiem Papier aus nachhaltiger Forstwirtschaft.

Bildquellen

Alamy, Abingdon (HWG.2 alle Bild 4: International Photobank; HWG.5 S. 3 alle Robbe: Krisken; 1.6 S. 1 Level 1 und Level 2 Bild 5 und Level 3 2. v. li.: Design Pics Inc., Level 1 und Level 2 Bild 1 und Level 3 re.: WoodyStock; 3.1 S. 1 Level 1 und Level 2 Hockey (u. Lösungen S. 41–42 li.): Enigma, Judo (u. Lösungen S. 41–42 li.): Andrzej Gorzkowski; 4.1 S. 1 Level 1 Bild 4: ACE STOCK LIMITED, Bild 1: Dave Porter; 4.2 S. 1 alle Strand: Robert Harding World Imagery; 4.6 S. 1 alle: digitalunderwater.com; 4.7 alle Mitte: 2d Alan King, re.: Classic Image); **Trevor Burrows Photography Ltd**, Plymouth (HWG.2 alle Bild 3, 8, 10; 3.7 Bild 7); **Copyright © 2012 www.all-free-download.com** (1.3 S. 1 Level 1); Corbis, Düsseldorf (4.1 S. 1 Level 1 Bild 3: Loop Images/LOOP IMAGES/Jon Bower); **Getty**, München (5.6 S. 1 Level 1: Getty Images); **iStockphoto**, Calgary (HGW.5 S. 1 alle Ratte: Pakhnyushchyy, Ameise: Antagain; S. 3 alle Affen: Madzia71; HWG.7 S. 1 alle Stift (u. Lösungen S. 9–10 re.): Ivantsov, Pullover (u. Lösungen S. 9–10 re.): studyoritim, Federtasche (u. Lösungen S. 9–10 re.): hatman12; 1.5 S. 2 Level 2 und Level 3: monkeybusinessimages; 1.6 S. 1 Level 1 und Level 2 Bild 4 und Level 3 Mitte: jacomstephens, Level 1 und Level 2 Bild 3 und Level 3 2. v. re.: kali9, Level 1 und Level 2 Bild 2 und Level 3 li.: TatyanaGl; 1.9 S. 1 alle: narvikk; 3.1 S. 1 Level 1 und Level 2 Orchester (u. Lösungen S. 41–42 li.): JoseGirarte, Cricket (u. Lösungen S. 41–42 li.): hadynyah; S. 4 Level 3 Hund: GlobalP, Elefant: xLabrador, Skier: walik; 4.1 S. 1 Level 1 Bild 5: gerenme; 4.2 S. 1 alle Westminster Abbey: peterspiro; 4.3 S. 2 alle Rad: A_nik, Schach: acilo, Skier: walik, Schokolade: nilsz; 5.1 S. 2 alle: oneclearvision; 5.2 S. 3 Level 3 Warnsignal: KristinaVelickovic; 5.4 S. 1 alle: Miiicha; 5.5 S. 1 alle Gorillas: carolgaranda; S. 2 Level 2 und Level 3 Erdmännchen: pjmalsbury; 5.6 S. 1 Level 2 und Level 3: MattStansfield); **Picture Alliance**, Frankfurt/Main (4.7 alle li.: akg-images); **Shutterstock**, New York (HWG.2 alle Bild 5: JMiks, Bild 2: jaroslava V, Bild 1: Eric Isselee, Bild 9: prapass, Bild 6: M. Unal Ozem, Bild 11: aquariagirl 1970, Bild 7: Andrew Scherbackov; HWG.5 S. 1 alle Wal: Mike Price, Schlange: Twin Design, Schwein: Tsekhmister, Pferd: mariait, Vogel: Sari ONeal, Frosch: Tsekhmister, Elefant: Four Oaks, Löwe, Katze, Affe, Bär: Eric Isselee, Schmetterling: Ambient Ideas, Hund: DoLevel 1tya Mathe, Meerschwein: Vasily Kovalev, Hase: Stefan Petru Andronache, Giraffe: jaroslava V; S. 3 alle Elefant: Regien Paassen, Löwe: Zdenek Krchak, Frosch: Gucio_55, Giraffe: Dean Pennala; HWG.6 S. 1 alle Affe, Pferd, Frosch, Storch: Eric Isselee, Tiger: BMCL, Schwein: Tsekhmister; S. 2 Level 3 Zahn: Yulia Glam, Ohr, Mund, Nase, Auge: nikolae, Haare: Lonely; HWG.7 alle Banane (u. Lösungen S. 9–10 re.): eye-blink, Kleber: Alexandr Makarov, Radierer (u. Lösungen S. 9–10 re.): Picsfive, Bücher (u. Lösungen S. 9–10 re.): Hong Vo, Level 2 und Level 3 Apfel: Maks Narodenko;1.2 S. 2 alle: vector illustration; 1.5 S. 2 Level 1 und Level 2 Torte: Elena Elisseeva; 1.7 alle: Monkey Business Images; 2.1 Lösungen S. 27–28 re. Haltestelle: Stephen Rees; 3.1 S. 1 Level 1 und Level 2 Fußball (u. Lösungen S. 41–42 li.): Fotokostic; S. 4 alle Tischtennis: Silhouette Lover, Badmintonschläger: Alexander Dashewsky, Level 1 und Level 2 Inline Skates: Shapiro Svetlana, Pferd: Olga_i, Level 3 Kartoffeln: Nattika, Pizza: Africa Studio, Äpfel: Valentyn Volkov; 3.3 alle Aktivitäten: Virinaflora; 3.4 S. 1 Level 3 Mann: rui vale sousa, Junge: Jorg Hackemann, Mädchen: theerasakj; 3.5 S. 2 Level 1 und Level 2 Kind: Alan Uster, Frosch: Sarawut Padungkwan, Fragezeichen: HitToon.Com, Level 3: vector illustration; 3.7 Level 2 Bild 2: Zoltan Fabian, Bild 4: SoRad, Bild 5: primopiano, Bild 8: Pete Spiro, Bild 1: Globe Turner; 4.1 S. 1 Level 1 Bild 2: ian woolcock; 4.2 S. 1 alle Big Ben: Claudio Divizia, Dartmoor: DavidYoung, Thames: Georgi Djadjarov, Tower Bridge: Apurva Madia; 4.3 S. 2 alle Rucksack: Podfoto, Volleyball: Aptyp_koK, Tennis: Bragin Alexey, TV: Ioan Panaite, Buch: Amero, Bananen: Tatiana Popova, Toast: RusGri, Äpfel: Valentyn Volkov, Tischtennis: Silhouette Lover, Eimer: Timmary; 4.6 S. 2 alle: badztua; 5.2 S. 3 Level 3 Biene: stockshoppe; 5.5 S. 1 alle Bären: Lustra, Tiger: Rat007, Papagei: Marcin Sylwia Ciesielski; S. 2 alle Jaguar: Pal Teravagimov, Level 1 Waschbär: Xavier MARCHANT, Level 1 und Level 2 Fuchs: JacintaPhoto, Level 3 Strauß: Nina B)

Illustrationen

Christian Bartz, Berlin (HWG.1; HWG.2 S. 1 Level 3; HWG.4 Level 1; HWG.5 S. 2 alle (u. Lösungen S. 5–6 re.); S. 3 alle Spiel; HWG.8 Level 1 und Level 2 oben; HWG.9 S. 1 Level 1 oben, Level 2; S. 2 alle; 1.1 alle; 1.2 S. 1 alle; 1.4 S. 1 alle oben; 1.5 S. 1 alle; S. 2 alle; S. 3 alle (u. Lösungen S. 21–22 re.); 1.6 S. 1 alle; S. 2 alle; 1.7 alle; 1.8 alle; 2.1 S. 1 alle; 2.2 S. 1 alle; 2.3 S. 1 alle; 2.4 alle; 2.5 Text; 2.7 alle; 2.8 alle; 2.9 alle; 3.1 S. 1 Level 3; S. 2 alle; S. 4 li.; 3.2 S. 1 Level 1; 3.5 S. 1 Level 1 und Level 2; 3.6 alle; 3.7 Level 1 und Level 3 (u. Lösungen S. 49– 50 re.), Level 2 Bild 3 und 6; 3.8 Level 1 und Level 2; 3.9 S. 2 alle; 3.10 alle; 4.1 S. 2 alle; 4.2 S. 1 alle (u. Lösungen S. 57–58 re. u. 59–60 li.); 4.3 S. 1 alle; 4.4 Level 1 und Level 2, Level 3; 4.5 S. 1 alle; S. 2 alle oben; 4.8 Text; 5.2 S. 2 alle; 5.3 S. 1 alle; S. 2 alle; 5.5 S. 3 alle; 5.7 alle); **Roland Beier**, Berlin (HWG.5 S. 3 Level 1 und Level 2 Tiere; 2.6 koop S. 2); **Judy Brown**, Sutton (HWG.6 S. 2 Level 1 (u. Lösungen S. 7–8 re.), Level 2 (u. Lösungen S. 9–10 li.), Level 3 (u. Lösungen S. 9–10 li.); HWG.8 alle unten; HWG.9 S. 1 Level 1 unten (u. Lösungen S. 11–12 re.); 3.2 S. 1 Level 2 und Level 3; S. 2 alle; 3.4 S. 2 alle (u. Lösungen S. 45–46 re., 47–48 re. u. li.); **Tobias Dahmen**, Utrecht, Niederlande, www.tobidahmen.de (HWG.5 S. 1 alle; 1.2 S. 2 alle; 1.4 S. 1 Level 1 und Level 2 unten; S. 2 Level 2; 1.5 S. 2 Level 3; 1.9 alle; 1.10; 2.1 S. 2 alle; 2.2 S. 2 alle; 2.3 S. 2 Level 1; 3.1 S. 4 Level 1 und Level 2 re.; 3.3 alle; 4.3 S. 2 Level 1 und Level 2; 4.5 S. 2 alle unten; 5.3 S. 2 Level 3); **Elke Hanisch**, Köln (2.6 koop. S. 1); **Jane Smith**, London (HWG.3 alle)

Titelbild

Trevor Burrows Photography Ltd, Plymouth

Here we go!

Meine Lernlandkarte für Here we go!

Name: ____________________ Klasse: __________

Wie gut bist du in den Lernfeldern dieser Unit?
Schätze dich darin ein und male die entsprechende Anzahl an Kreisen auf der Ampel aus.
So findest du dein Übungsblatt.

Das lief nicht gut, ich muss mehr üben.	Das war OK, aber ich könnte besser werden.	Das habe ich gut geschafft.

Setze ein Häkchen, wenn du fertig bist. ✓

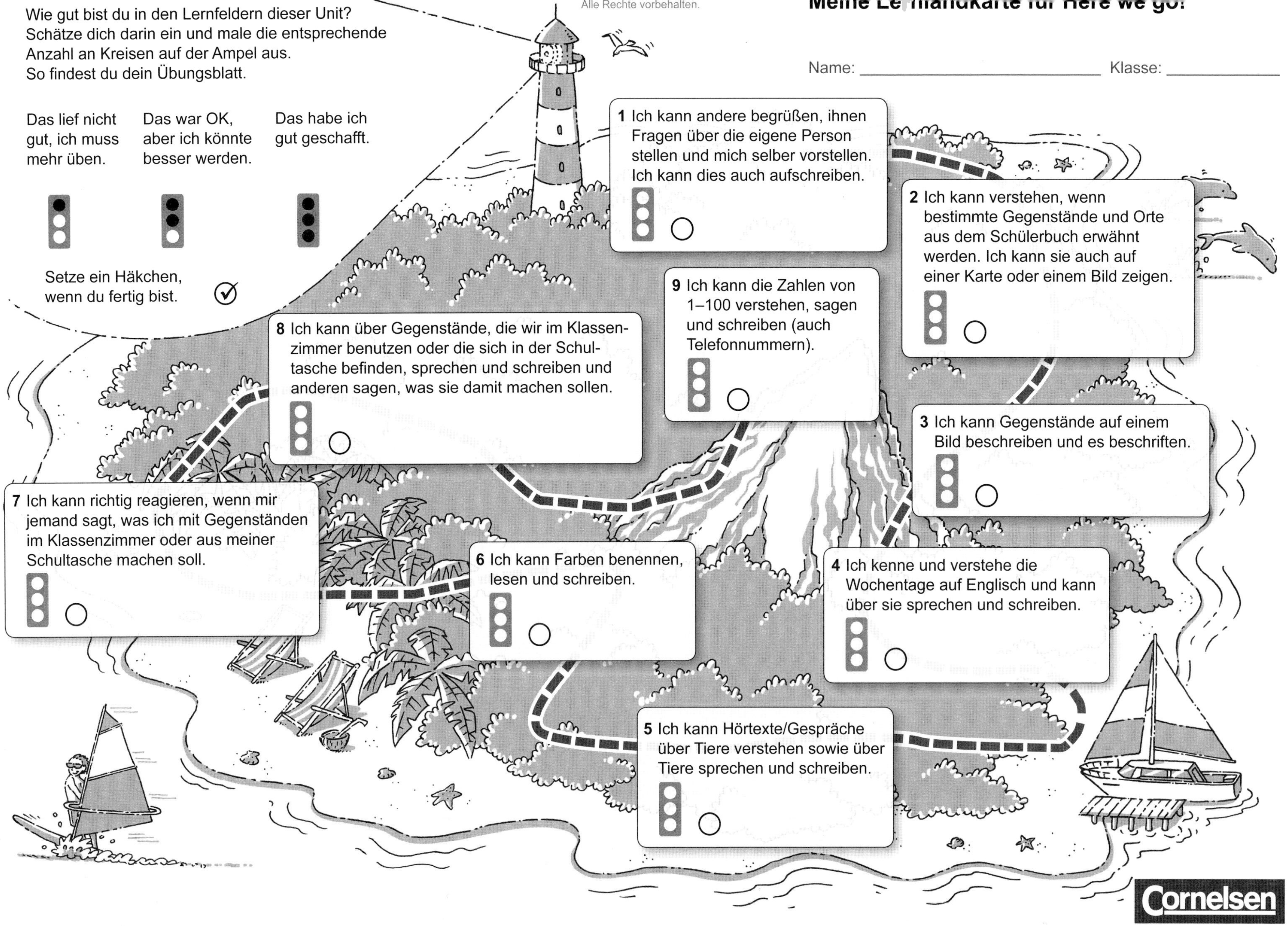

1 Ich kann andere begrüßen, ihnen Fragen über die eigene Person stellen und mich selber vorstellen. Ich kann dies auch aufschreiben.

2 Ich kann verstehen, wenn bestimmte Gegenstände und Orte aus dem Schülerbuch erwähnt werden. Ich kann sie auch auf einer Karte oder einem Bild zeigen.

3 Ich kann Gegenstände auf einem Bild beschreiben und es beschriften.

4 Ich kenne und verstehe die Wochentage auf Englisch und kann über sie sprechen und schreiben.

5 Ich kann Hörtexte/Gespräche über Tiere verstehen sowie über Tiere sprechen und schreiben.

6 Ich kann Farben benennen, lesen und schreiben.

7 Ich kann richtig reagieren, wenn mir jemand sagt, was ich mit Gegenständen im Klassenzimmer oder aus meiner Schultasche machen soll.

8 Ich kann über Gegenstände, die wir im Klassenzimmer benutzen oder die sich in der Schultasche befinden, sprechen und schreiben und anderen sagen, was sie damit machen sollen.

9 Ich kann die Zahlen von 1–100 verstehen, sagen und schreiben (auch Telefonnummern).

Cornelsen

Ich kann andere begrüßen, ihnen Fragen über die eigene Person stellen und mich selber vorstellen.
Ich kann dies auch aufschreiben.

1 Meet my friend Philip

a) FF 02 **Mia and Sophie meet Mia's friend Philip. Listen to Mia, Sophie and Philip.**

b) FF 02 **Listen again and finish the sentences.**

name • cat • from • are you

Philip: Hi Mia!

Mia: Hello Philip. This is my new friend.

Philip: Hello, I'm Philip. What's your (1) ______________?

Sophie: Hi, my name is Sophie.

Philip: Where are you (2) ______________?

Sophie: I'm from London.

Philip: Really? I'm from Plymouth. How old (3) ______________ ______________, Sophie?

Sophie: I'm eleven years old. What about you?

Philip: I'm twelve. What's your favourite animal?

Sophie: My favourite animal is a (4) ______________.

Mia: Oh, it's late. Don't you have football training, Philip?

Philip: Uh, that's true. I have to run. Bye!

Sophie

Mia

Philip

2 Meet Poppy!

Act out the dialogue. Partner A: You are Poppy. Read out the questions. Partner B: Answer the questions. Take turns.

Hello! My name is Poppy. What's your name?

(1) Hello! My name ________ ________.

I'm ten years old. How old are you?

(2) I'm ________ ________ ________.

I come from Plymouth. Where do you come from?

YOU!

(3) I come ________ ________.

My favourite animal is a rabbit. But I like horses too. What's your favourite animal?

(4) My favourite animal ________ ________ ________.

3 That's me!-Card

Write about yourself. What's your name? Where are you from? How old are you? What are your favourite animals?

Draw a picture of yourself next to your text. You can hang up your card in the classroom or put it in your exercise book.

	Hello! My name is Philip and I'm twelve years old. I'm from Plymstock in England. My favourite animals are dogs and bears. I like frogs too.
	Hello! My name is ... I'm ... years old. I'm from ... I like ... ☺ I don't like ... ☹

Ich kann andere begrüßen, ihnen Fragen über die eigene Person stellen und mich selber vorstellen.
Ich kann dies auch aufschreiben.

1 Meet my friend Philip

a) FF 02 **Mia and Sophie meet Mia's friend Philip. Listen to Mia, Sophie and Philip.**

b) FF 02 **Listen again and finish the sentences.**

Philip: Hi, Mia!

Mia: Hello, Philip. This is my new friend.

Philip: Hello, I'm Philip. What's (1) ________________ ________________?

Sophie: Hi, my name is Sophie.

Philip: Where are (2) ________________ ________________?

Sophie: I'm from London.

Philip: Really? I'm from Plymouth. How old (3) ________________ ________________, Sophie?

Sophie: I'm eleven years old. What about you?

Philip: I'm (4) __________________. What's your favourite animal?

Sophie: My favourite (5) __________________ is a cat.

Mia: Oh, it's late. Don't you have football training, Philip?

Philip: Uh, that's true. I have to run. Bye!

Sophie

Philip

Mia

2 A bus ride to school

a) **You meet Poppy on the school bus to Plymstock School. Complete the questions and ask Poppy some questions. Answer Poppy's questions at the end.**

You: Hello!

(1) ____________________?

Poppy: Hello! My name is Poppy.

You: (2) ____________________?

Poppy: I'm ten years old.

You: (3) ____________________?

Poppy: I come from Plymouth.

You: (4) ____________________?

Poppy: My favourite animal is a rabbit. But I love horses too. What about you? What's your name and where do you come from? What's your favourite animal?

You: (5) ____

____

b) **Act out the dialogue. Partner A: You're Poppy. Ask your partner some questions. Partner B: You answer the questions. Take turns.**

3 That's me!-Card

Write a That's me!-Card in your exercise book. Draw a picture of yourself next to your text.

Hello!
My name is … and I'm … years old.
I'm from …
My favourite animal is …
I like … too.

fold here

More help

My name is… • I'm … years old. • I'm from… • My favourite animal is… What's your name? How old are you? Where do you come from? What's your favourite animal?

Ich kann verstehen, wenn bestimmte Gegenstände und Orte aus dem Schülerbuch erwähnt werden.
Ich kann sie auch auf einer Karte oder einem Bild zeigen.

Where to go on a sunny day in Plymouth?

a) Look at the pictures and label them.

1 ____________________

2 ____________________

3 ____________________

4 ____________________

5 ____________________

6 ____________________

7 ____________________

8 ____________________

9 ____________________

10 ____________________

11 ____________________

b) FF 03 Listen to the text and circle the things Philip and Mia talk about.

c) FF 03 Cut out the things they talk about. Listen again and put them in the right order.

fold here

More help

Barbican • Big Wheel • Plymouth Sound • Aquarium • boat • clock • ice cream • monkey • fish • elephant • zebra • giraffe

Ich kann verstehen, wenn bestimmte Gegenstände und Orte aus dem Schülerbuch erwähnt werden.
Ich kann sie auch auf einer Karte oder einem Bild zeigen.

Where to go on a sunny day in Plymouth?

a) Look at the pictures and label them.

1 ____________ 2 ____________ 3 ____________ 4 ____________

5 ____________ 6 ____________ 7 ____________ 8 ____________

9 ____________ 10 ____________ 11 ____________

b) FF 03 Listen to the text and circle the things Philip and Mia talk about.

c) FF 03 Cut out the things they talk about. Listen again and put them in the right order.

Ich kann andere begrüßen, ihnen Fragen über die eigene Person stellen und mich selber vorstellen. Ich kann dies auch aufschreiben.

1 Meet my friend Philip

a) FF 02 Mia and Sophie meet Mia's friend Philip. Listen carefully.

b) FF 02 Listen again and finish the sentences.

Philip: Hi, Mia!

Mia: Hello, Philip. This is my new friend.

Philip: Hello, I'm Philip. (1)______________________________?

Sophie: Hi, my name is Sophie.

Philip: (2)______________________________?

Sophie: I'm from London.

Philip: Really? I'm from Plymouth. (3)______________________, Sophie?

Sophie: I'm eleven years old. What about you?

Philip: I'm twelve. (4)__________________ your favourite animal?

Sophie: My favourite (5) ______________ is a cat.

Mia: Oh, it's late. Don't you have football training, Philip?

Philip: Uh, that's true. I have to run. Bye!

Sophie

Mia

Philip

2 A bus ride to school

You meet Poppy on the school bus to Plymstock School. Act out a dialogue with a partner. Partner A: You are Poppy. Ask the questions. Partner B: Answer the questions. Take turns.

3 That's me!-Card

Write about yourself. Draw a picture next to your text. You can hang up your card in the classroom or put it in your exercise book.

Ich kann verstehen, wenn bestimmte Gegenstände und Orte aus dem Schülerbuch erwähnt werden.
Ich kann sie auch auf einer Karte oder einem Bild zeigen.

Where to go on a sunny day in Plymouth?

a) Look at the pictures and label them.

1 ____________ 2 ____________ 3 ____________ 4 ____________

5 ____________ 6 ____________ 7 ____________ 8 ____________

9 ____________ 10 ____________ 11 ____________

b) FF 03 Listen to the text. Circle the things Philip and Mia talk about.

c) FF 03 Listen again and write down where Mia wants to go and where Philip wants to go. Where do they go together in the end?

____________ ____________ ____________

____________ ____________ ____________

Ich kann Gegenstände auf einem Bild beschreiben und es beschriften.

WORDS Plymouth places

Fill in the crossword.

DOWN

1 

2 

3 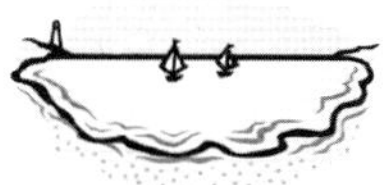

4 

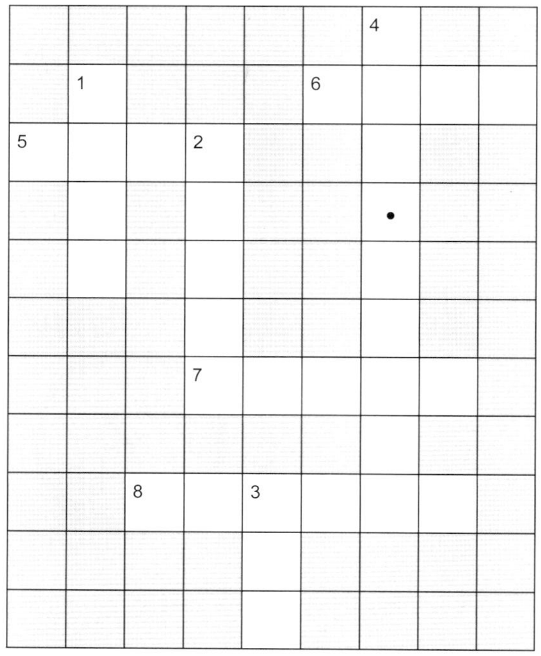

ACROSS

5 

6 

7 

8 

fold here

More help

Big Wheel • boat • castle • hill • pool • river • sea • tower

Ich kann Gegenstände auf einem Bild beschreiben und es beschriften.

WORDS Plymouth places

Fill in the crossword.

DOWN ↓

1 

2 

3 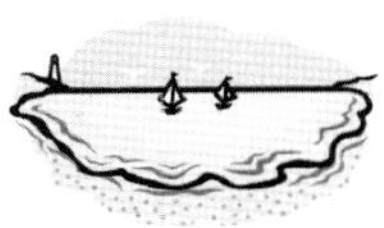

4 

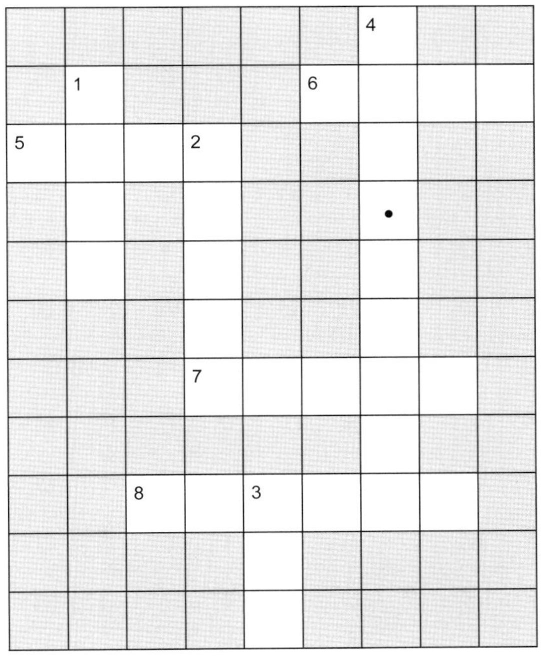

ACROSS →

5 

6 

7 

8 

fold here

More help

igB ehWel • aobt • lcsate • ilhl • loop • rrvie • esa • wteor

Ich kann Gegenstände auf einem Bild beschreiben und es beschriften.

WORDS Plymouth places

a) Look at the pictures. Circle the words for them in the grid.

K	P	J	F	S	D	B	P	A
L	P	W	O	M	H	I	L	L
B	O	A	T	W	H	G	E	B
A	O	H	O	R	G	•	X	P
Z	L	K	W	U	T	W	P	J
U	Y	C	E	F	C	H	L	V
H	F	E	R	I	V	E	R	R
G	L	N	F	E	I	E	I	D
K	M	C	A	S	T	L	E	U
I	P	A	D	E	Y	T	J	M
K	T	N	R	A	M	E	G	D

b) Now make a puzzle like this for your partner on a paper.

Ich kenne und verstehe die Wochentage auf Englisch und kann über sie sprechen und schreiben.

1 WORDS Oops!

Finish the days of the week. The letters in the box can help you.

1) S _ t _ _ d a y

2) _ _ u r _ d _ _

3) S _ _ d _ _

4) _ r i _ _ _

5) T _ e _ d a _

6) _ o n _ _ y

7) _ e d _ e _ d a _

M y d a u W s s y n y T a h s y F y d a a u u r n a

fold here

2 Oh no! Snake eats days of the week

a) **Cut out the cards and put them in the right order. Then find a partner and read your week snakes. Are they right?**

b) **Write the days of the week in the right order in your timetable. What are your favourite days of the week? Draw green smileys ☺.**

My Timetable

Monday	T...					

c) **Talk to a partner. What days does your partner like? Draw blue smileys for your partner. Talk like this:**

Partner A: *I like Mondays. What about you?* **Partner B:** *I like Tuesdays.*
Partner A: *I like Wednesday.* **Partner B:** *I don't like Wednesday.*

Ich kenne und verstehe die Wochentage auf Englisch und kann über sie sprechen und schreiben.

1 WORDS Oops!

Write down the days of the week.

1) T _ e _ d a y

2) S _ t _ _ d a y

3) S _ _ d _ _

4) _ r i _ _ _

5) _ _ u r s d _ _

6) _ e d _ e _ d a _

7) _ o n _ _ y

M y d a W s n y T a h s y F y d a a u u r n a u

2 WHATLRDARESFTHEWEDDAYSSLKOFYXTHEAFWEEKFT

a) Find and circle the days of the week. Write the days down in the right order.

WATSGTDLSATURDAYASTSUMSRTUESDAYRMONDAYIEDSKWEDNESDAYLKT
SUNDAYASJTHTHUDSEFRIDAYOSSARDYSTHURSDAYENS

b) Write the days of the week in your timetable. What are your favourite days of the week? Draw green smileys: ☺ = I like.

Monday	T...					

c) Talk to a partner. Tell him or her about your week. Draw blue smileys for your partner. You don't know a word? You can use your hands and feet.

Partner A: *I like Mondays.*
Partner B: *Where are you on Monday?*
Partner A: *I play tennis.*
Partner B: *I like Tuesday.*

Ich kenne und verstehe die Wochentage auf Englisch und kann über sie sprechen und schreiben.

1 Your Weekday Puzzle

a) WORDS Make your own puzzle with the days of the week. You can start like this:

										F									
						S	a	t	u	r	d	a	y						
										i									
										d									
										a									
										y									

b) Draw the puzzle without the words on a paper. Write one day in the middle.
Now find a partner and give your partner your puzzle. Ready – steady – go! The first one wins the game!

2 My week

a) Fill in the days of the week in your timetable. What are your favourite days of the week? Where are you then? Draw green smileys.

M...						

b) Find a partner and tell him or her about your week. Take turns.
You don't know a word? You can use your hands and feet.

Partner A: I like Mondays.
Partner B: Where are you on Monday?
Partner A: I play tennis.
Partner B: I like Tuesday.

Ich kann Hörtexte/Gespräche über Tiere verstehen und über Tiere sprechen und schreiben.

1 WORDS Covered animals game

Look at the picture for 10 seconds. Cover it and write down six animals you can remember.
Look at the picture again and check your answers with your partner.
Talk to your partner like this:

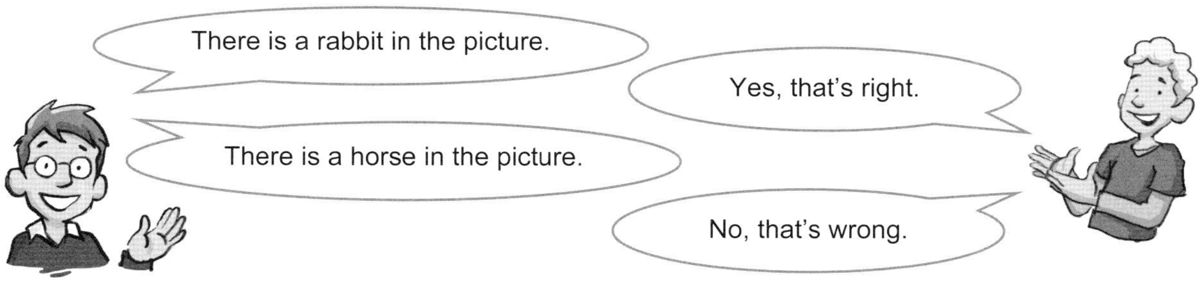

fold here

More help

b _ tt _ _ f _ y • fr _ g • _ ig • ra _ _ it • r _ t • _ nake • gi _ _ ffe • e _ _ phan _ •
hor _ e • li _ n • guin _ a p _ _ • m _ _ key • wh _ le • _ nt • _ ear • b _ rd • ca _ • _ og

2 Philip and Mia at the Zoo

a) **Philip and Mia are at the Zoo. Mia wants to see the baby giraffe. They are at the entrance with their map. Look at their map. Can you find the entrance[1]?**

b) **FF 04 Listen to the text and draw a line to show where Mia and Philip walk.**

[1]entrance ['entrəns] *Eingang*

c) FF 04 Look at the pictures and read the sentences. Then listen again and finish the sentences.

1) The ______________ are funny.	2) The ______________ have a red ball.	3) The ______________ are number six.

4) There's a baby ______________.	5) Philip likes ______________.	6) The ______________ is in the water.

3 WORDS Guess what I am!

Find a partner. Look at the box and pick out one animal. Make the sound your animal makes. You can mime too. Your partner has to guess what animal you are. Take turns.

You can start like this:

Partner A: What am I? … roarr, roarr
Partner B: You are an elephant.
Partner A: No, try again. … roarr, roarr
Partner B: You are a lion!
Partner A: Yes, that's right.

fold here

More help

Ich kann Hörtexte/Gespräche über Tiere verstehen und über Tiere sprechen und schreiben.

1 WORDS Covered animals game

Look at the picture for 10 seconds. Cover it and write down ten animals you can remember.
Look at the picture again and check your answers with your partner.
Talk to your partner like this:

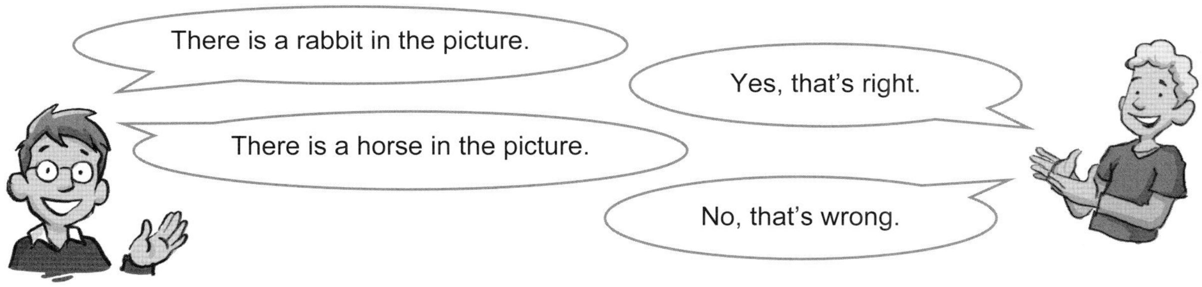

2 Philip and Mia at the Zoo

a) Philip and Mia are at the Zoo. Mia wants to see the baby giraffe. They are at the entrance[1] with their map. Look at their map. Can you find the entrance[1]?

b) FF 04 Listen to the text and draw a line to show where Mia and Philip walk.

[1]entrance ['entrəns] *Eingang*

c) FF 04 **Look at the pictures and read the sentences. Listen again and tick (✓) all the right sentences.**

 1	 2	 3
☐ The monkeys are funny.	☐ The seals have a red ball.	☐ The lions are number six.
☐ The monkeys are red.	☐ There's a baby seal.	☐ The lion is six years old.

 4	 5	 6
☐ There's a baby giraffe.	☐ Mia loves snakes.	☐ The elephant has a pool.
☐ The giraffes are number nine.	☐ Philip's favourite animal is a green frog with red eyes.	☐ The elephant has fun in the water.

3 WORDS Guess what I am!

Find a partner. Look at the pictures and pick out one animal. Partner A: make the sound your animal makes. You can mime too. Partner B: guess what animal you are. Take turns.

You can start like this:

Partner A: What am I? … roarr, roarr
Partner B: You are an elephant.
Partner A: No, try again. … roarr, roarr
Partner B: You are a lion!
Partner A: Yes, that's right.

fold here

More help

Ich kann Hörtexte/Gespräche über Tiere verstehen und über Tiere sprechen und schreiben.

1 WORDS Covered animals game

Look at the picture for 10 seconds. Cover it and write down ten animals you can remember.
Look at the picture again and check your answers with your partner.
Talk to your partner like this:

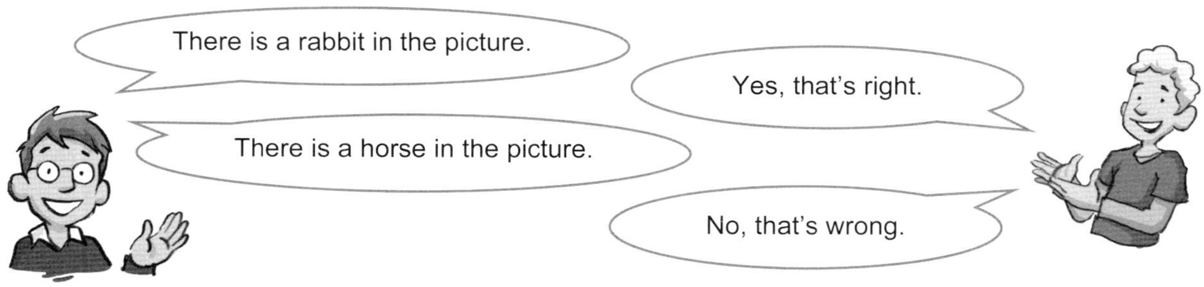

2 Philipp and Mia at the Zoo

a) Philipp and Mia are at the Zoo. Mia wants to see the baby giraffe. They are at the entrance with their map. Look at their map too. Can you find the entrance[1]?

b) FF 04 Listen to the text and draw a line to show where Mia and Philip walk.

[1]entrance ['entrəns] *Eingang*

c) FF 04 **Listen again and tick (✓) all the right sentences.**

1

a) The monkeys are funny. ☐
b) The monkeys are red. ☐
c) The zookeeper has oranges for the monkeys. ☐

2

a) The seals have a red ball. ☐
b) The seals have a blue ball too. ☐
c) There's a baby seal. ☐

3

a) The lions are number six. ☐
b) The lion has a green ball. ☐
c) The lion is six years old. ☐

4

a) The giraffes are in the pool. ☐
b) There's a baby giraffe. ☐
c) The giraffes are number nine. ☐

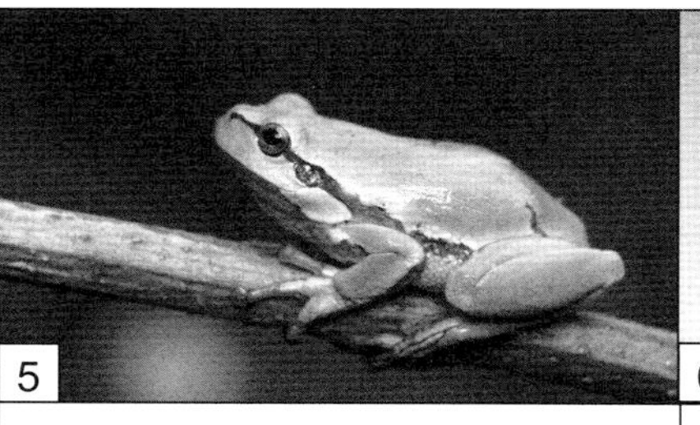

5

a) Mia loves frogs. ☐
b) Philip's favourite animal is a green frog with red eyes. ☐
c) Philip's favourite animal is a yellow frog. ☐

6

a) The elephant has a pool. ☐
b) There's a mouse in the pool. ☐
c) The elephant has fun in the water. ☐

3 Guess what I am!

Write down 5 animals. Find two or three partners. Partner A: mime the animal. You can make sounds. Take turns. One point for every right answer!

You can start like this:

Partner A: What am I? … roarr, roarr
Partner B: You are an elephant.
Partner A: No, try again. … roarr, roarr
Partner B: You are a lion!
Partner A: Yes, that's right.

Ich kann Farben benennen, lesen und schreiben.

1 What's my colour?

a) Write down the colours of the animals and write a sentence too.

animal	colour	sentence
	black + white	It's a black and white animal.
		It's a ____________
		____________
		____________
		____________
		____________

b) Write down three more animals plus their colours.

____

____

____

fold here

More help

yellow • red • orange • blue • brown • black • green • grey • pink • white

2 Colour me in!

Colour the picture. Then write the colour names in Froggy's speech bubble – with the right colour pen or pencil.

1 = blue	2 = orange	3 = yellow	4 = red	5 = brown	6 = green	7 = pink	8 = black	9 = grey

Ich kann Farben benennen, lesen und schreiben.

1 WORDS What's my colour?

a) Write down the colours of the animals and write a sentence too.

animal	colour	sentence
	black + white	It's a black and white animal.
		It's a
		______________________________
		______________________________
		______________________________
		______________________________

b) Write down three more animals plus their colours.

____

____

____

2 Colour Safari

Read the text and colour the picture.

Hi, and welcome to African Park! Come with me on a short safari. Look! The two grey elephants are in the water and the green crocodile is in the sun. The yellow lion and the orange and black tiger are playing cards. Wait! Is that normal? The orange snake has pink glasses and the red birds have brown hats! And look at this! The black and white zebra has a blue T-shirt and an orange cap. I'm sorry, but I have to take you back. Something is wrong here. Bye bye!

Ich kann Farben benennen, lesen und schreiben.

1 WORDS What's my colour?

a) Match the colours of the animals. Sometimes you can use two or more colours for one animal. Write a sentence too.

animal	colour	sentence
	black + white	It's a black and white animal.
		______________________
		______________________
		______________________
		______________________
		______________________

b) Write down three more animals plus their colours.

____

____

____

2 Meet Gulp!

a) Read the text and colour the picture.

Hi! I'm Gulp and I'm an alien. This is a picture of me. But I'm not black and white!!! My ears are pink and my eyes are green. My nose is orange and my mouth is purple. My teeth are yellow and my hair is blue. I'm soooooooooooo hairy, but I hate shampoo. What about you? Are you black and white?

b) You are an alien too. Write an e-mail to Gulp and tell him about you. What do you look like? What colour is your hair, your mouth and your nose? What colour are your ears, your eyes and your teeth?

Ich kann richtig reagieren, wenn mir jemand sagt, was ich mit Gegenständen im Klassenzimmer oder aus meiner Schultasche machen soll.

Poppy packs her bag

a) FF 05 Poppy packs her bag for school. Read the words in the box. Then listen to Poppy. Circle the things she packs in her bag.

banana • book • card • carrot • fruit • glue stick • pen • pencil • pencil case • picture • poster • pullover • rabbit • rubber • scissors • seal • sharpener • T-shirt • two books • two carrots

b) The pictures show things Poppy packs in her bag. Label the pictures and then listen again. Put the pictures in the right order. Write the numbers under the pictures.

__ ________________

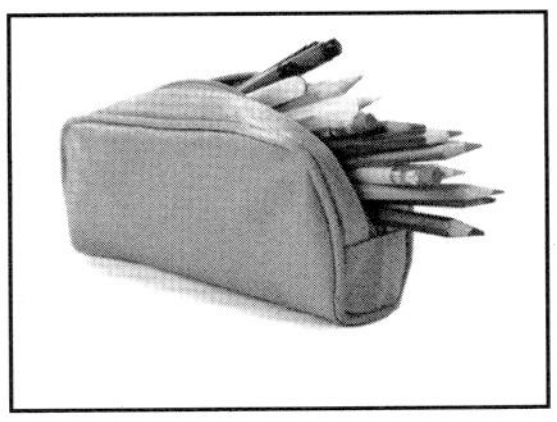
__ ________________

__ ________________

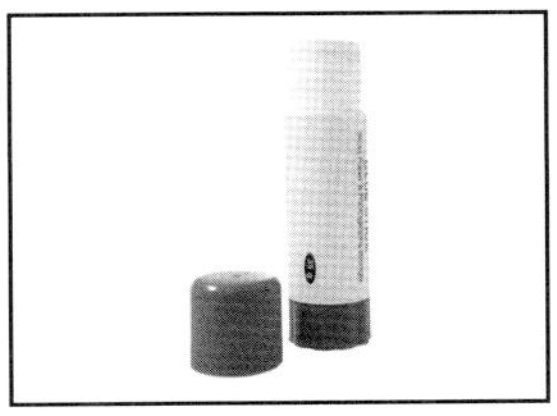
__ ________________

__ ________________

__ ________________

__ ________________

c) What's in Poppy's school bag? Write four sentences on a paper.

Start like this: In Poppy's school bag there is …

Ich kann richtig reagieren, wenn mir jemand sagt, was ich mit Gegenständen im Klassenzimmer oder aus meiner Schultasche machen soll.

Poppy packs her bag

a) FF 05 Right or wrong? Listen to Poppy. What's in her bag?

In her bag there is …	right	wrong
her pencil case		
a yellow pencil		
a blue pencil		
a grey sharpener		
two yellow rubbers		
her glue stick		
two books		
one carrot and one banana		
her purple pullover		

b) FF 05 The pictures show things Poppy packs in her bag. Label the pictures and then listen again. Put the pictures in the right order. Write the numbers under the pictures. But there is one thing Poppy doesn't pack in her bag!

_ ______________

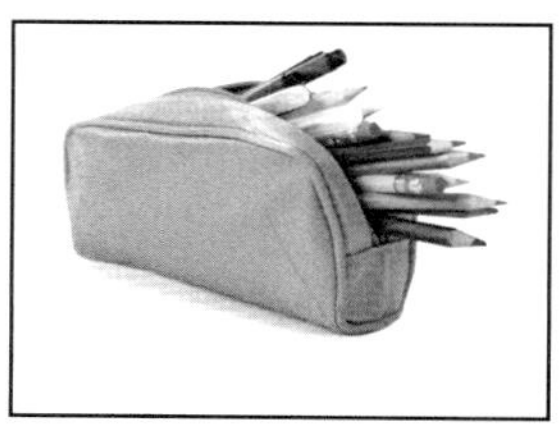
_ ______________

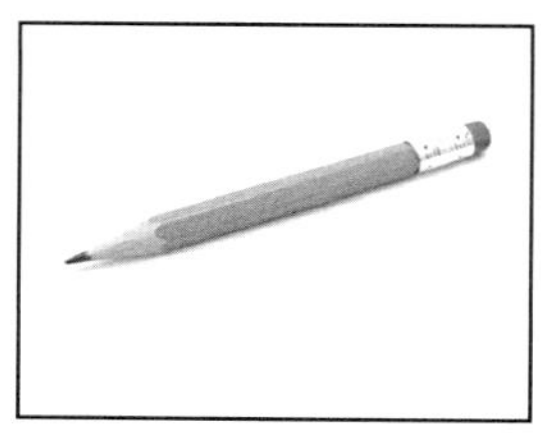
_ ______________

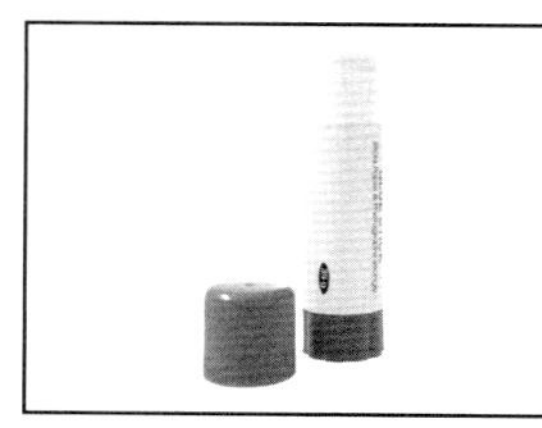
_ ______________

_ ______________

_ ______________

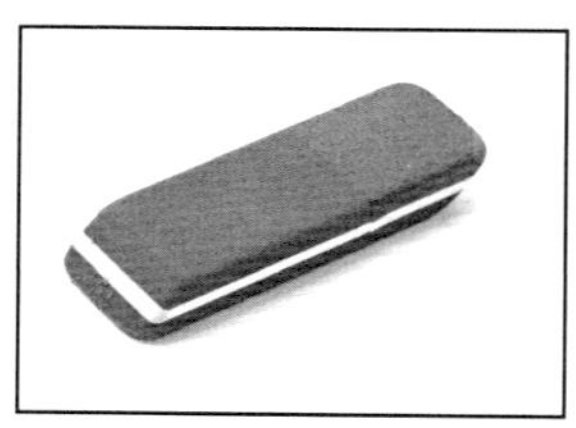
_ ______________

_ ______________

c) What's in Poppy's school bag? Write four sentences on a paper.

Start like this: In Poppy's school bag there is …

Ich kann richtig reagieren, wenn mir jemand sagt, was ich mit Gegenständen im Klassenzimmer oder aus meiner Schultasche machen soll.

Poppy packs her bag

a) FF 05 The pictures show some things Poppy packs in her bag. Look at the pictures and label them. Listen to the text and put the pictures in the right order. Write the numbers under the pictures. Be careful: there is one thing Poppy doesn't pack in her bag.

__ ______________

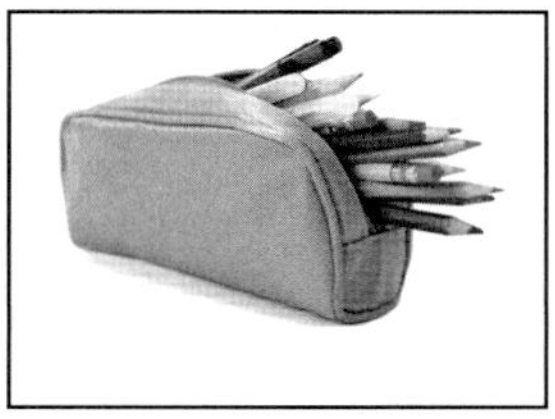
__ ______________

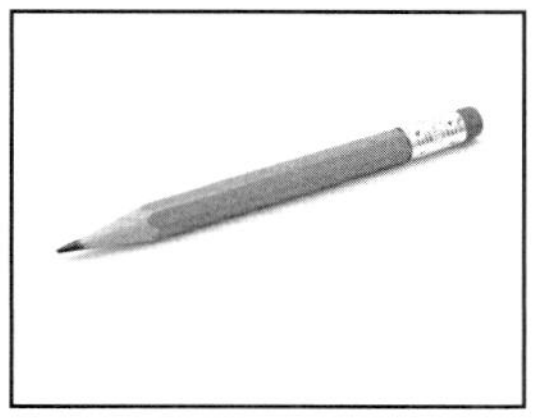
__ ______________

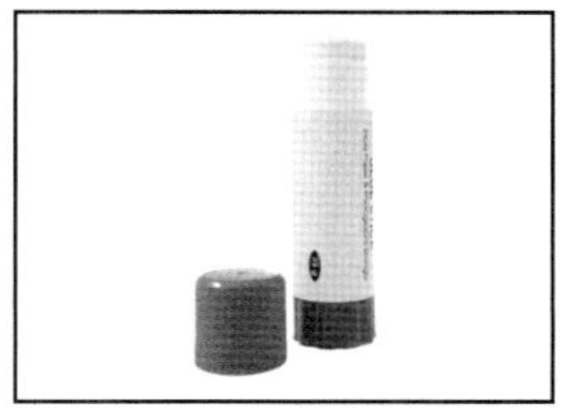
__ ______________

__ ______________

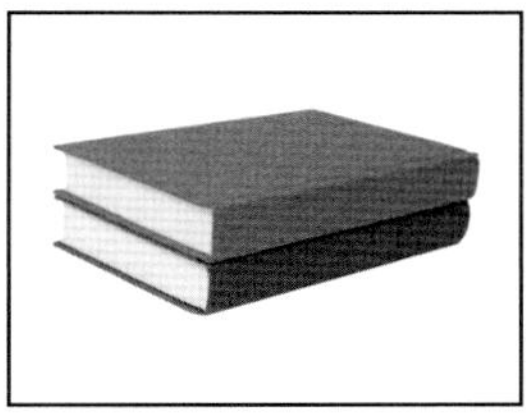
__ ______________

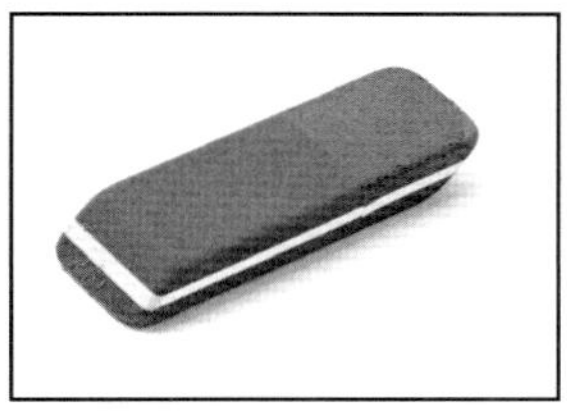
__ ______________

__ ______________

b) Read the sentences. Listen again and tick (✓) the right sentences.

1 Today is	
a) Monday.	
b) Tuesday.	

2 Poppy puts	
a) a black pencil in her pencil case.	
b) a green pencil in her pencil case.	

3 She has	
a) a yellow rubber.	
b) a brown rubber.	

4 She needs	
a) three books.	
b) two books.	

5 Poppy packs	
a) two carrots and an apple in her bag.	
b) two carrots and a banana in her bag.	

6 Poppy packs	
a) her scissors in her bag.	
b) her pullover in her bag.	

c) What's in Poppy's school bag? Name five things that are in her bag.

Start like this: In Poppy's school bag there is ...

Ich kann über Gegenstände, die wir im Klassenzimmer benutzen oder die sich in der Schultasche befinden, sprechen und schreiben und anderen sagen, was sie damit machen sollen.

1 What's on the desk?

a) Look at Mia's desk. Write the letters in the right order.

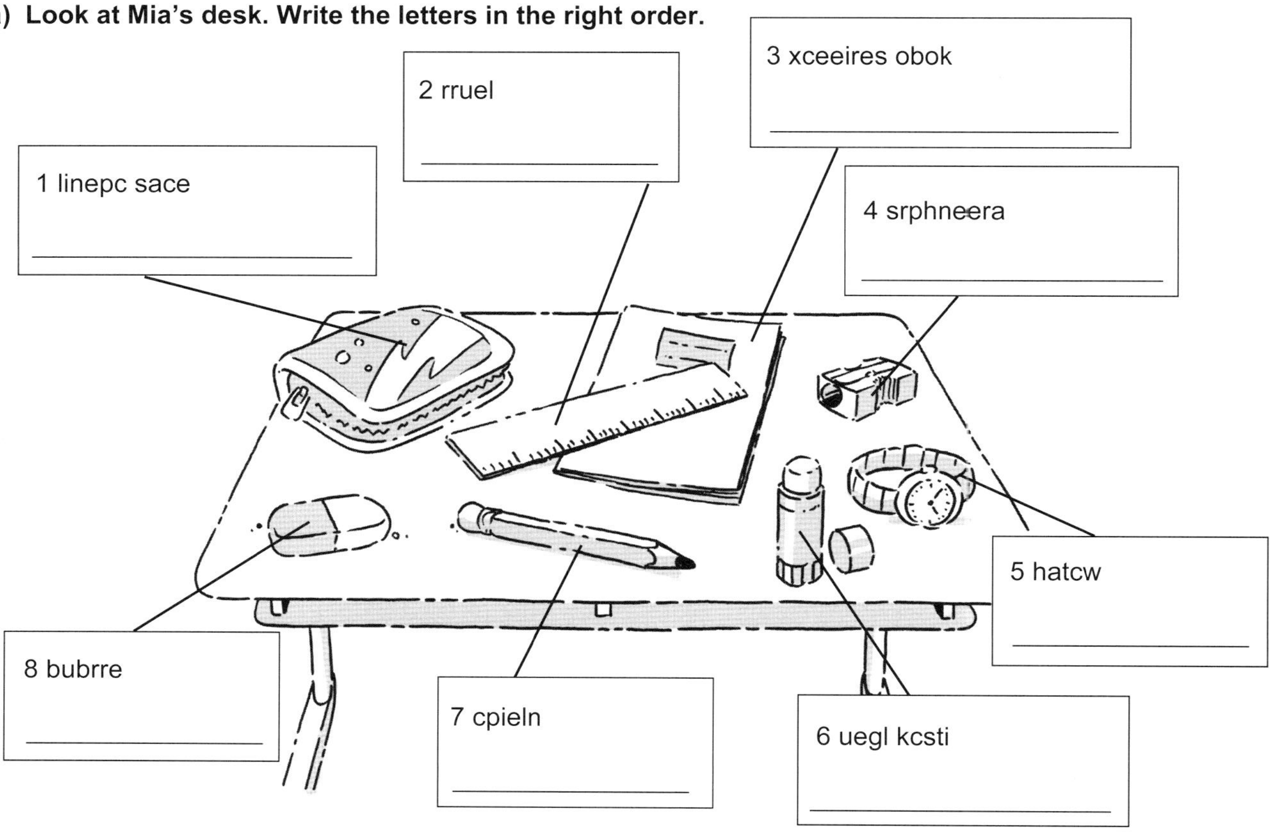

b) Now look at your desk. What can you see? Write three sentences on a separate paper.
You can start like this: *On my desk I can see …*

2 Little ant says …

a) Write down seven things you can tell your partner to do. Use the words from the box.

b) Find a partner. Partner A: You read out the things you want your partner to do. Partner B: You do what your partner says. Take turns.

touch
give me
open
show me

the door	a classmate	a sharpener
a glue stick	a watch	an exercise book
a book	a blue thing	your school bag
the window	the board	a pencil

Ich kann über Gegenstände, die wir im Klassenzimmer benutzen oder die sich in der Schultasche befinden, sprechen und schreiben und anderen sagen, was sie damit machen sollen.

1 My school bag

a) Look at Mia's desk. Write the letters in the right order.

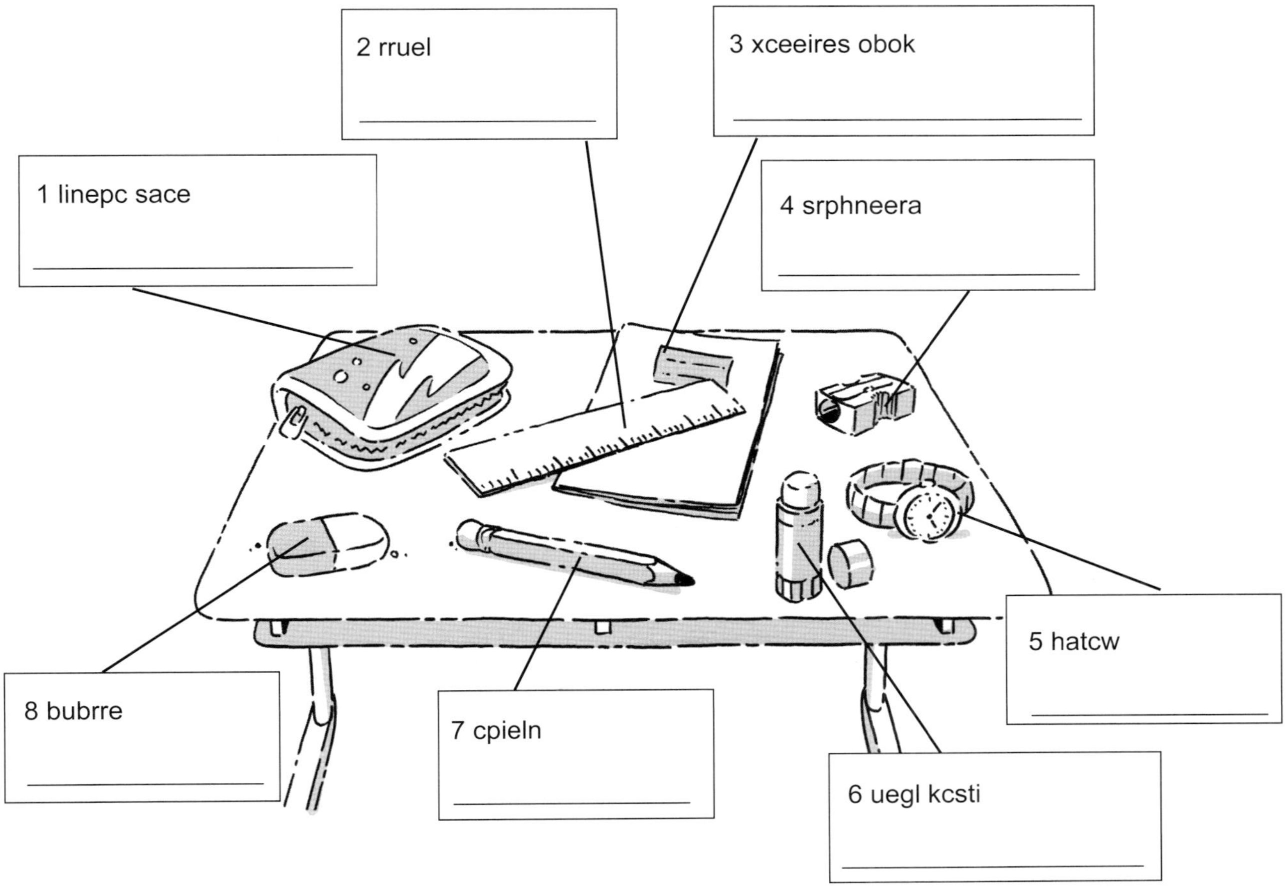

b) Write four sentences on a separate paper about things in your school bag and say what colours they are.
Start like this: *In my school bag there is a red …*

2 Little ant says

Find two or three partners. One of you is the teacher for 10 seconds now. The others do what you say. Take turns.

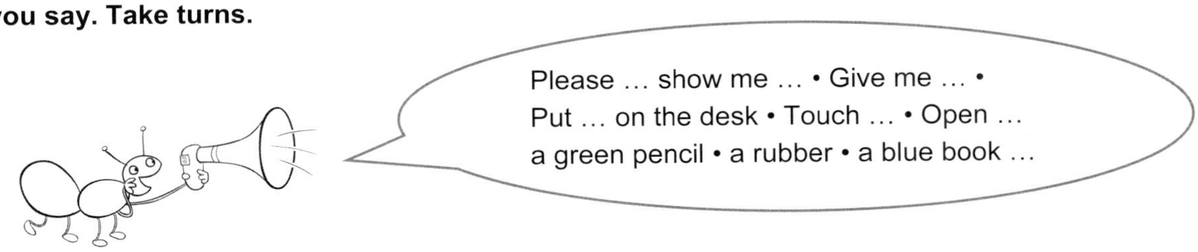

Ich kann über Gegenstände, die wir im Klassenzimmer benutzen oder die sich in der Schultasche befinden, sprechen und schreiben und anderen sagen, was sie damit machen sollen.

1 My school bag

a) Write four sentences about things in your school bag and say what colours they are.
Start like this: *In my school bag there is a red …*

b) Find a partner. Partner A: Read your text to your partner. Partner B: You listen. You have one minute to write down all the things Partner A has in her/his bag.
Check with your partner and take turns.

2 Little ant says …

a) Write down seven things you can tell your partner to do. Use the words from the box.

b) Find a partner. Partner 1: You read out the things you want your partner to do. Partner 2: You do what your partner says.

talk to
give me
open
show me
close
touch

a pencil	a classmate	a chair
a ruler	a watch	a yellow thing
a book	a blue thing	a picture
the window	a red pen	a sharpener
the door	the board	an exercise book
a glue stick	a pencil	your school bag

Ich kann die Zahlen 1–100 verstehen, sagen, schreiben (auch Telefonnummern).

TIP
You know the numbers. But watch out for the tricky bits!

1	one	11	eleven	21	twenty-one
2	two	12	twelve	22	twenty-two
3	three	13	thirteen	30	thirty
4	four	14	fourteen	40	forty
5	five	15	fifteen	50	fifty
6	six	16	sixteen	60	sixty
7	seven	17	seventeen	70	seventy
8	eight	18	eighteen	80	eighty
9	nine	19	nineteen	90	ninety
10	ten	20	twenty	100	one hundred

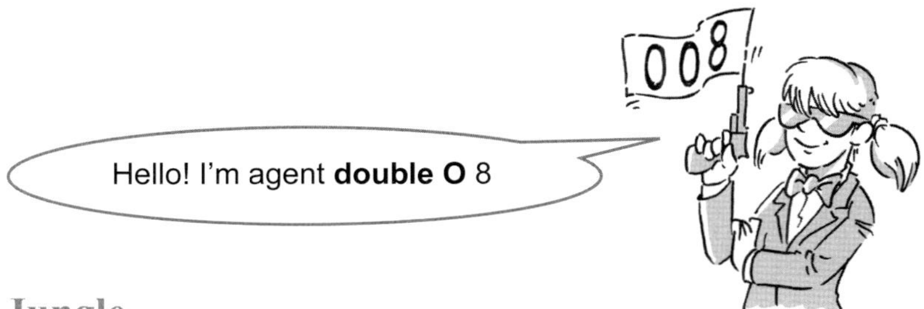

1 WORDS Number Jungle

Can you find the ten numbers in the jungle?
Colour the numbers and write them in words on a separate paper.

15 • 9 • 88 • 47 • 36 • 79 • 52 • 61 • 26

2 Telephone numbers

a) **Write down Philip's telephone number.**

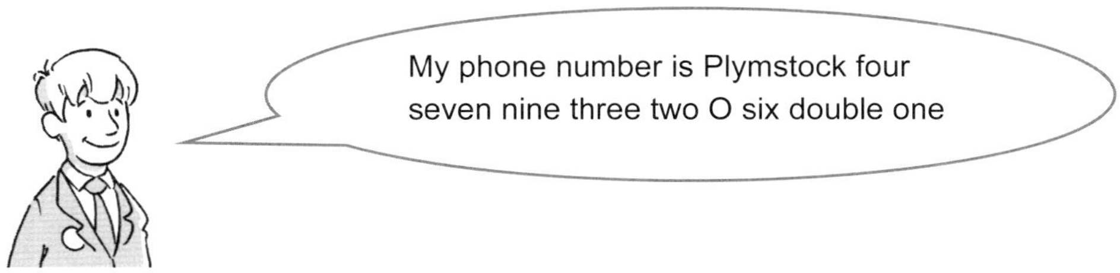

b) **Find a partner. Partner A: Dictate your telephone number. Partner B: Write down your partner's telephone number.**
Check with your partner. Take turns.

Partner A: *What's your telephone number?*
Partner B: *My telephone number is O one five …*

3 Stretch, count, smile

1 **Stand up.**

2 **Count from 1 to 20 in English. Smile! Then bend forward.**

3 **Count from 20 to 40. Smile! Slowly roll up again.**

4 **Count from 40 to 60. Smile! Stand straight and stretch out your hands to the side.**

5 **Count from 60 to 80. Smile! Shake out your hands in front of you.**

6 **Count from 80 to one hundred. Smile! Sit down.**

7 **Smile!**

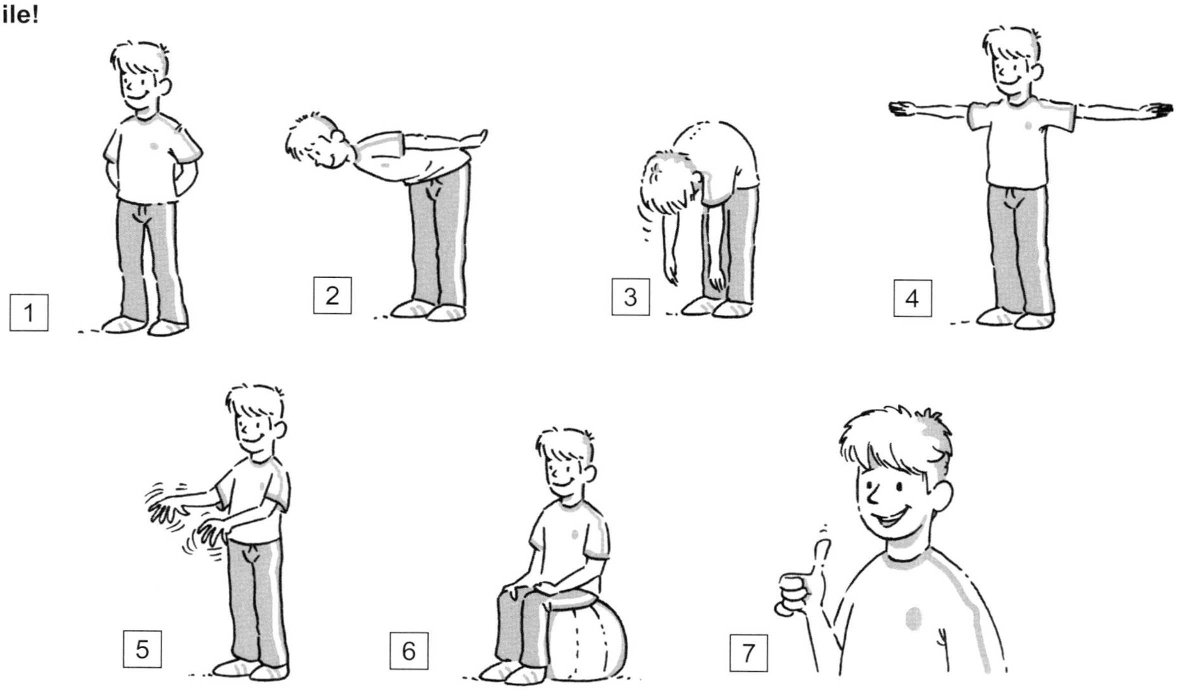

Ich kann die Zahlen 1–100 verstehen, sagen, schreiben (auch Telefonnummern).

TIP
You know the numbers. But watch out for the tricky bits!

1	one	11	eleven	21	twenty-one
2	two	12	twelve	22	twenty-two
3	three	13	thirteen	30	thirty
4	four	14	fourteen	40	forty
5	five	15	fifteen	50	fifty
6	six	16	sixteen	60	sixty
7	seven	17	seventeen	70	seventy
8	eight	18	eighteen	80	eighty
9	nine	19	nineteen	90	ninety
10	ten	20	twenty	100	one hundred

1 Warm up!

Look at Poppy's cupboard and write down what she has.

one	glue stick		balls
	pens		rabbits
	books		CDs
	games		flowers
	photos		clocks
	boats		school bag

2 Telephone numbers

a) Write down Philip's telephone number.

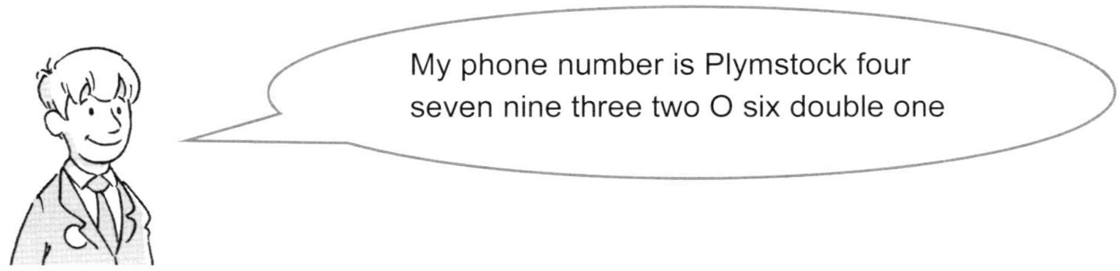

b) Find <u>two</u> partners. Partner A: dictate your telephone number. Partner B and C: write down your partner's telephone number. Take turns.

Partner B/C: *What's your telephone number?*
Partner A: *My telephone number is O one five …*

3 Stretch, count, smile

1 Stand up.

2 Count from 1 to 20 in English. Smile! Then bend forward.

3 Count from 20 to 40. Smile! Slowly roll up again.

4 Count from 40 to 60. Smile! Stand straight and stretch out your hands to the side.

5 Count from 60 to 80. Smile! Shake out your hands in front of you.

6 Count from 80 to one hundred. Smile! Sit down.

7 Smile!

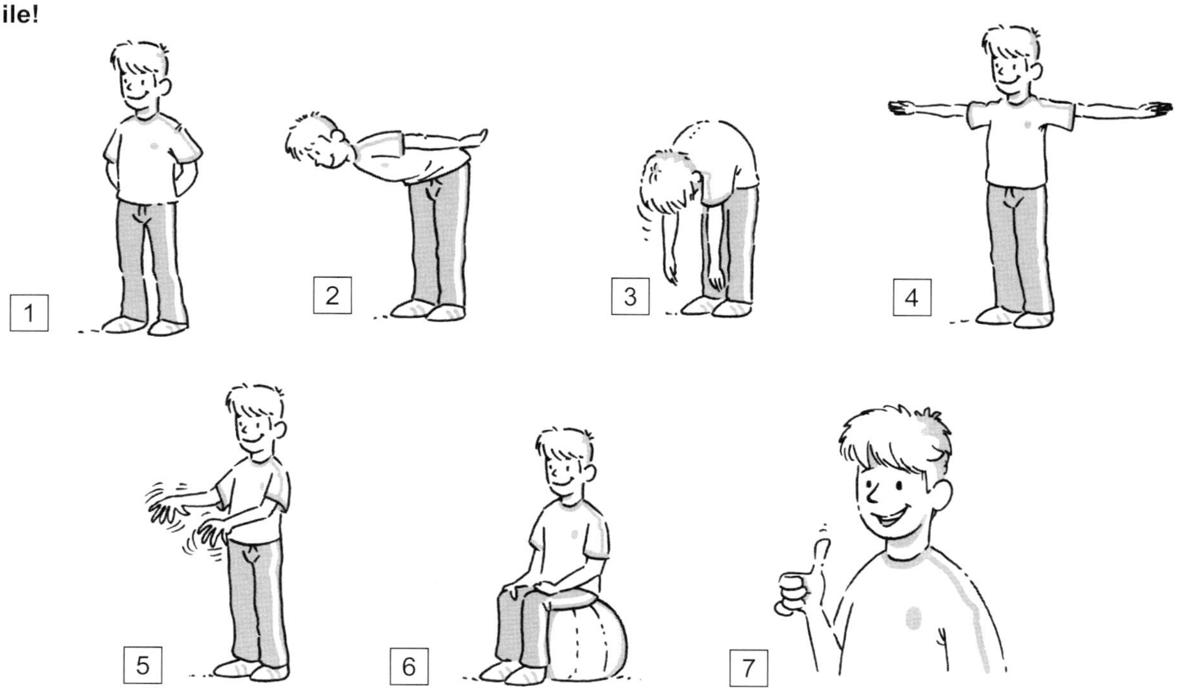

Unit 1

The first day at school

Meine Lernlandkarte für Unit 1

Name: ______________________ Klasse: ____________

Wie gut bist du in den Lernfeldern der Unit 1?
Schätze dich darin ein und male die entsprechende Anzahl an Kreisen auf der Ampel aus.
So findest du dein Übungsblatt.

Das lief nicht gut, ich muss mehr üben.	Das war OK, aber ich könnte besser werden.	Das habe ich gut geschafft.
●○○	●●○	●●●

Setze ein Häkchen, wenn du fertig bist. ✓

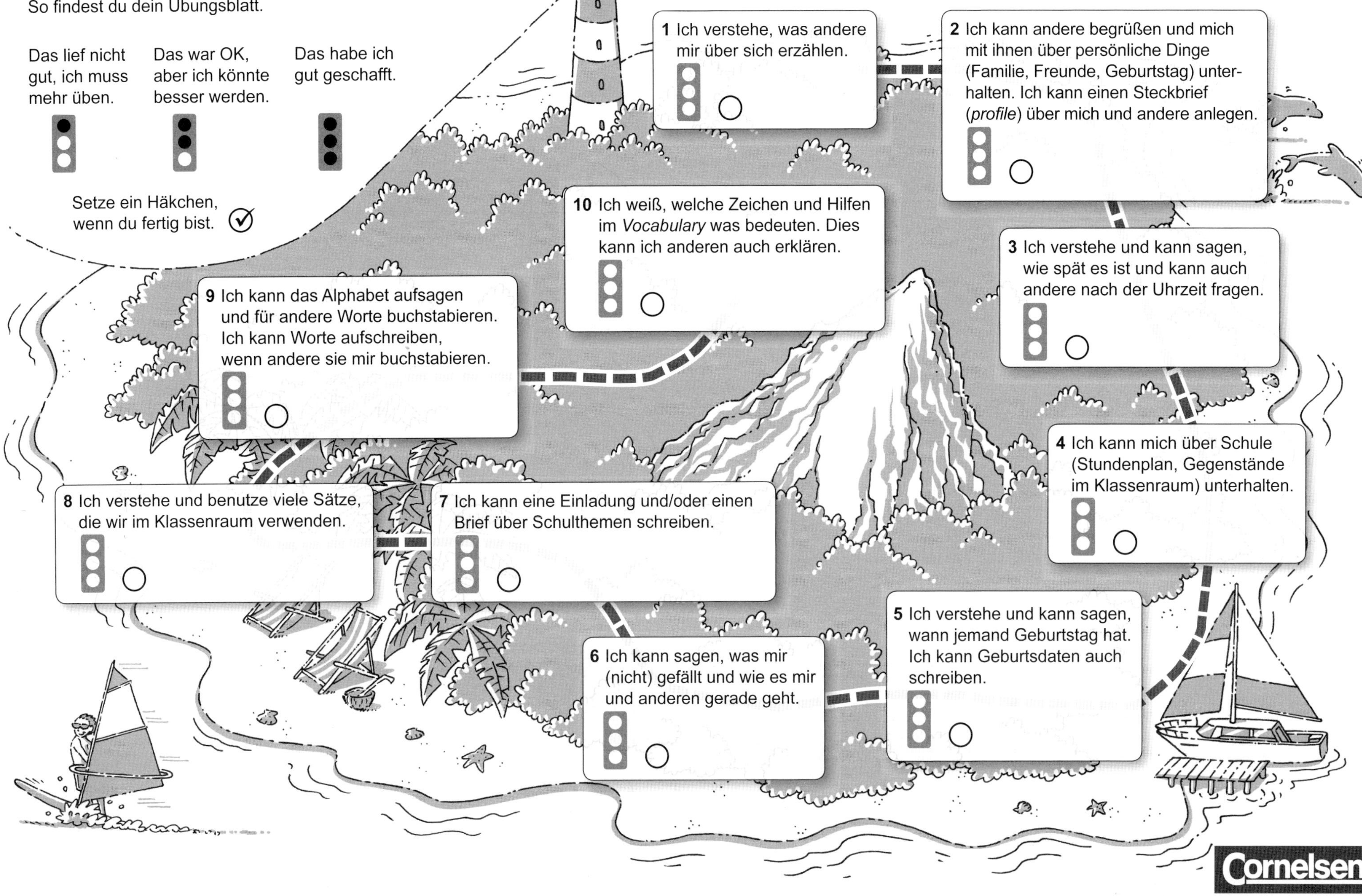

Cornelsen

Ich verstehe, was andere mir über sich erzählen.

1 LANGUAGE At the aquarium

a) Jeremy and his mum are at Plymouth Aquarium. Write six sentences.

(1) Sunday • (2) Jeremy and his mum: Plymouth Aquarium • (3) many fish • (4) Jeremy: happy • (5) fish: Jeremy's favourite animals • (6) little fish: happy

b) At home Jeremy's father has some questions. Finish the sentences.

Dad: Is ______ the aquarium big?
Jeremy: (+) Yes, it is ______.
Dad: ________ you happy?
Jeremy: (+) ____________.

Dad: ________ seals great?
Jeremy: (+) ____________________.
Dad: ________ you and the seals friends now?
Jeremy: (–) ________________, Dad. You are silly!

2 A workshop 🎧

At the aquarium there are lots of kids in one room. They all have the same T-shirt. The T-shirt says: "Plymouth Aquarium – meet the fish – a workshop for kids". Jeremy is interested and listens to the woman who is with the group.

a) FF 06 Listen to the woman and the kids to find out about them. Then tick (✓) the correct boxe Two answers are correct.

1 The girl talks about …
a) her hobbies. ☐
b) her friends. ☐
c) her hometown. ☐
d) how old she is. ☐
e) her parents. ☐
f) her pets. ☐

2 The boy talks about …
a) his hobby. ☐
b) his sports club. ☐
c) his holidays. ☐
d) a fishing trip. ☐
e) his family. ☐
f) his friends. ☐

b) FF 06 Listen again to find out more about the girl and the boy. Finish the sentences.

The girl's name is (1) Jenny ________. She doesn't have a brother, but she has a (2)____________. Her name is (3)____________. She is (4)____________ years old. Phil and his mum and dad like (5)____________. They have a (6)____________ and they often go (7)____________.

Ich verstehe, was andere mir über sich erzählen.

1 LANGUAGE At the aquarium

a) Jeremy and his mum are at Plymouth Aquarium. Circle the correct verb forms.

It are / is Sunday. Jeremy and his mum is / are at Plymouth Aquarium. There is / are many seals. Jeremy is / are happy. Seals are / is Jeremy's favourite animals. The little seal are / is happy too.

b) At home Jeremy's father has some questions. Circle the correct verb forms.

Dad: Is / Are the aquarium big?
Jeremy: Yes, it is / are.
Dad: Am / Are you happy?
Jeremy: Yes, I am / are.

Dad: Is / Are seals great?
Jeremy: Yes, they is / are.
Dad: Are / Is you and the seals friends now?
Jeremy: No, we isn't / aren't, Dad. You am / are silly!

2 A workshop

At the aquarium there are lots of kids in one room. They all have the same T-shirt. The T-shirt says: "Plymouth Aquarium – meet the fish – a workshop for kids". Jeremy is interested and listens to the woman who is with the group.

a) FF 06 Listen to the woman and the kids to find out about them. Tick (✓) the correct boxes.

The girl talks about …
- ☐ her hobbies.
- ☐ her friends.
- ☐ her hometown.

The boy talks about …
- ☐ his holidays.
- ☐ his family.
- ☐ his friends.

b) FF 06 Listen again to find out more about the girl and the boy. Tick (✓) the correct boxes.

1 The girl's name is …
a) Jenny. ☐
b) Sandra. ☐
c) Catherine. ☐

2 She has …
a) no brothers or sisters. ☐
b) a brother. ☐
c) a sister. ☐

3 Phil likes …
a) fishing. ☐
b) chips. ☐
c) football. ☐

4 He has …
a) a boat. ☐
b) friends in Germany. ☐
c) a lot of pets. ☐

Ich verstehe, was andere mir über sich erzählen.

1 LANGUAGE At the aquarium

a) Jeremy and his mum are at Plymouth Aquarium. Finish the sentences.

It ____ Sunday. Jeremy and his mum ________ at Plymouth Aquarium. There __________ many seals. Jeremy ________ happy. Seals ________ Jeremy's favourite animals. The little seal ______ happy too.

b) At home Jeremy's father has some questions. Finish the questions.

Dad: Is ________ the aquarium big?
Jeremy: Yes, it ________.
Dad: ________ you happy?
Jeremy: Yes, I ________.

Dad: ________ seals great?
Jeremy: Yes, they ________.
Dad: ________ you and the seals friends now?
Jeremy: No, we ________, Dad. You are silly!

2 A workshop

At the aquarium there are lots of kids in one room. They all have the same T-shirt. The T-shirt says: "Plymouth Aquarium – meet the fish – a workshop for kids". Jeremy is interested and listens to the woman who is with the group.

a) FF 06 Listen to the woman and the kids to find out about them. Tick (✓) the correct boxes (two answers are correct).

1 The girl talks about …
a) her hobbies. ☐
b) her friends. ☐
c) her hometown. ☐
d) how old she is. ☐

2 The boy talks about …
a) his hobby. ☐
b) his holidays. ☐
c) his family. ☐
d) his friends. ☐

b) FF 06 Listen again to find out more about the girl and the boy. Tick (✓) the correct boxes (only one answer is correct).

1 The girl's name is …
a) Sharon. ☐
b) Jenny. ☐
c) Gina. ☐
d) Jessica. ☐

2 She has …
a) two sisters. ☐
b) an older sister. ☐
c) a brother. ☐
d) a sister. ☐

3 Phil likes …
a) Plymouth. ☐
b) fishing. ☐
c) chips. ☐
d) his brother. ☐

4 He has …
a) a boat. ☐
b) a dog, Telly. ☐
c) a friend in London. ☐
d) a fish at home. ☐

Ich kann andere begrüßen und mich mit ihnen über persönliche Dinge (Familie, Freunde, Geburtstag) unterhalten. Ich kann einen Steckbrief *(profile)* über mich und andere anlegen.

1 LANGUAGE In the classroom

Look at the picture. What can you say about the students in the classroom? Finish the sentences with I, you, he, she, it, we or they.

(1) We 're classmates now.
(2) _____'m your English teacher.
(3) _____'re my new class.
(4) _____'s nice!
(5) _____'s Tuesday.
(6) _____'m English.
(7) _____'re my books.
(8) _____'s my sister.
(9) _____'re eleven.
(10) _____'s the first day at Plymstock.

2 Who is it?

a) Read the four profiles of Gary, Susan, Sophie and Lorcan. They are friends.

My name is Gary.
I'm from Plymouth in England.
My hobby is football.
I have 0 pets.
I like pizza.
My mum works at the Lido.
My dad is in the Navy.

My name is Sophie.
I'm from Swindon in England.
My hobby is playing the piano.
I have a snake.
I like blue.
No carrots for me!
My mum works in a shop.
My dad is from New York.

My name is Susan.
I'm from Dover in England.
My hobby is sailing.
I have two mice.
I like French, but not Science.
My mum has a boat.
My dad is a teacher.

My name is Lorcan.
I'm from Dublin in Ireland.
My hobby is dancing.
I have a dog.
I like Art.
I like dogs, but not cats.
My mum is from Ireland.
My dad is from England.

b) Now look at these speech bubbles. Who says what?

(1) Susan: My dad goes to school every day.

(2) ______________: My mum works at a swimming pool. I do sports in a team.

(3) ______________: My dad is from America. Carrots are for rabbits!

(4) ______________: My mother isn't from England.

(5) ______________: I often go sailing with my mum.

3 GAME My new life

Do you want a new life? Let's play a game! You need a dice ⚅.

a) Choose four categories (e.g. age, mum, likes and friends).

b) Throw your dice ⚅ for each of your four categories and highlight the information your dice shows (e.g.: ⚁ : age 10, ⚄ : mum works in a shop, ...)

c) Give your person a name.

	age	mum	dad	pets	hobbies	likes	doesn't like	hometown	friends
⚀	9	from Scotland	from Germany	dog	tennis	animals	school uniforms	London	Sally
⚁	10	teacher	---	2 cats	football	computers	milk	Bristol	Tom
⚂	11	---	lives in Liverpool	3 guinea pigs	swimming	dogs	ants	Plymouth	Chris and Ewan
⚃	12	in the Navy	works in a museum	rabbits	playing	rock music	Geography	Bath	Amanda
⚄	13	works in a shop	in the Navy	rat	German	Art	pink	Manchester	Emily
⚅	14	works in a canteen	has a boat	snake	sailing	DVDs	kung fu	Newcastle	Jake

d) You are your person. Find a partner in the classroom. You meet on the first day of school. Talk to each other and ask your partner questions. Look at e) for more help.

Hi, my name is ... .
What's your name?

Oh, hello! My ... . I have a pet. It's a ... . What about you?

e) Your person needs a profile for a chatroom. Help him or her to write the profile.

fold here

More help

I'm from ... • I have ... • My hobby is • hobbies are ... • I like ... • I don't like ... • My mum/dad is from ... • My friend is • friends are ...

Ich kann andere begrüßen und mich mit ihnen über persönliche Dinge (Familie, Freunde, Geburtstag) unterhalten. Ich kann einen Steckbrief (*profile*) über mich und andere anlegen.

1 LANGUAGE In the classroom

Finish the sentences about the picture with personal pronouns and forms of *(to) be*.

(1) ________ classmates now.
(2) ________ your English teacher.
(3) ________ my new class.
(4) ________ nice!
(5) ________ Tuesday.
(6) ________ English.
(7) ________ my books.
(8) ________ my sister.
(9) ________ eleven.
(10) ________ the first day at Plymstock.

2 Who is it?

a) Read the four profiles of Gary, Susan, Sophie and Lorcan. They are friends.

My name is Gary and I'm from Plymouth in England. Football is my hobby. I like pizza. It's my favourite food. I have 0 pets. No shopping! My mum works at the Lido and my dad is in the Navy. They both like swimming.

My name is Sophie.
I'm from Swindon in England, but my dad is from New York.
My mum works in a shop. She likes it very much.
I have a snake and playing the piano is my hobby.
I like blue things.
No carrots for me!

My name is Susan and I'm from Dover in England.
My mum has a boat and my hobby is sailing too.
My dad is a teacher at my school.
I like French but not Science.
I have two mice at home.

My name is Lorcan.
I'm from Dublin in Ireland.
My mum is from Ireland but my dad is from England.
I have two dogs but no cats.
My hobby is dancing and I also like Art.

b) Now look at these speech bubbles. Who says what?

(1) Susan: My dad goes to school every day.

(2) ____________: My father wears a uniform and works at sea. When we go to a restaurant I normally choose Italian food.

(3) ____________: My teacher likes my pictures. When I throw a ball for Ben he runs and brings it back.

(4) ____________: My pet sometimes eats normal pet food but mice are its favourite food.

(5) ____________: We always go to Paris in the summer and the food there is great.

3 GAME My new life

Do you want a new life? Let's play a game! You need dice ⚅.

a) Throw your dice ⚅ for each category (e. g. age, mum, ..., friends).

b) Highlight the information your dice shows (e.g.: ⚁ : age 10, ⚄ : mum works in a shop, ...).

c) Give your person a name.

	age	mum	dad	pets	hobbies	likes	doesn't like	hometown	friends
⚀	9	from Scotland	from Germany	dog	tennis	animals	school uniforms	London	Sally
⚁	10	teacher	---	2 cats	football	computers	milk	Bristol	Tom
⚂	11	---	lives in Liverpool	3 guinea pigs	swimming	dogs	ants	Plymouth	Chris and Ewan
⚃	12	in the Navy	works in a museum	rabbits	playing	rock music	Geography	Bath	Amanda
⚄	13	works in a shop	in the Navy	rat	German	Art	pink	Manchester	Emily
⚅	14	works in a canteen	has a boat	snake	sailing	DVDs	kung fu	Newcastle	Jake

d) You are your person. Find a partner in the classroom.
You meet on the first day of school. Talk to each other and ask your partner questions.

Hi, my name is ... .
What's your name?

Oh, hello! My ... .
I have a pet. It's a ... .
What about you?

e) Your person needs a profile for a chatroom. Help him or her to write the profile.
Use the information from the table. You can give extra information.

Ich kann andere begrüßen und mich mit ihnen über persönliche Dinge (Familie, Freunde, Geburtstag) unterhalten. Ich kann einen Steckbrief *(profile)* über mich und andere anlegen.

1 LANGUAGE In the classroom

Finish the sentences about the picture with personal pronouns and forms of *(to) be*.

(1) We're classmates now.
(2) ________ your English teacher.
(3) ________ my new class.
(4) ________ nice!
(5) ________ Tuesday.
(6) ________ English.
(7) ________ my books.
(8) ________ my sister.
(9) ________ eleven.
(10) ________ the first day at Plymstock.

2 Who is it?

a) Read the four profiles of Gary, Susan, Sophie and Lorcan. They are friends.

My name is Gary and I'm from Plymouth in England.
My hobby is football.
I like pizza.
I have 0 pets.
My mum works at the Lido and my dad is in the Navy.

My name is Sophie.
I'm from Swindon in England.
My dad is from New York.
My mum works in a shop.
I have a snake.
My hobby is playing the piano and I like blue.
No carrots for me!

My name is Susan and I'm from Dover in England.
My mum has a boat and my hobby is sailing.
My dad is a teacher.
I like French but not Science.
I have two mice.

My name is Lorcan.
I'm from Dublin in Ireland.
My mum is from Ireland but my dad is from England.
My hobby is dancing.
I also like Art.
I have two dogs but no cats.

b) Now look at these speech bubbles. Who says what?

(1) Susan________: My dad goes to school every day.

(2)____________: My father works on a boat. I like Italian food.

(3)____________: My pet eats mice.

(4)____________: I'm good at drawing. I always go to the park with my pet.

(5)____________: We always go to Paris in the summer.

3 GAME My new life

Do you want a new life? Let's play a game! You need dice ⚅.

a) Choose six categories (e.g. age, mum, likes, friends, doesn't like and hobby).

b) Throw your dice ⚅ for each of your six categories and highlight the information your dice shows (e.g.: ⚁ age 10, ⚄ mum works in a shop, ...)

c) Give your person a name.

	age	mum	dad	pets	hobbies	likes	doesn't like	hometown	friends
⚀	9	from Scotland	from Germany	dog	tennis	animals	school uniforms	London	Sally
⚁	10	teacher	---	2 cats	football	computers	milk	Bristol	Tom
⚂	11	---	lives in Liverpool	3 guinea pigs	swimming	dogs	ants	Plymouth	Chris and Ewan
⚃	12	in the Navy	works in a museum	rabbits	playing	rock music	Geography	Bath	Amanda
⚄	13	works in a shop	in the Navy	rat	German	Art	pink	Manchester	Emily
⚅	14	works in a canteen	has a boat	snake	sailing	DVDs	kung fu	Newcastle	Jake

d) You are your person. Find a partner in the classroom. You meet on the first day of school. Talk to each other and ask your partner questions.

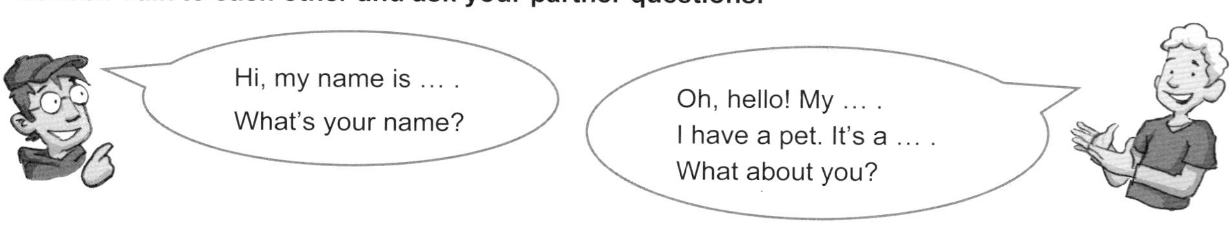

e) Your person needs a profile for a chatroom. Help him or her to write the profile. Use linking words like *and* or *but*.

Ich verstehe und kann sagen, wie spät es ist und kann auch andere nach der Uhrzeit fragen.

1 At what time?

TIP

quarter past

half past

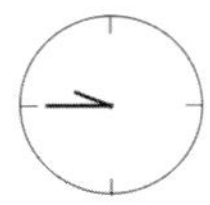
quarter to

8 : 25
eight twenty-five

FF 07 **Listen. Then circle the correct times.**

a)
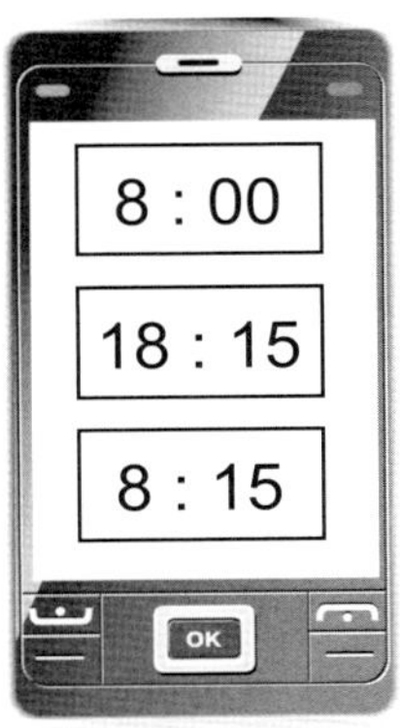

b)
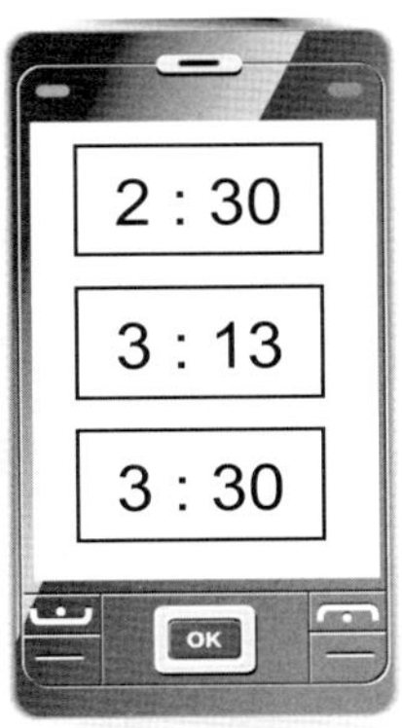

c)
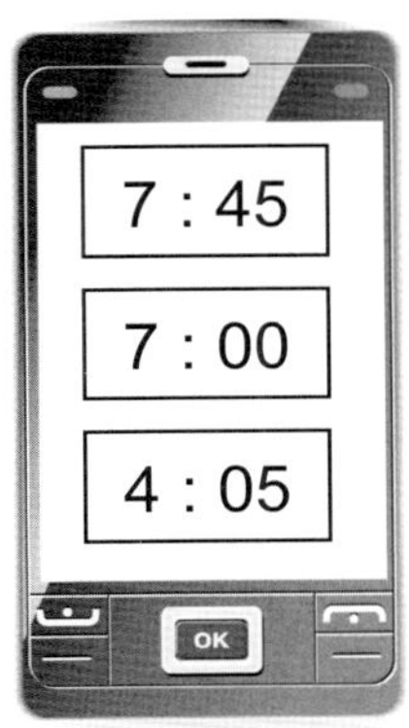

d)
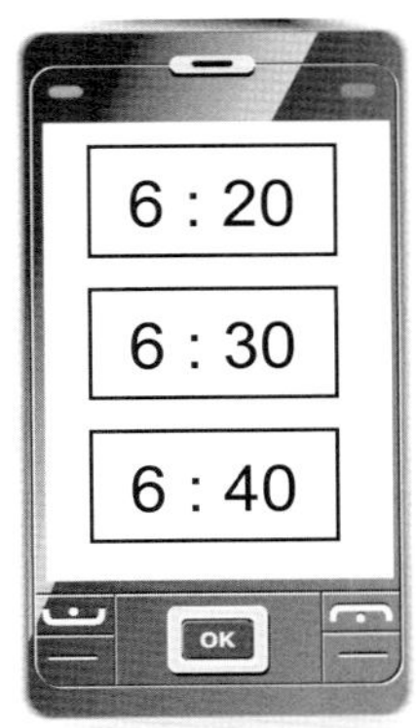

e)
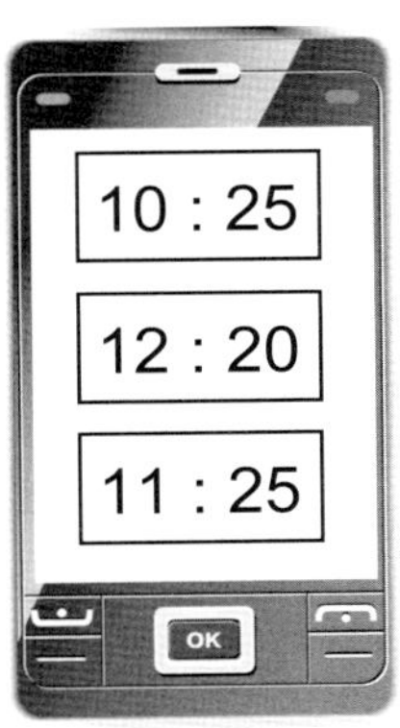

f)
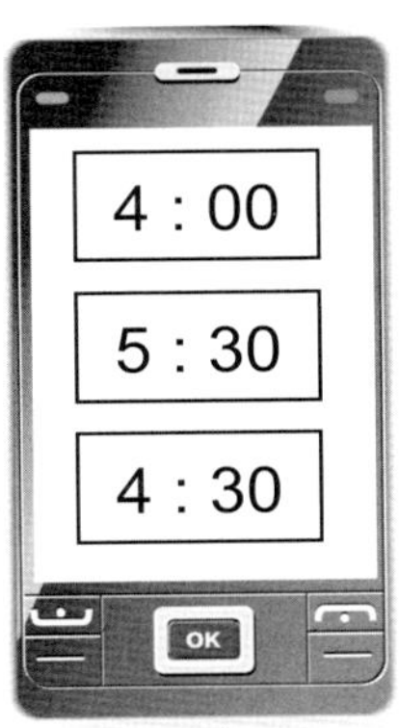

g)
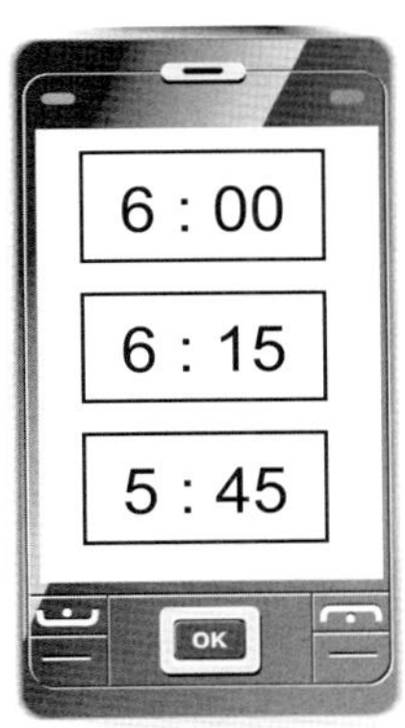

h)
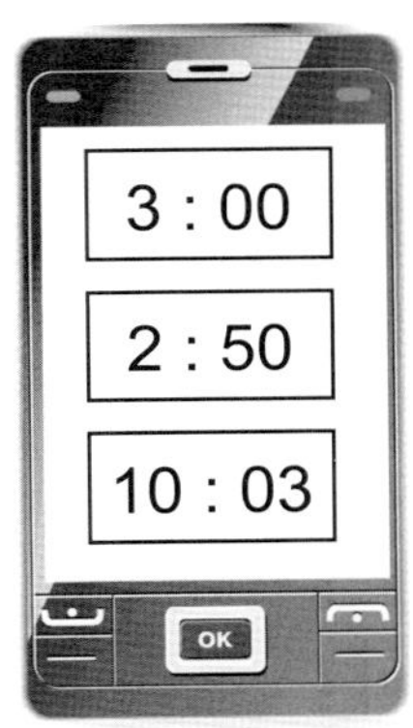

2 What time is it, please?

Cut out the table and fold it in the middle. Partner B starts.

Partner A	Partner B
Partner B starts.	You start: "What time is it, please?"
Say these times: It's eleven twenty. / … ten past six. … a quarter to eleven. … half past ten. … five to three. / … four thirty-five.	Listen, say "Thank you!" and draw the clocks: 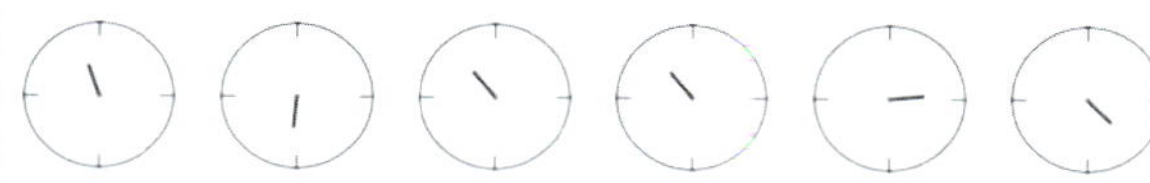
"What time is it, please?"	Partner A speaks.
Listen, say "Thank you!" and draw the clocks: 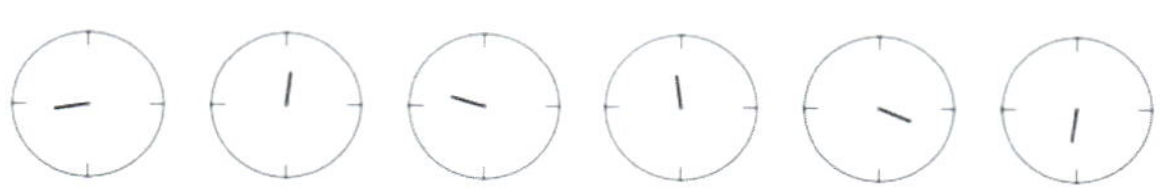	Say these times: It's a quarter to nine. / … twelve fifteen. … half past nine. … ten to twelve. … three forty-five. … twenty past six
Check your partner's clocks.	Check your partner's clocks.

Ich verstehe und kann sagen, wie spät es ist und kann auch andere nach der Uhrzeit fragen.

1 At what time?

FF 07 **Listen. Then finish the clocks.**

a) 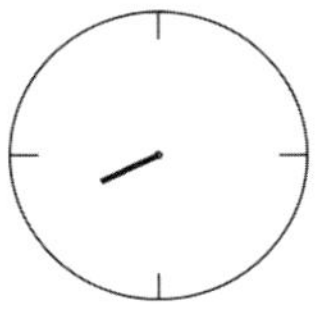
b) 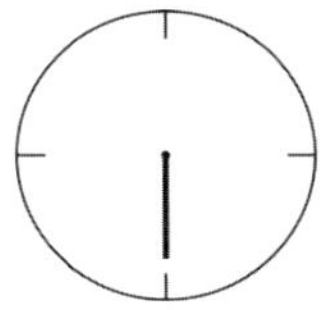
c) 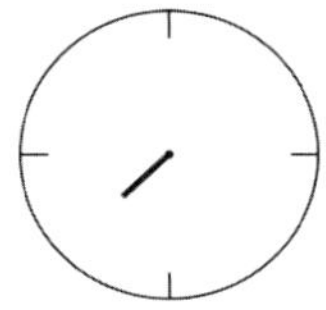
d) 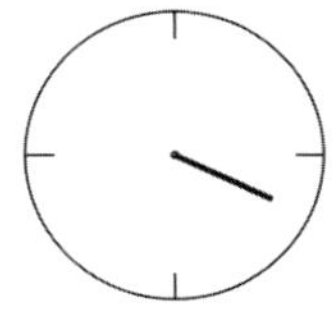

e) 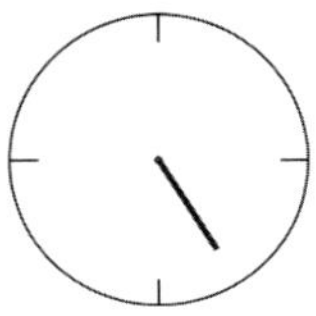
f) 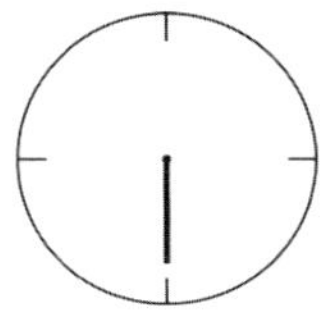
g) 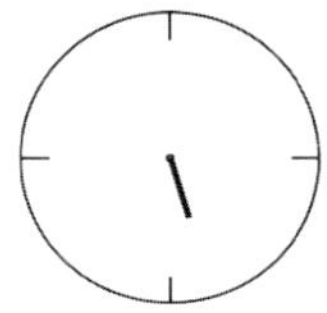
h) 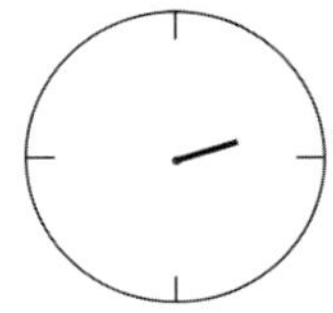

2 What time is it, please?

Cut out the table and fold it in the middle. Partner B starts.

Partner A	**Partner B**
Finish your clocks. 08:____ 02:____ 11:____	Finish your clocks. ____:23 ____:45 ____:52
Partner B starts.	You start: "What time is it, please?"
Tell your partner your times: "It's …"	Listen, say "Thank you!" and draw the clocks: 08:____ 02:____ 11:____
Listen to your partner and draw the clocks. ____:23 ____:45 ____:52	Tell your partner your times: "It's …"
Check your partner's clocks.	Check your partner's clocks.

Ich verstehe und kann sagen, wie spät es ist und kann auch andere nach der Uhrzeit fragen.

1 At what time?

FF 07 **Listen. Then draw the correct clocks.**

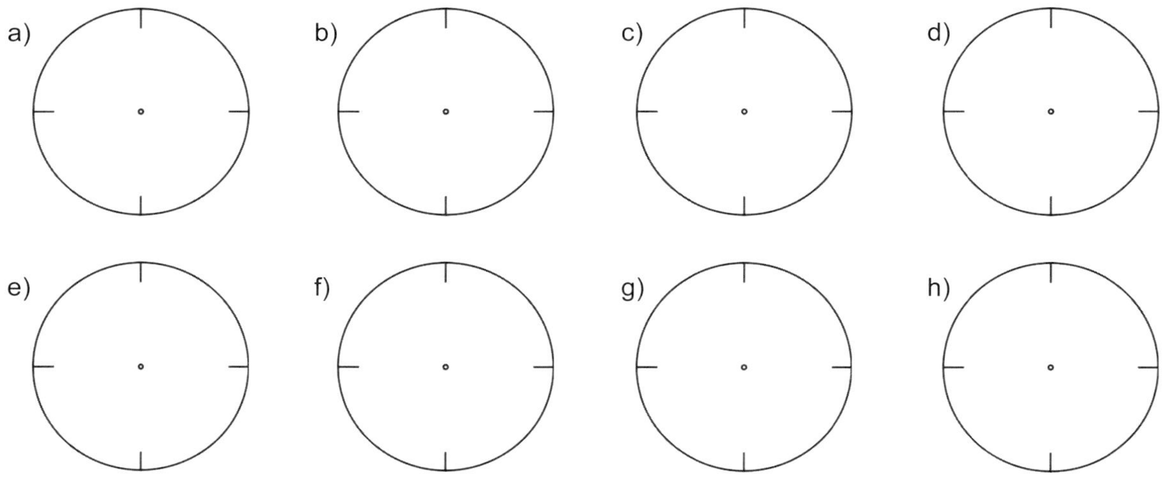

2 The time game

Make a "clock" and play a game with a partner. You need paper and scissors.

01	05
02	10
03	15
04	20
05	25
06	30
07	35
08	40
09	45
10	50
11	55
12	

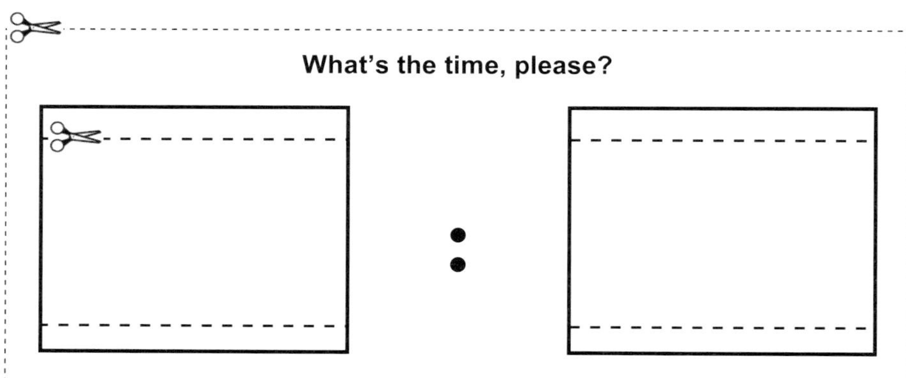

Partner A: You start. Set a time on your clock and give it to your partner. Ask your partner: "What's the time, please?" / "What time is it, please?" / "Can you tell me the time, please?" / "Have you got the time, please?"

Partner B: Answer the question: "It's … ."

Partner A: Check the time on the clock. "No, that's wrong." / "Yes, that's right."

Partner B: You get a point for a correct answer. Now you can ask your partner.

Ich kann mich über Schule (Stundenplan, Gegenstände im Klassenraum) unterhalten.

1 WORDS In the classroom

a) Here are Philip's and Mia's classrooms. Twelve things are different. What are they? Colour the things. Then choose one classroom and write sentences.

There is … / There are (three) … in Philip's/Mia's classroom.

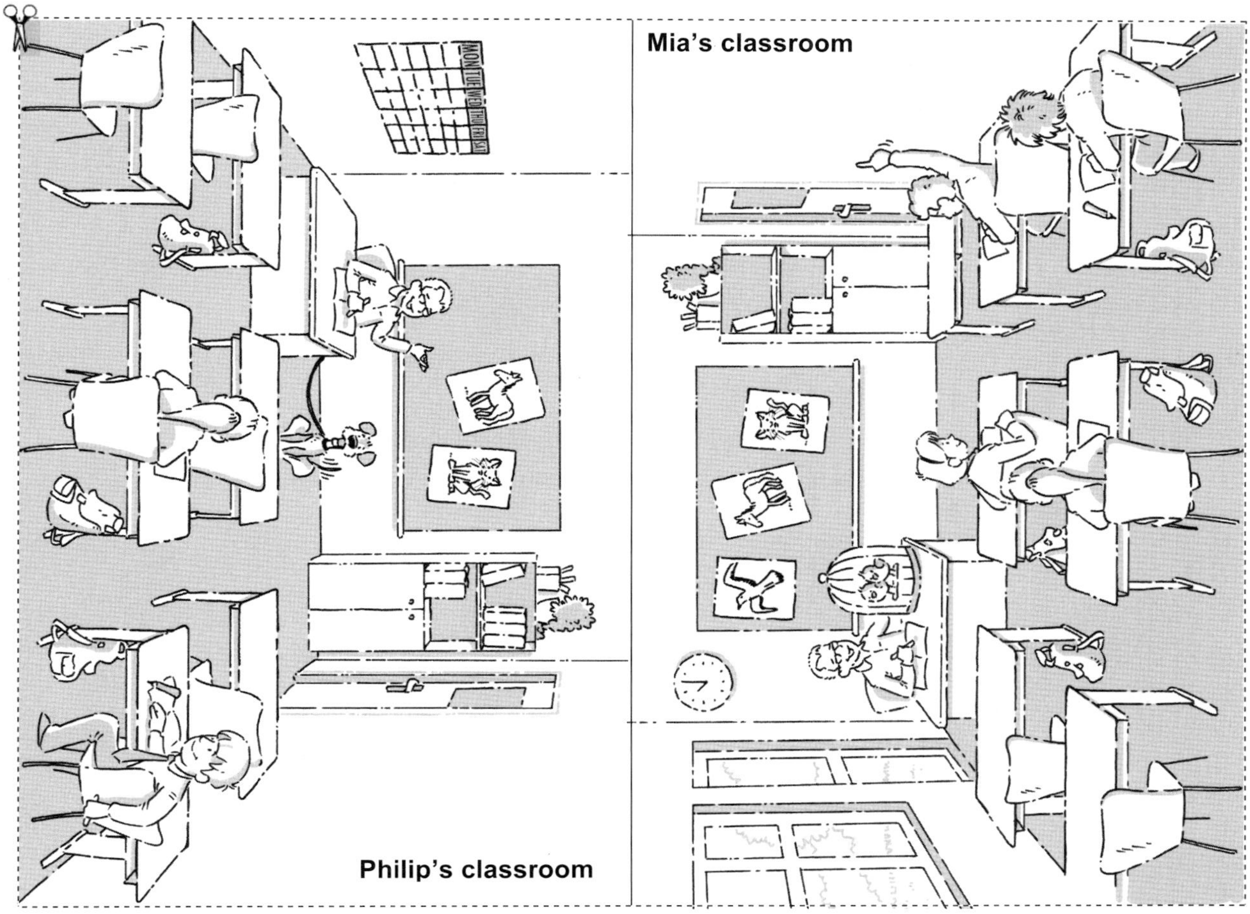

b) Find a partner and talk about the two classrooms. What is different? Talk about six things.

There is a clock / are six desks in my classroom. What about your classroom?

In my classroom there isn't a clock. / are seven desks. There is / are … in my classroom. What about your classroom?

In my classroom there is /are …

2 A school in Liverpool

Look at this timetable from Woodpark High in Liverpool. Then talk to your partner about lessons, breaks and times. You can use these questions:

What's lesson 1 on Monday? • How many lessons do the students have every day? • At what time is the first lesson? • At what time is the first break? • How long is it? • How long are the lessons? • At what time is it time to go home?

Lesson	Monday	Tuesday	Wednesday	Thursday	Friday
8:30 – 9:25	Biology	Science	D & T	Geography	Maths
9:25 – 10:20	English	Art	German	Music	German
BREAK 10:20 – 10:40					
10:40 – 11:35	Geography	History	English	ICT	French
11:35 – 12:30	German	Maths	Maths	PE	Art
LUNCH 12:30 – 1:10					
1:10 – 2:05	D & T	French	Spanish	Spanish	Science
2:05 – 3:00	PE	ICT	Drama	Religion	English

fold here

More help The first lesson on Monday is … . • We have … lessons every day. • The first lesson starts at … . • The first break is at … . • It's … minutes long. • The lessons are … long. • It's time to go home at … .

Ich kann mich über Schule (Stundenplan, Gegenstände im Klassenraum) unterhalten.

1 WORDS In the classroom

a) Here are Philip's and Mia's classrooms. How many different things can you find? What are they? Then choose one classroom and write sentences.

There is a … / There isn't a … / There are (three) … / There aren't any …
in Philip's/Mia's classroom.

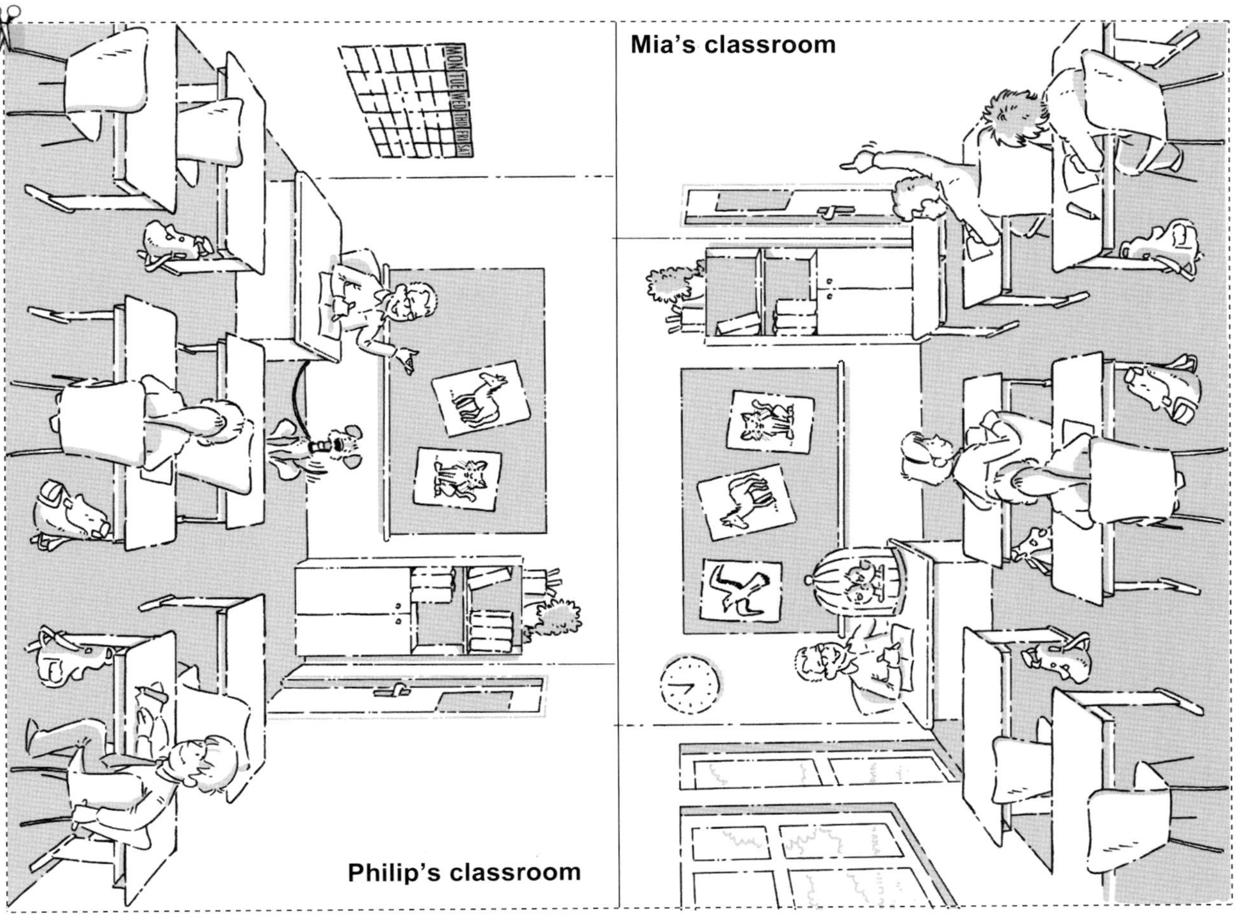

b) Find a partner and talk about the two classrooms. What is different? Talk about six things.

There is/isn't a clock / are/aren't any desks in my classroom. What about your classroom?

In my classroom there is/isn't (only) … . There is / are … in my classroom. What about your classroom?

In my classroom there is /are (only) … .

2 Different schools

Choose a school. Then talk to your partner about lessons, break and times. You can start like this:

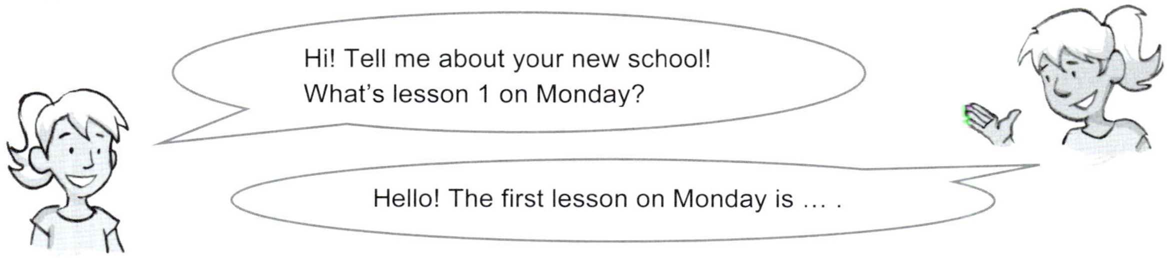

Partner A: You're at Royal Grammar School, Manchester.

Lesson	Monday	Tuesday	Wednesday	Thursday	Friday
9:00 – 10:00	Biology	French	English	ICT	Art
10:00 – 11:00	English	PE	Science	Maths	D & T
BREAK 11:00 – 11:20					
11:20 – 12:20	Music	Maths	Biology	French	Maths
12:20 – 1:20	German	ICT	History	German	English
LUNCH 1:20 – 1:55					
1:55 – 2:55	Science	Religion	D & T	Geography	Maths

Partner B: You're at Woodpark High, Liverpool.

Lesson	Monday	Tuesday	Wednesday	Thursday	Friday
8:30 – 9:25	Biology	Science	D & T	Geography	Maths
9:25 – 10:20	English	Art	German	Music	German
BREAK 10:20 – 10:40					
10:40 – 11:35	Geography	History	English	ICT	French
11:35 – 12:30	German	Maths	Maths	PE	Art
LUNCH 12:30 – 1:10					
1:10 – 2:05	D & T	French	Spanish	Spanish	Science
2:05 – 3:00	PE	ICT	Drama	Religion	English

fold here

More help The first lesson on Monday is … . • We have … lessons every day. • The first lesson starts at … . • The first break is at … . • It's … minutes long. • The lessons are … long. • It's time to go home at … .

Ich kann mich über Schule (Stundenplan, Gegenstände im Klassenraum) unterhalten.

1 WORDS In the classroom

a) Here are Philip's and Mia's classrooms. How many different things can you find? Then choose one classroom and write sentences.

There is a ... / There isn't a ... / There are (three) ... / There aren't any ... in Philip's/Mia's classroom.

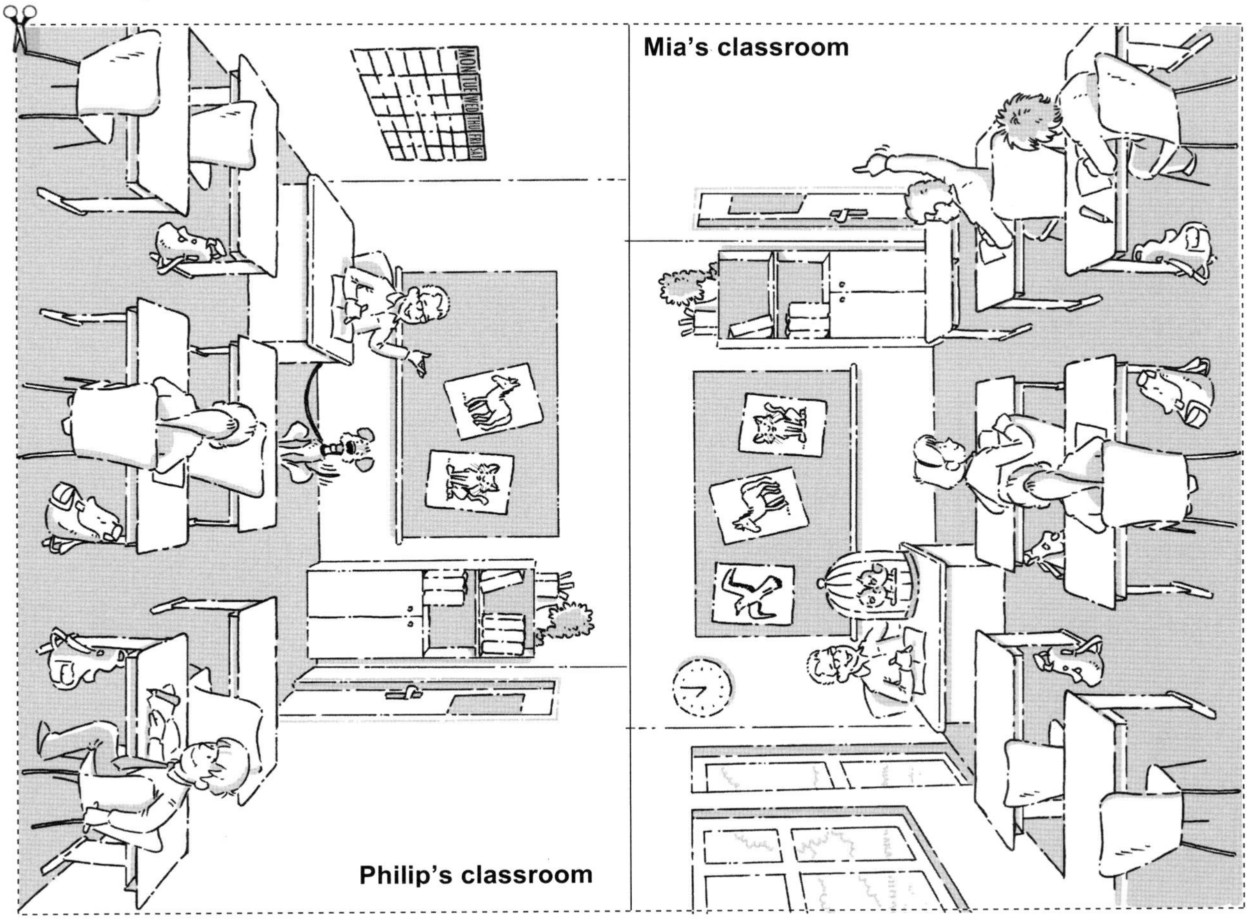

b) Find a partner and talk about eight different things in the classrooms. You can use your sentences from a), questions (Are there any ... / Is there a ... in your classroom?) and short answers (Yes, there is/are. / No, there isn't/aren't.)

2 Different schools

You are staying in Manchester with an English family. Your friend is in Liverpool. You are both visiting schools. You want to meet for an afternoon and go shopping.
Talk about your lessons and times and find a good day to meet. You can talk like this:

There are … lessons every day/on … day. Are there … at your school on …? • Yes, there are … / No, there aren't … . • What about …? • The lessons at … are … long. • It's time to go home at … on … day. • I can come to … . • Good. Let's meet in … . / No, … .

Partner A: You're at Royal Grammar School, Manchester.

Lesson	Monday	Tuesday	Wednesday	Thursday	Friday
9:00 – 10:00	Biology	French	English	ICT	Art
10:00 – 11:00	English	PE	Science	Maths	D & T
BREAK 11:00 – 11:20					
11:20 – 12:20	Music	Maths	Biology	French	Maths
12:20 – 1:20	German	ICT	History	German	English
LUNCH 1:20 – 1:55					
1:55 – 2:55	Science	Religion	D & T	–	–

Partner B: You're at Woodpark High, Liverpool.

Lesson	Monday	Tuesday	Wednesday	Thursday	Friday
8:30 – 9:25	Biology	Science	D & T	Geography	Maths
9:25 – 10:20	English	Art	German	Music	German
BREAK 10:20 – 10:40					
10:40 – 11:35	Geography	History	English	ICT	French
11:35 – 12:30	German	Maths	Maths	PE	Art
LUNCH 12:30 – 1:10					
1:10 – 2:05	D & T	French	Spanish	Spanish	–
2:05 – 3:00	–	ICT	Drama	Religion	–

Ich verstehe und kann sagen, wann jemand Geburtstag hat. Ich kann Geburtsdaten auch schreiben.

1 WORDS Months

Find eleven months in the word grid (↓→). Which month is missing?

M	G	B	C	V	L	J	U	N	O	A
A	U	G	U	S	T	C	R	O	K	B
Y	W	S	S	E	M	I	B	V	H	M
Q	O	B	B	P	J	D	B	E	T	I
D	M	H	T	T	D	F	V	M	G	T
Q	A	M	D	E	C	E	M	B	E	R
F	R	V	T	M	M	B	P	E	A	R
O	C	T	O	B	E	R	X	R	A	J
H	H	I	F	E	I	U	X	E	W	U
R	M	U	F	R	R	A	P	R	I	L
Y	T	Q	Q	X	K	R	P	X	A	Y
J	A	N	U	A	R	Y	M	Y	U	U

2 WORDS Noah's Ark[1]

a) Put the animals in front of the boat. Don't show them to your partner.

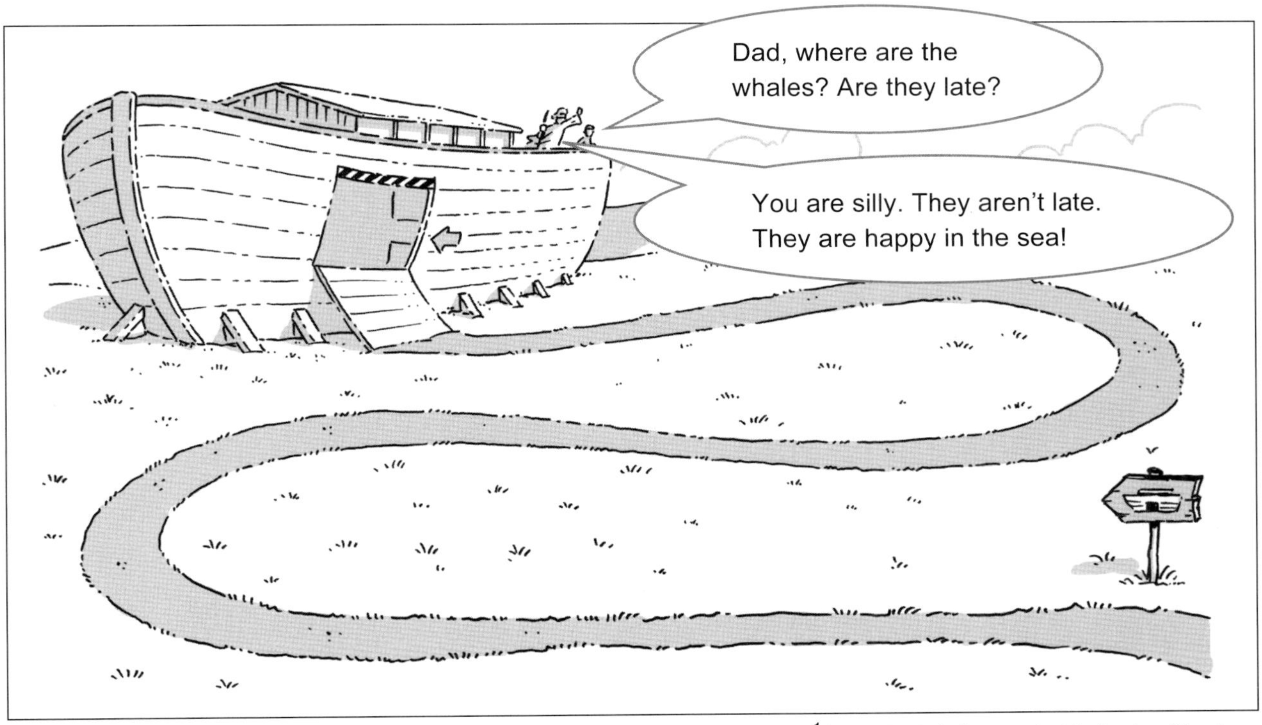

[1]Noah's Ark [nəʊəz 'ɑːk] *Arche Noah*

b) Talk to your partner.

A: Are the … your first/second/… pair?
B: Yes, they are. / No, they aren't, the … are my … pair.

B: Are the … your first/second/… pair?
A: Yes, they are. / No, they aren't, the … are my … pair.

TIP
Schau dir die Übersicht über die Zahlen und Ordinalzahlen auf S. 233 in deinem Englischbuch dazu an.

3 In the new class

a) FF 08 Listen to class 7AF. It's their first lesson. What do they talk about?

☐ animals ☐ holidays ☐ birthdays

b) FF 09 Listen to class 7AF again. When are the children's birthdays? Listen and find out.

Anna:	☐ 5th November	☐ 16th November	☐ 4th November
Tim:	☐ 11th March	☐ 12th March	☐ 20th March
Harry:	☐ 2nd July	☐ 20th July	☐ 31st July
Mary:	☐ 23rd May	☐ 13th May	☐ 3rd May
Ben:	☐ 2nd May	☐ 22nd March	☐ 2nd March
Indira:	☐ 2nd January	☐ 20th July	☐ 20th January

4 When are their birthdays?

Answer the questions for your family and friends.

My best friend's birthday is the ____________ of ______________.
My mother's birthday is the ______________ of ______________.
My grandfather's birthday is the ___________ of ______________.
My ____________ 's birthday is the _______ of ______________.
My ____________ 's birthday is the _______ of ______________.
My ____________ 's birthday is the _______ of ______________.
My birthday is the ______________________ of ______________.

b) Talk to your partner.

A: Are the … your first/second/… pair?
B: Yes, they are. / No, they aren't, the … are my … pair.

B: Are the … your first/second/… pair?
A: Yes, they are. / No, they aren't, the … are my … pair.

3 In the new class

a) FF 08 Listen to class 7AF. It's their first lesson. What do they talk about?

☐ names ☐ holidays ☐ birthdays

b) FF 09 Listen to class 7AF again. When are the children's birthdays? Listen and find out. Write down the names.

16th November ______________

12th March ______________

31st July ______________

3rd May ______________

20th January ______________

2nd March ______________

4 When are their birthdays?

Answer the questions for your family and friends.

My best friend's birthday is the __________ of __________.

My mother's birthday is the __________ of __________.

My grandfather's birthday is the __________ of __________.

My __________ 's birthday is the ________ of __________.

My __________ 's birthday is the ________ of __________.

My __________ 's birthday is the ________ of __________.

My birthday is the __________ of __________.

5 LANGUAGE *a* [ə] or *an* [ən]?

Colour all numbers for words with *an*. There are thirteen words with *an*.

1. appointment	2. grey seal	3. answer	4. animal
5. ant	6. elephant	7. English song	8. MP3 player
9. yellow ruler	10. new appointment	11. timetable	12. strange answer
13. pink elephant	14. hour	15. Art lesson	16. river
17. uniform	18. ICT teacher	19. guinea pig	20. rhyme
21. brown sharpener	22. orange rubber	23. exercise book	24. whale
25. history book	26. open window		

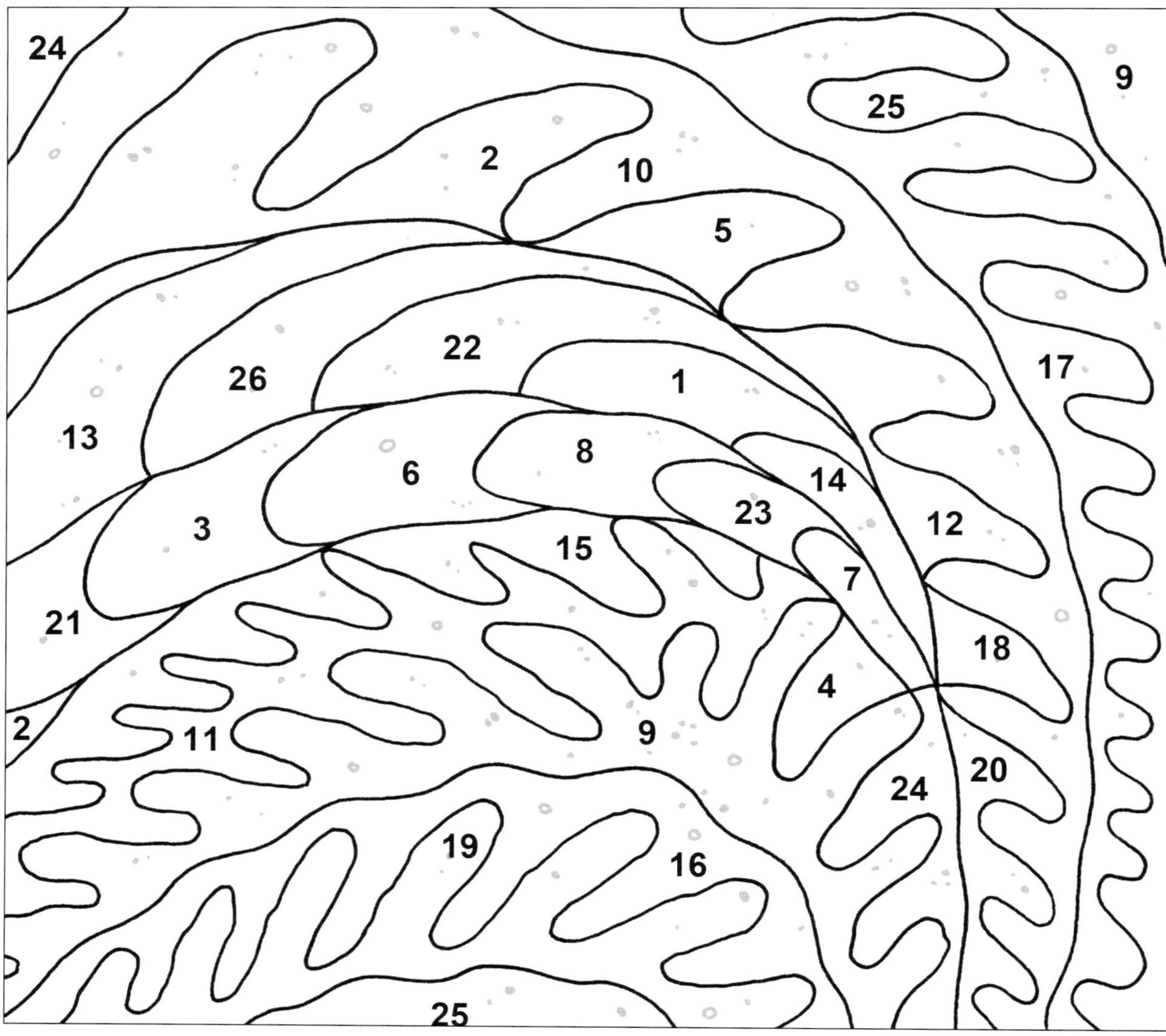

5 LANGUAGE *a* [ə] or *an* [ən]?

Colour words with *an*.
There are thirteen words with *an*.

TIP
an elephant • an ant • an animal •
a bear • a horse • a monkey

1. appointment	2. grey seal	3. answer	4. animal
5. ant	6. elephant	7. English song	8. MP3 player
9. yellow ruler	10. new appointment	11. timetable	12. strange answer
13. pink elephant	14. hour	15. Art lesson	16. river
17. uniform	18. ICT teacher	19. guinea pig	20. rhyme
21. brown sharpener	22. orange rubber	23. exercise book	24. whale
25. history book	26. open window		

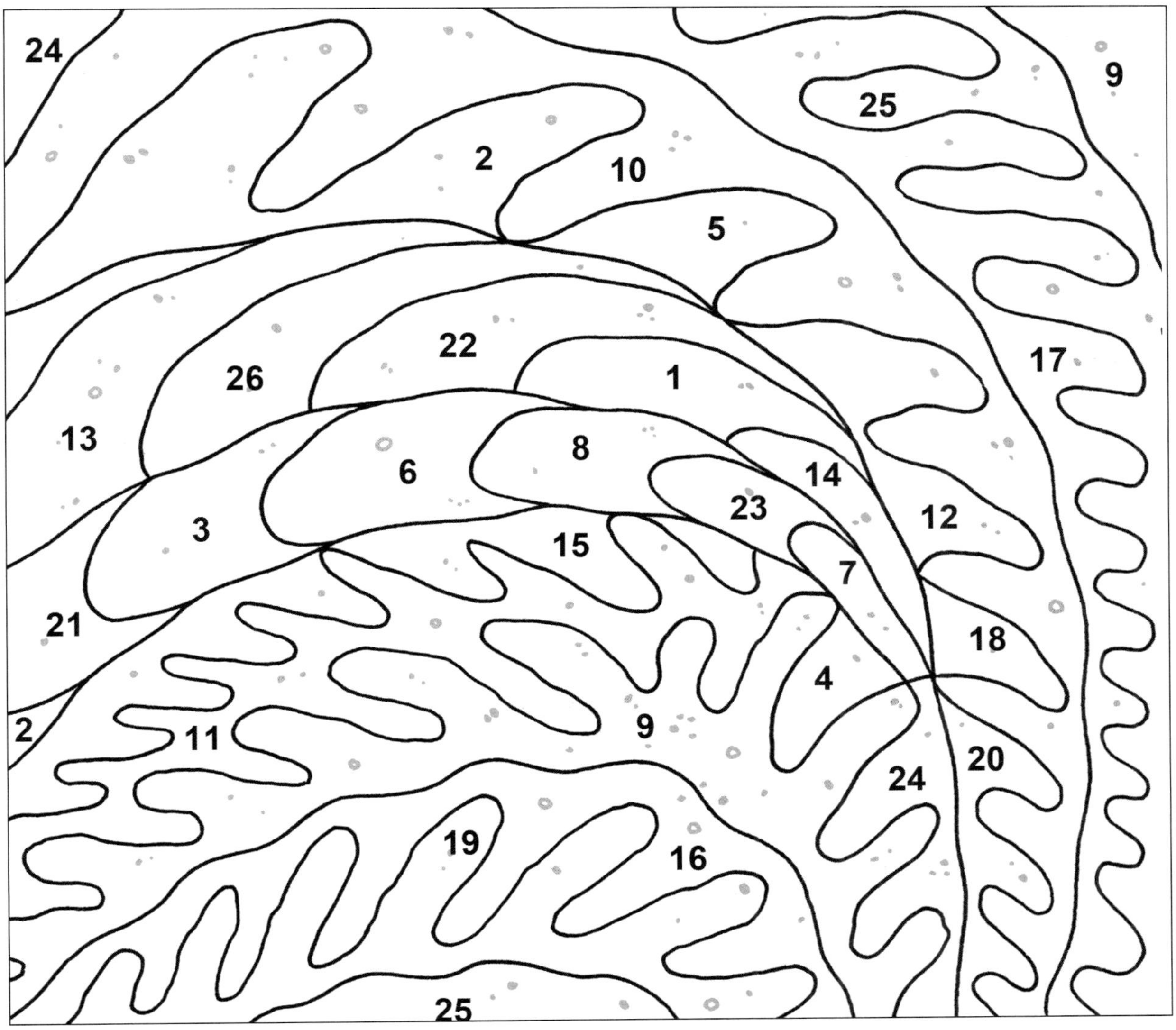

Ich verstehe und kann sagen, wann jemand Geburtstag hat. Ich kann Geburtsdaten auch schreiben.

1 WORDS Months

Find the twelve months of the year in the word grid (↓→↘).

M	G	B	C	V	J	X	U	N	E	A
A	U	G	U	S	T	U	R	O	K	B
Y	W	S	S	E	M	I	N	V	H	M
Q	O	B	B	P	J	D	B	E	T	I
M	M	H	T	T	D	F	V	M	G	T
Q	A	M	D	E	C	E	M	B	E	R
F	R	Y	T	M	M	B	P	E	A	R
O	C	T	O	B	E	R	X	R	A	J
H	H	I	F	E	I	U	X	E	W	U
R	M	U	F	R	R	A	P	R	I	L
Y	T	Q	Q	X	K	R	P	X	A	Y
J	A	N	U	A	R	Y	M	Y	U	U

2 WORDS Noah's Ark[1]

a) Put the animals in front of the boat. Don't show them to your partner.

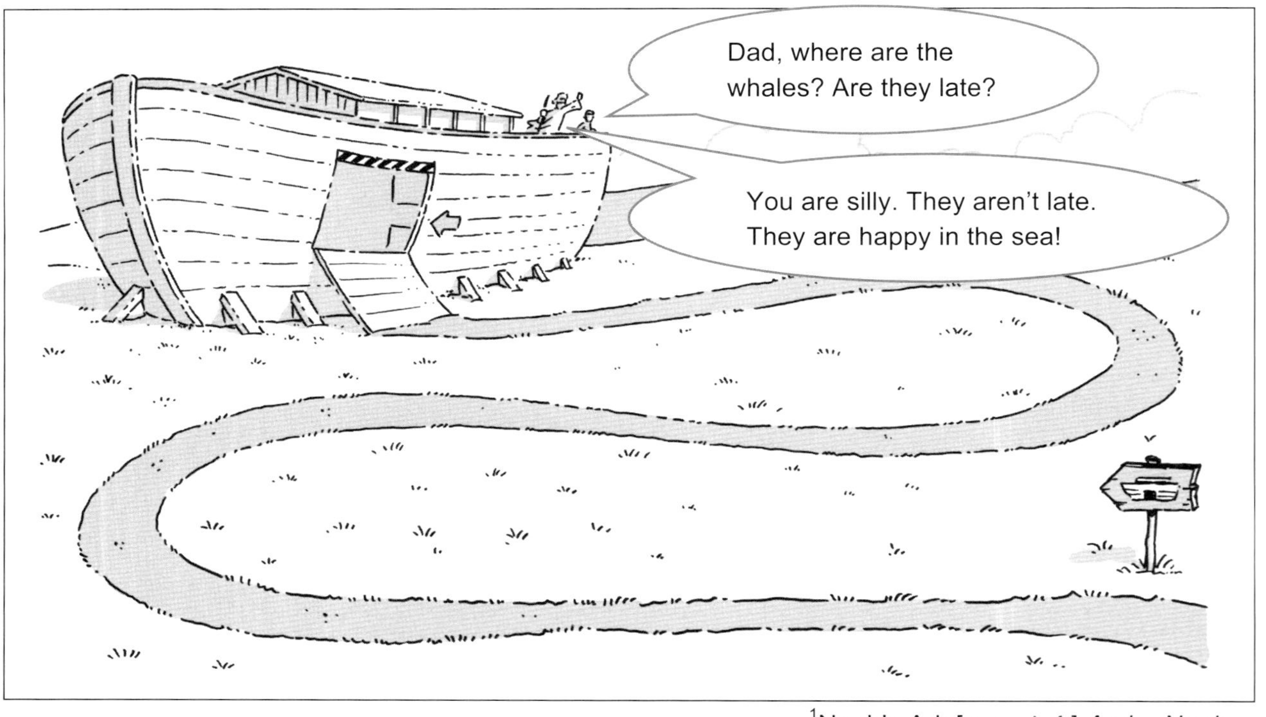

[1]Noah's Ark [nəʊəz 'ɑːk] *Arche Noah*

4 LANGUAGE *a* [ə] or *an* [ən]?

Colour all numbers for words with *an*. There are thirteen words with *an*.

1. appointment	2. grey seal	3. answer	4. animal
5. ant	6. elephant	7. English song	8. MP3 player
9. yellow ruler	10. new appointment	11. timetable	12. strange answer
13. pink elephant	14. hour	15. Art lesson	16. river
17. uniform	18. ICT teacher	19. guinea pig	20. rhyme
21. brown sharpener	22. orange rubber	23. exercise book	24. whale
25. history book	26. open window		

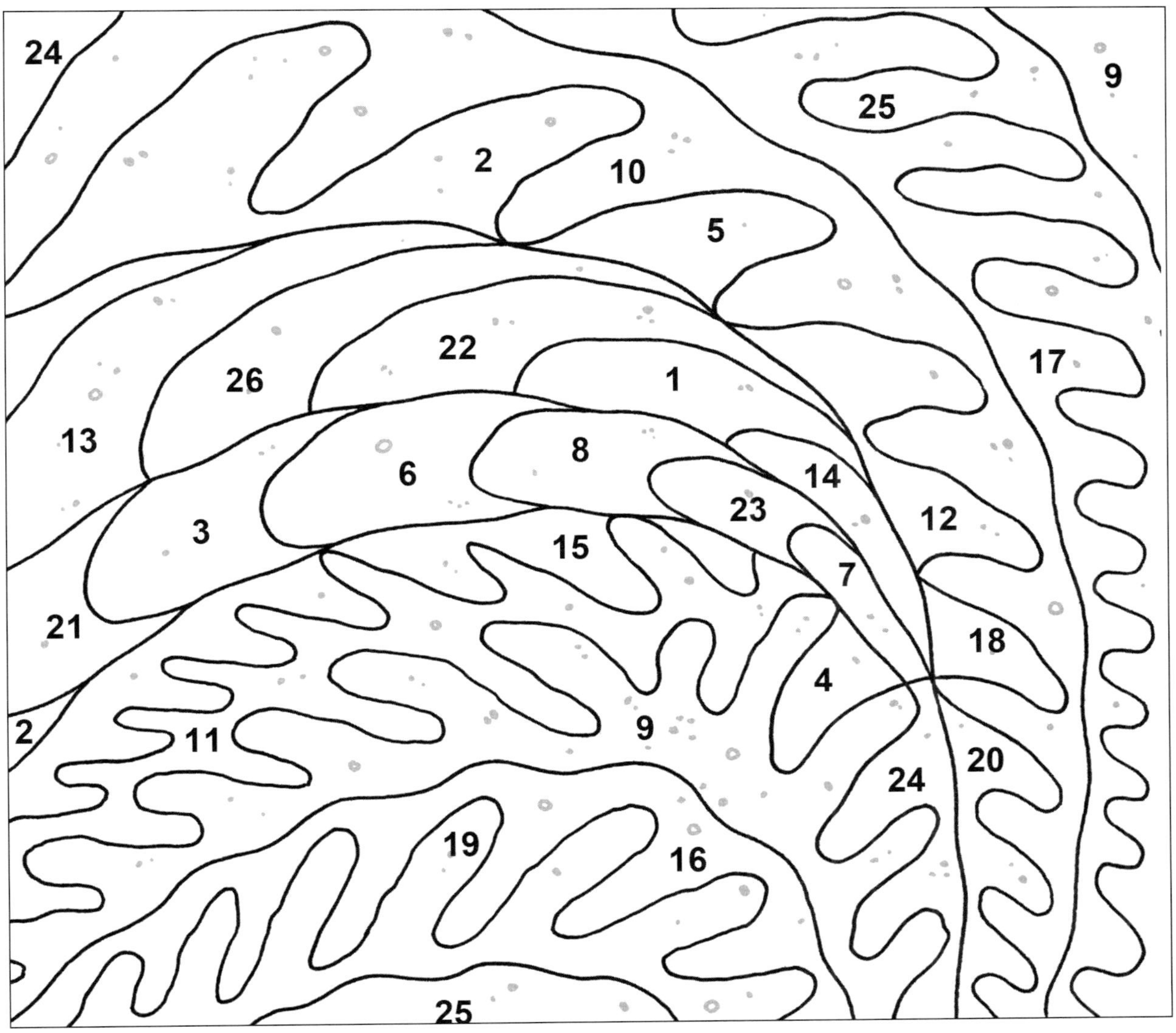

Ich verstehe und kann sagen, wann jemand Geburtstag hat. Ich kann Geburtsdaten auch schreiben.

1 WORDS Months

Find 15 months in the word grid.

J	G	B	C	V	J	J	U	N	E	A
A	U	G	U	S	T	U	R	O	K	B
Y	W	L	S	E	M	I	N	V	H	M
Q	O	B	Y	P	J	D	B	E	T	A
M	M	A	Y	T	D	F	V	M	G	P
Q	A	M	D	E	C	E	M	B	E	R
F	R	Y	T	M	M	B	P	E	A	I
O	C	T	O	B	E	R	X	R	A	L
H	H	I	F	E	I	U	X	E	W	U
R	M	U	F	R	R	A	P	R	I	L
Y	T	Q	Q	M	A	R	C	H	A	Y
J	A	N	U	A	R	Y	M	Y	U	U

2 WORDS Noah's Ark[1]

a) Put twelve animals in front of the boat. Don't show them to your partner.

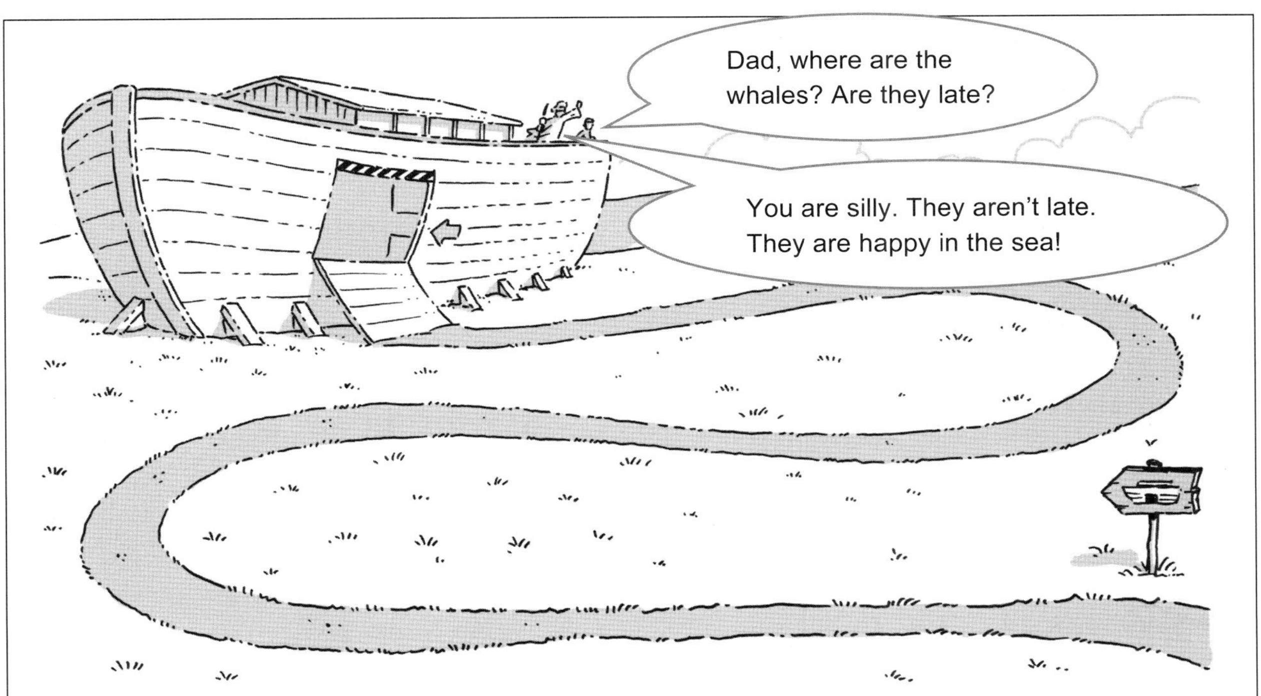

[1]Noah's Ark [nəʊəz 'ɑːk] *Arche Noah*

You have four more animals:

b) **Talk to your partner.**

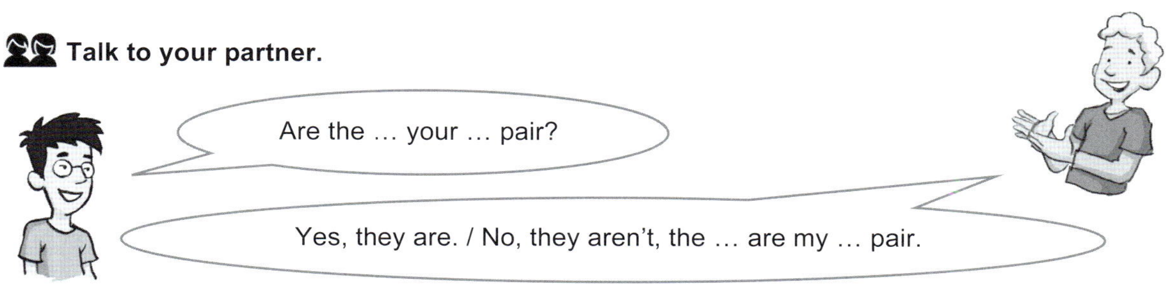

c) **You have four more animals. Write numbers from the list on them. Then talk to your partner again.**

20 • 31 • 36 • 42 • 50 • 53 • 67 • 73 • 79 • 85 • 91 • 100

B: Are the … your first/second/… pair?
A: Yes, they are. / No, they aren't, the … are my … pair.

3 In the new class

a) FF 08 **Listen to class 7AF. It's their first lesson. What do they talk about?**

☐ birthday parties ☐ birthdays ☐ birthday cakes

b) FF 09 **Listen to class 7AF again. When are the children's birthdays? Listen and find out. Write down the dates.**

Anna: ____________________
Tim: ____________________
Harry: ____________________
Mary: ____________________
Indira: ____________________
Ben: ____________________

Ich kann sagen, was mir (nicht) gefällt und wie es mir und anderen gerade geht.

1 I like it

a) Draw lines. What do you like? What don't you like?

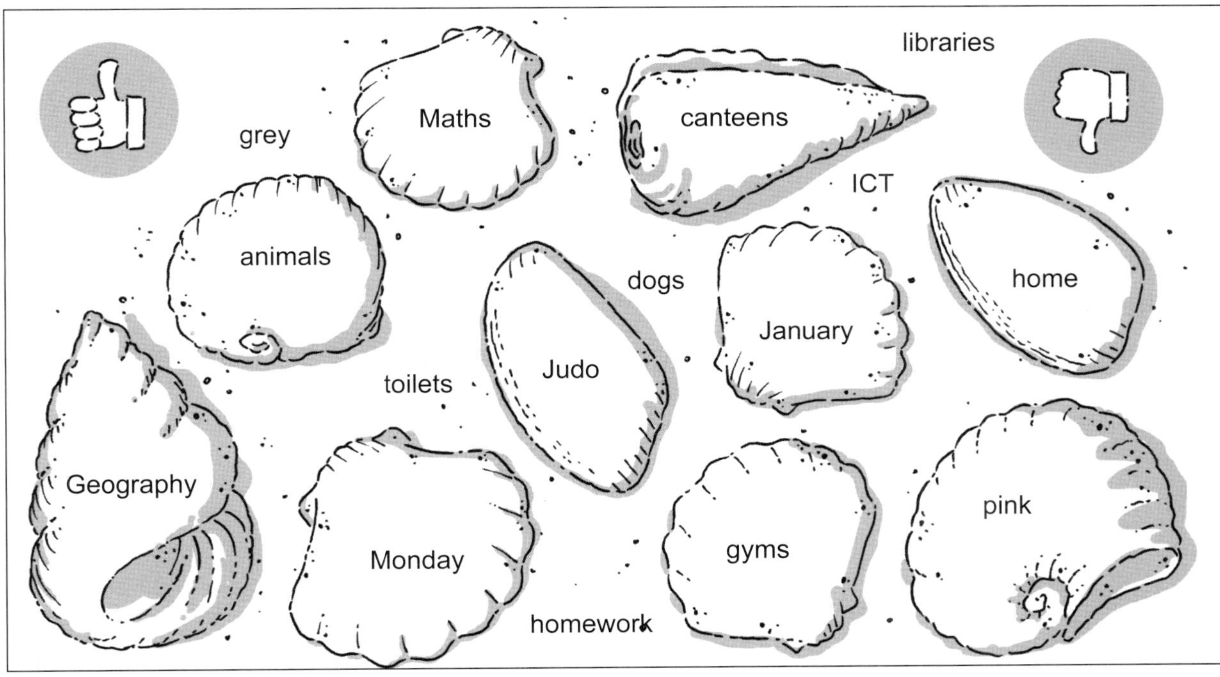

b) Tell your partner what you like and don't like. Find two examples where you think the same as your partner and two where you don't think the same.

2 Feelings

FF 10 **Listen to the people. They are surprised or sad or angry or sorry or happy. Tick (✓) the correct boxes.**

	 1	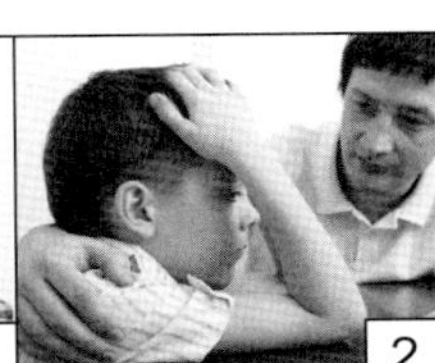 2	 3	 4	 5
sad					
surprised					
sorry					
happy					
angry					

3 WORDS Friendly or unfriendly?

a) Charlie Rud and Fred Snap are very unfriendly. Act out their dialogue with a partner. Be unfriendly!

Charlie Rud: My name is Charlie. I'm new here.
Fred Snap: Oh.
Charlie Rud: Where is the canteen?
Fred Snap: It's near the library.
Chalie Rud: The library? Hm. I like books.
Fred Snap: Oh.

b) Help Mr Rud and Mr Snap to be friendly now. You can use the words from the box.

> That's cool. • Goodbye! (2x) • Nice to meet you. • Let me show you. • What about you? • My name is Fred. • Thank you. • Here's the canteen, OK? • Hello! • What's your name? • Can you help me, please? • Hi! • I like books about cars.

Charlie Rud: (1) ____________ My name is Charlie.
I'm new here.
(2) What's ____________
Fred Snap: Oh. (3) ____________
(4) ____________
Charlie Rud: (5) ____________
(6) Can ____________
Where is the canteen?
Fred Snap: It's near the library.
(7) Let ____________
Charlie Rud: The library? Hm.
(8) ____________ I like books.
(9) ____________
Fred Snap: Oh. (10) I ____________
(11) Here ____________
I have to go now.
(12) ____________
Charlie Rud: (13) ____________
(14) ____________

c) Act out their friendly dialogue. Show your friends or your teacher. Be nice and smile!

Ich kann sagen, was mir (nicht) gefällt und wie es mir und anderen gerade geht.

1 I like it

a) Draw lines. What do you like? What don't you like?

b) Tell your partner what you like and don't like. Find two examples where you think the same as your partner and two where you don't think the same.

2 Feelings

FF 10 Listen to the people. They are surprised or sad or angry or sorry or happy. Finish the sentences.

1 The boy is ____________________.

2 The boy is ____________________.

3 The girl is ____________________.

4 The boy is ____________________.

5 The boy is ____________________.

3 WORDS Friendly or unfriendly?

a) Charlie Rud and Fred Snap are very unfriendly. Act out their dialogue with a partner. Be unfriendly!

Charlie Rud:	My name is Charlie. I'm new here.
Fred Snap:	Oh.
Charlie Rud:	Where is the canteen?
Fred Snap:	It's near the library.
Chalie Rud:	The library? Hm. I like books.
Fred Snap:	Oh.

b) Help Charlie Rud and Fred Snap to be friendly now. Choose phrases from the box.

That's cool. • Goodbye! (2x) • Nice to meet you. • Let me show you. • What about you? • Come in, please. • My name is Fred. • Thank you. • Here's the canteen, OK? • Hello! • What's your name? • Can you help me, please? • Hi! • I like books about cars. • Can you speak louder, please?

Charlie Rud: (1) ____________ My name is Charlie.
I'm new here.
(2) ____________________

Fred Snap: Oh. (3) ____________________
(4) ____________________

Charlie Rud: (5) ____________________
(6) ____________________
Where is the canteen?

Fred Snap: (7) ____________________
It's near the library.

Charlie Rud: The library? Hm.
(8) ____________ I like books.
(9) ____________________

Fred Snap: Oh. (10) ____________________
(11) ____________________
I have to go now.
(12) ____________________

Charlie Rud: (13) ____________________
(14) ____________________

c) Act out their friendly dialogue. Show your friends or your teacher. Be nice and smile!

Ich kann sagen, was mir (nicht) gefällt und wie es mir und anderen gerade geht.

1 I like it

a) Draw lines. What do you like? What don't you like? You don't know some of the words. Try to find words. Example: Ritter – a man on a horse.

b) Tell your partner what you like and don't like. Find two examples where you think the same as your partner and two where you don't think the same.

2 Feelings

FF 10 Listen to the people. They are surprised or sad or angry or sorry or happy. Finish the sentences.

1 The boy is ______________________________.

2 The boy is ______________________________.

3 The girl is ______________________________.

4 The girl is ______________________________.

5 The boy is ______________________________.

3 WORDS Friendly or unfriendly?

a) Charlie Rud and Fred Snap are very unfriendly. Act out their dialogue with a partner. Be unfriendly!

Charlie Rud: My name is Charlie. I'm new here.
Fred Snap: Oh.
Charlie Rud: Where is the canteen?
Fred Snap: It's near the library.
Chalie Rud: The library? Hm. I like books.
Fred Snap: Oh.

b) Help Charlie Rud and Fred Snap to be friendly now. You can use the words from the box. Write the dialogue again. You need paper.

Charlie Rud:

Thank you • Goodbye! • Can you help me, please? • Hi! • My name is … • What's your name? • That's cool. • What about you? • I'm new here.

Fred Snap:

Nice to meet you. • Let me show you. • My name is … . • Goodbye! • Here's the canteen, OK? • Hello! • I like books about cars. • Oh.

c) Write a new friendly dialogue with a partner. Act it out. Show your friends or your teacher. Be nice and smile!

TIP
- What are your names?
- Where are you?
- Who starts the dialogue?
- You can use words from **b)**.

Ich kann eine Einladung und/oder einen Brief über Schulthemen schreiben.

1 WORDS New schools

Paul and Oliver are new in Plymouth. Finish the text. Use the words in the box.

at (5x) • in • from • to (3x) • with • on (2x)

Paul and Oliver Newman are (1) _____ home (2) _____ Plymouth. They are new here. They come (3) _____ London. Now they live (4) _____ 17 Alvington Street. Paul is twelve. He goes (5) _____ Plymstock School. His first day (6) _____ the new school is (7) _____ Monday. The lessons start (8) _____ 9 o'clock.

Oliver is four years old. He goes (9) _____ Beechwood Primary School. Mrs Newman is a teacher (10) _____ Oliver's new school. Oliver goes (11) _____ school (12) _____ his mum. It's his first day (13) _____ Monday too.

2 You choose The last day of school

It's the last day of school before your holidays.
What do you do? Do you have a party?

Choose a) or b):

a) Write a letter to a friend in England or the USA about your last day of school.

You can write about …
- the lessons and subjects you have that day,
- what you do,
- the times,
- what you do in the breaks,
- what rooms you are in,
- what you like/don't like.

b) Write a party invitation for your last-day-of-school-party.

What? ______________________________

Where? ______________________________

When? ______________________________

Ich kann eine Einladung und/oder einen Brief über Schulthemen schreiben.

1 WORDS New schools

Paul and Oliver are new in Plymouth. Finish the text with these prepositions.

at • in • from • to • with • on

Paul and Oliver Newman are (1) _____ home (2) _____ Plymouth. They are new here. They come (3) _____ London. Now they live (4) _____ 17 Alvington Street. Paul is twelve. He goes (5) _____ Plymstock School. His first day (6) _____ the new school is (7) _____ Monday. The lessons start (8) _____ 9 o'clock.

Oliver is four years old. He goes (9) _____ Beechwood Primary School. Mrs Newman is a teacher (10) _____ Oliver's new school. Oliver goes (11) _____ school (12) _____ his mum. It's his first day (13) _____ Monday too.

2 You choose The last day of school

**It's the last day of school before your holidays.
What do you do? Do you have a party?**

Choose a) or b):

a) Write a letter to a friend in England or the USA about your last day of school.

You can write about …
- the lessons and subjects you have that day,
- what you do,
- the times,
- what you do in the breaks,
- what rooms you are in,
- what you like/don't like.

b) Write a party invitation for your last-day-of-school-party.

What? ______________________________

____

____

Ich kann eine Einladung und/oder einen Brief über Schulthemen schreiben.

1 WORDS New schools

Paul and Oliver are new in Plymouth. Finish the text with prepositions.

Paul and Oliver Newman are (1) _____ home (2) _____ Plymouth. They are new here. They come (3) _____ London. Now they live (4) _____ 17 Alvington Street. Paul is twelve. He goes (5) _____ Plymstock School. His first day (6) _____ the new school is (7) _____ Monday. The lessons start (8) _____ 9 o'clock.

Oliver is four years old. He goes (9) _____ Beechwood Primary School. Mrs Newman is a teacher (10) _____ Oliver's new school. Oliver goes (11) _____ school (12) _____ his mum. It's his first day (13) _____ Monday too.

2 You choose The last day of school

It's the last day of school before your holidays.
What do you do? Do you have a party?

Choose a) or b):

a) Write a letter to a friend in England or the USA about your last day of school.

You can write about …
- the lessons and subjects you have that day,
- what you do,
- the times,
- what you do in the breaks,
- what rooms you are in,
- what you like/don't like.

b) Write a party invitation for your last-day-of-school / winter / summer / … party. Add drawings and pictures. You need paper.

You can use words from the box.

See you! • Let's • Come! • on Monday, … • lots of fun/… • Please bring/come/wear/…/don't wear … • 1 o'clock • I live …

Ich verstehe und benutze viele Sätze, die wir im Klassenraum verwenden.

1 WORDS In the classroom

A friend goes to school in England for two weeks. Write down some good phrases for him.

Was soll er sagen, wenn …

1 … er das Fenster öffnen möchte? C_____ I o______ t___ w________, p________?

2 … er zu spät kommt? S_________, I'm l_________.

3 … er wissen möchte, was als Hausaufgabe auf ist? W______ f_____ h____________?

4 … der Lehrer oder ein Mitschüler zu leise spricht? C_____ y_____ s_________ l_________, p_________?

5 … er eine Antwort nicht weiß? S_________, I d________ k_________.

6 … er einen Stift ausleihen möchte? C_____ I h________ a p_________, p_________?

7 … er wissen möchte, wie man das englische Wort für „Boot" buchstabiert? C_____ y_____ s_________ "boat", p_________?

8 … er noch nicht fertig ist? S_________, I h__________ f__________.

9 … er auf die Toilette muss? C_____ I g_____ t____ t___ toilet, p_________?

10 … er wissen möchte, was „Klassenkamerad" auf Englisch heißt? W______ "Klassenkamerad" i _____ E___________?

2 LANGUAGE Signs[1]

Look at the pictures. Can you explain what the signs say?

1 (forget / –) Don't forget to write ____________.

2 (have / +) ______________________________ here.

3 (talk / –) ______________________________.

4 (win / +) ______________________________ a teddy bear.

5 (open / –) ______________________________ the window.

6 (like / +) ______________________________ me.

[1] sign [saɪn] *Zeichen, Informationsschild*

Ich verstehe und benutze viele Sätze, die wir im Klassenraum verwenden.

1 WORDS In the classroom

A friend goes to school in England for two weeks. Write down some good phrases for him.

Was soll er sagen, wenn …

1 … er das Fenster öffnen möchte? ▸ Can I ______________________________?

2 … er zu spät kommt? ▸ Sorry, ______________________________.

3 … er wissen möchte, was als Hausaufgabe auf ist? ▸ What's ______________________________?

4 … der Lehrer oder ein Mitschüler zu leise spricht? ▸ Can you ______________________________?

5 … er eine Antwort nicht weiß? ▸ Sorry, ______________________________.

6 … er einen Stift ausleihen möchte? ▸ Can I ______________________________?

7 … er wissen möchte, wie man das englische Wort für „Boot“ buchstabiert?
▸ Can I ______________________________?

8 … er noch nicht fertig ist? ▸ Sorry, ______________________________.

9 … er auf die Toilette muss? ▸ Can I ______________________________?

10 … er wissen möchte, was „Klassenkamerad“ auf Englisch heißt?
▸ What's ______________________________?

2 LANGUAGE Signs[1]

Look at the pictures. Can you explain what the signs say?

1 (forget) Don't forget to write______________________________.

2 (have) ______________________________ here.

3 (talk) ______________________________.

4 (win) ______________________________ a teddy bear.

5 (open) ______________________________ the window.

6 (like) ______________________________ me.

[1]sign [saɪn] *Zeichen, Informationsschild*

Ich verstehe und benutze viele **Sätze, die wir im Klassenraum** verwenden.

1 WORDS In the classroom

A friend goes to school in England for two weeks. Write down some good phrases for him. You need paper.

Was soll er sagen, wenn …
1 … er das Fenster öffnen möchte?
2 … er zu spät kommt?
3 … er wissen möchte, was als Hausaufgabe auf ist?
4 … der Lehrer oder ein Mitschüler zu leise spricht?
5 … er eine Antwort nicht weiß?
6 … er einen Stift ausleihen möchte?
7 … er wissen möchte, wie man das englische Wort für „Boot" buchstabiert?
8 … er noch nicht fertig ist?
9 … er auf die Toilette muss?
10 … er wissen möchte, was „Klassenkamerad" auf Englisch heißt?

2 LANGUAGE Signs[1]

Look at the pictures. Can you explain what the signs say? Choose verbs from the box.

ask • eat • like • open • start • talk • touch • win • have

1 Don't forget to write ______________________.
2 ______________________ here.
3 ______________________.
4 ______________________ a teddy bear.
5 ______________________ the window.
6 ______________________ me.

[1] sign [saɪn] *Zeichen, Informationsschild*

Ich kann das Alphabet aufsagen und für andere Worte buchstabieren. Ich kann Worte aufschreiben, wenn andere sie mir buchstabieren.

1 At the airport

FF 11 **You're at an airport. Listen and tick (✓) the right flight numbers.**

1 ☐ EE 6178 ☐ AA 6178 ☐ EA 6178 to Washington

2 ☐ EB 7447 ☐ AB 7447 ☐ IB 7447 to Madrid

3 ☐ AC 6551 ☐ IC 6551 ☐ CA 6551 to Dublin

4 ☐ LA 907 ☐ LE 907 ☐ LH 907 to Frankfurt

5 ☐ DF 4381 ☐ GF 4381 ☐ JF 4381 to Boston

2 Codes

You need some codes for a computer game. Some are on your list, but some aren't.

a) Find a partner and complete your lists.

You can talk like this:

Is code MAD5F on your list?

Yes, it is. / No, it isn't. Can I write it down, please? / Sorry, say it again, please! … What about code ARP5N? Is it on your list?

Yes, it is. / No, it isn't. Can I write it down, please? / Sorry, say it again, please! What about …?

b) Then look at your list and your partner's list. Are all the codes the same?

Partner A's list

MAD5F	KHD1A	ARP5M
MAD7P	WOL8M	LKE3P
ESG9T	WUL8N	ESJ9T

Partner B's list

ARP5N	ESJ9T	MAD5F
MAD7P	WUL8N	LOE3G
ESG9T	WOL8Z	WHD1A

Ich kann das Alphabet aufsagen und für andere Worte buchstabieren. Ich kann Worte aufschreiben, wenn andere sie mir buchstabieren.

1 At the airport

FF 11 **You're at an airport. Listen and tick (✓) the right flight numbers.**

1	☐ EE 6178	☐ AA 6178	☐ AE 6178	☐ EA 6178 to Washington
2	☐ EB 7447	☐ AB 7447	☐ ET 7447	☐ IB 7447 to Madrid
3	☐ AC 6551	☐ IC 6551	☐ IS 6551	☐ CA 6551 to Dublin
4	☐ LA 907	☐ LE 907	☐ LE 907	☐ LH 907 to Frankfurt
5	☐ DF 4381	☐ GF 4381	☐ ATF 4381	☐ JF 4381 to Boston

2 Codes

You need some codes for a computer game. Some are on your list, but some aren't.

a) Find a partner and complete your lists.

You can talk like this:

Is code MAD5F on your list?

Yes, it is. / No, it isn't. Can I write it down, please? / Sorry, say it again, please! …
What about code ARP5N? Is it on your list?

Yes, it is. / No, it isn't. Can I write it down, please? / Sorry, say it again, please! What about …?

b) Then look at your list and your partner's list. Are all the codes the same?

Partner A's list

MAD5F	KHD1A	ARP5M
MAD7P	WOL8M	LKE3P
ESG9T	WUL8N	ESJ9T

Partner B's list

ARP5N	ESJ9T	MAD5F
MAD7P	WUL8N	LOE3G
ESG9T	WOL8Z	WHD1A

Ich kann das Alphabet aufsagen und für andere Worte buchstabieren. Ich kann Worte aufschreiben, wenn andere sie mir buchstabieren.

1 At the airport

FF 11 **You're at an airport. Listen to the messages. Can you find out the right flight numbers?**

1 AA 6178 to Washington
2 _____ 7447 to Madrid
3 _____ 6551 to Dublin
4 _____ 907 to Frankfurt
5 _____ 4381 to Boston

2 Codes

You need some codes for a computer game. Some are on your list, but some aren't.
a) Find a partner and complete your lists.

You can talk like this:

Is code MAD5F on your list?

Yes, it is. / No, it isn't. Can I write it down, please? / Sorry, say it again, please! … What about code ARP5N? Is it on your list?

Yes, it is. / No, it isn't. Can I write it down, please? / Sorry, say it again, please! What about …?

b) Then look at your list and your partner's list. Are all the codes the same?

Partner A's list

YARP5N	HESJ9T	GMAD5F
VMUO7P	WUL8N	ILQE3G
PESG9Y	WVOL8M	EWHD1A

Partner B's list

GMAD5F	YKHD1A	ZARP5M
VMUO7P	XWOL8M	YLZE3P
VESG9I	WUL8N	HESJ 9T

Ich weiß, welche Zeichen und Hilfen im *Vocabulary* was bedeuten. Dies kann ich anderen auch erklären.

GAME Dominoes

Make a line of cards. Talk to your partner like this:

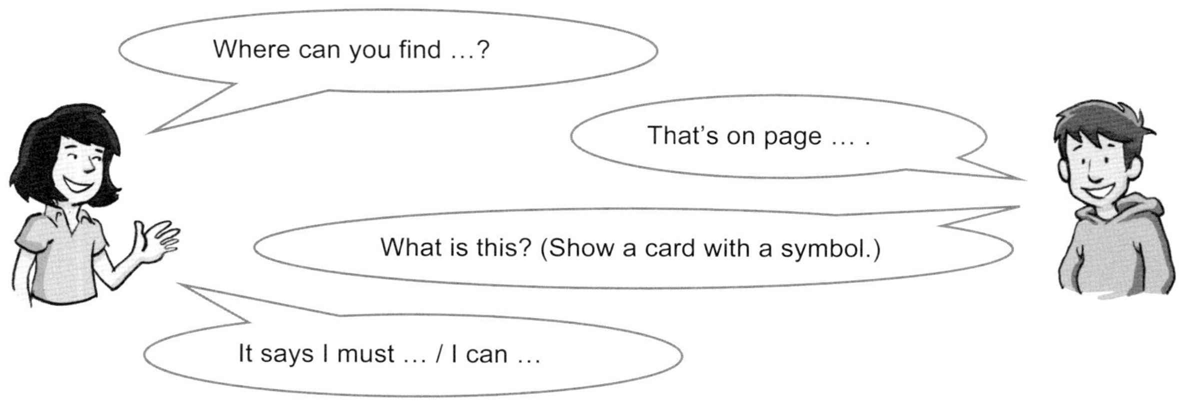

ENGLISH G access 1	*The Vocabulary*	*pp. 172-205*	*sb.*
somebody …	Bedeutung und Aussprache englischer Wörter	*English-German Dictionary, pp. 206-219*	Plural (Mehrzahl)
pl	*Sounds • Numbers*	*p. 233*	Die Zeichen in eckigen Klammern [ ] zeigen die …
Aussprache.	Diese Vokabeln sind blau gedruckt.	Vokabeln, die du in der Grundschule gelernt hast.	*opposite* (Gegenteil)
◂▸	Eingerückte Vokabeln, z.B. clock [klɒk] watch [wɒtʃ]	Diese Wörter solltest du zusammen lernen.	*p. 236*
Classroom English	Wie heißt … auf Englisch?	*German-English Dictionary, pp. 220-230*	*something*
sth.	Blaue Kästen enthalten …	Vokabeln zu einem bestimmten Thema / Tipps zur Verwendung.	Vorsicht, hier macht man leicht Fehler!
!	In der rechten Spalte stehen …	Beispielsätze.	*I can do it!*

Unit 2

Homes and families

Meine Lernlandkarte für Unit 2

Name: ______________________ Klasse: ____________

Wie gut bist du in den Lernfeldern der Unit 2?
Schätze dich darin ein und male die entsprechende Anzahl an Kreisen auf der Ampel aus.
So findest du dein Übungsblatt.

Das lief nicht gut, ich muss mehr üben.	Das war OK, aber ich könnte besser werden.	Das habe ich gut geschafft.

Setze ein Häkchen, wenn du fertig bist. ✓

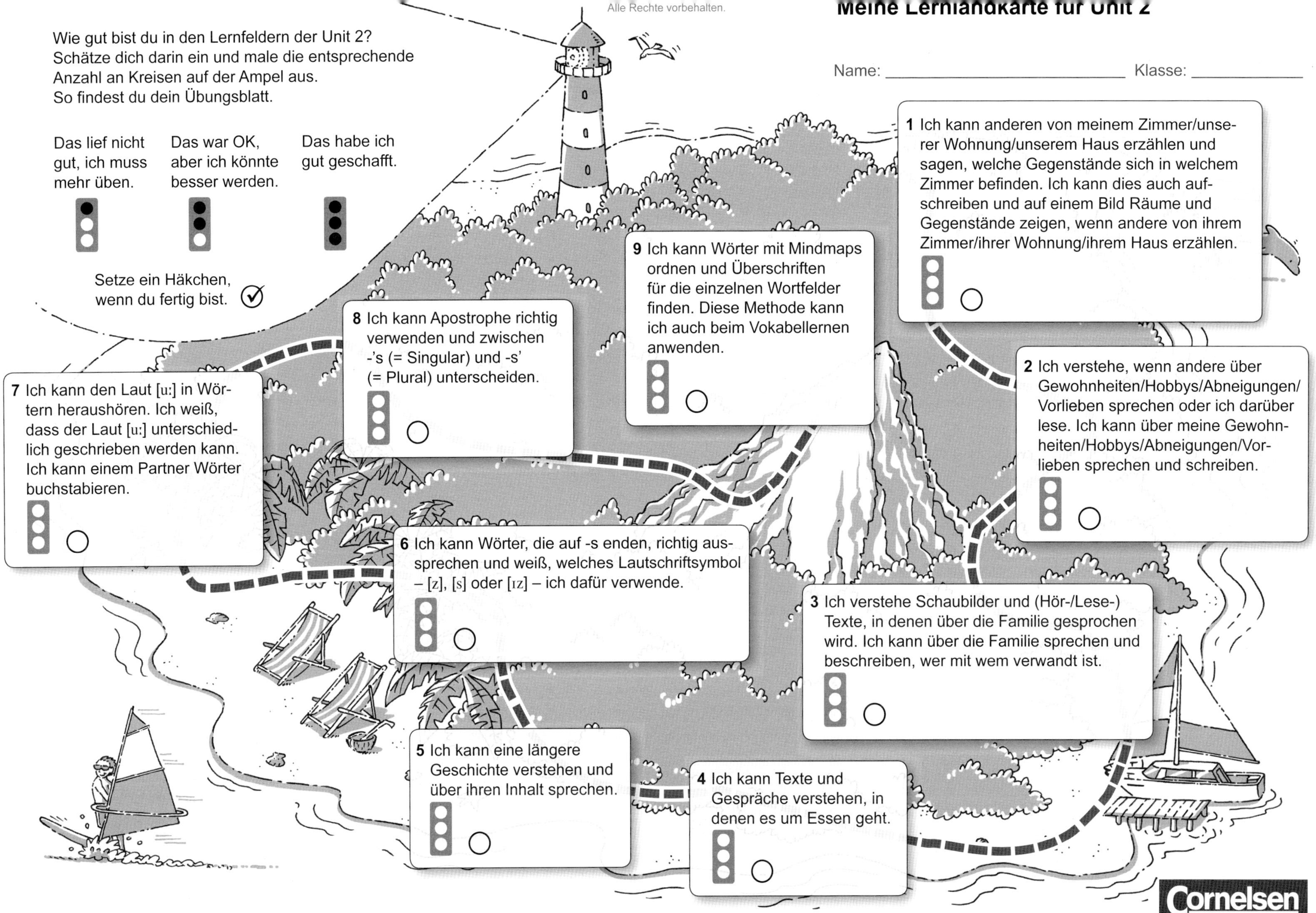

1 Ich kann anderen von meinem Zimmer/unserer Wohnung/unserem Haus erzählen und sagen, welche Gegenstände sich in welchem Zimmer befinden. Ich kann dies auch aufschreiben und auf einem Bild Räume und Gegenstände zeigen, wenn andere von ihrem Zimmer/ihrer Wohnung/ihrem Haus erzählen.

2 Ich verstehe, wenn andere über Gewohnheiten/Hobbys/Abneigungen/Vorlieben sprechen oder ich darüber lese. Ich kann über meine Gewohnheiten/Hobbys/Abneigungen/Vorlieben sprechen und schreiben.

3 Ich verstehe Schaubilder und (Hör-/Lese-)Texte, in denen über die Familie gesprochen wird. Ich kann über die Familie sprechen und beschreiben, wer mit wem verwandt ist.

4 Ich kann Texte und Gespräche verstehen, in denen es um Essen geht.

5 Ich kann eine längere Geschichte verstehen und über ihren Inhalt sprechen.

6 Ich kann Wörter, die auf -s enden, richtig aussprechen und weiß, welches Lautschriftsymbol – [z], [s] oder [ɪz] – ich dafür verwende.

7 Ich kann den Laut [uː] in Wörtern heraushören. Ich weiß, dass der Laut [uː] unterschiedlich geschrieben werden kann. Ich kann einem Partner Wörter buchstabieren.

8 Ich kann Apostrophe richtig verwenden und zwischen -'s (= Singular) und -s' (= Plural) unterscheiden.

9 Ich kann Wörter mit Mindmaps ordnen und Überschriften für die einzelnen Wortfelder finden. Diese Methode kann ich auch beim Vokabellernen anwenden.

Cornelsen

Ich kann anderen von meinem Zimmer/unserer Wohnung/unserem Haus erzählen und sagen, welche Gegenstände in welchem Zimmer sind. Ich kann dies auch aufschreiben und auf einem Bild Räume und Gegenstände zeigen, wenn andere von ihrem Zimmer/ihrer Wohnung/ihrem Haus erzählen.

A tree house

a) WORDS Look at the tree house and label the rooms and things.

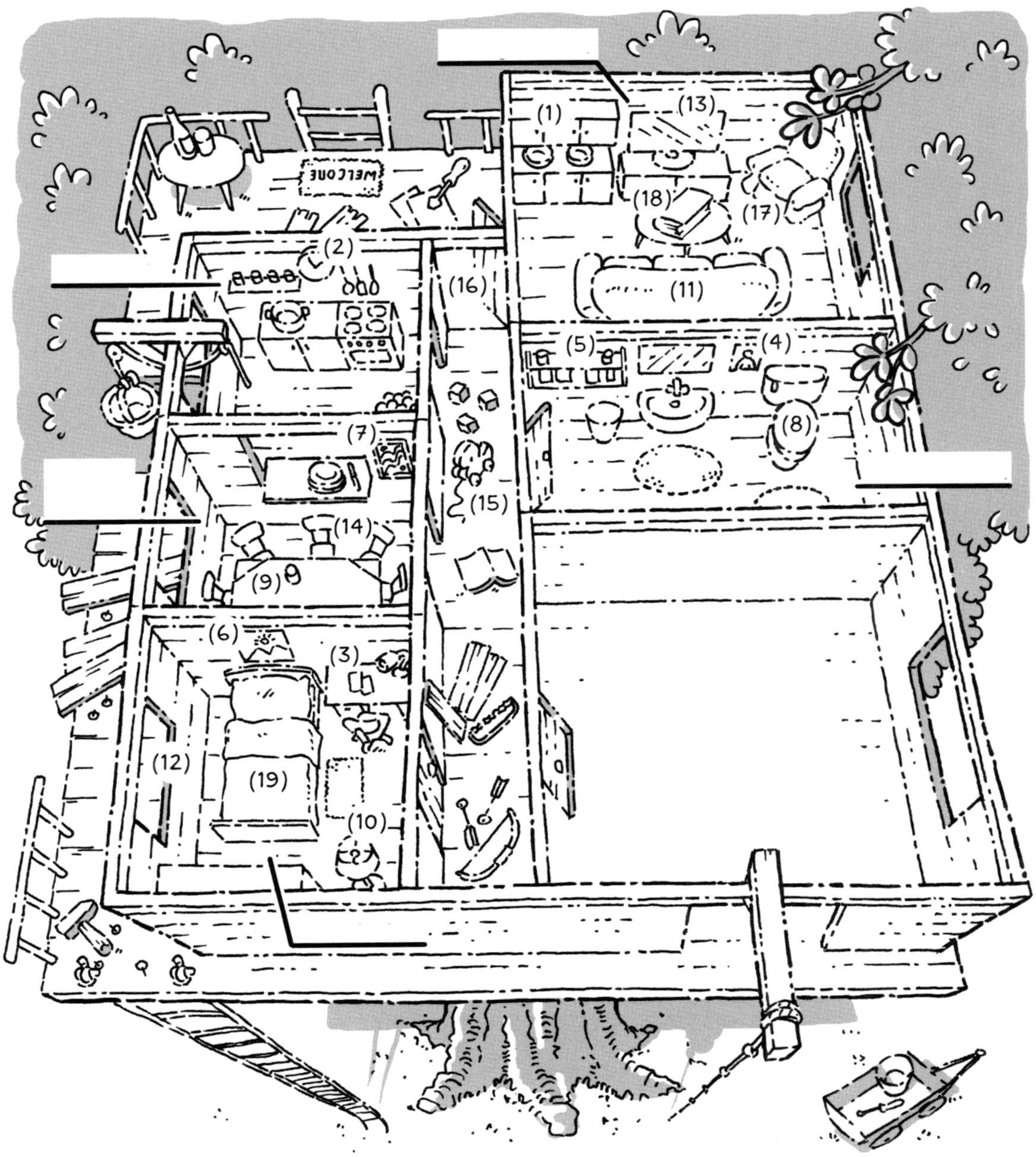

fold here

More help bdrm • bthrm • dnng rm • ktchen • lvng rm • rmchr • bd • bk • chr • clck • cpbrd • dsk • dr • lmp • pht • pctr • pstr • shlf • sf • tbl • tlt • ty • TV • wndw

b) Take your picture and a pencil and work with a partner. Check the words together. Is the spelling correct? Then work on c).

fold here

> **More help** What's this? • This is a … • Yes, that's right. / No, it isn't. It's a/an . . . •
> What do you think? Can you help me with the spelling?

c) Draw your own bedroom in the empty room of the tree house. Label the things.

d) Work with a new partner. Describe your pictures to each other.

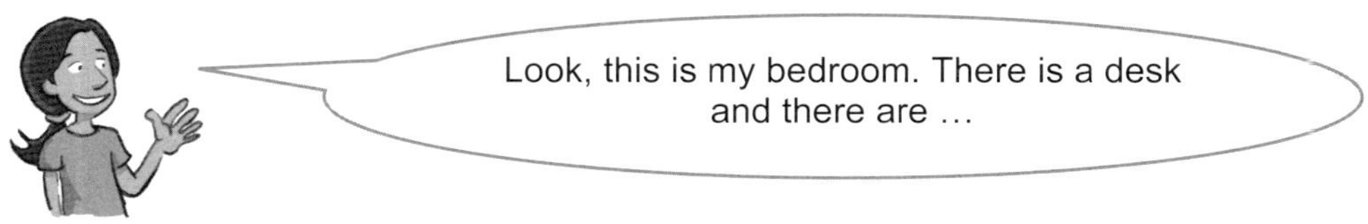

e) Colour the things in the treehouse.

f) Work with a new partner. What colour are the things in your tree houses?

g) Write a short text about your dream house. You need paper.

fold here

> **More help**
> My dream house/bedroom/garden/… is … • In my dream house/Downstairs/Upstairs there is … / there are … • … live/lives in my dreamhouse. • In my bedroom / In the kitchen / In the garden … there is / there are …
>
> new • old • big • small • green • red • colourful • made of wood/stone •
> my best friends • my family • famous pop stars • play computer games • watch TV • CD player •
> listen to music • eat what I like • magical room • game room • swimming-pool • helicopter landing site • …

h) Work with a new partner. Read out your texts. Then say what you remember about your partner's dream house.

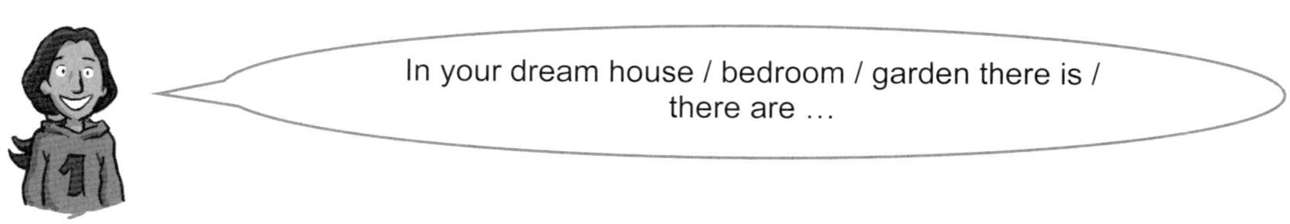

EXTRA Draw a big, colourful picture of your dream house to go with the text.

Ich verstehe, wenn andere über Gewohnheiten/Hobbys/Abneigungen/Vorlieben sprechen oder ich darüber lese. Ich kann über meine Gewohnheiten/Hobbys/Abneigungen/Vorlieben sprechen und schreiben.

LANGUAGE Around the week

a) Look at the pictures of Mia's week. Then fill in the missing information about your week and Mia's week in the table.

	Me	**Mia**	**Partner 1: ______**	**Partner 2: ______**
On Mondays	I wake up at ______	wakes up at ______	wakes up at ______	wakes up at ______
On Tuesdays	I have breakfast ______	has breakfast ______	has breakfast ______	has breakfast ______
On Wednesdays	I play ______ ______	plays ______ ______	plays ______ ______	plays ______ ______
On Thursdays	I meet ______	meets ______	meets ______	meets ______
On Fridays	I often have ______ ______ for lunch.	often has ______ ______ for lunch.	often has ______ ______ for lunch.	often has ______ ______ for lunch.
On Saturdays	I fall asleep ______	falls asleep ______	falls asleep ______	falls asleep ______
On Sundays	I watch ______ ______ on TV.	watches ______ ______ on TV.	watches ______ ______ on TV.	watches ______ ______ on TV.

b) **Find two partners and talk to them about your weeks. Add your partners' information to the table.**

c) **Tell the class about your partner's weekend.**

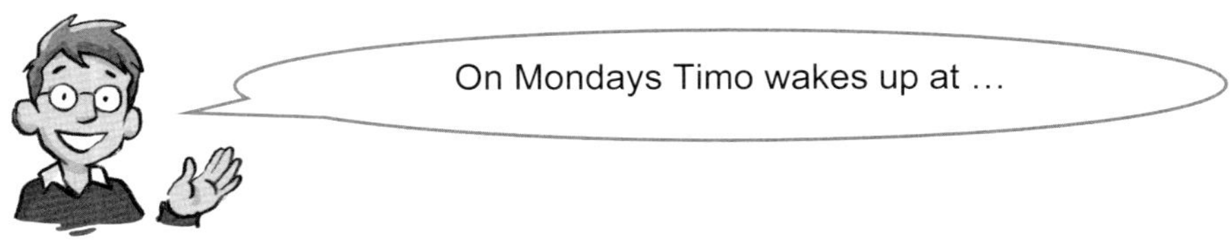

d) **Write a text about your partners' weekend. You need paper.**

fold here

More help

On Mondays	seven o'clock • quarter past six • quarter to seven • half past seven • …
On Tuesdays	in the kitchen • in my bedroom • at home • at school • with my family • alone
On Wednesdays	football • basketball • computer games • with my friends • with my dog • in the garden • …
On Thursdays	my friends • my best friend Thomas • my classmates • my little sister • …
On Fridays	fish • pizza • spaghetti • a sandwich • pancakes • …
On Saturdays	at ten o'clock • at midnight • very late • …
On Sundays	The Simpsons • football • a film • game shows • …

Ich verstehe, wenn andere über Gewohnheiten/Hobbys/Abneigungen/Vorlieben sprechen oder ich darüber lese. Ich kann über meine Gewohnheiten/Hobbys/Abneigungen/Vorlieben sprechen und schreiben.

LANGUAGE Around the week

a) Look at the pictures of Mia's week. Then fill in the missing information about your week and Mia's week in the table.

	Me	Mia	Partner 1: _____	Partner 2: _____
On Mondays wake up/wakes up				
On Tuesdays have/has breakfast				
On Wednesdays play/plays				
On Thursdays meet/meets				
On Fridays often have/has … for lunch				
On Saturdays fall/falls asleep				
On Sundays watch/watches … on TV				

b) Find two partners and talk to them about your weeks. Fill in your partners' information.

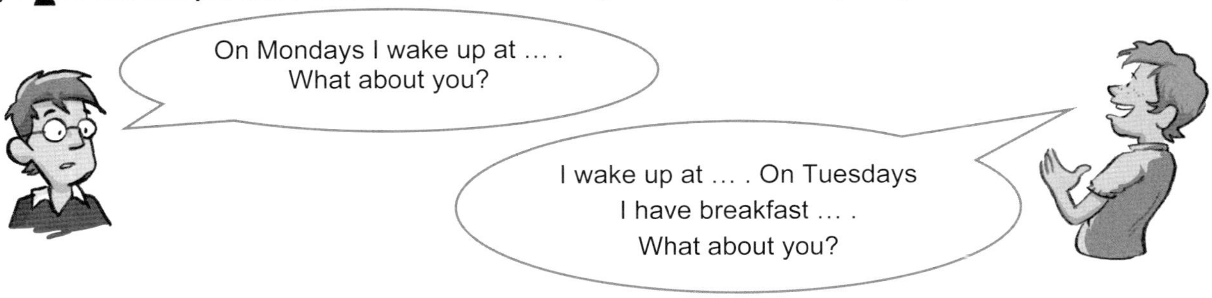

c) Tell the class about your partner's weekend.

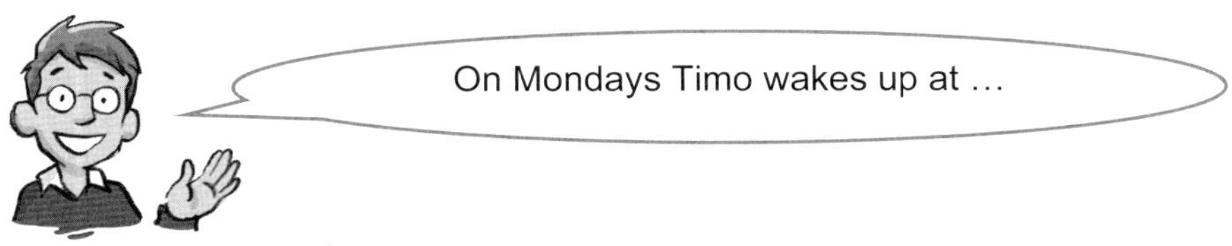

d) Write a text about your partner's weekend. You need paper .

fold here

More help

On Mondays	seven o'clock • quarter past six • quarter to seven • half past seven • …
On Tuesdays	in the kitchen • in my bedroom • at home • at school • with my family • alone • at 7 o'clock • …
On Wednesdays	football • basketball • computer games • with my friends • with my dog • in the garden • …
On Thursdays	my friends • my best friend Thomas • my classmates • my little sister • …
On Fridays	fish • pizza • spaghetti • a sandwich • pancakes • …
On Saturdays	at ten o'clock • at midnight • very late • …
On Sundays	The Simpsons • football • a film • game shows • …

Ich verstehe, wenn andere über Gewohnheiten/Hobbys/Abneigungen/Vorlieben sprechen oder ich darüber lese. Ich kann über meine Gewohnheiten/Hobbys/Abneigungen/Vorlieben sprechen und schreiben.

LANGUAGE Around the week

a) Look at the pictures of Mia's week. Then fill in the missing information about your week and Mia's week in the table.

	Me	Mia	Partner 1: _____	Partner 2: _____
On Mondays (to) wake up				
On Tuesdays (to) have breakfast				
On Wednesdays (to) play				
On Thursdays (to) meet				
On Fridays (to) often have … for lunch				
On Saturdays (to) fall asleep				
On Sundays (to) watch … on TV				

b) Find two partners and talk to them about your weeks. Fill in your partners' information.

c) Tell the class about your partner's weekend.

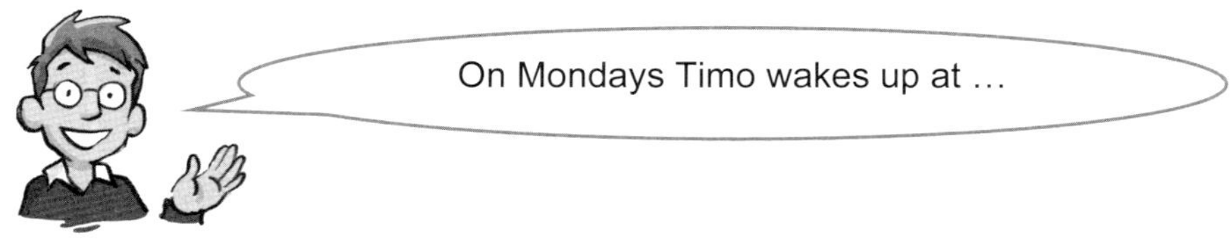

d) Write a text about a person that you know, somebody in your family or a famous person: a pop star, a film character or a comic-strip character. Write about this person's typical week. Find a good title for your text.

You can start like this:

On Mondays … always gets up at … . On Tuesdays …

Ich verstehe Schaubilder und (Hör-/Lese-)Texte, in denen über die Familie gesprochen wird. Ich kann über die Familie sprechen und beschreiben, wer mit wem verwandt ist.

1 You choose Family life

TIP
Entscheide selbst, welche Aufgabe zum Thema *family* du bearbeitest!
Welche Aufgabe …
- unterstützt mich, mehr zum Thema *family* zu lernen?
- hilft mir beim Üben, damit ich die neu gelernten Wörter zum Thema *family* besser behalten kann?
- macht mir richtig Spaß, so dass ich mich gerne mit dem Thema *family* beschäftige?
- fordert mich heraus, so dass ich so dass ich zeigen kann, wozu ich fähig bin?
- passt zu mir, weil ich durch sie das Thema *family* gut begreifen kann?
- finde ich spannend, weil ich darüber mehr wissen möchte?

Choose one or two tasks.

a) WORDS Write an alphabetical list of family words. Look in a dictionary and write down the German word too. Then write one sentence for every word.

b) Write about your family or a famous family you know about. How many people are there? What are their names? Where do they live? How old are they? Give one or two more facts about hobbies, favourite food/music/pet/colour … .
Then read your text to your partner. What does she/he remember[1]?

c) Draw a picture *This is my crazy[2] family*. Label the people.
Uncle Dracula, Cousin Superman … . Then describe it to your partner.

d) Work with a partner and write a dialogue about your families or about a famous family. Act out the dialogue.

e) Write about someone in your family you like very much.
Read it out to a partner.

f) Make a survey[3]:
How many "only-children"[4] are there in your class? How many have brothers or sisters? How many do they have? Draw a poster and tell your partner about it.

	Number
Only children	
Children with brothers or sisters	
1 brother or sister	
2 brothers or sisters	
3 / > 3 brothers or sisters	

A survey

g) Write about your dream family.
Read your text to a partner.

h) Draw a comic-strip *One day with my family*. Make speech bubbles. You can look at pp. 34–35 in your English book for ideas.

[1](to) remember [rɪ'membə] sich (an jdn./etw.) erinnern • [2]crazy ['kreɪzɪ] verrückt • [3]survey ['sɜːveɪ] *Umfrage* • [4]only-children ['əʊnlɪ] ['tʃɪldən] *Einzelkinder*

Ich verstehe Schaubilder und (Hör-/Lese-)Texte, in denen über die Familie gesprochen wird. Ich kann über die Familie sprechen und beschreiben, wer mit wem verwandt ist.

2 Think Pair Share: The simple present

TIP

THINK Was weißt Du noch über das *Simple present*? Wann wird es benutzt? Wie werden bejahte Aussagen gebildet? Was ist besonders in der 3. Person Singular? Wie werden verneinte Aussagen gebildet? Und wie werden Aussagen in der 3. Person Singular verneint? Mache Dir Notizen.

PAIR Benutze Deine Notizen und tausche Dich mit Deinem Partner aus. Notiert, was Ihr voneinander Neues lernt.

SHARE Tragt Eure Ergebnisse gemeinsam in der Klasse zusammen.

→ Vergleicht eure Ergebnisse mit dem **Grammar File 6, Seite 160–162** in eurem Englischbuch.

3 Meet Barney

Poppy has a dog. His name is Barney. Here are some facts about him. Use the *simple present* and write about what Barney does and likes and what he doesn't do and like.

1 Barney likes ____________________
2 ____________________
3 ____________________
4 ____________________
5 ____________________
6 ____________________

fold here

More help

sleeps in a basket / doesn't sleep in a basket • eats carrots / doesn't eat carrots • jumps when he is happy / doesn't jump when he is happy • plays with other dogs / doesn't play with other dogs • likes cats / doesn't like cats • likes swimming / doesn't like swimming

4 What about you?

a) Draw four pictures that show what you normally like or do and what you normally don't like or don't do. Show your pictures to your partner. Can she/he guess what it is?

b) Write your sentences next to your pictures.

fold here

More help

I like / I don't like • I play / I don't play • I meet / I don't meet • I have / I don't have • I wake up at / I don't wake up at • I feed / I don't feed • I watch / I don't watch • …

Ich verstehe Schaubilder und (Hör-/Lese-)Texte, in denen über die Familie gesprochen wird. Ich kann über die Familie sprechen und beschreiben, wer mit wem verwandt ist.

2 Think Pair Share: The simple present

TIP

THINK Was weißt Du noch über das *Simple present*? Wann wird es benutzt? Wie werden bejahte Aussagen gebildet? Was ist besonders in der 3. Person Singular? Wie werden verneinte Aussagen gebildet? Und wie werden Aussagen in der 3. Person Singular verneint? Mache Dir Notizen.

PAIR Benutze Deine Notizen und tausche Dich mit Deinem Partner aus. Notiert, was Ihr voneinander Neues lernt.

SHARE Tragt Eure Ergebnisse gemeinsam in der Klasse zusammen.

→ Vergleicht eure Ergebnisse mit dem **Grammar File 6, Seite 160–162** in eurem Englischbuch.

3 Meet Barney

Poppy has a dog. His name is Barney. Here are some facts about him. Use the *simple present* and write about what Barney does and likes and what he doesn't do and like. You need paper.

1 Barney likes ...

fold here

More help

(to) sleep in a basket • (to) eat carrots • (to) jump when he is happy • (to) play with other dogs • (to) like cats • (to) like swimming

4 You choose What about you?

Choose a) or b).

a) **Work with a partner. Talk about what you normally do and like and what you normally don't do and don't like. Act out the dialogue in front of the class.**

b) **Write about *What I like and what I don't like at school.* Read your text to the class.**
You can make a table first. Then write your text.

What I like	What I don't like
friends	Maths
teacher	small school yard
breaks	homework

Ich verstehe Schaubilder und (Hör-/Lese-)Texte, in denen über die Familie gesprochen wird. Ich kann über die Familie sprechen und beschreiben, wer mit wem verwandt ist.

2 Think Pair Share: The simple present

TIP
THINK Make notes about what you know about the *simple present*.
You can write them in English or German.
PAIR Use your notes and talk to your partner. You can speak English or German.
Add to your notes what your partner has in her/his notes.
SHARE Check your results together in class.
→ Now read **Grammar File 6, pp. 160–162** in your English book.

3 Meet Barney

Poppy has a dog. His name is Barney. Here are some facts about him. Use the *simple present* and write down what Barney does and likes and what he doesn't do and like. You need paper.

1 Barney likes ...

4 You choose Help your classmates

Choose a), b) or c).
a) Work as a *learning assistant*: Help your classmates with their exercises!

TIP
Als *learning assistant* hilfst du deinen Mitschülern, die Lösung selber zu finden, indem du die Regel erklärst und sie durch kluge Fragen unterstützt, z. B.: "Welche Person ist das – erste, zweite oder dritte?"

b) Make a poster about "The simple present". You can make a mind map or use pictures. Do you have a better idea? Go ahead! Tell the class about your poster. Then put up the poster in the classroom.

c) Work out exercises about the simple present for your classmates. Look into your Englishbook/workbook for good examples. Do you have better ideas? Go ahead! Now write your exercises on the board and help your classmates as their learning assistant.

Ich kann Texte und Gespräche verstehen, in denen es um Essen geht.

1 Would you like some tea?

A typical morning in Mia's family!
FF 12 Listen to Mia and her parents.
Then choose the right answer.

1 Today Mia is …
a) tired. ☐ b) happy. ☐ c) hungry. ☐

2 In the afternoon Mia has a …
a) piano lesson. ☐ b) violin lesson. ☐ c) guitar lesson. ☐

3 Mia drinks …
a) orange juice. ☐
b) tea. ☐
c) milk. ☐

4 For breakfast Mia wants …
a) cornflakes. ☐
b) yoghurt. ☐
c) scones. ☐

5 For dinner Mia's dad wants …
a) spaghetti. ☐
b) roast beef. ☐
c) pizza. ☐

6 In the end Mia forgets to take the …
a) bread and cheese. ☐
b) money. ☐
c) banana. ☐

2 That's how easy it is!

Here are three recipes – for a sandwich, a milkshake and a pizza. Which is which? Write the food names over the recipes.

(1) ____________________

1 Use ready-made dough[1] and put some tomato sauce on it.
2 Put mixed vegetables on the sauce.
3 Top with cheese.
4 Bake at 225 degrees for 20 to 25 minutes.

(2) ____________________

1 Take one piece of bread and put peanut butter on it.
2 Put jam on the other piece of bread.
3 Put the pieces of bread together.

(3) ____________________

1 Cut two bananas into pieces and put them into a blender[2].
2 Add two spoons of chocolate spread[3] and one cup of cold milk.
3 Now add two scoops of vanilla ice-cream.
4 Blend until the drink is frothy[4].

[1]ready-made-dough [dəʊ] *Fertigteig*
[2]blender ['blendə] *Mixer*
[3]chocolate spread ['tʃɒklət spred] *Nuss-Nougat-Crème*
[4]frothy [frɒθi] *schaumig*

Ich kann Texte und Gespräche verstehen, in denen es um Essen geht.

1 Would you like some tea?

A typical morning in Mia's family!
FF 12 Listen to Mia and her parents.
Then finish the sentences.

Today Mia is (1) ____________________.

In the afternoon Mia has a (2) ____________________.

Mia drinks (3) ____________________.

For breakfast Mia wants (4) ____________________.

For dinner Mia's dad wants (5) ____________________.

In the end Mia forgets to take the (6) ____________________.

2 That's how easy it is!

Here are three recipes – for a sandwich, a milkshake and a pizza. Which is which? Write the food names over the recipes.

(1) ______________________________

Use ready-made dough[1] and put some tomato sauce on it.

1 Put mixed vegetables on the sauce.
2 Top with cheese.
3 Bake at 225 degrees for 20 to 25 minutes.

(2) ______________________________

1 Take one piece of bread and put peanut butter on it.
2 Put jam on the other piece of bread.
3 Put the pieces of bread together.

(3) ______________________________

1 Cut two bananas into pieces and put them into a blender[2].
2 Add two spoons of chocolate spread[3] and one cup of cold milk.
3 Now add two scoops of vanilla ice-cream.
4 Blend until the drink is frothy[4].

[1]ready-made-dough [dəʊ] *Fertigteig*
[2]blender ['blendə] *Mixer*
[3]chocolate spread ['tʃɒklət spred] *Nuss-Nougat-Crème*
[4]frothy ['frɒθi] *schaumig*

Ich kann Texte und Gespräche verstehen, in denen es um Essen geht.

1 Would you like some tea?

a) A typical morning in Mia's family!
FF 12 Listen to Mia and her parents.
What happens in the text?

We can hear ______________________________.

The family ______________________________.

They talk about ______________________________.

In the end ______________________________.

b) What do Mia and her mum disagree[1] about?

Mia ______________________________.

But her mother thinks ______________________________.

c) Why does Mia's mother say "I think I have two kids here!"?

Mia's mother says that because ______________________________.

d) Is this a realistic conversation for a girl and her parents?
What is realistic, and what is not realistic?

I (don't) think this is a realistic conversation because ______________________________

______________________________.

2 That's how easy it is!

The recipes for pizza, a sandwich and a milkshake are mixed up. Cut out the lines of the recipes.

a) Find out which lines go with which recipes.
b) Put the lines of each recipe in the right order.

Now add two scoops of vanilla ice-cream.
Put jam on the other piece of bread.
Add two spoons of chocolate spread[2] and one cup of cold milk.
Cut two bananas into pieces and put them into a blender[3].
Put the pieces of bread together.
Use ready-made dough[4] and put some tomato sauce on it.
Put mixed vegetables on the sauce.
Top with cheese.
Blend until the drink is frothy[5].
Bake at 225 degrees for 20 to 25 minutes.
Take one piece of bread and put peanut butter on it.

[1](to) disagree [ˌdɪsəˈgrɪː] *verschiedener Meinung sein* •
[2]chocolate spread [ˈtʃɒklət spred] *Nuss-Nougat-Crème* • [3]blender [ˈblendə] *Mixgerät* •
[4]ready-made-dough [dəʊ] *Fertigteig* • [5]frothy [frɒθi] *schaumig*

Ich kann Texte und Gespräche verstehen, in denen es um Essen geht.

3 Tandem activity: I love our garden in the summer

Fold the worksheet. Take turns and use the correct English *possessive pronoun*.
Read out the sentence. Your partner checks your answers. Then swap roles and start again.

Partner A	Partner B
Look at this photo. This is … family. (meine)	Look at this photo. This is *my* family. (meine)
Chen is very hungry. *His* plate is full of spaghetti. (sein)	Chen is very hungry. … plate is full of spaghetti. (sein)
I love … garden in the summer! (unseren)	I love *our* garden in the summer! (unseren)
Emma likes sailing. *Her* trophies are on the shelf. (ihre)	Emma likes sailing. … trophies are on the shelf. (ihre)
Hurry up and give the rabbit … food. (sein)	Hurry up and give the rabbit *its* food. (sein)
The Bakers have a TV in *their* kitchen. (ihrer)	The Bakers' have a TV in … kitchen. (ihrer)
… task is to finish the sentences. (deine)	*Your* task is to finish the sentences. (deine)
Don't come into *my* bedroom! (mein)	Don't come into … bedroom! (mein)
My brother and I visit … uncle every Tuesday. (unseren)	My brother and I visit *our* uncle every Tuesday. (unseren)
Barney doesn't sleep in a basket. He sleeps in *his* armchair. (seinem)	Barney doesn't sleep in a basket. He sleeps in … armchair. (seinem)
Stop talking and eat … dinner. (dein)	Stop talking and eat *your* dinner. (dein)
The twins play a lot. Look at *their* toys. (ihre)	The twins play a lot. Look at … toys. (ihre)
This is my rat. … name is Speedy. (sein)	This is my rat. *Its* name is Speedy. (sein)
My sister is five years old. *Her* name is Isabella. (ihr)	My sister is five years old. … name is Isabella. (ihr)
Wow, … sandwich looks yummy! (dein)	Wow, *your* sandwich looks yummy! (dein)
The students like *their* English teacher. (ihren)	The students like … English teacher. (ihren)
Give Barney … dog biscuit. (seinen)	Give Barney *his* dog biscuit. (seinen)
Do you like living on *your* farm? (eure)	Do you like living on … farm? (eure)

More help

my	mein/meine	This is my house.
your	dein/deine	This is your house.
his	sein/seine	This is his house. (Philip's house)
her	ihr/ihre (von einer Frau oder einem Mädchen)	This is her house.(Poppy's house)
its	sein/seine (Sache oder Tier, das keinen Namen hat)	This is its basket. (That cat's basket)
our	unser/unsere	This is our house.
your	euer/eure	This is your house. (your and your family's house)
their	ihr/ihre	This is their house. (the Bakers' house)

Ich kann eine längere Geschichte verstehen und über ihren Inhalt sprechen.

1 The Legend of Little Al

a) Look at the pictures. What can you see? Tell a partner about the pictures.

b) Read the story about Little Al.

1

Little Al is unhappy. She sits at the beach and watches the sea. Her father, Pirate Sid, is late. The sky is cloudy[1] and there is a cold wind. Al is worried. She thinks, 'I hope Dad can find Plymouth! What can I do to help him?' Before the sun goes down, she sees a ship! It is far out on the sea. She has an idea. She makes a bonfire[2]. After it gets dark, she goes home. A great storm[3] comes, but the bonfire burns[4] into the night.

2

In the morning, Al sees sails in the harbour. She is very excited! She runs to the water. She looks for the *Sea Dog*, her father's pirate ship, but it is not there. She sees a big ship that she does not know. It is called the *Beacon*. It is beautiful[5], but its sails are torn[6] from the storm. The captain asks the people about the bonfire. He finds Little Al and says, 'I'm Captain Cooper. You saved us[7] from the storm. Thank you.' He puts three gold coins in her hand. Little Al is surprised. 'Th-thank you, Captain!' she says. But she is not really happy. 'What's wrong?' the captain asks. 'My father is still at sea,' Al tells him. 'I'm afraid[8] he's in trouble.'

3

For three days, the captain and his men help Little Al. They make a big bonfire every evening. Captain Cooper watches with her, but they do not see any ships. Every evening, Al walks home very sad.
The third night, Al wakes up. She hears loud sounds. She runs to the harbour. It is dark, but she can see two ships together on the water. One is the *Beacon* – and the other is the *Sea Dog*! Sid's pirates are in a fight[9] with Captain Cooper's men! The pirates shout, 'Give us the gold! Give us the gold!' Little Al jumps into her small boat and goes out to the ships. Sid and his pirates take a chest[10] of gold from the *Beacon*. Al's boat goes between[11] the two ships. She shouts, 'Stop, Dad! Stop!'

4

The pirates are so surprised that the chest falls[12] out of their hands – and into Al's boat! They look down. Pirate Sid shouts, 'Little Al!' The fighting stops. The pirates take Al and the chest of gold onto the *Sea Dog*. Al is angry. 'Give the chest back to Captain Cooper!' she says. 'He helped me[13] make the bonfire and look for you! He's my friend!' Then Sid understands. He says, 'The fire on the beach that helped us find Plymouth in the night ... *You* made that fire[14]!' Al looks to Captain Cooper and says, 'Yes, we made that fire!' Then Sid says to his men, 'Do as Little Al says! Give the chest back to the Captain!'

Al is happy to have her father back. She tells him about the bonfire, the *Beacon* and the three gold coins. Pirate Sid says, 'I'm sorry, Captain. It was wrong to attack[15] you. I want to help you now. What can I do?' The captain thinks for a moment and says, 'There are lots of pirate ships on the sea. Can you sail to London with us?' Sid smiles and says, 'Yes, we can! When other pirates see the *Sea Dog*, they will not attack[16] you!' The two men shake hands[17]. 'But first,' Sid says, 'let's have a bonfire and a great party for you and your men!' Captain Cooper says, 'And don't forget: for your Little Al!' Al smiles from ear to ear.

5

Everyone is excited about the party. When all is ready, Captain Cooper and his men come from the *Beacon* – with a big chest! They put[18] the chest down in front of Sid and Al. The captain says, 'This is a present for you.' Al opens the chest. In it are hundreds and hundreds of gold coins! Al and Sid's eyes open up as big as the coins. 'Thank you,' Sid says to the captain, 'but this gold is not only for Al and me. It's for all of Plymouth! Let's build[19] a great lighthouse[20] so ships at sea can find our good harbour. Let's bring lots of ships here and make Plymouth a great city!' The people are very happy. They make the bonfire and everyone eats, drinks and dances into the night.

The next day, the *Beacon* leaves the Plymouth harbour with beautiful new sails. In front of it is the *Sea Dog* – with Pirate Sid and Little Al.

[1]cloudy ['klaʊdi] *bewölkt* • [2]bonfire ['bɒnfaɪə] *Leucht-/Signalfeuer* • [3]storm [stɔːm] *Sturm* • [4](to) burn [bɜːn] *brennen* • [5]beautiful [bjuːtɪfl] *schön* • [6]torn [tɔːn] *zerrissen* • [7]You saved us! *Du hast uns gerettet!* • [8](to) be afraid [ə'freɪd] *befürchten, Angst haben* • [9]fight [faɪt] *Kampf* • [10]chest [tʃest] *Truhe, Kiste* • [11]between [bɪ'twiːn] *zwischen* • [12](to) fall [fɔːl] *fallen* • [13]He helped me. *Er hat mir geholfen.* • [14]You made that. *Du hast das gemacht.* • [15](to) attack sb. [ə'tæk] *jn. angreifen* • [16]They will not attack you. *Sie werden dich nicht angreifen.* • [17](to) shake hands [ʃeɪk] *sich die Hand geben/schütteln* • [13](to) put sth. down [ˌpʊt 'daʊn] *hinstellen* • [19](to) build [bɪld] *bauen* • [20]lighthouse [laɪthaʊs] *Leuchtturm*

Ich kann eine längere Geschichte verstehen und über ihren Inhalt sprechen.

2 Right or wrong

Tick (✓) the correct answer. Then check with a partner.

	Right	Wrong
Little Al is unhappy because Pirate Sid is late.		
Before the sun goes down, Al sees two ships.		
Al makes a bonfire and goes home.		
The next morning Al's father's pirate ship is not there.		
For three days Al is alone when she makes a bonfire.		
Pirate Sid and Captain Cooper fight for a bag of gold.		
Pirate Sid and Captain Cooper make friends and shake hands.		
There is a party, but only for Al's father and his men.		
With the gold coins they build a lighthouse in Plymouth.		
The story is real. What do you think?		

3 Story titles

Then check with a partner. Put the titles for the five parts of the story into the correct order.

The fight • A present • New friends • A big ship • Father is late

4 You choose The Legend-of-Little-Al-booklet

Make a booklet for The Legend of Little Al and write/draw your answers in the booklet.
Make a cover page and number the pages.
Write clearly[1] so that others can read your texts.

Choose THREE TO FIVE tasks from a)–h).

a) Find a better title for the story.

b) Make a list of words you want to remember.

c) Make a list of the feeling words.

[1] clearly ['klɪəli] *deutlich*

d) Make a mind map that shows what happens in the story. You can use words from the box.

Captain Cooper • unhappy • Beacon • Sea Dog • (to) fight • (to) become friends • bonfire • party • (to) help • at sea • (to) be late • gold • lighthouse • (to) save • (to) see • ship

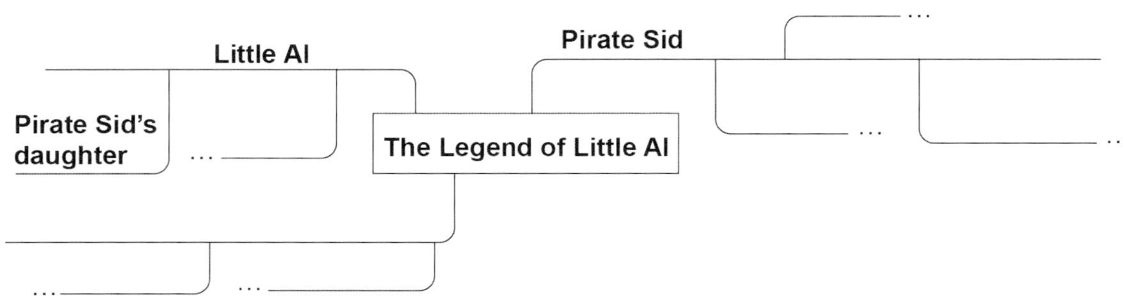

e) Draw a comic with speech bubbles.

f) Draw a picture of a person in the story.
Write down all the things you know about this person around the picture.

g) Write a new dialogue for two people in the story and act it out.

h) Write a new ending.

Ich kann eine längere Geschichte verstehen und über ihren Inhalt sprechen.

2 Right or wrong

Tick (✓) the correct answer. Then check with a partner.

	Right	Wrong
Little Al is sad because her father is late.		
When it gets dark, Al sees a ship.		
The storm blows out the bonfire.		
Cooper is the captain of the *Beacon*.		
Captain Cooper steals a chest of gold from Sid and his pirates.		
The *Sea Dog's* captain wants to help Captain Cooper on his way to London.		
There's a party.		
The lighthouse can make Plymouth rich.		
The *Sea Dog* is behind the *Beacon*.		
The story is real. What do you think?		

3 Story titles

Then check with a partner. Choose five titles for the five parts of the story from the box.

The fight • A present • New friends • A family • A big ship • Father is late • A party • The beach
A strange animal

4 You choose The Legend-of-Little-Al-booklet

Make a booklet for The Legend of Little Al and write/draw your answers in the booklet.
Make a cover page and number the pages.
Write clearly[1] so that others can read your texts.

Choose THREE TO FIVE tasks from a)–h).

a) Find a better title for the story.

b) Make a list of words you want to remember.

c) Make a list of the feeling words.

[1]clearly ['klɪəli] *deutlich*

d) Make a mind map that shows what happens in the story. You can use words from the box.

Captain Cooper • unhappy • Beacon • Sea Dog • (to) fight • (to) become friends • bonfire • party •
(to) help • at sea • (to) be late • gold • lighthouse • (to) save • (to) see • ship

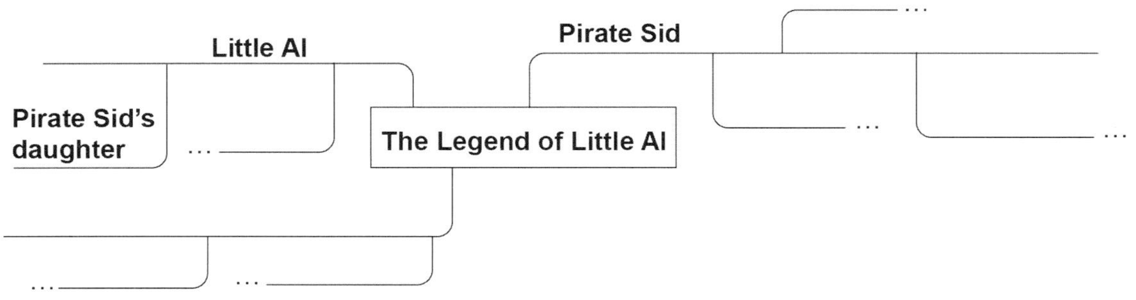

e) Draw a comic with speech bubbles.

f) Draw a picture of a person in the story.
Write down all the things you know about this person around the picture.

g) Write a new dialogue for two people in the story and act it out.

h) Write a new ending.

Ich kann eine längere Geschichte verstehen und über ihren Inhalt sprechen.

2 Right or wrong

Tick (✓) the correct answer. Then check with a partner.

	Right	Wrong	Not in the text
Little Al is worried because she can't see her father's ship.			
When Al sees a ship she thinks it's her father's and she tries to give him a sign that shows him where Plymouth is.			
The *Beacon's* captain doesn't know that it was Al's bonfire.			
The Sea Dog isn't in Plymouth because of the storm.			
Al's father is very surprised that his daughter and the *Beacon's* captain are friends.			
London is the *Beacon's* home harbour.			
Sid wants to give a party because he is so proud[1] of his little daughter.			
They build a lighthouse to help the ships to find Plymouth, like the bonfires.			
Captain Cooper wants to come back to Plymouth.			
The story is real. What do <u>you</u> think?			

3 Story titles

Then check with a partner. Write five titles for the five parts of the story from the box.

The fight • A present • New friends • …

4 You choose The Legend-of-Little-Al-booklet

Make a booklet for The Legend of Little Al and write/draw your answers in the booklet.
Make a cover page and number the pages.
Write clearly[2] so that others can read your texts.

Choose THREE TO FIVE tasks from a)-h).

a) Find a better title for the story.

b) Make a list of words or sentences you want to remember.

c) Make a list of the feeling words.

[1]proud ['praʊd] *stolz*
[2]clearly ['klɪəli] *deutlich*

d) Make a mind map that shows what happens in the story. You can use words from the box.

Captain Cooper • unhappy • *Beacon* • *Sea Dog* • (to) fight • (to) become friends • bonfire • party • (to) help • at sea • (to) be late • gold • lighthouse • (to) save • (to) see • ship

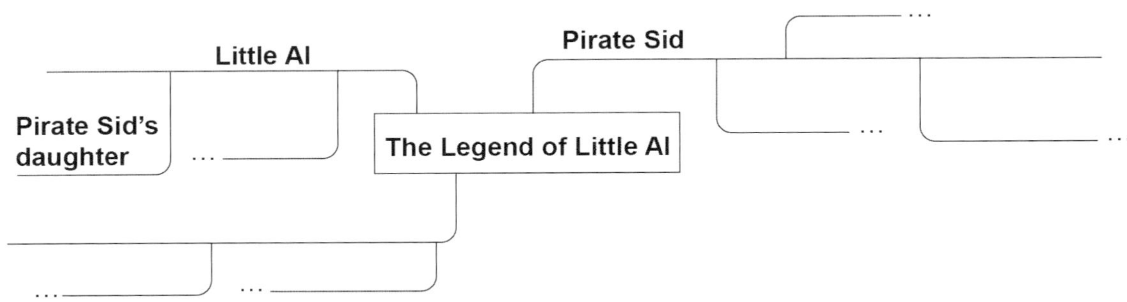

e) Draw a comic with speech bubbles.

f) Choose two people from the story. Write down how they feel.

g) Choose a scene from the story. Write down and draw the dialogues in your booklet, then act out the scene.

h) Write a new ending.

Ich kann Wörter, die auf -s enden, richtig aussprechen und weiß, welches Lautschriftsymbol – [z], [s] oder [ɪz] – ich dafür verwende.

PRONUNCIATION A poem and a riddle

a) FF 13–14 Listen to the poem and the riddle. Can you hear the "special sounds"?

A poem: Silky the Seal

Silky the seal
wakes up at six,
jumps into the water
and does some tricks.

She watches whales,
swims around,
and counts the seagulls
over the Sound.

She finds her friends,
plays in the sun,
chases[1] boats,
has lots of fun.

She catches crabs,
eats lots of fish,
sees an evening star
and makes a wish.

When the sun goes down,
she dives down deep,
then comes back up
and goes to sleep.

A riddle: Who is this?

He runs on eight pointy[2] feet, dances on rocks,
and thinks he's the coolest kid under the docks.

He waits for dinner, catches it, puts it in his mouth –
but when dinner doesn't come to him, he goes out!

He isn't big, but he's hard to crack[3]
because he wears a shell[4] across his back.

He shows his claws[5], says 'Stay away!'
and gives you a pinch[6] when you don't obey[7].

One more tip:
Maybe *you* don't want him on *your* plate,
but Silky the seal thinks he tastes great!

[1](to) chase [tʃeɪs] *jagen* • [2]pointy [pɔɪntɪ] *spitz zulaufend* • [3](to) crack [kræk] *knacken* • [4]shell [ʃel] *Schale, Hülse, Muschel*; hier: *Panzer* • [5]claw [klɔː] *Kralle, Klaue, Schere, Zange* • [6]pinch [pɪntʃ] *Kniff, Zwicken* • [7](to) obey [əˈbeɪ] *gehorchen*

You choose Do b), c), d), e) or f).

b) Read the poem and the riddle. Can you find all the special sounds? Put the words in the right place in the table.

Silky the Seal

Snake sounds [s]	Bee sounds [z]	Special bee sounds [ɪz]

A riddle

Snake sounds [s]	Bee sounds [z]	Special bee sounds [ɪz]

TIP
Sprich die Wörter beim Zuordnen nach und lege deine Hand an deinen Hals.
Wenn dein Hals dabei vibriert, ist es ein stimmhafter s-Laut, also ein *bee sound* [z].

c) Copy the poem OR riddle and underline the "special sounds" [s], [z] and [ɪz] in different colours. Draw a picture next to the text and put it up in the classroom.

d) Practise the "special sounds" [s], [z] and [ɪz]. Read out the poem and the riddle.

e) Practise reading with a partner. Check how your partner says the "special sounds" [s], [z] and [ɪz].

f) You can work with a partner. Choose a part of the poem OR the riddle and learn it by heart[1]. If you want, you can rap it or act it out while you say it. Now present it in class. Be careful with the "special sounds" [s], [z] and [ɪz].

[1] by heart [baɪ ˈhɑːt] *auswendig*

Ich kann den Laut [uː] in Wörtern heraushören. Ich weiß, dass der Laut [uː] unterschiedlich geschrieben werden kann. Ich kann einem Partner Wörter buchstabieren.

SPELLING The odd one out

a) FF 15 Listen to the word groups with [uː]-sounds. One word is wrong. Underline the word that sounds different.

1 you – soup – book – shoe

2 glue – zoo – food – go

3 pool – group – double – who

4 fruit – touch – Lucy – do

5 look – two – Tuesday – blue

6 school – door – room – new

7 uniform – student – afternoon – but

b) Choose five words with [uː]-sounds. Write them down.

1 ______________________________

2 ______________________________

3 ______________________________

4 ______________________________

5 ______________________________

c) Take turns and write your five words on your partner's back.

Can your partner say and spell the word?

Ich kann den Laut [uː] in Wörtern heraushören. Ich weiß, dass der Laut [uː] unterschiedlich geschrieben werden kann. Ich kann einem Partner Wörter buchstabieren.

SPELLING The odd one out

a) FF 15 Listen to the word groups with [uː]-sounds. One word is wrong. Finish the words. Then underline the word that sounds different.

1 y____ – s____ p – b____ k – sh____

2 gl____ – z____ – f____ d – g____

3 p____ l – gr____ p – d____ ble – wh____

4 fr____ t – t____ ch – L____ cy – d____

5 l____ k – tw____ – T____ sday – bl____

6 sch____ l – d____ r – r____ m – n____ w

7 ____ niform – st____ dent – aftern____ n – b____ t

b) Choose five words with [uː]-sounds. Write them down.

1 ____________________

2 ____________________

3 ____________________

4 ____________________

5 ____________________

c) Take turns and write your five words on your partner's back.

Can your partner say and spell the word?

Ich kann den Laut [uː] in Wörtern heraushören. Ich weiß, dass der Laut [uː] unterschiedlich geschrieben werden kann. Ich kann meinem Partner Wörter buchstabieren.

SPELLING The odd one out

a) FF 15 **Listen to the word groups with [uː]-sounds. One word is wrong. Write down the words. Underline the word that sounds different.**

1 __________

2 __________

3 __________

4 __________

5 __________

6 __________

7 __________

b) Choose five words with [uː]-sounds. Write them down.

1 __________

2 __________

3 __________

4 __________

5 __________

c) Take turns and write your five words on your partner's back.

Can your partner say and spell the word?

Ich kann Apostrophe richtig verwenden und zwischen –'s (Singular) und s' (Plural) unterscheiden.

LANGUAGE The Bakers' crazy house

a) FF 16 **Listen and point to the things in the picture. Check with your partner.**

b) Now finish the sentences. Use words from the box. Colour the things that you write about in the picture.

the Bakers' • Lucy's • the dog's • mum's • Jack's • dad's

This is (1) ___________ cupboard.	This is (2) ___________ bed.	This is (3) ___________ basket.
Here is (4) ___________ paper.	These are (5) ___________ trophies.	This is (6) ___________ TV.
This is (7) ___________ toilet.	This is (8) ___________ uniform.	This is (9) ___________ dining room.
This is (10) ___________ bedroom.	This is (11) ___________ clock.	These are (12) ___________ books.
This is (13) ___________ bathroom.	This is (14) ___________ watch.	This is (15) ___________ desk.
This is (16) ___________ kitchen.	This is (17) ___________ ball.	This is (18) ___________ garden.

TIP

's = Nomen im Singular

dad's shoes

s' = Nomen im Plural

the Bakers' dog

Ich kann Apostrophe richtig verwenden und zwischen -'s (Singular) und s' (Plural) unterscheiden.

LANGUAGE The Bakers' crazy house

a) FF 16 Listen and point to the things in the picture. Check with your partner.

b) Now finish the sentences. Colour the things that you write about in the picture.

This is (1) ___________ cupboard.	This is (2) ___________ bed.	This is (3) ___________ basket.
Here is (4) ___________ paper.	These are (5) ___________ trophies.	This is (6) ___________ TV.
This is (7) ___________ toilet.	This is (8) ___________ uniform.	This is (9) ___________ dining room.
This is (10) ___________ bedroom.	This is (11) ___________ clock.	These are (12) ___________ books.
This is (13) ___________ bathroom.	This is (14) ___________ watch.	This is (15) ___________ desk.
This is (16) ___________ kitchen.	This is (17) ___________ ball.	This is (18) ___________ garden.

c) Write some more sentences about the picture.

____

____

____

Ich kann Apostrophe richtig verwenden und zwischen -'s (Singular) und s' (Plural) unterscheiden.

LANGUAGE The Bakers' crazy house

a) FF 16 Listen and point to the things in the picture. Check with your partner.

b) Write some more sentences about the picture.

c) When do we use 's and when do we use s'? Write a TIP in German or English

d) Work as a *learning assistant*: Go around and help your classmates with their exercises.

TIP
Als *learning assistant* sollst du nicht die Aufgaben für Deine Mitschüler erledigen, sondern ihnen helfen, dies selbst zu tun, indem Du die Regel erklärst und sie durch kluge Fragen unterstützt, z. B.: „Sind das mehrere oder ist das einer?"

Ich kann Wörter mit Mindmaps ordnen und Überschriften für die einzelnen Wortfelder finden. Diese Methode kann ich auch beim Vokabellernen anwenden.

1 STUDY SKILLS Umbrella words

Find the correct umbrella word for each list. Write them over the lists.

(1)__________	(2)__________	(3)__________	(4)__________	(5)__________	(6)__________	(7)__________
bear	child	breakfast	cool	Can I say it in German?	birthday	big wheel
farm	girl	drink	dark	Sorry, I'm late.	Christmas	England
seal	man	sandwich	friendly	Can I read, please?	month	Silky
zoo	teacher	vegetable	nice	What page are we on?	weekend	river
cow	woman	fruit	worried	It's your turn.	summer holidays	aquarium

fold here

More help

adjectives • animals • around the year • body parts • books • cars • classroom phrases • colours • countries • drinks • Europe • family • food • in the house • London • months • people • places • Plymouth • question words • at school • school things • time • in the town • in the zoo

2 STUDY SKILLS Your mind map

a) Choose one list from 1 or write a new one. Write each word on a small card.

b) Look in your English book and add more words.

c) Make a mind map and glue it on a piece of paper. Use colours and pictures, too.

d) Put up your mind map poster in the classroom.

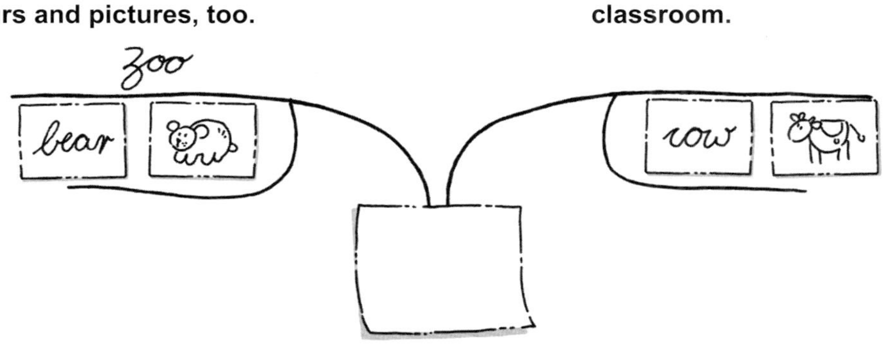

Ich kann Wörter mit einer Mindmap ordnen und Überschriften für die einzelnen Wortfelder finden. Diese Methode kann ich auch selbst beim Vokabellernen anwenden.

1 STUDY SKILLS Umbrella words

Find the correct umbrella word for each list. Write them over the lists.

(1)________ ________	(2)________ ________	(3)________ ________	(4)________ ________	(5)________ ________	(6)________ ________	(7)________ ________
bear	child	breakfast	cool	Can I say it in German?	birthday	big wheel
farm	girl	drink	dark	Sorry, I'm late.	Christmas	England
seal	man	sandwich	friendly	Can I read, please?	month	Silky
zoo	teacher	vegetable	nice	What page are we on?	weekend	river
cow	woman	fruit	worried	It's your turn.	summer holidays	aquarium

2 STUDY SKILLS Your mind map

a) Choose one list from 1 or write a new one. Write each word on a small card.

b) Look in your English book and add more words.

c) Make a mind map and glue it on a piece of paper. Use colours and pictures, too.

d) Put up your mind map poster in the classroom.

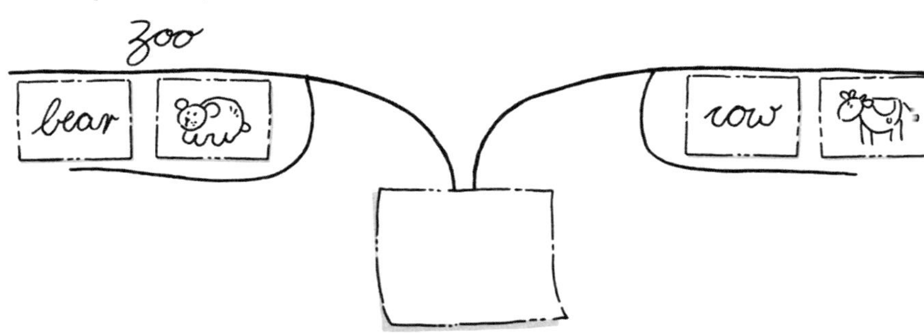

Ich kann Wörter mit einer Mindmap ordnen und Überschriften für die einzelnen Wortfelder finden. Diese Methode kann ich auch selbst beim Vokabellernen anwenden.

1 STUDY SKILLS Umbrella words

Find the correct umbrella word for each list. Write them over the lists.

(1) ______	(2) ______	(3) ______	(4) ______	(5) ______	(6) ______	(7) ______
bear	child	breakfast	cool	Can I say it in German?	birthday	big wheel
farm	girl	drink	dark	Sorry, I'm late.	Christmas	England
seal	man	sandwich	friendly	Can I read, please?	month	Silky
zoo	teacher	vegetable	nice	What page are we on?	weekend	river
cow	woman	fruit	worried	It's your turn.	summer holidays	aquarium

2 STUDY SKILLS Your mind map

a) Find a new umbrella word and write a word list.

b) Write each word on a small card.

c) Make a mind map and glue it on a piece of paper. Use colours and pictures, too.

d) Put up your mind map poster in the classroom.

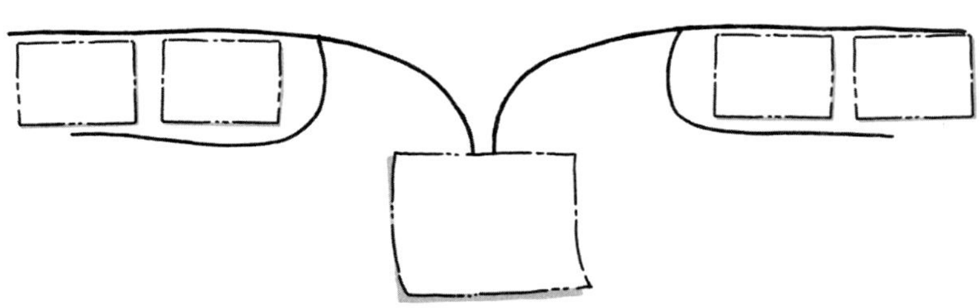

Unit 3

Clubs and hobbies

Meine Lernlandkarte für Unit 3

Name: ______________________ Klasse: ____________

Wie gut bist du in den Lernfeldern der Unit 3?
Schätze dich darin ein und male die entsprechende Anzahl an Kreisen auf der Ampel aus.
So findest du dein Übungsblatt.

Das lief nicht gut, ich muss mehr üben.	Das war OK, aber ich könnte besser werden.	Das habe ich gut geschafft.
●○○	●●○	●●●

Setze ein Häkchen, wenn du fertig bist. ✓

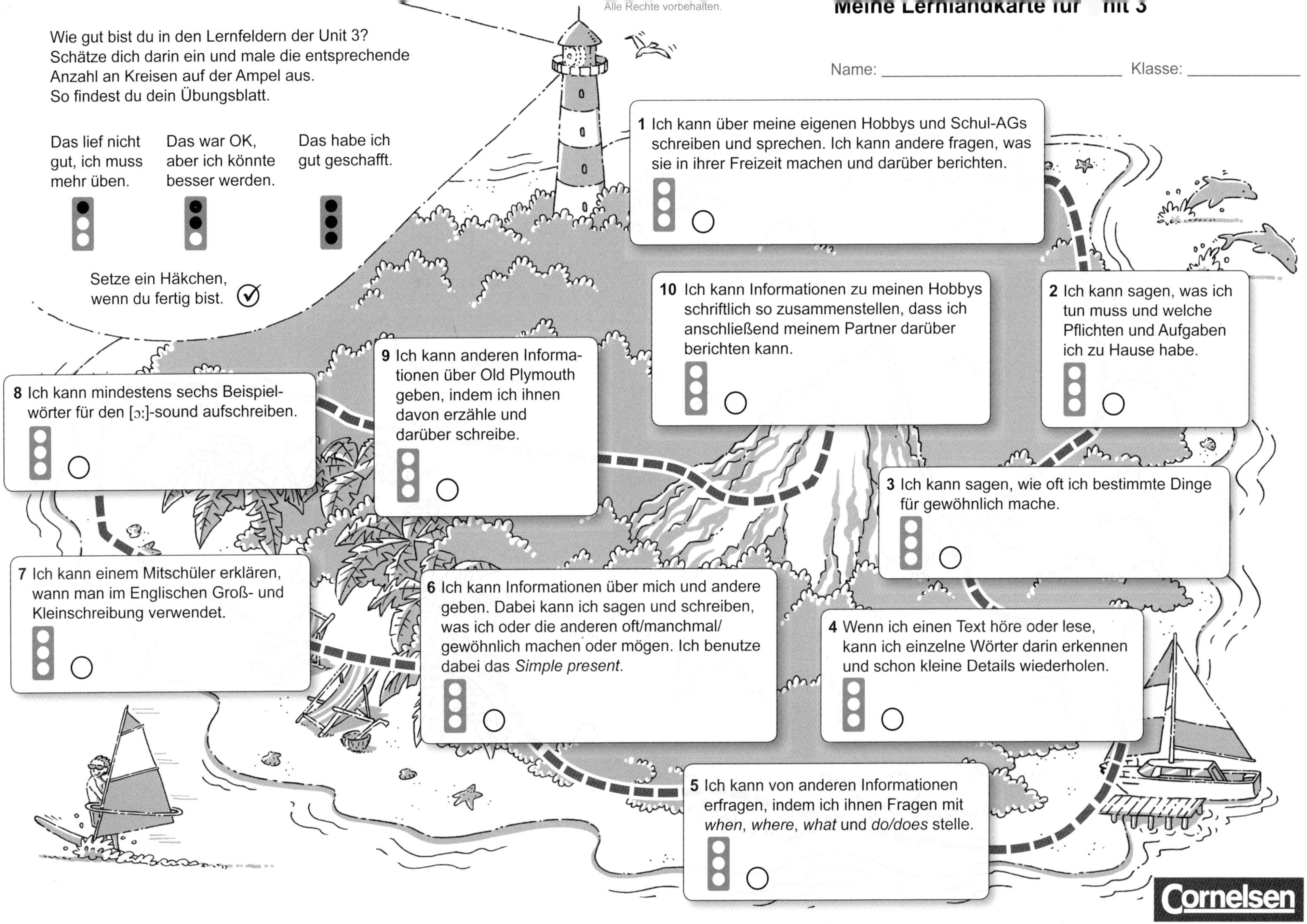

1 Ich kann über meine eigenen Hobbys und Schul-AGs schreiben und sprechen. Ich kann andere fragen, was sie in ihrer Freizeit machen und darüber berichten.

2 Ich kann sagen, was ich tun muss und welche Pflichten und Aufgaben ich zu Hause habe.

3 Ich kann sagen, wie oft ich bestimmte Dinge für gewöhnlich mache.

4 Wenn ich einen Text höre oder lese, kann ich einzelne Wörter darin erkennen und schon kleine Details wiederholen.

5 Ich kann von anderen Informationen erfragen, indem ich ihnen Fragen mit *when*, *where*, *what* und *do/does* stelle.

6 Ich kann Informationen über mich und andere geben. Dabei kann ich sagen und schreiben, was ich oder die anderen oft/manchmal/gewöhnlich machen oder mögen. Ich benutze dabei das *Simple present*.

7 Ich kann einem Mitschüler erklären, wann man im Englischen Groß- und Kleinschreibung verwendet.

8 Ich kann mindestens sechs Beispielwörter für den [ɔː]-sound aufschreiben.

9 Ich kann anderen Informationen über Old Plymouth geben, indem ich ihnen davon erzähle und darüber schreibe.

10 Ich kann Informationen zu meinen Hobbys schriftlich so zusammenstellen, dass ich anschließend meinem Partner darüber berichten kann.

Ich kann über meine eigenen Hobbys und Schul-AGs schreiben und sprechen. Ich kann andere fragen, was sie in ihrer Freizeit machen und darüber berichten.

1 Join my club

a) Mia and Philip meet at the Plymstock School pin board. There are the new clubs for year 7 students. Mia wants to join a new club. Philip helps her. Label the pictures.

cricket club

____

____

____

____

b) 17 Listen to Mia and Philip and put the pictures in the right order (1, 2, 3, …).

c) 17 Listen again. Are the sentences right or wrong?

	Right	Wrong
1 Mia wants to join a sport club.		
2 Philip goes to the hockey club every Wednesday.		
3 The hockey club starts at 3 pm.		
4 The cricket club meets on Tuesday.		
5 Chen is in the judo club.		
6 Poppy plays in the girls' football team too.		

d) 17 Listen again. Finish the sentence. Tick (✓) two answers.

Mia goes to the football club because …
a) she can play football.
b) Poppy is her friend and is in the girls' team too.
c) Philip says she can try and the students are nice.
d) Chen doesn't want her in the judo club.
e) the cricket club doesn't want new students.

2 Fit for Christmas? Not yet.

Santa Claus loves chocolate cookies but he has to get fit during summer. He wants to go to a school sport club to train his muscles and to lose some extra pounds. Look at his pin board and read the emails he has from different schools.

Dear Mr Claus,
you don't know Plymouth in summer?
You have to come here and go to our sport clubs at Plymstock School. We have a trampoline club and a swimming club. You can do kung fu, yoga and gymnastics too. And you can play chess to relax.
Please come to our school!
See you soon!
Mia

Don't forget!
2 x milk,
3 bananas,
4 x chocolate,
5 x vanilla ice cream,
3 x chocolate ice cream,
15 carrots for the reindeer and 1 small carrot for Santa,
5 x chocolate cookies (light)

Dear Mr Santa Claus,
we have a great volleyball club on Mondays at our school in Dover. On Tuesdays you can go swimming and do yoga. On Thursdays we play badminton and tennis. On Fridays we have a book club where you can relax with a good book. Or you can go to the modern dance club. It's fun!
Love, Anne

Dear Santa Claus,
please come to Southampton School over summer. We have a sailing club on Tuesdays and we play basketball at 5 o'clock on Thursdays. It's great! You can do judo and yoga too.
On Mondays and Wednesdays you can go skating along the beach with the skating club.
Bye-bye, Neville

CLAUS,
FEED THE REINDEER BEFORE YOU GO OUT AND DON'T FORGET TO CALL YOUR MUM IN THE EVENING.

Dear Mr Claus, please come to Brighton School as a special student over summer. We will help you get rid of those extra pounds from Christmas in our Zumba club on Mondays or our biking club on Thursdays. We have a sailing club and a swimming club too.
Best regards,
Mr Radamaker

Santa Claus doesn't know where to go. Can you help him? Tick (✓) the right answer.

1) You can go swimming	a) at Brighton School, at Dover School and at Plymstock School.	
	b) at Plymstock School and Southampton School.	
	c) at Southampton School and Brighton School.	

2) At Dover School you can	a) go swimming, join the kung fu club and do gymnastics.	
	b) play volleyball, you can go swimming and do yoga.	
	c) play badminton and basketball.	

3) You play basketball at Southampton School on	a) on Monday at 5 o'clock.	
	b) on Tuesday at 4 o'clock.	
	c) on Thursday at 5 o'clock.	

4) You can play badminton	a) at Plymstock School.	
	b) at Dover School.	
	c) at Southampton School.	

5) At Brighton School you can	a) go biking, you can do yoga and gymnastics.	
	b) join the Zumba club, go sailing or play basketball and volleyball.	
	c) go to a Zumba club, you can go biking or sailing too. You can go swimming at Brighton School.	

6) You do kung fu	a) at Plymstock School.	
	b) at Dover School.	
	c) at Brighton School.	

7) In the evening Santa Claus has to	a) wash the dishes and the reindeer. With shampoo!	
	b) clean the living-room and buy some flipflops for the reindeers' summer holiday.	
	c) feed the reindeer and he has to call his mum this evening.	

3 Meet Penny Pencil

a) Look at the table. Find a partner. Act out the interview. One of you is Penny Pencil, the other one is a friend of all the kids and can answer Penny's questions. Choose three students you want to talk about.

You can start like this:

Hello, dear! I'm Penny Pencil. I'm a journalist. Today I want to know all about the students' hobbies. Does Mia go to the judo club?

No, she doesn't. She goes to the music club.

And does Mia go to the football club too?

Yes, she does.

Does Poppy go to ______________?

	judo club	music club	book club	hockey club	football club
Mia		X	X		X
Poppy		X			X
Philip				X	
Sophie	X		X		
Chen	X			X	

b) Collect information about your school clubs. What clubs do you have and what can you do there? When and where do they meet? Talk to your partner. You can take notes.

4 Silent dialogue about sports

Partner A: Write a question on the paper and give it to your partner.
Partner B: Read the question and write your answer under the question.
Now it's partner B's turn. Write a question on the paper and Partner A has to answer it. Go on.
You can start like this:
Partner A: Do you like football?
Partner B: Yes, I do. Do you play tennis?
Partner A: No, I don't. Do you …

Ich kann über meine eigenen Hobbys und Schul-AGs schreiben und sprechen. Ich kann andere fragen, was sie in ihrer Freizeit machen und darüber berichten.

1 Join my club

a) Mia and Philip meet at the Plymstock School pin board. There are the new clubs for year 7 students. Mia wants to join a new club. Philip helps her to find a new one.
Label the pictures.

cricket club

____

____

____

____

b) FF 17 Listen to Mia and Philip. Who joins which club? Write five sentences.

(1) Mia: ____________________

(2) Philip: ____________________

(3) Emma: ____________________

(4) Chen: ____________________

(5) Poppy: ____________________

c) FF 17 Read the sentences. Then listen again and finish the sentences.

1 ____________________ wants to join a new sports club.

2 Philip goes to the hockey club every ____________________.

3 Sophie is in the cricket club every ____________________.

4 Mia can't go to the cricket club because she goes to the __________ club on Monday.

5 The ____________________ club is on Tuesday.

d) Do you know why Mia wants to join the girls' football club? Write it down.

Mia wants to join the girls' football club because ____

____.

2 Fit for Christmas? Not yet.

Santa Claus loves chocolate cookies but he has to get fit during summer. He wants to go to a school sport club to train his muscles and to lose some extra pounds. Look at his pin board and read the emails he has from different schools.

Dear Mr Claus,
you don't know Plymouth in summer?
You have to come here and go to our sport clubs at Plymstock School. We have a trampoline club and a swimming club. You can do kung fu, yoga and gymnastics too. And you can play chess to relax.
Please come to our school!
See you soon!
Mia

Don't forget!
2 x milk,
3 bananas,
4 x chocolate,
5 x vanilla ice cream,
3 x chocolate ice cream,
15 carrots for the reindeer and 1 small carrot for Santa,
5 x chocolate cookies (light)

Dear Mr Santa Claus,
we have a great volleyball club on Mondays at our school in Dover. On Tuesdays you can go swimming and do yoga. On Thursdays we play badminton and tennis. On Fridays we have a book club where you can relax with a good book. Or you can go to the modern dance club. It's fun!
Love, Anne

CLAUS,
FEED THE REINDEER BEFORE YOU GO OUT AND DON'T FORGET TO CALL YOUR MUM IN THE EVENING.

Dear Santa Claus,
please come to Southampton School over summer. We have a sailing club on Tuesdays and we play basketball at 5 o'clock on Thursdays. It's great!
You can do judo and yoga too.
On Mondays and Wednesdays you can go skating along the beach with the skating club.
Bye-bye, Neville

Dear Mr Claus, please come to Brighton School as a special student over summer. We will help you get rid of those extra pounds from Christmas in our Zumba club on Mondays or our biking club on Thursdays. We have a sailing club and a swimming club too.
Best regards,
Mr Radamaker

Santa Claus doesn't know where to go. Can you help him answer his questions? Tick (✓) the right answer.

1) You can go swimming	a) at Brighton School, at Dover School and at Plymstock School.	
	b) at Plymstock School and Southampton School.	
	c) at Southampton School and Brighton School.	

2) At Dover School you can	a) go swimming, join the kung fu club and do gymnastics.	
	b) play volleyball, you can go swimming and do yoga.	
	c) play badminton and basketball.	

3) You play basketball at Southampton School	a) on Monday at 5 o'clock.	
	b) on Tuesday at 4 o'clock.	
	c) on Thursday at 5 o'clock.	

4) You can play badminton	a) at Plymstock School.	
	b) at Dover School.	
	c) at Southampton School.	

5) At Brighton School you can	a) go biking, you can do yoga and gymnastics.	
	b) join the Zumba club, go sailing or play basketball and volleyball.	
	c) go to a Zumba club, you can go biking or sailing too. You can go swimming at Brighton School.	

6) You do kung fu	a) at Plymstock School.	
	b) at Dover School.	
	c) at Brighton School.	

7) In the evening Santa Claus has to	a) wash the dishes and the reindeer. With shampoo!	
	b) clean the living-room and buy some flipflops for the reindeers' summer holiday	
	c) feed the reindeer and call his mum.	

8) Anne goes to	a) Plymstock School.	
	b) Brighton School.	
	c) Dover School.	

3 Meet Penny Pencil

a) Look at the table. Find a partner and act out the interview. One of you is Penny Pencil, the other one is a friend of all the kids and can answer her questions. Choose three students you want to talk about. Take turns.

Hello, dear! I'm Penny Pencil. I'm a journalist. Today I want to know all about the students' hobbies. Does Mia go to the judo club?

No, she doesn't. She goes to the music club.

And does Mia go to …?

	judo club	music club	book club	hockey club	football club
Mia		X	X		X
Poppy		X			X
Philip				X	
Sophie	X		X		
Chen	X			X	

b) Collect information about your school clubs. What clubs do you have and what can you do there? When and where do they meet?

4 Silent dialogue about sports

Partner A: Write a question on the paper and give it to your partner.
Partner B: Read the question and write your answer under the question.
Now it's partner B's turn. Write a question on the paper and Partner A has to answer it. Go on.
You can start like this:
Partner A: Do you like football?
Partner B: Yes, I do. I play football every Monday. Do you play tennis?
Partner A: No, I don't. I never play tennis. Do you …

Ich kann über meine eigenen Hobbys und Schul-AGs schreiben und sprechen. Ich kann andere fragen, was sie in ihrer Freizeit machen und darüber berichten.

1 Join my club

a) Mia and Philip meet at the Plymstock School pin board. There are the new clubs for year 7 students. Mia wants to join a new club. Philip helps her to find a new one.
FF 17 First read the sentences. Then listen to Mia and Philip and finish the sentences.

Emma • Philip • Poppy • Mia • Chen

1 Mia ______ wants to join a new club.
2 ______ goes to the hockey club.
3 ______ plays cricket in the cricket club.
4 ______ plays the violin in the orchestra.
5 ______ does judo.
6 ______ plays football in a girls' team.

b) FF 17 Listen again. Are the sentences right or wrong? Tick (✓) the correct answers. Then correct the wrong sentences. Write them in your exercise book.

	Right	Wrong
1 Mia is in the music club and in the book club.		
2 Philip loves hockey and he usually plays on Thursday.		
3 Mia doesn't want to join the hockey club because she can't run after lunch.		
4 The hockey club starts Wednesday at 3 pm.		
5 Plymstock School has a girls' football team. They usually play football on Thursday.		
6 Emma plays football in the girls' team too.		

c) FF 17 Do you know the answer? Write it down.

Mia wants to join the girls' football club because ______________________

____

2 Fit for Christmas? Not yet.

Santa Claus loves chocolate cookies but he has to get fit during summer. He wants to go to a school sport club to train his muscles and to lose some extra pounds. Look at his pin board and read the emails he has from different schools.

Dear Mr Claus,
you don't know Plymouth in summer?
You have to come here and go to our sport clubs at Plymstock School. We have a trampoline club and a swimming club. You can do kung fu, yoga and gymnastics too. And you can play chess to relax.
Please come to our school!
See you soon!
Mia

Don't forget!
2 x milk,
3 bananas,
4 x chocolate,
5 x vanilla ice cream,
3 x chocolate ice cream,
15 carrots for the reindeer and 1 small carrot for Santa,
5 x chocolate cookies (light)

Dear Mr Santa Claus,
we have a great volleyball club on Mondays at our school in Dover. On Tuesdays you can go swimming and do yoga. On Thursdays we play badminton and tennis. On Fridays we have a book club where you can relax with a good book. Or you can go to the modern dance club. It's fun!
Love, Anne

CLAUS,
FEED THE REINDEER BEFORE YOU GO OUT AND DON'T FORGET TO CALL YOUR MUM IN THE EVENING.

Dear Santa Claus,
please come to Southampton School over summer. We have a sailing club on Tuesdays and we play basketball at 5 o'clock on Thursdays. It's great!
You can do judo and yoga too.
On Mondays and Wednesdays you can go skating along the beach with the skating club.
Bye-bye, Neville

Dear Mr Claus, please come to Brighton School as a special student over summer. We will help you get rid of those extra pounds from Christmas in our Zumba club on Mondays or our biking club on Thursdays. We have a sailing club and a swimming club too.
Best regards,
Mr Radamaker

Santa Claus doesn't know where to go. Can you help him answer his questions? Tick (✓) the right answer.

1) Which schools have a sailing club?	a) Dover School and Brighton School have a sailing club.	
	b) Southampton School and Plymstock School have a sailing club.	
	c) Brighton School and Southampton School have a sailing club.	

2) What can you do to relax at the different schools?	a) At Dover School you can relax with a good book at the book club.	
	b) At Southampton School you can relax doing kung fu.	
	c) At Brighton School you can relax on a skating tour at high speed.	

3) What can you do at Southampton School?	a) You can join a sailing club, a basketball club and a cook club.	
	b) You can join a sailing club, a basketball club and a judo club.	
	c) You can join a yoga club and a biking club.	

4) What can you do Thursday at Dover School?	a) You can go to the book club or join the modern dance club.	
	b) You can go swimming and do yoga.	
	c) You can play badminton and tennis.	

5) What can you do at Plymstock School to get fit?	a) You can go to the trampoline club and the sailing club to get fit. You can do kung fu, judo or gymnastics too.	
	b) You can go to the trampoline club and the swimming club to get fit. You can do kung fu, yoga or gymnastics too.	
	c) You can join the sailing club and the basketball club to get fit. You can do Zumba, yoga or gymnastics too.	

6) What does Claus has to do before he goes out?	a) He has to feed the reindeer.	
	b) He has to call his father.	
	c) He has to wash the dishes.	

3 Meet Penny Pencil

Look at the table. Find a partner and act out the interview. Choose three students you want to talk about.

Partner A is Penny Pencil, Partner B is a friend of all the kids and can answer Penny's questions.
Talk like this:
Penny Pencil: Does Mia go to the judo club?
Friend: No, she doesn't. She goes to the music club.
Penny Pencil: And does Mia go to the book club?
Friend: Yes, she does.

	judo club	music club	book club	hockey club	football club
Mia		X	X		X
Poppy		X			X
Philip				X	
Sophie	X		X		
Chen	X			X	

4 Silent dialogue about hobbies

Partner A: Write a question on the paper and give it to your partner.
Partner B: Read the question and write a long answer under the question.
Now it's partner B's turn. Write a question on the paper and Partner A has to answer it. Go on.
You can start like this:
Partner A: Do you like football?
Partner B: Yes, I do. I play football every Monday. Do you play the violin?
Partner A: No, I don't. I never play the violin. Do you ...

Ich kann sagen, was ich tun muss und welche Pflichten und Aufgaben ich zu Hause habe.

1 LANGUAGE Fox calls duck

Hungry Fixy Fox calls Ducky Duck. Fixy Fox wants to meet her because he is really hungry but Ducky Duck is clever and is very busy. What do the duck and her friends have to do?
Finish the dialogue and act it out. Use *have to* or *has to*.

Oh, I'm so hungry. I hope Ducky Duck is there. Maybe we can meet …

Oh no – it's Fixy Fox. What does he want from me?

Hello, sweety! Do you want to play tennis with me on Monday?

Oh, sorry. I can't. I have to clean the kitchen on Monday.

Do you and Ritzo Rat want to go swimming on Tuesday?

1 No, we can't because

____

____

Do you, Bernie Bear and Ritzo Rat want to have lunch on Wednesday?

2 Oh sorry. Bernie Bear and I can't because ______________

____

Oh, what about Ritzo Rat? Does he want to have a nice lunch in the park?

3 Erm, yes, erm, no, I think he can't because ______________

____

Maybe next time. Bye, Fixy Fox.

Oh, OK. Bye.

2 House elf meets fairy[1]

Read little fairy's email. She wants to go out with the busy house elf. But look at his to do list: the house elf has no time. Write his email to the fairy and say why you don't have time. Use *because*.

My dear house elf,
I hope you like your new family. Do you have many things to do? I want to go out with you. When do you have time?

See you soon, Fairy

after breakfast:
clean kitchen: orange juice on the table
at lunchtime:
make lunch: family is hungry
in the afternoon:
clean living room: books on the floor
Sunday: free ☺

You can start like this:

Dear fairy,
Thank you for your email. I want to go out with you but I can't because in the morning I have to clean the bedrooms.

Love, your friend, the house elf

[1]fairy ['feəri] *Fee*

Ich kann sagen, was ich tun muss und welche Pflichten und Aufgaben ich zu Hause habe.

1 LANGUAGE What do they have to do?

a) What do they have to do? Make sentences and use *have to* or *has to*.

Chen and Philip: do their homework • Poppy and Mia: go shopping on Thursday • Sophie: clean her room • Poppy: go for a walk with her dog, Barney • Sophie: visit her grandparents on Sunday

Chen and Philip have to ...

b) What do you have to do? Write three sentences.

fold here

More help

clean the bathroom • work in the garden • clean the car • go for a walk with the dog

2 House elf meets fairy[1]

Read little fairy's email. She wants to go dancing with the busy house elf. But the house elf has no time. Write his email to the fairy.

My dear house elf,
I hope you like your new family. Do you have many things to do? I want to go dancing with you. Can we go on Tuesday? Or when do you have time to meet?
Love, fairy

Dear fairy,

Thank you for your email.

I want to go dancing with you but I can't go on Tuesday because I have to clean the child's room.

don't have time – I – because – clean all the windows – on Thursday – have to.

____

on Friday – because – have to make dinner – can't go dancing – I – for my family – I.

____

Sunday – but – what about?

____

Do you have time on Sunday?

Love,

your friend, the house elf

[1] fairy ['feəri] *Fee*

Ich kann sagen, was ich tun muss und welche Pflichten und Aufgaben ich zu Hause habe.

1 LANGUAGE Fox calls duck

Hungry Fixy Fox calls Ducky Duck. Fixy Fox wants to meet her because he is really hungry but Ducky Duck is clever and is very busy. What do the duck and her friends have to do?
Finish the dialogue and act it out. Use *have to* or *has to*.

Oh, I'm so hungry. I hope Ducky Duck is there. Maybe we can meet …

Oh no – it's Fixy Fox. What does he want from me?

Hello, sweety! Do you want to play tennis with me on Monday?

Oh, sorry. I can't. I have to clean the kitchen on Monday.

Do you and Ritzo Rat want to go swimming on Tuesday?

1 No, we can't because

____

____

Do you, Bernie Bear and Ritzo Rat want to have lunch on Wednesday?

2 Oh sorry. Bernie Bear and I can't because ______________

____

Oh, what about Ritzo Rat? Does he want to have a nice lunch in the park?

3 Erm, yes, erm, no, I think he can't because ______________

____

Maybe next time. Bye, Fixy Fox.

Oh, OK. Bye.

fold here

More help clean the bathroom • work in the garden • feed the frogs • clean the car

2 House elf meets fairy[1]

Read little fairy's email. She wants to go dancing with the busy house elf. But look at his to do list: the house elf has no time. Write his email to the fairy and say why you don't have time. Use *because*.

My dear house elf,
I hope you like your new family. Do you have many things to do? I want to go dancing with you. When do you have time to meet?
See you soon, Fairy

Tuesday:
work in the garden
Thursday:
clean all windows
Friday:
make dinner for family
Sunday: free ☺

You can start like this:

Dear fairy,
Thank you for your email. I want to go dancing with you but I can't go on Monday because I have to clean the child's room.

____

____

____

____

____

____

Do you have time on Sunday?
Love, your friend, the house elf

[1] fairy ['feəri] *Fee*

Ich kann sagen, wie oft ich bestimmte Dinge für gewöhnlich mache.

LANGUAGE What I never, sometimes, often, usually and always do

TIP: Adverbs of frequency
In simple present-Sätzen stehen oft sogenannte Häufigkeitsadverbien: **always**, **usually**, **often**, **sometimes**, **never**.
Sie stehen in der Regel direkt vor dem Vollverb. *Tim often plays football.*
Sie stehen nie zwischen Verb und Objekt. *I never play chess.*
Aber aufgepasst bei ***be***: Häufigkeitsadverbien stehen hinter **am/are/is**.
On Mondays, Mr Tomololo is usually at school.

Look at the table and tick (✓) the boxes that are right for you. Find a partner and talk about your table. Take turns.
Talk like this:

I never go swimming.
What about you?

I sometimes go swimming.
But I never …

	never	sometimes	usually	often	always
go swimming					
play football					
listen to music					
do homework					
read comics					

Ich kann sagen, wie oft ich bestimmte Dinge für gewöhnlich mache.

LANGUAGE What I never, sometimes, often, usually and always do

Find a partner and add two activities. Tick (✓) the boxes that are right for you and then talk about your tables.
Talk like this:

	never	sometimes	usually	often	always
go swimming					
play football					
do homework					
read comics					
eat pizza					

Ich kann sagen, wie oft ich bestimmte Dinge für gewöhnlich mache.

LANGUAGE What I never, sometimes, often, usually and always do

Find a partner. Tick (✓) the boxes that are right for you and add two activities. Then talk about your tables.
Talk like this:

I never go swimming.
What about you?

I sometimes go swimming.
But I never …

	never	sometimes	usually	often	always
go swimming					
play football					
listen to music					
read comics					
eat pizza					
____________					
____________					

Wenn ich einen Text höre oder lese, kann ich einzelne Wörter darin erkennen und schon kleine Details wiederholen.

1 On air

a) Anne und Dave talk about their favourite school club on Radio PLYM, the radio station in Plymouth. FF 18 First read the three flyers for school clubs. Then listen to part 1 and tick (✓) the right flyer. Is the radio show about club A, B or C?

adventure [əd'ventʃə] *Abenteuer* • on air [ɒn_'eə] *auf Sendung* • crime story ['kraɪm ˌstɔːri] *Krimi*

A
Boat club

Do you like water, wind and sport? Go sailing with us! Join the boat club. We have boats and you have fun! You can learn everything about boats and sailing. We try to go sailing every Friday afternoon, just bring along some sunshine.

B
Book club

Do you like good books? Great! This is your club! You can meet people who love great books, too. We read together, talk about books and have extra activities around books. You see, it's all about books in the book club!

C
Photo club

Do you want to take good photos? Yes? Join us and you are master of the camera in three months. We can take wonderful photos of Plymouth and of people, or what would you like? Create your own photos – it's really fun!

Fold your paper here before you start working on this exercise.

b) FF 19 Read the table. Then listen to part 2 and circle the right answers.

1 Anne and Dave are in a club where you can eat	a) breakfast.	
	b) lunch.	
	c) biscuits and fruit.	

2 Dave	a) doesn't like books.	
	b) doesn't like romantic stories.	
	c) loves old books.	

3 At the book club the students talk about	a) adventure stories.	
	b) books they don't have in the book club.	
	c) their lunch.	

4 You usually get good ideas what	a) to do Saturday morning.	
	b) music you can listen to.	
	c) to read next.	

c) FF 20 Read the table. Then listen to part 3. Are the sentences right or wrong? Circle the wrong word too.

	Right	Wrong
We usually read to the kindergarten children.		
They sometimes have funny questions about the book.		
We also have book nights where lots of pupils always come to.		
We usually meet every Friday from 2 to 4 pm in the book club …		
… or in Anne's garden when it's sunny and warm.		

2 Aliens' athletic centre

a) Warm up your brain! Read the text and match sentences 1–4 to the pictures.

HOME | ABOUT | SERVICES | OUR BOSS | CONTACT

Welcome to the alien world of sports! You are on the homepage of the Aliens' Athletic Centre and it doesn't matter how many arms, legs, eyes or ears you have, you can join anytime! Get to know our members and join our centre. Warm up with a little quiz …

Ready – steady – go!

1 **TRAIN YOUR EARS WITH JOE!**
2 Play basketball with Oscar!
3 *Go swimming with* Mando!
4 Try to win against Ivy: **Play hockey in the sand!**

b) **Good! Your brain is warm. Go on! Read this text about Walli on our homepage and fill out his *That's me! card.* Draw a picture of Walli.**

HOME | ABOUT | SERVICES | **OUR BOSS** | CONTACT

Our boss:

Hi! I'm Walli! I'm eighty-seven years old and I'm the boss here because I'm the best.
I am the best in tennis and I'm good at basketball too. My arms are long and I get every ball. My favourite sport is football but I don't have football partners who want to play with me. I don't know why! I like table tennis and judo.
I don't like swimming because my arms and legs don't know what to do in the water.
Do you have questions about the Aliens' Athletic Centre? Come to me and I help you.
There isn't a photo on the homepage. I look like this: I'm three metres high. I have five arms and four feet. I have three eyes and two antennas on my head. Do I have hair? No, I don't have hair but I'm blue. I put a photo of me on my *That's me! card*.

That's me! card

name: ____________________

age: ____________________

best in: ____________________

favourite sport: ____________________

sport I like: ____________________

sport I don't like: ____________________

my photo:

Wenn ich einen Text höre oder lese, kann ich einzelne Wörter darin erkennen und schon kleine Details wiederholen.

1 On air

Anne und Dave talk about their favourite school club on Radio PLYM, the radio station in Plymouth.

a) FF 18 Read the sentences. Then listen to part 1. Circle the wrong word and write down the right word.

adventure [əd'ventʃə] *Abenteuer* • on air [ɒn_'eə] *auf Sendung* • crime story ['kraɪm ˌstɔːri] *Krimi*

1 Anne is in the show to talk about the photo club. ____________________

2 Dave is in three sport clubs. ____________________

3 When you read a book, you can meet aliens that can talk and join great adventures.

____

4 Dave: "In the book club we read and talk about new books and have extra activities around boats too."

____

b) FF 19 Read the table. Then listen to part 2 and circle the right answers.

1 There is a special room for the book club	a) with chairs and desks.	
	b) with sofas.	
	c) with beds.	

2 We talk about the books	a) we read.	
	b) we have.	
	c) we want.	

3 Dave doesn't like	a) adventure stories.	
	b) dogs.	
	c) romantic stories.	

4 At the book club there are	a) four or five people.	
	b) six or seven people.	
	c) eight or nine people.	

5 You usually get good ideas	a) what to read at the weekend.	
	b) what to read in the English lesson.	
	c) what to read next.	

c) FF 20 **Read the ideas about part 3. Then listen to part 3. What's right: 1, 2 or 3? Tick (✓) the right sentence.**

1 The book club goes to old people and reads to them. They bring books to the kindergarten too.	

2 The book club goes to the kindergarten and reads to the children. They have book nights too.	

3 The book club chooses books for the English lesson. They have book weekends too.	

2 Aliens' athletic centre

a) **Warm up your brain! Complete the four sentences and match them to the pictures.**

HOME | ABOUT | SERVICES | OUR BOSS | CONTACT

Welcome to the alien world of sports! You are on the homepage of the Aliens' Athletic Centre and it doesn't matter how many arms, legs, eyes or ears you have, you can join anytime! Get to know our members and join our centre. Warm up with a little quiz …

Ready – steady – go!

1 **TRAIN YOUR __________ WITH JOE!**

2 Play _____________ with Oscar!

3 _____ *swimming with* Mando!

4 Try to win against Ivy: ________ **hockey in the sand!**

A

B

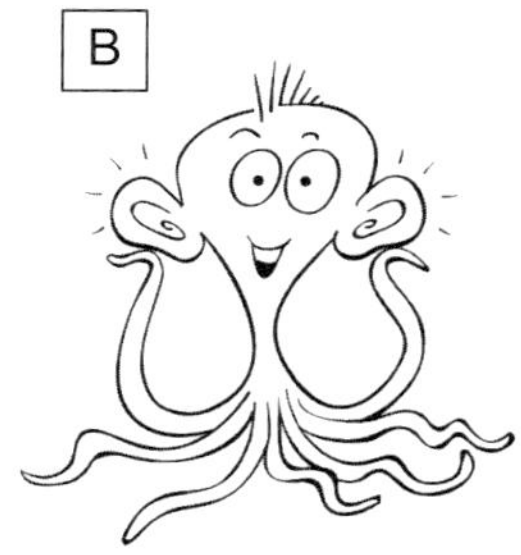

C

D

b) Good! Your brain is warm. Go on! Read this text about Walli on our homepage and fill out his *That's me! card.* Draw a picture of Walli.

HOME ABOUT SERVICES **OUR BOSS** CONTACT

Our boss:
Hi! I'm Walli! I'm eighty-seven years old and I'm the boss here because I'm the best.
I am the best in tennis and I'm good at basketball too. My arms are long and I get every ball. My favourite sport is football but I don't have football partners who want to play with me. I don't know why! I like table tennis and judo.
I don't like swimming because my arms and legs don't know what to do in the water. And water is usually wet. I don't like wet water.
Do you have questions about the Aliens' Athletic Centre? Come to me and I help you.
There isn't a photo on the homepage. I look like this: I'm three metres high. I have five arms and four feet. I have three eyes and two antennas on my head. Do I have hair? No, I don't have hair but I'm blue. I put a photo of me on my *That's me! card.*

That's me! card

name: ______________________

age: ______________________

best in: ______________________

favourite sport: ______________________

sport I like: ______________________

____

sport I don't like: ______________________

____

my photo:

Wenn ich einen Text höre oder lese, kann ich einzelne Wörter darin erkennen und schon kleine Details wiederholen.

1 On air

a) Anne und Dave talk about their favourite school club on Radio PLYM, the radio station in Plymouth. Look at the picture and read the thought bubbles.
FF 18 Then listen to Golo, Anne and Dave. Who thinks what? Match the person to the thought bubbles.

adventure [əd'ventʃə] *Abenteuer* • on air [ɒn_'eə] *auf Sendung* • crime story ['kraɪm ˌstɔːri] *Krimi*

1 My guests are here. Let's welcome them to my show on Radio PLYM!

2 I love fantasy stories with talking animals or great adventure stories.

Golo
Anne
Dave

5 I love books and I like to meet people who love books too.

4 Sport is great, but with a good book you can relax.

3 What are the boy's and girl's favourite club at Plymstock School? Let's find out!

b) FF 19 Listen to part 2. In every sentence there is a wrong word. Circle the wrong word and write down the right word.

1 You can drink tea and eat bananas anytime. ____________________

2 We never have a book talk where we talk about the books we read. ____________________

3 I don't watch romantic stories. ____________________

4 We're usually three or five people. ____________________

5 You usually get good ideas what to eat next. ____________________

c) FF 20 Read the list of extra activities. Then listen to part 3. What are the extra activities around books? Tick (✓) all activities Anne and Dave talk about.

	Tick (✓) here:
1 We usually read to the kindergarten children.	
2 We have book weekends at school.	
3 We also have book nights.	
4 We often read to old people.	

2 Aliens' Athletic Centre

a) Warm up your brain! Read the four sentences. Make sentences and match them to the pictures.

HOME | ABOUT | SERVICES | OUR BOSS | CONTACT

Welcome to the alien world of sports! You are on the homepage of the Aliens' Athletic Centre and it doesn't matter how many arms, legs, eyes or ears you have, you can join anytime! Get to know our members and join our centre. Warm up with a little quiz …

Ready – steady – go!

1 ears – Joe. – your – train – with ______________________

2 Oscar. – play – with – basketball ______________________

3 swimming – Mando. – with – go ______________________

4 Try to win against Ivy: – sand. – hockey – in – play – the ______________________

____

A

B

C

D

1		2		3		4	

b) Good! Now read this text about Walli on our homepage and fill out his *That's me! card.* Draw a picture of Walli.

HOME ABOUT SERVICES **OUR BOSS** CONTACT

Our boss:

Hi! I'm Walli! I'm eighty-seven years old and I'm the boss here, because I'm the best. I'm good-looking, I have muscles and I have grey material on my head.

I am the best in tennis and basketball. My arms are long and I get every ball. My favourite sport is football but I don't have football partners who want to play with me. I don't know why! I like table tennis, kung fu and judo. Do you know any table tennis players who want to play with me? I need a kung fu and a judo partner too. Do you have time on Thursday? I'm free!!!

I don't like swimming because my arms and legs don't know what to do in the water. And water is usually wet. I don't like wet water. And I don't like dancing, I never know what to do with my four feet.

Do you have questions about the Aliens' Athletic Centre? Come to me and I help you. I can show you everything. There isn't a photo of me on the homepage. I look like this: I'm three metres high. I have five arms and four feet. I have three eyes and two antennas on my head. Do I have hair? No, I don't have hair but I'm blue. I put a photo of me on my *That's me! card*.

That's me! card

name: ______________________

age: ______________________

best in: ______________________

favourite sport: ______________________

sport I like: ______________________

sport I don't like: ______________________

my photo:

Ich kann von anderen Informationen erfragen, indem ich ihnen Fragen mit *when*, *where*, *what* und *do/does* stelle.

1 Penny Pencil interviews Busy Lizzie

Penny Pencil interviews Busy Lizzie for a sport magazine and asks her about sports. Read the interview first. Then find the questions to Lizzie's answers. Use questions with *where*, *when*, *do*, *why* and *what*.

Penny Pencil: Good morning, Lizzie! Our magazine is all about sport. So Lizzie, (1) do ______ you like sport?

Busy Lizzie: Good morning, Penny. Yes, I do.

Penny Pencil: (2)__________ sports do you like?

Busy Lizzie: I like tennis and badminton. (3)__________ about you?

Penny Pencil: Oh, I like tennis. (4)__________ you play tennis in a club?

Busy Lizzie: No, I don't. I sometimes meet friends and we play tennis together.

Penny Pencil: (5)__________ you like dancing, Lizzie?

Busy Lizzie: Yes, I do. I like dancing very much.

Penny Pencil: (6)__________ do you like dancing?

Busy Lizzie: I like dancing because I love music. I'm in a dancing club.

Penny Pencil: That's a nice hobby. (7)__________ is the dancing club?

Busy Lizzie: The club is in Foxtrot Street.

Penny Pencil: And (8)__________ does it meet?

Busy Lizzie: It meets on Monday evening.

Penny Pencil: (9)__________ you have other hobbies too?

Busy Lizzie: Yes, I have other hobbies too.

Penny Pencil: (10)__________ are your other hobbies?

Busy Lizzie: My other hobbies are sailing and reading.

Penny Pencil: This is funny – I like books too. (11)__________ do you usually read?

Busy Lizzie: I usually read ghost stories. But I also like funny books very much.

Penny Pencil: Thank you very much for the interview, Lizzie. You are very nice.

Busy Lizzie: Thank you!

2 Ask me!

Cut out the cards. Put all cards together that have the same symbol.
Partner A: Take one card of each symbol and make a question. Put the cards back.
Partner B: Now it's your turn. Take one card of each symbol and make a question.
Now it's partner A's turn again. Go on.

You can make funny questions, of course. But be careful: the word order has to be correct!

Partner A: Does the frog go skating?
Partner B: When do we go surfing?
Partner A: Why do you …

question word cards

(do / does)

pronoun / name cards

verb + activity cards

When	I	Walli	go for a walk with the dog	go swimming
Why	you	the house elf	clean Pfiffy's room	do judo
Where	he	we	go sailing	do gymnastics
Do/Does	she	the frog	make breakfast	play football
go dancing	Mr Donald	your friend	do gardening	cook dinner
read a good book	read a comic	listen to music	play the guitar	help in the kitchen

Ich kann von anderen Informationen erfragen, indem ich ihnen Fragen mit *when*, *where*, *what* und *do/does* stelle.

1 Penny Pencil interviews Busy Lizzie

Penny Pencil interviews Busy Lizzie for a sport magazine and asks her about sports. Read the interview first. Then find the questions to Lizzie's answers. Use questions with *where*, *when*, *do*, *why* and *what*.

Penny Pencil: Good morning, Lizzie! Our magazine is all about sport. So Lizzie, do you like sport?

Busy Lizzie: Good morning, Penny. Yes, I like sport very much.

Penny Pencil: (1) ______________________________?

Busy Lizzie: I like tennis and badminton. (2) ______________________________?

Penny Pencil: Oh, I like tennis too. (3) ______________________________?

Busy Lizzie: No, I don't play tennis in a club. I sometimes meet friends and we play tennis together.

Penny Pencil: (4) ______________________________, Lizzie?

Busy Lizzie: Yes, I do. I like dancing very much.

Penny Pencil: (5) ______________________________?

Busy Lizzie: I like dancing because I love music.

Penny Pencil: (6) ______________________________?

Busy Lizzie: Yes, I'm in a dancing club.

Penny Pencil: That's a nice hobby. (7) ______________________________?

Busy Lizzie: The dancing club is in Foxtrot Street.

Penny Pencil: And (8) ______________________________?

Busy Lizzie: It meets on Monday evening.

Penny Pencil: (9) ______________________________ too?

Busy Lizzie: Yes, I have other hobbies too.

Penny Pencil: (10) ______________________________?

Busy Lizzie: My other hobbies are sailing and reading.

Penny Pencil: This is funny – I like books too. (11) ______________________________?

Busy Lizzie: I usually read ghost stories. But I also like funny books very much.

Penny Pencil: Thank you very much for the interview, Lizzie. You are very nice.

Busy Lizzie: Thank you!

2 Ask me!

Cut out the cards. Put all cards together that have the same symbol.
Partner A: Take one card of each symbol and make a question. Put the cards back.
Partner B: Now it's your turn. Take one card of each symbol and make a question.
Now it's partner A's turn again. Go on.

You can make funny questions and answers, of course. But be careful: the word order has to be correct!

Partner A: Does the frog go skating?
Partner B: When do we go surfing?
Partner A: Why do you …

question word cards

(do / does)

pronoun / name cards

verb + activity cards

When	I	Walli	go for a walk with the dog	go swim-ming
Why	you	the house elf	clean Pfiffy's room	do judo
Where	he	we	go sailing	do gym-nastics
Do/Does	she	the frog	make break-fast	play football
go dancing	Mr Donald	your friend	do garde-ning	cook dinner
read a good book	read a comic	listen to music	play the guitar	help in the kitchen

Ich kann von anderen Informationen erfragen, indem ich ihnen Fragen mit *when*, *where*, *what* und *do/does* stelle.

1 What's the question? What's your answer?

a) In this question and answer table there are some questions and some answers missing. Finish the table with the right questions and your answers. Use adverbs of frequency too.

Question	Answer
What's your favourite colour?	
	No, I **hate** pink!
	I live in Bonn.
When do you go to sleep?	
	I often play football at the weekend.
	I read books because I like ghost stories.
Where do you go to school?	
	I usually go home at four o'clock.
	I have to go shopping because I need a new ruler.
When do you get angry?	

b) Now write three questions and three answers in the table for your partner. Then swap the table with your partner and write in your partner's table.

Question	Answer
•	
•	
•	
	•
	•
	•

2 Question dice

Partner A: Throw the dice. Use the question word, choose a pronoun and an activity if you need it and make a question.
Partner B: Answer the question. Now it's your turn to ask a question. You can make funny questions and answers, of course!

Each number of the dice is a question word:

⚀ = where; ⚁ = what; ⚂ = when; ⚃ = why;

⚄ = do / does; ⚅ = Joker: choose your favourite question word.

Partner A: Ok, I throw the dice … It's a five, a five is: do or does. I have to make a question with do or does. Hmmm. Does Walli clean Pfiffi's room?

Partner B: No, he doesn't. He does judo. Now it's my turn. I have a four, a four is: why …

Pronoun	Activity
we	go for a walk with the dog
she	go sailing
he	clean Pfiffy's room
you	help in the kitchen
I	make breakfast
the house elf	cook dinner
Walli	do gardening
frog	go swimming
your friend	play the guitar
Mr Donald	do judo
	do gymnastics
	play football

Ich kann Informationen über mich und andere geben. Dabei kann ich sagen und schreiben, was ich oder die anderen oft/manchmal/gewöhnlich machen oder mögen. Ich benutze dabei das *Simple present*.

Hello, love!

a) Please answer Penny Pencil's questions. Make the sentences and use *never*, *sometimes*, *usually*, *often* and *always*. Your answers can be funny, of course!

Penny Pencil: Hello, love! My next article is about German students. Please answer my questions. Do you fly to the moon on Sundays?

You: No, I never fly to the moon on Sundays.

Penny Pencil: Do you sit on a tree?

You: on a tree – sit – I – never/sometimes/usually/often/always.

(1)______________________________

Penny Pencil: Do you eat with your fingers?

You: I – with my fingers – eat – never/sometimes/usually/often/always.

(2)______________________________

Penny Pencil: Do you drink water?

You: drink – water – I – never/sometimes/usually/often/always.

(3)______________________________

Penny Pencil: Do you sleep at seven o'clock in the evening?

You: I – at seven o'clock – sleep – in the evening – never/sometimes/usually/often/always.

(4)______________________________

Penny Pencil: Do you eat ice cream?

You: I – eat – ice cream – never/sometimes/usually/often/always.

(5)______________________________

Penny Pencil: Do you go to school by bike?

You: by bike – to school – I – go – never/sometimes/usually/often/always.

(6)______________________________

b) Swap your exercise with a partner. Read your partner's answers and write Penny's article about him/her in your exercise book..

Start like this: Lisa never flies to the moon on Sundays. She often sits on a tree.

Ich kann Informationen über mich und andere geben. Dabei kann ich sagen und schreiben, was ich oder die anderen oft/manchmal/gewöhnlich machen oder mögen. Ich benutze dabei das *Simple present.*

Hello, love!

a) **Please answer Penny Pencil's questions. Use *never*, *sometimes*, *usually*, *often* and *always* at the right time. Your answers can be funny, of course!**

Penny Pencil: Hello, love! My next article is about German students. Please answer my questions. Do you fly to the moon on Sundays?

You: No, I never fly to the moon on Sundays.

Penny Pencil: Do you sit on a tree?

You: (1)____________________

Penny Pencil: Do you eat with your fingers?

You: (2)____________________

Penny Pencil: Do you drink water?

You: (3)____________________

Penny Pencil: Do you do your homework at four o'clock in the morning?

You: (4)____________________

Penny Pencil: Do you go to bed at seven o'clock in the evening?

You: (5)____________________

Penny Pencil: Do you eat roast beef, scones or cakes?

You: (6)____________________

Penny Pencil: Do you eat ice cream?

You: (7)____________________

Penny Pencil: Do you play basketball or do you sometimes do gymnastics?

You: (8)____________________

Penny Pencil: Do you do sport at school?

You: (9)____________________

Penny Pencil: Do you go to school by bike?

You: (10)____________________

Penny Pencil: Thank you for this interview.

b) **Swap your exercise with a partner. Read your partner's answers and write Penny's article about him/her in your exercise book. Use *never*, *sometimes*, *usually*, *often* and *always*.**
Start like this: Lisa never flies to the moon on Sundays. She often sits on a tree.

Ich kann Informationen über mich und andere geben. Dabei kann ich sagen und schreiben, was ich oder die anderen oft/manchmal/gewöhnlich machen oder mögen. Ich benutze dabei das *Simple present.*

Hello, love!

a) **Please answer Penny Pencil's questions. Use *never*, *sometimes*, *usually*, *often* and *always* at the right time. You answers can be funny, of course!**

Penny Pencil: Hello, love! My next article is about German students. Please answer my questions. Do you fly to the moon on Sundays?

You: No, I never fly to the moon on Sundays.

Penny Pencil: Do you sit on a tree?

You: (1)____________________

Penny Pencil: Do you eat with your fingers?

You: (2)____________________

Penny Pencil: Do you drink water?

You: (3)____________________

Penny Pencil: Where do you usually do your homework?

You: (4)____________________

Penny Pencil: When do you often go to bed?

You: (5)____________________

Penny Pencil: Do you eat roast beef, scones or cakes?

You: (6)____________________

Penny Pencil: Do you eat ice cream?

You: (7)____________________

Penny Pencil: Do you play basketball or do you sometimes do gymnastics?

You: (8)____________________

Penny Pencil: Where do you never do sport?

You: (9)____________________

Penny Pencil: Do you go to school by bike?

You: (10)____________________

Penny Pencil: Thank you for this interview.

b) **Swap your exercise with a partner. Read your partner's answers and write Penny's article about him or her. Use *never*, *sometimes*, *usually*, *often* and *always*. You can start like this:**
Lisa never flies to the moon on Sundays. She often sits on a tree ...

Ich kann einem Mitschüler erklären, wann man im Englischen Groß- und Kleinschreibung verwendet.

LANGUAGE S-word snake says yummy

a) Look at this! Steven the snake loves s-words and all words in the snake are small. Draw a line after every word.

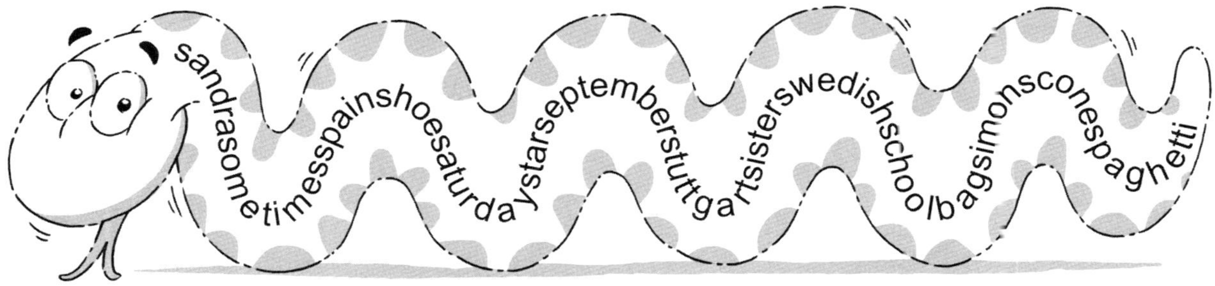

b) Write the words in the table. Use capital letters where you need them. Write down why you use a capital letter.

Find a partner and compare.

small letter	CAPITAL LETTER	Why do you use a capital letter?
	Sandra	name

TIP: CAPITAL LETTERS, small letters

CAPITAL LETTERS:
- **names** (*Mr Owen, Amy*)
- **country adjectives** (*French bread*)
- **countries** (*England*)
- **cities** (*Mannheim*)
- **names of schools**
- the word "I"
- **days and months** (*Friday, June*)

small letters:
- **nouns** (*letter, guitar*)

Ich kann einem Mitschüler erklären, wann man im Englischen Groß- und Kleinschreibung verwendet.

LANGUAGE Name it!

a) Look at the pictures. Then look at the word box. Match the words to the pictures. Then write down the words and use capital and small letters where you need them.

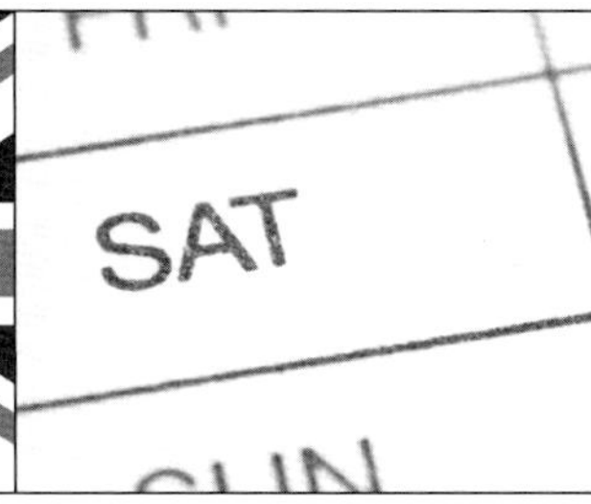

1 ______ 2 ______ 3 ______ 4 ______

5 ______ 6 ______ 7 ______ 8 ______

A GreaT cAStle • SaTuRDaY • peNNy penCil • amErIcan hAMburgeR • a fUnNy moNkey • sMeatOn's tower • sOPhIe • englaNd

b) Some words from the box in a) need a capital letter. Why? Write it down.
Now find a partner and compare your answers.

Words with a capital letter	Why do you write a capital letter?
	country

Ich kann einem Mitschüler erklären, wann man im Englischen Groß- und Kleinschreibung verwendet.

LANGUAGE S-word snake says yummy

a) Look at this! Steven the snake loves s-words and all words in the snake are small. Draw a line after every word.

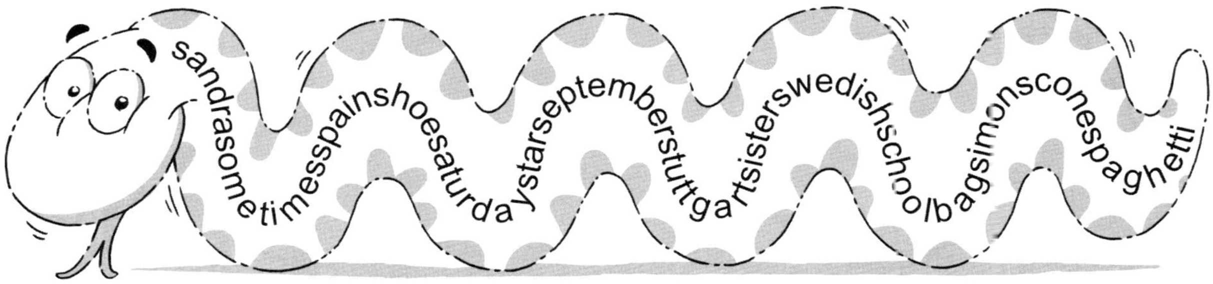

b) Write the words in the table and use capital letters where you need them. Write down why you use a capital letter.
Then compare your answers with a partner.

small letter	CAPITAL LETTER	Why do you use a capital letter?
	Sandra	name

c) Find a partner and draw a snake for your partner. Partner A draws Toby the t-word snake and partner B draws Melissa the m-word snake. Then do tasks a) and b) again.

Ich kann mindestens sechs Beispielwörter für den [ɔː]-sound aufschreiben.

1 PRONUNCIATION Sounds [ɔː]

Complete the words. They all have the [ɔː]-sound but the spelling is different.

w__ ll	f__ r
y__ __ r	sp__ rt
d__ __ r	sm__ ll
f__ __ r	h__ rse

2 PRONUNCIATION Sounds [ɔː] – the odd one out

In every line there are two words with an [ɔː]-sound. But there is always one wrong word too. Circle the word that doesn't have the [ɔː]-sound.
Compare with your partner, then check the words in your English book.

1 board – ball – mouse

2 hour – horse – fall

3 shower – talk – water

4 cornflakes – sometimes – floor

3 Rhyme with [ɔː]

Find a rhyming word for *walk*, *tall* and *floor*.

1 walk – t____________________

2 tall – b____________________

3 floor – d____________________

Ich kann mindestens sechs Beispielwörter für den [ɔː]-sound aufschreiben.

1 PRONUNCIATION Sounds [ɔː]

Complete the words. They all have the [ɔː]-sound but the spelling is different.

w __ ll	f __ r
y __ __ r	sp __ rt
d __ __ r	sm __ ll
f __ __ r	h __ rse

2 PRONUNCIATION Sounds [ɔː] – the odd one out

a) In every line there are two words with an [ɔː]-sound. But there is always one wrong word too. Circle the word that doesn't have the [ɔː]-sound.
Compare with your partner, then check the words in your English book.

1 board – ball – mouse

2 hour – horse – fall

3 shower – talk – water

4 cornflakes – sometimes – floor

b) Can you make one more line like in a) for your partner? The words in the box can help you.

____

small • group • water • more • talk • food • soup • sport • clothes • board • room

3 Rhyme with [ɔː]

Find a rhyming word for *walk*, *tall* and *floor*.

1 walk – ____________

2 tall – ____________

3 floor – ____________

Ich kann mindestens sechs Beispielwörter für den [ɔː]-sound aufschreiben.

1 PRONUNCIATION Sounds [ɔː]

Complete the words. They all have the [ɔː]-sound but the spelling is different.

w __ ll	*f __ r*
y __ __ r	*sp __ rt*
d __ __ r	*sm __ ll*
f __ __ r	*h __ rse*

2 PRONUNCIATION Sounds [ɔː] – the odd one out

a) In every line there are two words with an [ɔː]-sound. But there is always one wrong word too. Circle the word that doesn't have the [ɔː]-sound.
Compare with your partner, then check the words in your English book.

1 board – ball – mouse

2 hour – horse – fall

3 shower – talk – water

4 cornflakes – sometimes – floor

b) Can you make two more lines like in a) for your partner?

____

____

3 Rhyme with [ɔː]

Find rhyming words for *walk*, *tall* and *floor*.

1 walk – __________

2 tall – __________ – __________

3 floor – __________ – __________ – __________

Ich kann anderen Informationen über Old Plymouth geben, indem ich ihnen davon erzähle und darüber schreibe.

1 Come and see Plymouth Mayflower Exhibition

Du bist mit deinen Großeltern unterwegs in Plymouth. Ihr habt einen Flyer von der Plymouth Mayflower Exhibition[1]. Beantworte die Fragen deiner Großeltern auf Deutsch.

Plymouth Mayflower Exhibition
A fantastic tour of Plymouth's great harbour and the Barbican. Great sea adventures started here. And there is more to find out about the history of Plymouth.

* 1620: The Pilgrim Fathers sail from Plymouth Harbour to America on a big ship called the Mayflower.
* Read stories about some rich families from Plymouth
* Find information about the fishing industry and the military harbour
* Look at interactive graphics, photographies and documents on three levels in the museum

Open all year:
- April to October: Monday to Saturday 9.30 am to 5 pm, Sunday 10.30 am to 4 pm
- November to March, Monday to Friday 9.30am to 5pm Saturdays 10.30 am to 4pm
- last entry: 30 minutes before exhibition closes

Prices:
Adults: 2£, children (5–16 years): 1£, students and seniors: 1.50£, family ticket (2 adults + up to 3 children): 5£

[1] exhibition [ˌeksɪˈbɪʃn] *Ausstellung*

Opa: Worum geht es denn in der Ausstellung?

Du: Es geht um die Geschichte ______

Opa: Was macht denn Plymouth Harbour so besonders?

Du: Von hier aus ______

______

Oma : Ist die Ausstellung das ganze Jahr geöffnet?

Du: Ja, aber ______

______

______

Opa: Wir haben ja auch unsere kleine Carla dabei. Gibt es so etwas wie ein Familienticket?

Du: Ja, zwei Erwachsene und ______

______

2 A Saturday with Mia and Poppy

a) Read what Mia and Poppy say. Then cut out the speech bubbles and find the correct order for the dialogue. Who says what?

Hi, Poppy. Good to see you. How are you?

What is the exhibition about?	How much is it?
OK, sounds good. When can we go there?	It's two pounds.
Hi, Mia. Good, thanks. What do we want to do this afternoon?	We can go there now! Oh no, sorry we can't. It's already half past four. Let's meet there tomorrow at 3 pm.
It's about the history of the harbour. I know that many ships started their tours around the world from the harbour. The Mayflower with the Pilgrim Fathers for example.	I have no idea. But, hey, wait a minute. Look at that flyer from the Plymouth Mayflower Exhibition. Maybe we can go there?

b) Act out the dialogue.

Ich kann anderen Informationen über Old Plymouth geben, indem ich ihnen davon erzähle und darüber schreibe.

1 Come and see Plymouth Mayflower Exhibition

Du bist mit deinen Großeltern unterwegs in Plymouth. Ihr habt einen Flyer von der Plymouth Mayflower Exhibition[1]. Beantworte die Fragen deiner Großeltern auf Deutsch.

Plymouth Mayflower Exhibition
A fantastic tour of Plymouth's great harbour and the Barbican. Great sea adventures started here. And there is more to find out about the history of Plymouth.

* 1620: The Pilgrim Fathers sail from Plymouth Harbour to America on a big ship called the Mayflower.
* Read stories about some rich families from Plymouth
* Find information about the fishing industry and the military harbour
* Look at interactive graphics, photographies and documents on three levels in the museum

Open all year:
- April to October: Monday to Saturday 9.30 am to 5 pm, Sunday 10.30 am to 4 pm
- November to March, Monday to Friday 9.30am to 5pm Saturdays 10.30 am to 4pm
- last entry: 30 minutes before exhibition closes

Prices:
Adults: 2£, children (5–16 years): 1£, students and seniors: 1.50£, family ticket (2 adults + up to 3 children): 5£

[1]exhibition [ˌeksɪˈbɪʃn] *Ausstellung*

Opa: Worum geht es denn in der Ausstellung?

Du: Es geht um ______

Opa: Was macht denn Plymouth Harbour so besonders?

Du: ______

______

Oma: Und was können wir in der Ausstellung tun?

Du: Wir können ______

______

Opa: Ist die Ausstellung das ganze Jahr geöffnet?

Du: ______

______

Opa: Wir haben ja auch unsere kleine Carla dabei. Gibt es so etwas wie ein Familienticket?

Du: Ja, zwei ______

2 A Saturday with Mia and Poppy

a) Read Poppy's questions and write Mia's answers.

Mia: Hi, Poppy. Good to see you. How are you?

Poppy: Hi, Mia. Good, thanks. What do we want to do this afternoon?

Mia: I have no idea. But, hey, wait a minute. Look at that flyer from the Plymouth Mayflower Exhibition. Maybe we can go there?

Poppy: What is the exhibition about?

Mia: It's about ______________________________

____

Poppy: Why is it special?

Mia: Plymouth Harbour is special because ______________________________

____

Poppy: I don't have much money. How much is a ticket?

Mia: It's ______________________________

Poppy: OK, that sounds good. It's half past four now. Can we go there now?

Mia: No, we ______________. They close ______________

Poppy: OK, then let's meet there tomorrow. Maybe we can go and meet the others at the Barbican now.

Mia: OK, good idea.

b) Act out the dialogue.

Ich kann anderen Informationen über Old Plymouth geben, indem ich ihnen davon erzähle und darüber schreibe.

1 Come and see Plymouth Mayflower Exhibition

Du bist mit deinen Großeltern unterwegs in Plymouth. Ihr habt einen Flyer von der Plymouth Mayflower Exhibition[1]. Beantworte die Fragen deiner Großeltern auf Deutsch.

Plymouth Mayflower Exhibition
A fantastic tour of Plymouth's great harbour and the Barbican. Great sea adventures started here. And there is more to find out about the history of Plymouth.

* 1620: The Pilgrim Fathers sail from Plymouth Harbour to America on a big ship called the Mayflower.
* Read stories about some rich families from Plymouth
* Find information about the fishing industry and the military harbour
* Look at interactive graphics, photographies and documents on three levels in the museum

Open all year:
- April to October: Monday to Saturday 9.30 am to 5 pm, Sunday 10.30 am to 4 pm
- November to March, Monday to Friday 9.30am to 5pm Saturdays 10.30 am to 4pm
- last entry: 30 minutes before exhibition closes

Prices:
Adults: 2£, children (5–16 years): 1£, students and seniors: 1.50£, family ticket (2 adults + up to 3 children): 5£

[1] exhibition [ˌeksɪˈbɪʃn] *Ausstellung*

Opa: Worum geht es denn in der Ausstellung?

Du: ______________________________

____

Opa: Was macht denn Plymouth Harbour so besonders?

Du: ______________________________

____

Oma: Und was können wir in der Ausstellung tun?

Du: ______________________________

____

Opa: Ist die Ausstellung das ganze Jahr geöffnet?

Du: ______________________________

____

Opa: Wir haben ja auch unsere kleine Carla dabei. Gibt es so etwas wie ein Familienticket?

Du: ______________________________

2 A Saturday with Mia and Poppy

a) Read what Mia and Poppy say. Finish the dialogue with a partner.

Mia: Hi, Poppy. Good to see you. How are you?

Poppy: Hi, Mia. Good, thanks. What ______________________________ this afternoon?

Mia: I have no idea. But, hey, wait a minute. Look at that flyer from the Plymouth Mayflower Exhibition. Maybe we can go there?

Poppy: What is the exhibition about?

Mia: It's about ______________________________

____

Poppy: Why ______________________________?

Mia: Plymouth Harbour is special because ______________________________

____

Poppy: I don't have much money. How ______________________________?

Mia: ______________________________

Poppy: OK, that sounds good. It's half past four now. Can we ______________________________?

Mia: No, we ____________. They close ______________________________

Poppy: OK, then let's meet there tomorrow at 3 pm. Maybe we can go and meet the others at the Barbican now.

Mia: OK, good idea.

b) Act out the dialogue.

Ich kann Informationen zu meinen Hobbys schriftlich so zusammenstellen, dass ich anschließend meinem Partner darüber berichten kann.

STUDY SKILLS Let me tell you what I like

a) Look at Penny Pencil and Busy Lizzie. They want to talk about their free time. Can you help them collect their notes about their free-times activities?

basketball (ball, in the gym, Tuesday),
piano class (piano, at home, Wednesday),
art class (pens, at school, Friday afternoon)

dancing class (dancing shoes, at school, Monday),
singing class (voice, at music school, every day),
reading club (books, in the library, Saturday)

You choose **Collect their information in a table or a mind map.**

activity	basketball		
day			
place		at home	
what Penny needs			pens

activity			
day			
place			
what Lizzie needs	dancing shoes		

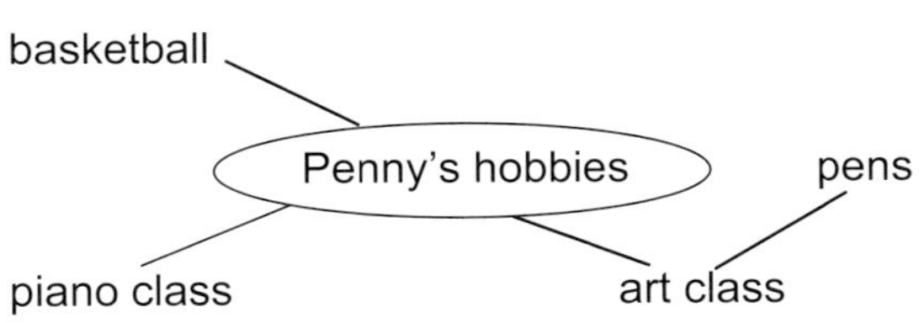

b) Partner A is Penny Pencil and Partner B is Busy Lizzie now. Tell your partner about your free time. You can start like this:

Hi there, I'm Penny Pencil! Let me tell you about my favourite hobbies. I play ...

fold here

More help

I play ... • I have ... • ... every Tuesday ... • in the evenings ... • in the gym ... • I need my ... • I use ...

Ich kann Informationen zu meinen Hobbys schriftlich so zusammenstellen, dass ich anschließend meinem Partner darüber berichten kann.

STUDY SKILLS Let me tell you what I like

a) Look at Penny Pencil and Busy Lizzie. They want to talk about their free time. Can you help them collect their notes about their free-time activities?

basketball (ball, in the gym, Tuesday),
piano class (piano, at home, Wednesday),
art class (pens, at school, Friday afternoon)

dancing class (dancing shoes, at school, Monday),
singing class (voice, at music school, every day),
reading club (books, in the library, Saturday)

You choose **Collect their information in a table or a mind map.**

activity			
day			
place			
what Penny needs			

activity			
day			
place			
what Lizzie needs			

Penny's hobbies: basketball, piano class, art class

Lizzie's hobbies: dancing class, singing class, reading

b) You are Penny Pencil or Busy Lizzie now. Tell your partner about your free time. You can start like this:

Hi there, I'm Penny Pencil! Let me tell you about my favourite hobbies. I play …

Ich kann Informationen zu meinen Hobbys schriftlich so zusammenstellen, dass ich anschließend meinem Partner darüber berichten kann.

STUDY SKILLS Let me tell you what I like

a) Look at Penny Pencil and Busy Lizzie. They want to talk about their free time. Can you help them collect notes about their free-time activities? Collect their information in a mind map or in a table.

basketball (ball, in the gym, Tuesday),
piano class (piano, at home, Wednesday),
art class (pens, at school, evenings)

dancing (dancing shoes, at school, Monday),
singing (voice, at music school, every day),
reading club (books, in the library, usually on Saturday)

b) Partner A is Penny Pencil and Partner B is Busy Lizzie now. Tell your partner about your free time. You can start like this:

Hi there, I'm Penny Pencil! Let me tell you about my favourite hobbies. I play …

Unit 4

Weekends

Meine Lernlandkarte für Unit 4

Name: ______________________ Klasse: ____________

Wie gut bist du in den Lernfeldern der Unit 4?
Schätze dich darin ein und male die entsprechende Anzahl an Kreisen auf der Ampel aus.
So findest du dein Übungsblatt.

Das lief nicht gut, ich muss mehr üben.	Das war OK, aber ich könnte besser werden.	Das habe ich gut geschafft.
●○○	●●○	●●●

Setze ein Häkchen, wenn du fertig bist. ✓

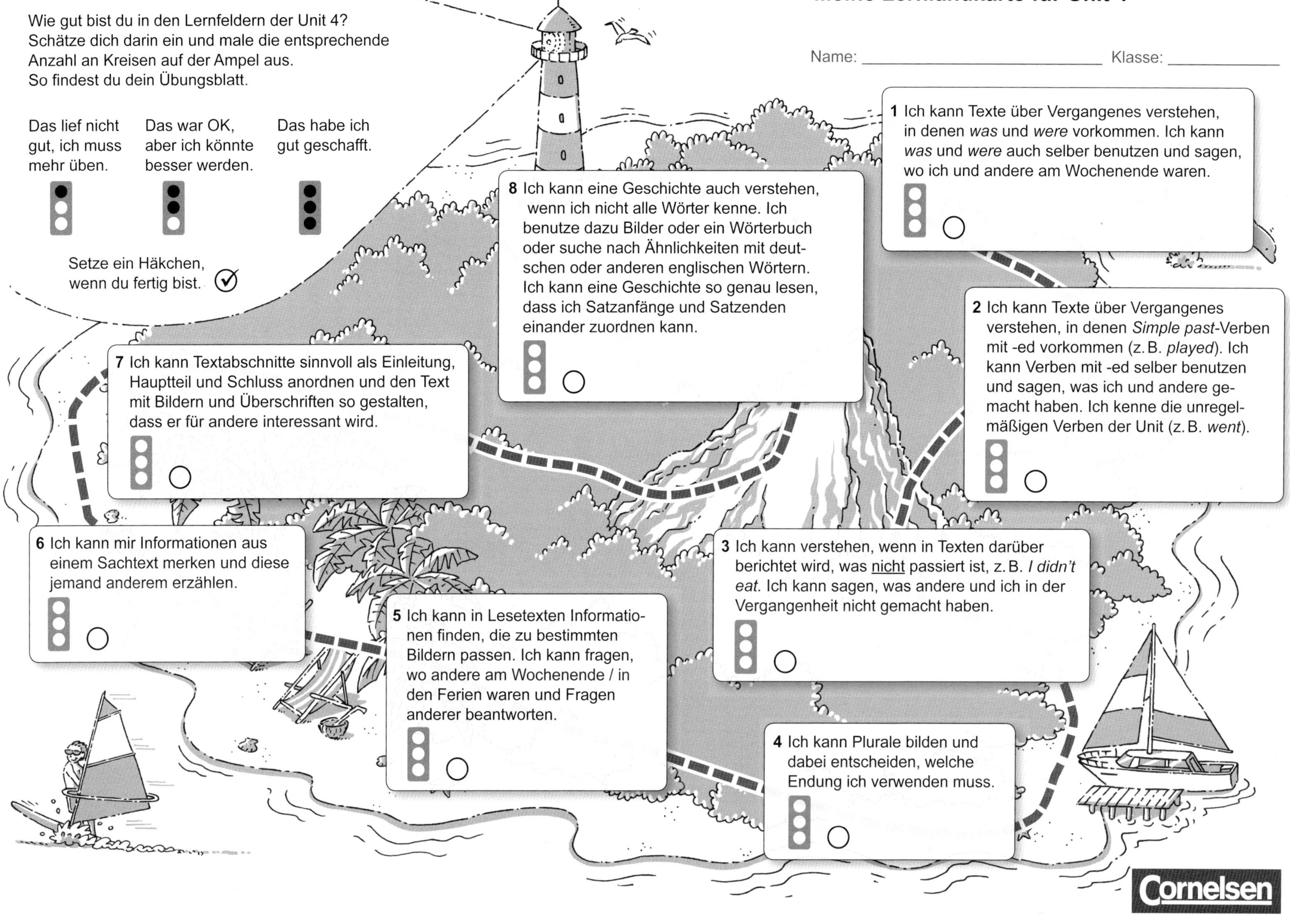

1 Ich kann Texte über Vergangenes verstehen, in denen *was* und *were* vorkommen. Ich kann *was* und *were* auch selber benutzen und sagen, wo ich und andere am Wochenende waren.
○○○ ○

2 Ich kann Texte über Vergangenes verstehen, in denen *Simple past*-Verben mit -ed vorkommen (z. B. *played*). Ich kann Verben mit -ed selber benutzen und sagen, was ich und andere gemacht haben. Ich kenne die unregelmäßigen Verben der Unit (z. B. *went*).
○○○ ○

3 Ich kann verstehen, wenn in Texten darüber berichtet wird, was nicht passiert ist, z. B. *I didn't eat.* Ich kann sagen, was andere und ich in der Vergangenheit nicht gemacht haben.
○○○ ○

4 Ich kann Plurale bilden und dabei entscheiden, welche Endung ich verwenden muss.
○○○ ○

5 Ich kann in Lesetexten Informationen finden, die zu bestimmten Bildern passen. Ich kann fragen, wo andere am Wochenende / in den Ferien waren und Fragen anderer beantworten.
○○○ ○

6 Ich kann mir Informationen aus einem Sachtext merken und diese jemand anderem erzählen.
○○○ ○

7 Ich kann Textabschnitte sinnvoll als Einleitung, Hauptteil und Schluss anordnen und den Text mit Bildern und Überschriften so gestalten, dass er für andere interessant wird.
○○○ ○

8 Ich kann eine Geschichte auch verstehen, wenn ich nicht alle Wörter kenne. Ich benutze dazu Bilder oder ein Wörterbuch oder suche nach Ähnlichkeiten mit deutschen oder anderen englischen Wörtern. Ich kann eine Geschichte so genau lesen, dass ich Satzanfänge und Satzenden einander zuordnen kann.
○○○ ○

Ich kann Texte über Vergangenes verstehen, in denen *was* und *were* vorkommen. Ich kann *was* und *were* auch selber benutzen und sagen, wo ich und andere am Wochenende waren.

1 Ella's homework

a) Last Saturday Ella's family was busy but she wasn't. She didn't do her homework and was on Skype for hours. But on Sunday Ella was busy too. She did her homework and wrote a text about "The jump from space"[1].
Read the following text to find out who was where.

The day of the first jump from space
The day Felix Baumgartner jumped from space was a busy day for my family.
That day my grandpa was the cameraman for a new film by his film club. Everybody in his club was at a lake and they filmed a love scene on the beach all day. I am happy my grandpa was the cameraman and not an actor in the film! But when he came home in the afternoon the jump was over!

My grandma didn't see Baumgartner's jump from space either. She was in Dartmoor walking with a friend. They walked and walked but they were home too late because they were too tired to catch an early bus back to Plymouth. So she was on the bus when Baumgartner jumped.

My dad was at a lunchtime party with people from work. The party was fun and the people were very happy. Dad was interested in the jump but the other people weren't interested. That was strange! Because Dad's watch was in his rucksack he didn't come home in time to watch TV.

On the day of the jump, my mum wasn't at the zoo where she works. She was in London because she took a dead monkey to the science museum. Her train back to Plymouth was late, so she couldn't watch TV. Maybe the train driver watched Felix Baumgartner too?

I wanted to watch the jump and I was at home all day. I was in my room and I was on Skype for hours. When I looked at my watch it was too late. The jump was already over!

b) Who was where? Write the names under the pictures.

Ella's mum • Ella's dad • Ella's grandpa • Ella's grandma • Ella

1

2

3

4

5

[1] jump from space [dʒʌmp frɒm speɪs] *Sprung aus dem All*

2 Different weekends

FF 21 **Listen to Jenny and Ella. Where was everybody on Saturday? Tick (✓) the correct answers. Listen again and check your answers.**

1 Jenny was …
a) at the cinema. ☐
b) at the shopping mall. ☐
c) at the theatre. ☐

2 Ella's father was …
a) away in his car. ☐
b) in the garage. ☐
c) in the garden. ☐

3 Ella's mother was …
a) in the car. ☐
b) in the kitchen. ☐
c) in the garden. ☐

4 Ella's grandparents were …
a) in the attic. ☐
b) at a book shop. ☐
c) at a museum. ☐

5 Ella's sister was …
a) at school. ☐
b) at the cinema. ☐
c) at a museum. ☐

6 Ella was …
a) in the garden. ☐
b) in her bedroom. ☐
c) in the park. ☐

3 GAME Their weekends

a) **Partner A: You are Sophie, Partner B: You are Philip. You had a very busy weekend. What did you do? Choose three places from the list and write them in your table – but don't let your partner see where you write them down! Then ask your partner what he or she did at the weekend. To win, you must find all your partner's places.**

places: cinema • park • café • beach • zoo • London

TIP
Fragen bildest du mit *Was I …?* und *Were you …?*. Die verneinten Formen von *to be* im *Simple past* heißen *I/he/she/it was* und *you/we/they were*. Wenn du mehr Hilfe brauchst, sieh dir das **Grammar File 11** in deinem Englischbuch an.

	Sophie's weekend	Philip's weekend
Saturday		
Sunday		

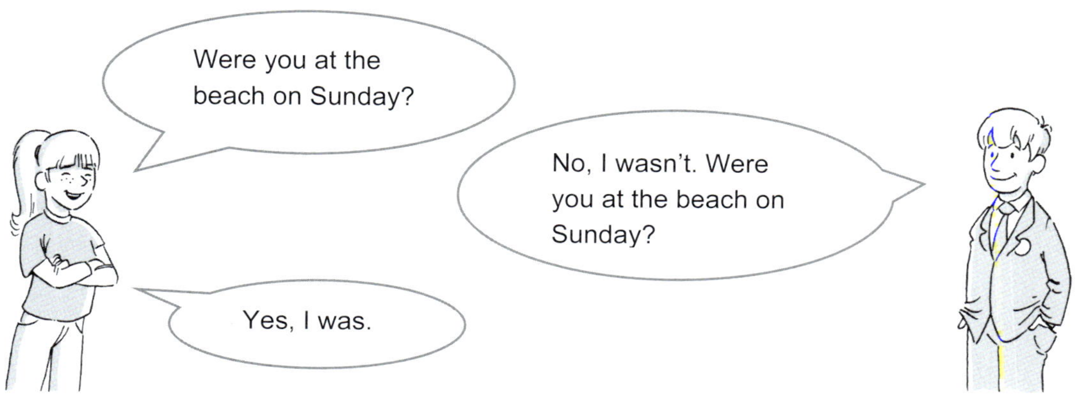

b) **Find another pair. Talk about your games: Tell the other pair where Sophie and Philip were at the weekend. You can start like this:**
Partner A: In our team, Philip was at the cinema on Sunday. He was …

Ich kann Texte über Vergangenes verstehen, in denen *was* und *were* vorkommen. Ich kann *was* und *were* auch selber benutzen und sagen, wo ich und andere am Wochenende waren.

1 Ella's homework

a) Last Saturday Ella's family was busy but she wasn't. She didn't do her homework and was on Skype for hours. But on Sunday Ella was busy too. She did her homework and wrote a text about "The jump from space"[1].
Read the following text and find out who was where.

The day of the first jump from space
The day Felix Baumgartner jumped from space was a busy day for my family.
That day my grandpa was the cameraman for a new film by his film club. Everybody in his club was at a lake and they filmed a love scene on the beach all day. I am happy my grandpa was the cameraman and not an actor in the film! But when he came home in the afternoon the jump was over!

My grandma didn't see Baumgartner's jump from space either. She was in Dartmoor walking with a friend. They walked and walked but they were home too late because they were too tired to catch an early bus back to Plymouth. So she was on the bus when Baumgartner jumped.

My dad was at a lunchtime party with people from work. The party was fun and the people were very happy. Dad was interested in the jump but the other people weren't interested. That was strange! Because Dad's watch was in his rucksack he didn't come home in time to watch TV.

On the day of the jump, my mum wasn't at the zoo where she works. She was in London because she took a dead monkey to the science museum. Her train back to Plymouth was late, so she couldn't watch TV. Maybe the train driver watched Felix Baumgartner too?

I wanted to watch the jump and I was at home all day. I was in my room and I was on Skype for hours. When I looked at my watch it was too late. The jump was already over!

b) Read the sentences and write down who was where.

1 On the day of the jump, this person wasn't on a train, this person wasn't at home, this person wasn't at a party and this person wasn't on a bus.

Who was it? It was ______________________________

2 On the day of the jump, this person wasn't at a museum, this person wasn't at a lake, this person wasn't on Skype and this person wasn't in Dartmoor.

Who was it? It was ______________________________

3 On the day of the jump, this person wasn't at a party, this person wasn't in London, this person wasn't in Dartmoor and this person wasn't outside all day.

Who was it? It was ______________________________

[1] jump from space [dʒʌmp frɒm speɪs] *Sprung aus dem All*

2 Different weekends

FF 21 **Listen to Jenny and Ella. Where was everybody on Saturday? Fill in *was* or *were* and circle the correct answer. Listen again and check your answers.**

1 Jenny ________
a) at the cinema.
b) at the shopping mall.
c) at the theatre.

2 Ella's father ________
a) away in his car.
b) in the garage.
c) in the garden.

3 Ella's mother ________
a) in the car.
b) in the kitchen.
c) in the garden.

4 Ella's grandparents ________
a) in the attic.
b) at a book shop.
c) at a museum.

5 Ella's sister ________
a) at school.
b) at the cinema.
c) at a museum.

6 Ella was ________
a) in the garden.
b) in her bedroom.
c) in the park.

3 GAME Our weeks

a) **Partner A: You are Sophie, Partner B: You are Philip. You had a very busy week. What did you do? Choose three places from the list and write them in your tables – but don't let your partner see where you write them down.**
Then ask your partner what his or her Philip or Sophie did in the week. To win, you have to find all your partner's places.

	Sophie's week	Philip's week
Monday		
Tuesday		
Wednesday		
Thursday		
Friday		
Saturday		
Sunday		

places
at cinema
in park
at café
at beach
at zoo
in London
in town

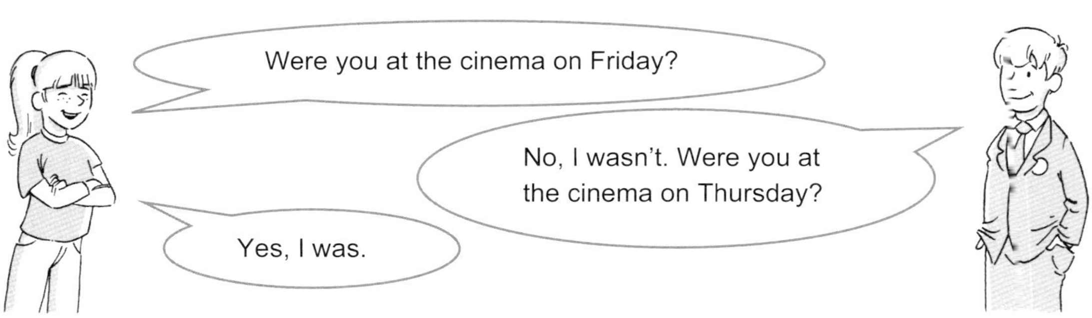

b) **Find another pair. Talk about your games: Tell the other pair where your Sophie or Philip was and wasn't in the week. You can start like this:**
Partner A: In our team, Philip wasn't at the cinema on Friday. He was at …

Ich kann Texte über Vergangenes verstehen, in denen *was* und *were* vorkommen. Ich kann *was* und *were* auch selber benutzen und sagen, wo ich und andere am Wochenende waren.

1 Ella's homework

a) Last Saturday Ella's family was busy but she wasn't. She didn't do her homework and was on Skype for hours. But on Sunday Ella was busy too. She did her homework and wrote a text about "The jump from space"[1].
Read the following text.

The day of the first jump from space
The day Felix Baumgartner jumped from space was a busy day for my family.
That day my grandpa was the cameraman for a new film by his film club. Everybody in his club was at a lake and they filmed a love scene on the beach all day. I am happy my grandpa was the cameraman and not an actor in the film! But when he came home in the afternoon the jump was over!

My grandma didn't see Baumgartner's jump from space either. She was in Dartmoor walking with a friend. They walked and walked but they were home too late because they were too tired to catch an early bus back to Plymouth. So she was on the bus when Baumgartner jumped.

My dad was at a lunchtime party with people from work. The party was fun and the people were very happy. Dad was interested in the jump but the other people weren't interested. That was strange! Because Dad's watch was in his rucksack he didn't come home in time to watch TV.

On the day of the jump, my mum wasn't at the zoo where she works. She was in London because she took a dead monkey to the science museum. Her train back to Plymouth was late, so she couldn't watch TV. Maybe the train driver watched Felix Baumgartner too?

I wanted to watch the jump and I was at home all day. I was in my room and I was on Skype for hours. When I looked at my watch it was too late. The jump was already over!

b) Read the sentences and write down who was where. Then make three more riddles[2] like this for your partner.

1 On the day of the jump, this person wasn't on a train, this person wasn't at home, this person wasn't at a party and this person wasn't on a bus.
Who was it? It was ______________________________.

2 On the day of the jump, this person wasn't at a museum, this person wasn't at a lake, this person wasn't on Skype and this person wasn't in Dartmoor.
Who was it? It was ______________________________.

3 On the day of the jump, this person wasn't ______________________________
______________________________.

4 On the day of the jump, this person wasn't ______________________________
______________________________.

5 On the day of the jump, this person wasn't ______________________________
______________________________.

[1]jump from space [dʒʌmp frɒm speɪs] *Sprung aus dem All* • [2]riddle [rɪdl] *Rätsel*

2 Different weekends

FF 21 **Listen to Jenny and Ella. Where was everybody on Saturday? Finish the sentences. Listen again and check your answers.**

1 Jenny ______________________________.

2 Ella's father ______________________________.

3 Ella's mother ______________________________.

4 Ella's grandparents______________________________.

5 Ella's sister ______________________________.

6 Ella ______________________________.

3 GAME Our weeks

a) **Partner A: You are Sophie, Partner B: You are Philip. You had a very busy week. What did you do? Choose three places from the list and write them in your tables – but don't let your partner see where you write them down!**
Then ask your partner what his or her Philip or Sophie did in the week. To win, you have to find all your partner's places.

	Sophie's week	Philip's week
Monday		
Tuesday		
Wednesday		
Thursday		
Friday		
Saturday		
Sunday		

places
cinema
park
café
beach
zoo
London
town

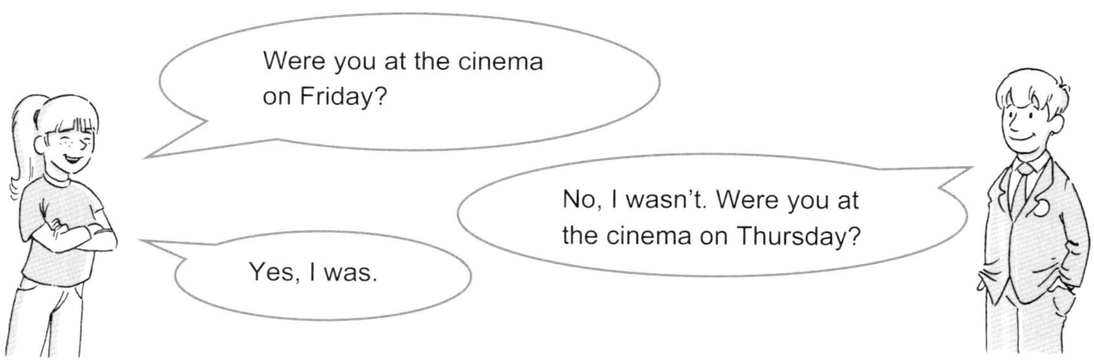

b) **Find another pair. Talk about your games: tell the other pair where your Sophie or Philip was and wasn't in the week. You can start like this:**
Partner A: In our team, Philip wasn't at the cinema on Friday. He was at …

Ich kann Texte über Vergangenes verstehen, in denen *Simple past*-Verben mit -ed vorkommen (z. B. *played*). Ich kann Verben mit -ed selber benutzen und sagen, was ich und andere gemacht haben. Ich kenne die unregelmäßigen Verben der Unit (z. B. *went*).

1 LANGUAGE Simple past

a) The simple past ending of regular verbs is -ed. But the snake also has irregular verbs that are different. Can you find them? (Circle) the five forms.

b) Copy the regular verb forms into the table. What are the -ed sounds?

[d]	[t]	[ɪd]
lived	looked	counted

c) Partner A: Read sentences 1–4 out to a partner. Partner B: Read sentences 5–8 out to your partner. Check your partner's pronunciation.

1) Tim wanted another ice cream.
2) Bob counted all his pens.
3) Claire looked at the tiger.
4) Tobi walked to the beach.

5) They lived in London.
6) Dilara spelled a new word.
7) Felix waited for a friend.
8) The sandwich tasted great.

2 Tony the traveller

a) FF 22 Tony is from Scotland and tells you about his holiday in southern England last summer. Listen to Tony.

Westminster Abbey

Big Ben

River Thames

Tower Bridge

Dartmoor National Park

Beach (southern England)

Find the correct answer.

1) On the first day he visited	a) Westminster Abbey.	
	b) the Tower.	
	c) London Bridge.	
2) In the afternoon he was at	a) the London Eye.	
	b) Trafalgar Square.	
	c) Big Ben.	
3) His walk across Tower Bridge on the second day was	a) boring.	
	b) exciting.	
	c) scary.	
4) In Dartmoor there were a lot of	a) mountains.	
	b) ponies.	
	c) trees.	
5) His last stop was Plymouth	a) at the weekend.	
	b) on a Friday.	
	c) on a Wednesday.	
6) The best thing at the beach was	a) the ice cream.	
	b) the warm water.	
	c) the hot sun.	

b) **Look at the pictures again. Tell your partner where Tony was on his holiday. You can also use the information from a). Use these verbs: visited, walked, saw, took a bus, went to.**

c) FF 22 **Now you are Tony. Listen to the text again and take notes on when Tony was where. Then write an email to your aunt Glenda in New Zealand about your holiday. Use your exercise book.**

You can start like this:
Dear Glenda,
How are you? I am fine. Last week I ...

You can end your email like this:
I want to go back next summer!
Lots of love from
Tony

fold here

More help

I ... to London by ... • On the first day, ... • In the afternoon, ... • On the next day, ... • That was ... • I really liked ... • The next morning ... • Then I ... • At the weekend ... • It was great when I ...

Ich kann Texte über Vergangenes verstehen, in denen *Simple past*-Verben mit -ed vorkommen (z. B. *played*). Ich kann Verben mit -ed selber benutzen und sagen, was ich und andere gemacht haben. Ich kenne die unregelmäßigen Verben der Unit (z. B. *went*).

1 LANGUAGE Simple past

a) Circle the irregular verbs and write down the past tense.

b) The regular simple past forms sound different. Make a mind map like this and write the simple past forms from a) in it. Use your exercise book.

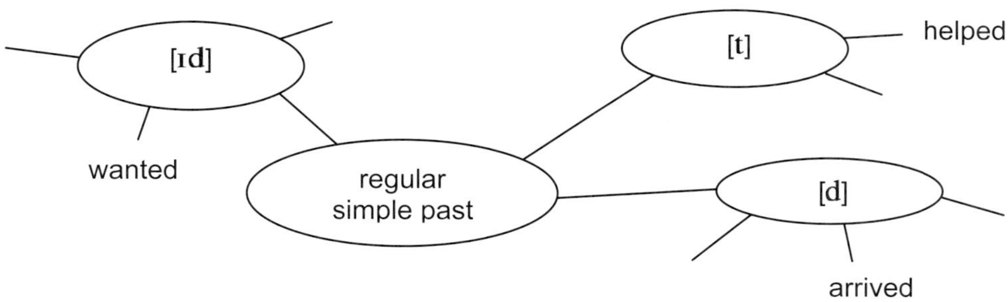

c) Finish the sentences with the simple past forms of the verbs. Partner A: You finish and then read out sentences 1–4 to your partner. Partner B: You finish and read out sentences 5–8 to your partner. Your partner writes down the sound of the past ([t], [d], [ɪd]) in his or her mindmap. Is the pronunciation correct?

1) Daniel ____________ (call) his dog.
2) Bob ____________ (count) his pencils.
3) Dilara ____________ (spell) a new word.
4) Tobi ____________ (walk) to the beach.

5) Sally ____________ (like) her new dress.
6) Claire ____________ (look) at the tiger.
7) Felix ____________ (wait) for a friend.
8) The sandwich ____________ (tast) great.

2 Tony the traveller

a) FF 22 Tony is from Scotland and tells you about his holiday in southern England last summer. Listen to Tony.

Westminster Abbey

Big Ben

River Thames

Tower Bridge

Dartmoor National Park

Beach (southern England)

Find the correct sentences.

1) At the beginning of his holiday, Tony was in	a) London for two days.	
	b) Leeds for three days.	
	c) London for four days.	
2) On the first day he was at	a) London Bridge.	
	b) Westminster Abbey.	
	c) Westminster Bridge.	
3) He was at	a) the London Eye in the afternoon.	
	b) Trafalgar Square in the evening.	
	c) Big Ben in the afternoon.	
4) His walk across Tower Bridge on the second day was	a) boring.	
	b) exciting.	
	c) scary.	
5) After his visit to London, he was in Dartmoor at a	a) bed & breakfast.	
	b) hotel.	
	c) holiday flat.	
6) His last stop was	a) Plymouth at the weekend.	
	b) Plymouth on a Friday.	
	c) Plymouth on a Wednesday	
7) The best thing at the beach was	a) the hot sun.	
	b) the warm water.	
	c) the ice cream.	

b) Look at the pictures again. Tell your partner where Tony was on his holiday. You can also use the information from a). Use these verbs:

visit • go to • walk • see • take a bus

c) FF 22 Now you are Tony. Listen to the text again and take notes on when Tony was where. Then write an email to your aunt Glenda in New Zealand about your holiday in your exercise book.

You can start like this:
Dear Glenda,
How are you? I am fine. Last week I ...

You can end your email like this:
I want to go back next summer!
Lots of love from Tony

fold here

More help I ... to London by ... • On the next day, ... • That was ... • I really liked .. • The next morning ... • Then I ... • At the weekend, ...

Ich kann Texte über Vergangenes verstehen, in denen *Simple past*-Verben mit -ed vorkommen (z. B. *played*). Ich kann Verben mit -ed selber benutzen und sagen, was ich und andere gemacht haben. Ich kenne die unregelmäßigen Verben der Unit (z. B. *went*).

1 LANGUAGE Simple past

a) Circle the irregular verbs.

b) The regular simple past forms sound different ([t], [d], [ɪd]). Write the simple past forms from a) into a mind map like this. Use your exercise book.

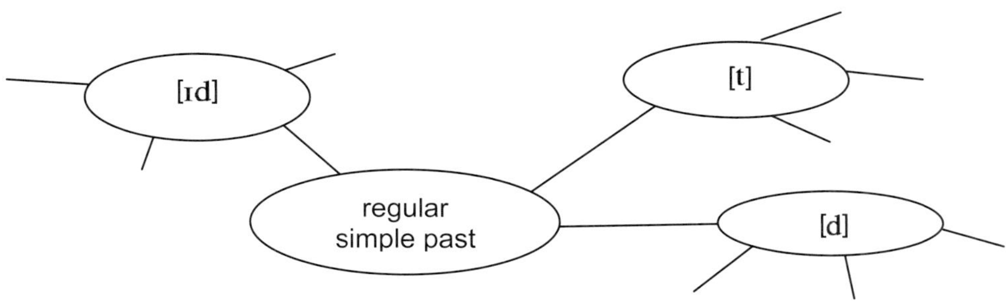

c) Use the verbs and make sentences in the simple past. Read them out to your partner. Your partner writes down the sound of the past ([t], [d], [ɪd]) in his or her mindmap. Is the pronunciation correct?
Partner A makes sentences with: count, walk, like, taste.
Partner B makes sentences with: want, spell, look, call.

2 Tony the traveller

a) FF 22 Listen to Tony. He is from Scotland and tells you about his holiday in southern England last summer.

Westminster Abbey

Big Ben

River Thames

Tower Bridge

Dartmoor National Park

Beach (southern England)

Find the correct sentences.

1) At the beginning of his holiday, Tony was in London for	a) two days.	
	b) three days.	
	c) four days.	
2) On the first day, he was at	a) Westminster Abbey.	
	b) the Tower.	
	c) London Bridge.	
3) In the afternoon, he was at	a) the London Eye.	
	b) Trafalgar Square.	
	c) Big Ben.	
4) His walk across Tower Bridge on the second day was	a) boring.	
	b) exciting.	
	c) scary.	
5) In Dartmoor, there were a lot of	a) mountains.	
	b) ponies.	
	c) trees.	
6) His last stop was Plymouth	a) at the weekend.	
	b) on Friday.	
	c) on Wednesday.	
7) There were some crabs	a) at the beach.	
	b) in an aquarium.	
	c) under some rocks.	
8) The best thing at the beach was	a) the ice cream.	
	b) the warm water.	
	c) the sun.	

b) **Look at the pictures again. Tell your partner what Tony did in his holiday. Use these verbs in the past tense:**

visit • go to • walk • take a bus • see

c) **Now you are Tony. Write an email to your aunt Glenda in New Zealand about your holiday. You can add more activities to Tony's email. You can write about what happened in London and what you saw in Dartmoor National Park. Try to use as many words as you can.**

adjectives: exciting • funny • nice • great • cool • big • busy • clean • fantastic • good
verbs: watch • visit • see • take a bus • play • go to • eat • walk • travel

Ich kann verstehen, wenn in Texten darüber berichtet wird, was nicht passiert ist, z. B. *I didn't eat*.
Ich kann sagen, was andere und ich in der Vergangenheit nicht gemacht haben.

1 A visit to Plymouth

a) It's Sunday. Mr Newman is taking Philip, his cousin Lauren and Chen to Plymouth Aquarium. They're on the bus now. Read the conversation.

Philip: Look, Lauren, there's the Hoe again.
Lauren: The Hoe? What's that?
Philip: It's the park with Smeaton's Tower and the Lido where we went for a walk. Didn't you listen to Dad when we arrived there yesterday morning?
Lauren: No, I didn't. I liked the things we saw but I can never remember names.
Philip Oops, I hope Dad didn't hear that!
Mr Newman: What was that?
Lauren: Errr … nothing, Uncle David. Where are we going?
Mr Newman: We didn't have time for the aquarium yesterday, so this is where we're going today.
Lauren: That's nice, Uncle David. I like fish!
Mr Newman: And they have a lot of fish there! And seals and sharks and …
Chen: … whales!
Mr Newman: Don't be silly, Chen! They didn't have whales last time and they don't have whales now. They're too big.
Chen: That was a joke, Mr Newman. I know that whales are too big for this aquarium.
Mr Newman: Ah! Very funny. Well, I didn't bring my book on the Plymouth Aquarium. But here's their website on my smartphone. You can have a look at what they really have.

b) Read the text and tick (✓) the right answer.

1) On Saturday Lauren	a) went to the Hoe.	
	b) didn't go to the Hoe.	
2) Lauren	a) didn't like the sights.	
	b) liked the sights.	
3) On the bus Chen	a) didn't talk about whales.	
	b) talked about whales.	
4) On Sunday Mr Newman	a) had his smartphone with him.	
	b) didn't have his smartphone with him.	

2 The "didn't-do-game"

Play the "didn't-do-game". You need a partner. Tell your partner what you didn't do last Thursday / weekend / week / summer / … Then your partner says what you didn't do and what he/she didn't do. Then it's your turn again. Who remembers the most things?

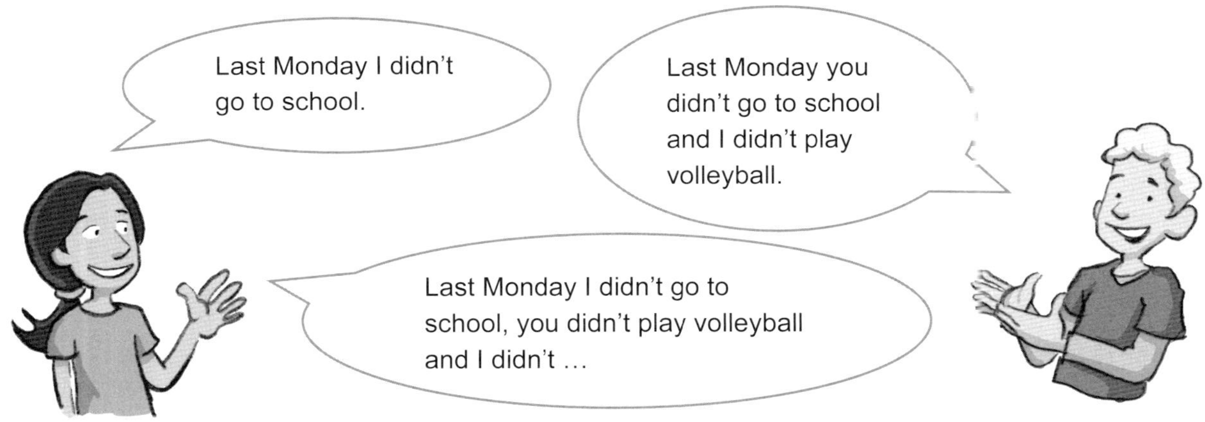

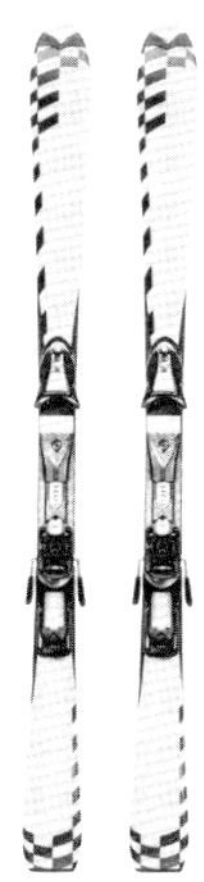

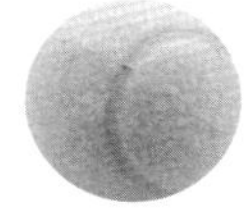

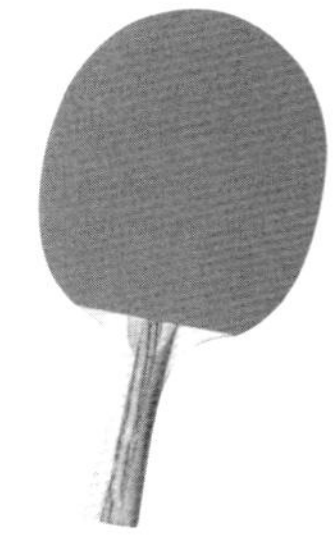

Ich kann verstehen, wenn in Texten darüber berichtet wird, was nicht passiert ist, z. B. *I didn't eat.*
Ich kann sagen, was andere und ich in der Vergangenheit nicht gemacht haben.

1 A visit to Plymouth

a) It's Sunday. Mr Newman is taking Philip, his cousin Lauren and Chen to the Plymouth Aquarium. They're on the bus now. Read the conversation.

Philip: Look, Lauren, there's the Hoe again.
Lauren: The Hoe? What's that?
Philip: It's the park with Smeaton's Tower and the Lido where we went for a walk. Didn't you listen to Dad when we arrived there yesterday morning?
Lauren: No, I didn't. I liked the things we saw but I can never remember names.
Philip: Oops, I hope Dad didn't hear that!
Mr Newman: What was that?
Lauren: Errr … nothing, Uncle David. Where are we going?
Mr Newman: We didn't have time for the Aquarium yesterday, so we're going there today.
Lauren: That's nice, Uncle David. I like fish!
Mr Newman: And they have a lot of fish there! And seals and sharks and …
Chen: … whales!
Mr Newman: Don't be silly, Chen! They didn't have whales last time and they don't have whales now. They're too big.
Chen: That was a joke, Mr Newman. I know that whales are too big for this aquarium.
Mr Newman: Ah! Very funny. Well, I didn't bring my book on the Plymouth Aquarium. But here's their website on my smartphone. You can have a look at what they really have.

b) Which sentences are correct? Read the conversation again if you need help.

1 On Saturday Lauren
a) didn't see the Lido. ☐
b) went on the Big Wheel. ☐
c) didn't go to the aquarium. ☐

2 On Sunday Mr Newman
a) had his smartphone. ☐
b) had a book on the aquarium. ☐
c) didn't want to go to the aquarium. ☐

3 On the bus Chen
a) didn't say a word. ☐
b) didn't tell a joke about whales. ☐
c) talked about whales. ☐

4 Lauren
a) didn't listen to Mr Newman. ☐
b) remembered the name of the park. ☐
c) didn't like the sights. ☐

2 The "didn't-do-game"

Play the "didn't-do-game". You need a partner. Tell your partner what you didn't do last Thursday / weekend / week / summer / ... Then your partner says what you didn't do and what he/she didn't do. Then it's your turn again. Who remembers the most things?

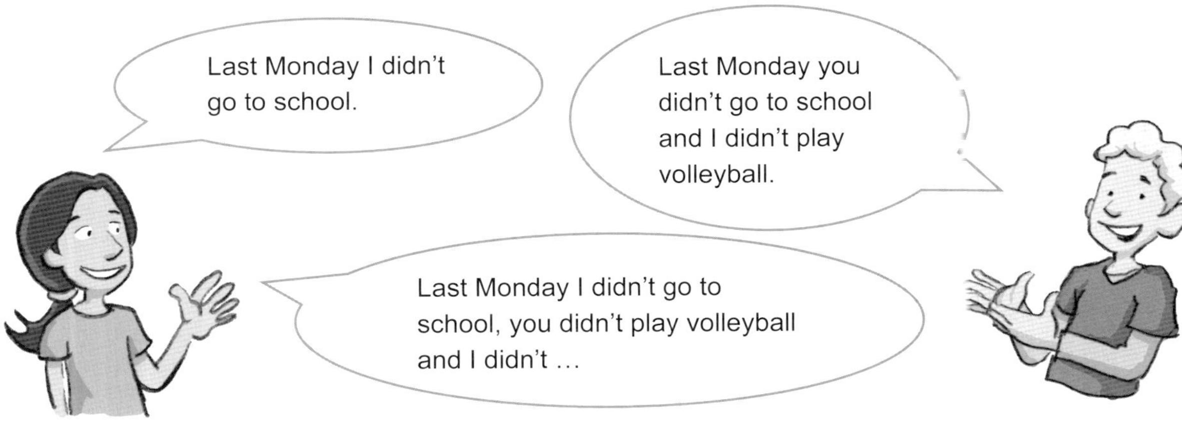

Ich kann verstehen, wenn in Texten darüber berichtet wird, was nicht passiert ist, z. B. *I didn't eat.*
Ich kann sagen, was andere und ich in der Vergangenheit nicht gemacht haben.

1 A visit to Plymouth

a) It's Sunday. Mr Newman is taking Philip, his cousin Lauren and Chen to the Plymouth Aquarium. Complete the conversation with the following sentences:

So we're going there today. • … I can never remember names. • No, I didn't. • Yes, I did. • I know that whales are too big for this aquarium. • … I don't want to be there the whole afternoon.

Philip: Look, Lauren, there's the Hoe again.
Lauren: The Hoe? What's that?
Philip: It's the park with Smeaton's Tower and the Lido where we went for a walk. Didn't you listen to Dad when we arrived there yesterday morning?
Lauren: (1)____________________. I liked the things we saw but (2)____.
Philip: Oops, I hope Dad didn't hear that!
Mr Newman: What was that?
Lauren: Errr… nothing, Uncle David.
Mr Newman: Ah, you talked about the Hoe. Did you like it, Lauren?
Lauren: (3)________________________. Where are we going now?
Mr Newman: We didn't have time for the aquarium yesterday. (4)____.
Lauren: That's nice, uncle David but (5)____.
Mr Newman: Yes, OK. But they have a lot of fish there, it's really nice! And they have seals and sharks and …
Chen: … whales!
Mr Newman: Don't be silly, Chen! They didn't have whales last time and they don't have whales now. They're too big.
Chen: That was a joke, Mr Newman. (6)____________________________________
Mr Newman: Ah! Very funny. Well, I didn't bring my book on the Plymouth Aquarium. But here's their website on my smartphone. You can have a look at what they really have.

b) Which sentences are right, wrong or not given in the text?

	Right	Wrong	Not given
1 On Saturday Lauren didn't go to the aquarium.			
2 On Sunday Mr Newman didn't have his computer.			
3 On the bus, Chen didn't make a joke.			
4 Lauren didn't listen to Mr Newman.			

2 The "didn't-do-game"

Play the "didn't-do-game". You need a partner. Tell your partner what you didn't do last Thursday / weekend / week / summer / … Then your partner says what you didn't do and what he/she didn't do. Then it's your turn again. You can also play this game with more partners.

Partner A: Last Monday I didn't go to school.
Partner B: Last Monday you didn't go to school and I didn't play volleyball.
Partner A: Last Monday I didn't go to school, you didn't play volleyball and I didn't …

Ich kann Plurale bilden und dabei entscheiden, welche Endung ich verwenden muss.

LANGUAGE What are the plurals?

What can you see? Find out what the plurals are.

TIP
Du bildest den Plural eines Nomens, indem du *-s/-es* anhängst. Bei Nomen, die auf *-y* enden, hängst du *-ies* an das Wort. Bei Nomen, die auf *-f* oder *-fe* enden, hängst du *-ves* an das Wort. Einige Nomen haben unregelmäßige Pluralformen – die musst du lernen.

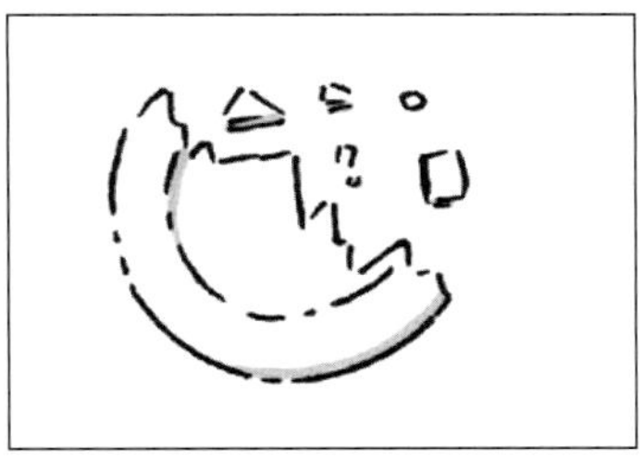

one half

____

one problem

____

one box

____

one child

____

one diary

____

Ich kann Plurale bilden und dabei entscheiden, welche Endung ich verwenden muss.

LANGUAGE What are the plurals?

What can you see? Find out what the plurals are.

TIP
Du bildest den Plural eines Nomens, indem du *-s/-es* anhängst. Bei Nomen, die auf *-y* enden, hängst du *-ies* an das Wort. Bei Nomen, die auf *-f* oder *-fe* enden, hängst du *-ves* an das Wort. Einige Nomen haben unregelmäßige Pluralformen – die musst du lernen.

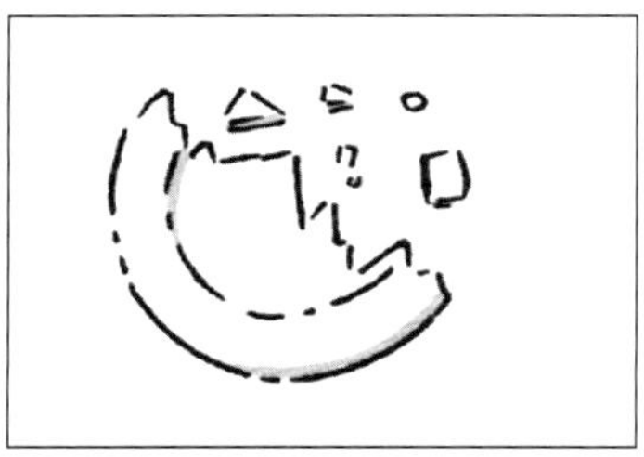
one half

____

one problem

____

one box

____

one child

____

one diary

____

Ich kann Plurale bilden und dabei entscheiden, welche Endung ich verwenden muss.

LANGUAGE What are the plurals?

Some people like to talk about everything they have and always want to be the winner. You too! Finish the sentences and use the numbers 2, 4, 7, 9, 14, 15 and 23.
Then find a partner and compare who has more. You can tick (✓) the box when you used a higher number than your partner. Who is the winner?

book • box • cake • car • child • party • trophy

1) I have __________ ______________ with gold at home. ☐

2) I have __________ ______________ at home. ☐

3) I went to __________ ______________ last week. ☐

4) I have __________ ______________ in my garage. ☐

5) I have __________ ______________ with trophies. ☐

6) I had __________ ______________ for my birthday. ☐

7) I have __________ ______________ . ☐

2 What did you do at the weekend?

a) Barney and his dog-friend Stella are in the park. This is what people hear: woof, woof – woof, woof. Find a partner and read out what they are really saying.

Stella: Hi, Barney. Did you have a good weekend?
Barney: Hi, Stella. Yes, I did. What about you? Did you have a good weekend too?
Stella: No, I didn't. So tell me, where were you on Saturday?
Barney: I went to Dartmoor with Poppy and her friends. What did you do at the weekend?
Stella: That's great! I went to Paris with Charlotte and her family. They went shopping and I watched them. That wasn't very nice. I didn't know what I could do.
Barney: Oh, that's too bad. Poppy and her friends played with me.
Stella: What did you play?
Barney: They threw a stick and I had to bring it back to them. I think they liked the game.
Stella: That sounds good. Charlotte didn't throw sticks for me. There were no sticks in Paris. I only walked for hours and hours.
Barney: I found a pony and helped to save it!
Stella: Wow, that's great! You're a very good dog – and you had an exciting weekend!

b) Now you are real people again. Talk to your partner about your last weekend or your last holiday. What did you do?

fold here

More help

What did …? • Did you walk …? • When did you …?
learn • listen • go • stay with • travel • walk • watch • win • play • see • have

Ich kann in Lesetexten Informationen finden, die zu bestimmten Bildern passen. Ich kann fragen, wo andere am Wochenende / in den Ferien waren und Fragen anderer beantworten.

1 An exciting day

a) Look at these scenes from the story. Find a sentence in the text for each picture. Colour the frame[1] of the picture and underline the sentence with the same colour.

b) Look at the sentences. Where do you find the information in the text? Give line numbers.

1 The kids had a snack on the rocks on Rippon Tor.	line ________
2 The pony couldn't move and looked at the kids.	line ________
3 The pony was small.	line ________
4 Poppy's dad called the ranger station.	line ________
5 The ranger had food for the pony.	line ________
6 The kids went home in the evening.	line ________

[1]frame [freɪm] *Rahmen*

2 What did you do at the weekend?

a) Barney and his dog-friend Stella are in the park. This is what people hear: woof, woof – woof, woof. Find a partner and read out what they are really saying.

Stella: Hi, Barney. Did you have a good weekend?
Barney: Hi Stella. Yes, I did. What about you? Did you have a good weekend too?
Stella: No, I didn't. So tell me, where were you on Saturday?
Barney: I went to Dartmoor with Poppy and her friends. What did you do at the weekend?
Stella: That's great! I went to Paris with Charlotte and her family. They went shopping and I watched them. That wasn't very nice. I didn't know what I could do.
Barney: Oh, that's too bad. Poppy and her friends played with me.
Stella: What did you play?
Barney: They threw a stick and I had to bring it back to them. I think they liked the game.
Stella: That sounds good. Charlotte didn't throw sticks for me. There were no sticks in Paris. I only walked for hours and hours.
Barney: I found a pony and helped to save it!
Stella: Wow, that's great! You're a very good dog – and you had an exciting weekend!

b) Now you are real people again. Talk to your partner about your last weekend or your last holiday. What did you do?

Ich kann in Lesetexten Informationen finden, die zu bestimmten Bildern passen. Ich kann fragen, wo andere am Wochenende / in den Ferien waren und Fragen anderer beantworten.

1 An exciting day

a) Look at these scenes from the story. Find a sentence in the text for each picture. Colour the frame[1] of the picture and underline the sentence with the same colour.

b) Look at the questions. Where do you find the information in the text? Give line numbers.

1 What did the pony do when it saw the kids?	Line ________
2 Who called the ranger station for help?	Line ________
3 Was the pony small?	Line ________
4 Where did the kids eat their snacks?	Line ________
5 What did the ranger give the pony?	Line ________
6 How many helpers arrived with the ranger?	Line ________

[1] frame [freɪm] *Rahmen*

Ich kann in Lesetexten Informationen finden, die zu bestimmten Bildern passen. Ich kann fragen, wo andere am Wochenende / in den Ferien waren und Fragen anderer beantworten.

An exciting day

"Bye! Have fun!" Poppy's dad called out as he left in the car. It was Poppy's first time in Dartmoor National Park without her mum and dad. She was happy that her friends Mia and Philip were with her – and her dog Barney too.

When they came to the rocks on Rippon Tor, they sat down and wanted to eat their snacks. They could see for many kilometres around them. Barney wanted to play, but the kids were tired of the game he always wanted to play. Barney jumped and barked. "Okay, okay!" said Philip. "One more time, Barney! Ready? Go!" He threw the stick down the hill as far as he could. Barney ran down the hill and out of sight.

"Now we can have a break!" said Mia. The three friends ate their sandwiches and watched the Dartmoor ponies on the next hill. "The last time we came here, the ponies were very near," Poppy said. "And there were some baby ponies too. They were so cute on their little legs."

When Barney came back, he didn't have the stick. He took the leg of Poppy's jeans in his mouth and pulled. Poppy got angry and shouted, "Stop it, Barney! Bad dog!" Barney barked at the kids. "I think he wants to show us something!" said Mia. "Let's follow him."

They came to the top of a slope. Barney looked down and barked again. The kids looked down the slope too. They saw an animal – a pony! It looked up at them, but it didn't move. "I think it's hurt!" said Philip.

"Come on!" said Poppy. "Let's go down there."

The slope was very steep, but they climbed down. The pony wasn't very big. Barney was excited. "Stay back, Barney," Poppy said. When the kids went near the pony, it tried to get up, but it couldn't. They saw that it had blood on its leg.

"The poor thing," Mia said. "We have to get help."

Poppy called her dad on her mobile phone, and he called the ranger station for help. Five minutes later, Poppy's mobile rang. It was the park ranger. She asked Poppy about the pony. Poppy gave her all the information. "Thank you, Poppy," she said. "We'll be there in half an hour."

The kids waited. After a few minutes the ranger arrived with three helpers. They came down the slope to the kids and the pony. The ranger was very friendly. She gave the pony food and medicine. Then they helped the pony to get up. They couldn't climb back up the slope to the trail, so they led the pony across the fields. Barney and the kids followed them. It was a long, slow walk back.

When they came to the road, Poppy's dad was there. "Will the pony be all right?" he asked.

"Yes," the ranger answered, "but only because you called us in time. So ... thank you. Thank you all!"

"We have to thank Barney," Poppy said. "*He* found the pony!"

The ranger and her helpers put the pony in a horse trailer. They shook hands with the kids and with Poppy's dad, and they shook Barney's paw. Barney wagged his tail and gave them a friendly bark. Then they left to take the pony to the animal clinic. The others got in the car and went home for dinner.

Ich kann in Lesetexten Informationen finden, die zu bestimmten Bildern passen. Ich kann fragen, wo andere am Wochenende / in den Ferien waren und Fragen anderer beantworten.

1 An exciting day

a) Look at these scenes from the story. Find a sentence in the text for each picture. Colour the frame[1] of the picture and underline the sentence with the same colour.

b) Look at the sentences. Where do you find the information in the text? Give line numbers.

1 The kids had a snack on the rocks on Rippon Tor.	line ___________
2 The pony couldn't move and looked at the kids.	line ___________
3 Poppy's dad called the ranger station.	line ___________
4 The ranger came with three helpers.	line ___________
5 The ranger had food for the pony.	line ___________

[1]frame [freɪm] *Rahmen*

2 What did you do at the weekend?

a) Barney and his dog-friend Stella are in the park. This is what people hear: woof, woof – woof, woof. Find a partner and read out what they are really saying.

Stella: Hi, Barney. Did you have a good weekend?
Barney: Hi Stella. Yes, I did. What about you? Did you have a good weekend too?
Stella: No, I didn't. So tell me, where were you on Saturday?
Barney: I went to Dartmoor with Poppy and her friends. What did you do at the weekend?
Stella: That's great! I went to Paris with Charlotte and her family. They went shopping and I watched them. That wasn't very nice. I didn't know what I could do.
Barney: Oh, that's too bad. Poppy and her friends played with me.
Stella: What did you play?
Barney: They threw a stick and I had to bring it back to them. I think they liked the game.
Stella: That sounds good. Charlotte didn't throw sticks for me. There were no sticks in Paris. I only walked for hours and hours.
Barney: I found a pony and helped to save it!
Stella: Wow, that's great! You're a very good dog – and you had an exciting weekend!

b) Now you're real people again. Talk to your partner about your last weekend or your last holiday. What did you do?

Ich kann mir Informationen aus einem Sachtext merken und diese jemand anderem erzählen.

1 Big fish

a) Read the text about basking sharks. Tick (✓) the correct answers and write down the line where you can find the information. More than one answer can be correct.

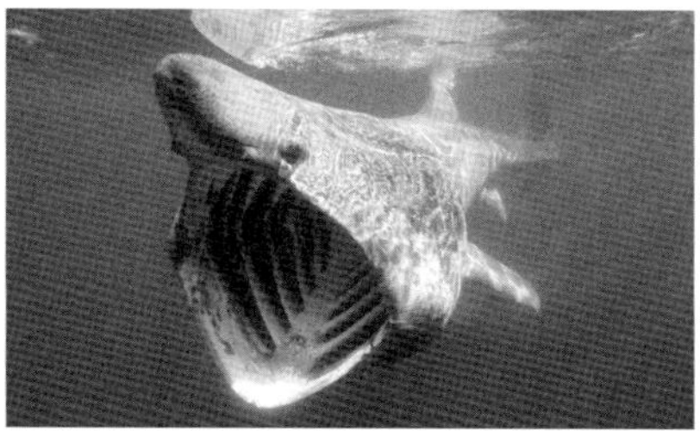

Basking sharks[1] are very big fish. Their colour is dark and light grey. Basking sharks can be 11 metres long and they can weigh up to 7,000 kg. That's very heavy! But they can jump out of the water! A basking shark filters very small animals from the water with its mouth and eats them. Look at the picture – the shark opens its great big mouth when it swims around. A basking shark can filter a lot of water in an hour, as much as in a 50 m-swimming pool. You can sometimes see these big sharks near the coast in Cornwall and Devon between May and October. They usually swim in pairs, but sometimes also in very large groups called schools. A school can have 100 sharks! When basking shark babies are born they are about 1.5 m long. A basking shark can live for over 50 years.

			Information in line …
1 Basking sharks eat (one correct answer)	a) animals like seals.		
	b) other sharks.		
	c) very small animals.		
2 Basking sharks swim in the sea near Plymouth (two correct answers)	a) in December.		
	b) in July.		
	c) in September.		
3 Basking sharks (one correct answer)	a) always swim in big groups.		
	b) have 100 babies.		
	c) filter water.		

b) Read the text one more time – now you're an expert on basking sharks. Find a partner and act out an interview.
Partner A: You ask questions. You can use the notes or ask other questions.
Partner B: You answer the questions.
Partner A: You can help your partner, of course and add information that you remember.

TIP
Do you think this is really hard? You can take notes on the text to work on this task. But try to write down only words, not sentences.

- what they look like
- what they eat
- what they can do
- where they live
- how big their babies are

[1]basking shark ['ba:skɪŋ ʃa:ks] *Riesenhai*

2 MEDIATION Shark Summer Event

You and your parents want to go to Devon in July. You find information about the Shark Summer Event on the internet and you want to go to it. Your parents ask you about the event. Read the information and take notes in German.

Shark Summer Event

Come and join us on North Sands Beach in Salcombe on the last weekend in August. Every year we have lots of fun together. We learn a lot about basking sharks and other fish. Let's find out how big basking sharks really are, make basking sharks out of sand on the beach, collect things on the beach and play games together.
We also make posters about basking sharks. The posters give tips for swimmers:

- Do not touch the sharks. Four metres between you and a shark is a good idea.
- Groups of swimmers must stay together.
- Take pictures! But remember that flash photography can be scary for sharks!
- Remember: for every shark you can see, there can be more under the water.

Wann findet das Shark Summer Event statt?

____

Wo findet das Shark Summer Event statt?

____

Was kann man beim Shark Summer Event machen? Gib zwei Beispiele an.

1. ____

2. ____

Was kann man beim Shark Summer Event lernen? Finde eine Regel für Schwimmer, wie man sich verhalten soll, wenn man auf einen Riesenhai trifft.

____

Ich kann mir Informationen aus einem Sachtext merken und diese jemand anderem erzählen.

1 Big fish

a) Read the text about basking sharks. Tick (✓) the correct answers and write down the line where you can find the information. More than one answer can be correct.

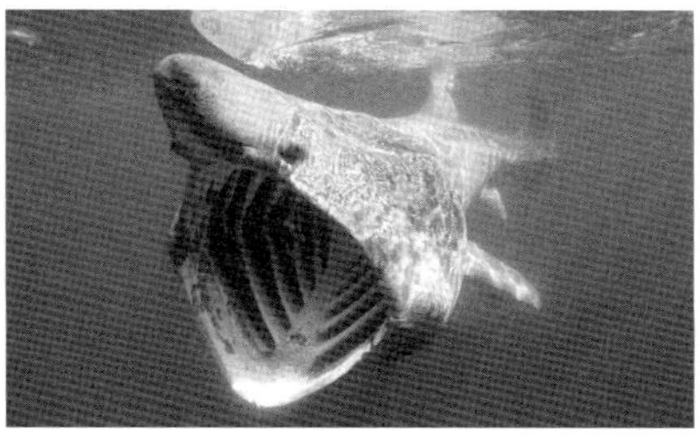

Basking sharks[1] are very big fish. Only whale sharks are bigger. Basking sharks are usually dark and light grey. They can be 11 metres long and can weigh up to 7,000 kg, but they can still jump out of the water!

Some people think that basking sharks look dangerous but they aren't dangerous to people. They swim around with their great big mouths open and filter little animals called zooplankton from the water. A basking shark can filter a lot of water in one hour, as much as in a whole Olympic-sized swimming pool.

You can sometimes see these big sharks near the coast in Cornwall and Devon between May and October. They usually swim in pairs but sometimes also in very large groups called schools. A school can have 100 sharks!

People don't know everything about basking sharks. But they know that baby sharks come out of their eggs inside their mother's body and when they are born they are about 1.5 m long. A basking shark can live for over 50 years.

			Information in line …
1 Basking sharks eat	a) animals like seals.		
	b) other sharks.		
	c) zooplankton.		
2 Basking sharks swim in the sea near Plymouth	a) in September.		
	b) in November.		
	c) in March.		
3 Basking sharks	a) always swim in big groups.		
	b) have 100 babies.		
	c) filter water.		
4 Basking sharks can	a) jump out of the water.		
	b) swim in large groups.		
	c) live in a swimming pool.		

[1] basking shark ['bɑːskɪŋ ʃɑːks] *Riesenhai*

b) Read the text one more time – now you're an expert on basking sharks. Find a partner and act out an interview.
Partner A: You ask questions about basking sharks. The pictures can help you.
Partner B: You answer the questions.
Partner A: You can help your partner, of course and add information that you remember.
You can talk about: their size, their babies, where they live, what they eat, what they look like.

TIP
Do you think this is really hard? You can take notes on the text to work on this task.
But try to write down only words, not sentences.

2 MEDIATION Shark Summer Event

You and your parents want to go to Devon in July. You find information about the Shark Summer Event on the internet and you want to go to it. Your parents ask you about the event. Read the information and take notes in German.

Shark Summer Event

Come and join us on North Sands Beach in Salcombe at the last weekend in August. Every year we have lots of fun together. We learn a lot about basking sharks and other fish. Let's find out how big basking sharks really are, make basking sharks out of sand on the beach, collect things on the beach and play games together.
We also make posters about basking sharks. The posters give tips for swimmers:

- Do not touch the sharks. Four metres between you and a shark is a good idea.
- Groups of swimmers must stay together.
- Take pictures! But remember that flash photography can be scary for sharks!
- Remember: for every shark you can see, there can be more under the water.

1. Wann und wo findet das Shark Summer Event statt?
2. Gib zwei Beispiele dafür, was man bei dieser Veranstaltung macht.
3. Zähle auf, was man lernen kann: finde zwei Verhaltensregeln für Schwimmer.

Ich kann mir Informationen aus einem Sachtext merken und diese jemand anderem erzählen.

1 Big fish

a) Read the text about basking sharks. Tick (✓) the correct answers and write down the line where you can find the information. More than one answer can be correct.

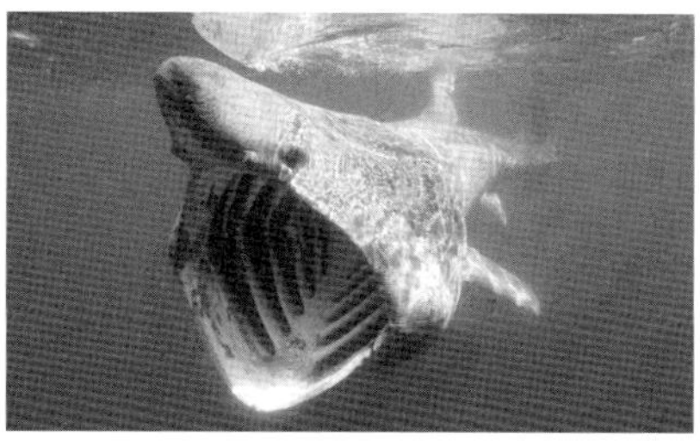

Basking sharks[1] are very big fish. Only whale sharks are bigger. Basking sharks are usually light grey with dark grey on top. They can be 11 metres long and can weigh up to 7,000 kg, but they can still jump out of the water!
A basking shark filters little animals called zooplankton from the water with its mouth. A basking shark can filter a lot of water, as much as a whole Olympic-sized swimming pool in one hour. So a basking shark can filter more water in one hour than you can find in the Lido. They swim around with their great big mouths open, which can look very dangerous. But the basking shark is not dangerous to people. It has only very small teeth and it doesn't use them to eat. You can sometimes see these big sharks near the coast in Cornwall and Devon between May and October. They usually swim in pairs, but sometimes also in very large groups called schools, which can have 100 sharks or more!
Even people at Plymouth Aquarium don't know very much about basking sharks. But they know that baby sharks come out of their eggs inside their mother's body and when they are born they are about 1.5 m long. A basking shark can live for over 50 years.

1 Basking sharks eat
- a) animals like seals. (line ____) ☐
- b) other sharks. (line ____) ☐
- c) zooplankton. (line ____) ☐
- d) shark eggs. (line ____) ☐

2 Basking sharks swim in the sea near Plymouth
- a) in winter. (line ____) ☐
- b) in summer. (line ____) ☐
- c) when they have babies. (line ____) ☐
- d) between October and May. (line ____) ☐

3 Basking sharks
- a) always swim in big groups. (line ____) ☐
- b) look very dangerous. (line ____) ☐
- c) have 100 babies. (line ____) ☐
- d) filter water (line ____) ☐

4 Basking sharks can
- a) jump out of the water. (line ____) ☐
- b) eat people. (line ____) ☐
- c) swim in large groups. (line ____) ☐
- d) live in a swimming pool. (line ____) ☐

basking shark ['bɑːskɪŋ ʃɑːks] *Riesenhai*

b) Read the text again – now you are an expert on basking sharks. Find a partner and act out an interview.
Partner A: You ask questions about basking sharks. The pictures can help you.
Partner B: You answer the questions.
Partner A: You can help your partner, and add information that you remember.
You can talk about: their size, their babies, where they live, what they eat, what they look like.

TIP
Do you think this is really hard? You can take notes on the text to work on this task.
But try to write down only words, not sentences.

2 MEDIATION Shark Summer Event

You and your parents want to go to Devon in July. Your parents heard about the Shark Summer Event. They ask you to find out more information. You find information about it on the internet. Read the information and take notes in German.

Shark Summer Event

Do you like sharks? There are some really big sharks in the sea at the Cornish and Devon coast. How exciting! Come and join us, the *Friends of Sharks* on North Sands Beach in Salcombe, Devon, on the last weekend in August. The action starts at 11 am on Saturday and the end of our Shark Summer Event is at 5 pm on Sunday.
Every year we have lots of fun together and learn a lot about basking sharks and other fish. Let's find out how big basking sharks really are, make life-sized basking sharks out of sand on the beach, collect things on the beach, take pictures and play games together.
We also make information posters for schools and give tourists information about basking sharks. The posters give useful tips for swimmers:

- Do not touch the sharks. A distance of four metres between you and a shark is a good idea.
- Groups of swimmers must stay together. Don't dive!
- Take pictures! But remember that flash photography is scary for sharks!
- We collect pictures to learn more about the sharks. Where do they eat? Where do they have babies? Where do they live in winter?
- Remember: for every shark you can see there can be more under the water.

1. Wann und wo findet das Shark Summer Event statt?
2. Gib zwei Beispiele dafür, was man bei dieser Veranstaltung macht.
3. Zähle auf, was man lernen kann: finde zwei Verhaltensregeln für Schwimmer.

Ich kann Textabschnitte sinnvoll als Einleitung, Hauptteil und Schluss anordnen und den Text mit Bildern und Überschriften so gestalten, dass er für andere interessant wird.

STUDY SKILLS Robert Falcon Scott

a) Read the paragraphs and put them in the right order. Write the numbers in the boxes.

☐ He made two journeys[1] to Antarctica. The first one was from 1901 to 1904 on a ship called Discovery. He travelled very far south with his team and when he came back to Britain he was a hero. He wanted to go to the South Pole again and he collected money so he could go.
The second journey started in June 1910. They used ponies and dogs to pull their things, but the ponies weren't happy in the cold weather and in the end the people had to pull all the things. Only Scott and four friends walked all the way to the South Pole. When they arrived, they found out that they weren't the first people there. People from Norway had been there before! On the way back to the ship, Scott and his friends died because they had no food and because of the bad weather. That's sad because they had only 20 km more to walk.

☐ Scott's dead body is still in Antarctica today. He wasn't the only man who died, but most people only remember him today.

☐ Robert Falcon Scott was a navy officer and an explorer who wanted to be the first to reach the South Pole. He was born on 6 June 1868 in Devonport, the naval part of Plymouth. He had five brothers and sisters.

b) Choose one of the titles for the text or write your own title.

A sad hero	A long way to go	A cold journey

c) Choose two of the pictures and a caption for each picture. You can write your own captions too.

At the South Pole	Young Scott in the navy	The first people at the South Pole
Hard work	No help from horses!	Keeping warm

d) Cut out ✂ all the parts you need and put them in the right order. You need paper.

[1]journey ['dʒɜːni] *Reise, hier: Expedition*

Ich kann Textabschnitte sinnvoll als Einleitung, Hauptteil und Schluss anordnen und den Text mit Bildern und Überschriften so gestalten, dass er für andere interessant wird.

STUDY SKILLS Robert Falcon Scott

a) Read the paragraphs and put them in the right order. Write the numbers in the boxes.

☐ He was born on 6 June 1868 in Devonport, the naval part of Plymouth. He had five brothers and sisters.

☐ The second journey[1] started in June 1910 and they used ponies and dogs to pull their things, but the ponies weren't happy in the cold weather and in the end the people had to pull all the things. Only Scott and four friends walked all the way and when they got to the South Pole. When they arrived, they found out that they weren't the first people there. People from Norway had been there before! On the way back to the ship, Scott and his friends died because they had no food and because of the bad weather. That's sad because they had only 20 km more to walk.

☐ He made two journeys to Antarctica. The first one was from 1901 to 1904 with a ship called Discovery. He travelled very far south with his team and when he came back to Britain he was a hero. He wanted to go to the South Pole again and he collected money so he could go.

☐ Scott's dead body is still in Antarctica today. He wasn't the only man who died, but most people only remember him today.

☐ Robert Falcon Scott was a navy officer and an explorer who wanted to be the first to reach the South Pole.

b) Choose one of the titles for the text or write your own title.

A sad hero	A long way to go	A cold journey

c) Choose two of the pictures and a caption for each picture. You can write your own captions too.

At the South Pole	Young Scott in the navy	The first people at the South Pole
Hard work	No help from horses!	Keeping warm

d) Cut out all the parts you need and put them in the right order. You need paper.

[1]journey ['dʒɜːni] *Reise hier: Expedition*

Ich kann Textabschnitte sinnvoll als Einleitung, Hauptteil und Schluss anordnen und den Text mit Bildern und Überschriften so gestalten, dass er für andere interessant wird.

STUDY SKILLS Robert Falcon Scott

a) Read the paragraphs and put them in the right order. Write the numbers into the boxes. Be careful: Two paragraphs belong to a different text!

☐ He was born on 6 June 1868 in Devonport, the naval part of Plymouth. He had five brothers and sisters.

☐ Many great sea captains came from Great Britain, and one of the most famous ones even came from the small town of Tavistock near Plymouth. Sir Francis Drake was born in 1540 and was the 12th son of his parents. People remember him today for being a pirate, a sailor and an English hero.

☐ The second journey[1] started in June 1910. They used ponies and dogs to pull their things, but the ponies weren't happy in the cold weather and in the end the people had to pull all the things. Only Scott and four friends walked all the way to the South Pole. When they arrived, they found out that they weren't the first people there. People from Norway had been there before! On the way back to the ship, Scott and his friends died because they had no food and because of the bad weather. That's sad because they had only 20 km more to walk.

☐ He made two journeys to Antarctica. The first one was from 1901 to 1904 with a ship called Discovery. He travelled very far south with his team and when he came back to Britain he was a hero. He wanted to go to the South Pole again and he collected money so he could go.

☐ Scott's dead body is still in Antarctica today. He wasn't the only man who died, but most people only remember him today.

☐ He died on board his ship, the Defiance, in 1596. He was ill and sad because his last journey was not successful. The people in South America now knew that he wanted their gold, and it was more difficult to get it. When he died, his body was thrown into the sea in Panama in a heavy box. So this famous British sailor never came home again.

☐ Robert Falcon Scott was a navy officer and an explorer who wanted to be the first to reach the South Pole.

b) Think of a good title for the text.

c) Choose two of the pictures and write captions for them.

d) Cut out ✂ all the parts you need and put them in the right order. You need paper.

[1]journey ['dʒɜːni] *Reise, hier: Expedition*

Ich kann eine Geschichte auch verstehen, wenn ich nicht alle Wörter kenne. Ich benutze dazu Bilder oder ein Wörterbuch oder suche nach Ähnlichkeiten mit deutschen oder anderen englischen Wörtern. Ich kann eine Geschichte so genau lesen, dass ich Satzanfänge und Satzenden einander zuordnen kann.

At Cawsand

A "It was a sunny day in the spring holiday. Philip, Chen, Mia and Poppy were on the ferry to Cawsand. Barney was with them. Philip knew about an old smugglers' cave near the village. He wanted to find it with his friends.
"Where is this cave?" Chen wanted to know.

"I don't know exactly, but I think it's somewhere near the villages," Philip said. The kids looked for a cave in the rocky cliffs along the coast, but they couldn't see one.

Mia said, "I can't see any beach to walk along there! So ... how can we find the cave?" Philip didn't answer.

"I just hope there aren't any smugglers in the cave," Poppy said.

B When the kids walked into Cawsand, they heard shouts from the pub up the street. Suddenly, a man ran out of the pub. He had long hair and wore strange clothes and shoes. It looked like he was in panic. He had a sack in his hand. A woman with a striped apron came out of the pub after him. She had a long knife in her hand! "Stop, thief!!" she shouted. "Give me the gold or you're a dead man!!" The kids were shocked. Barney barked wildly.

But a young man hurried over to them and said, "It's OK, it's OK!" The man and the woman from the pub stopped and smiled. The kids didn't understand. "It isn't real!" he said.

"They're actors! We're in a film club and we're making a film! See?" He pointed to a young woman with a film camera and a boy with a microphone on the other side of the street. Then the kids understood. But Barney still didn't understand. He ran around and barked and barked.

"Quiet, Barney!" Poppy shouted. "Sorry about my dog! We didn't know —"

"No problem!" the young man said. "We can do the scene again."

"What's the film about?" asked Mia.

"It's a story from the old times, about sailing ships and smugglers. When we're finished here, we have to go to the cave to film the last smuggling scene."

"Did you say … cave?" asked Philip.

"That's right." the man said. "It isn't far from here."

"Can … can we go with you?" Philip asked.

"Of course – but you have to help us with the film!" the man said with a smile.

"Cool!" said Chen.

"Let's do it!" the other kids said.

"Great!" said the man. "Welcome! My name's Jack. I'm the director."

C When they finished the scene, they went in two boats to a small sand beach with rocks all around it. "This is it!" said Jack. They climbed onto a rock. Philip looked around and saw the mouth of the cave. He wanted to go inside it, but first they had to do the film scene.

"OK, everybody," Jack said, "we have more people now – and a dog – so we can have a really great fight scene between the smugglers and the police. And we can use two cameras, not just one."

D The camerawoman showed Mia and Poppy how to use a camera and microphone. Philip and Chen had the role of policemen. Jack gave them their costumes, handcuffs and pistols. They looked funny in their costumes. Barney's role was to play the smugglers' dog. He waited on a soft blanket.

E When everybody was ready, the smugglers" took Barney into the cave. Jack stayed outside with the others. The cameras started. Jack held up a film pistol and shouted, "Action!" ...

When they finished the scene, the kids had time to go into the cave. The cave was long and very, very dark. The boys had one torch and the girls had another, but they still couldn't see to the back of the cave. Chen and Philip were in front of the girls. They all walked far into the cave. Chen said something to Philip. Suddenly, the boys ran away from the girls and hid behind some rocks – and turned off their torch!

"Where did they go?" asked Poppy.

"Hey!" shouted Mia. "Turn on your torch! No silly games now!"

When the girls came near, the boys jumped out and shouted, "Boo!" The girls screamed. The boys laughed. Then, suddenly, Mia took Philip's torch out of his hand and the two girls ran back to the mouth of the cave. It was too dark for the boys to follow them. Philip shouted, "Hey, come back here with my torch!" but the girls ran out of the cave.

They waited a minute and listened. Then they asked Jack to go into the cave and surprise the boys. The girls gave him a torch, but he didn't turn it on. He didn't make a sound.

The boys called out, "Hey, Mia! Poppy! Where are you?! We can't see! It's too dark in here!"

"The policemen sound worried!" laughed Poppy. Jack walked with careful, quiet steps and his hand on the side of the cave. The girls and the others waited at the mouth of the cave and listened.

"Poppy! Mia!" the boys shouted again. "Please, come back! Bring us a torch!" Jack was very near now. Chen said in a quiet voice, "Philip, I think somebody is here with us–"

"BOO!!" Jack shouted and turned on the bright torch to show his face.

"Aaaahhhhh!" screamed the two boys. ...

F Back in Cawsand, the kids thanked Jack and the others. Jack thanked the kids for their help. "Please come to the club and see the film when it's finished," he said. They said goodbye.

On the ferry back to Plymouth, Poppy said, "That was a great day!"

"Yeah!" said Mia. "You were right about the cave, Philip."

"It was so lucky that we met the people from the film club!" said Chen.

Mia said, "Barney was great. When Jack's pistol went *Boom! Boom! Boom!* and Barney ran out of the cave like a wild bear and chased Philip in that police costume, I laughed so hard, I almost couldn't hold the camera!"

"Yes, Barney, good boy!" said Poppy.

"No, Barney, *bad* boy!" said Philip.

"It was a lot of work," Chen said.

"I know," said Philip. "Jack made us film the fight again and again!"

"Chen," said Mia, "when you jumped off the rock and onto the sand, it looked like in the cinema! I thought you really *were* dead!"

"I thought I was too! All five times!" said Chen. "But when you screamed in the cave, that was also like in the cinema!"

"It was really cool in there," said Philip. "And dark!"

"Yeah, so dark that you two couldn't find the way out!" said Poppy. "We had to send Jack in to get you!" She and Mia laughed and laughed. "That was *so funny*!"

"Yeah, yeah – very funny!" said Chen.

Ich kann eine Geschichte auch verstehen, wenn ich nicht alle Wörter kenne. Ich benutze dazu Bilder oder ein Wörterbuch oder suche nach Ähnlichkeiten mit deutschen oder anderen englischen Wörtern. Ich kann eine Geschichte so genau lesen, dass ich Satzanfänge und Satzenden einander zuordnen kann.

At Cawsand

a) Read the text. Choose titles for the parts. Be careful: There is one more title than you need.

- A film scene ☐
- The kids' roles ☐
- Silly games ☐
- On the ferry to Cawsand ☐
- What a great day! ☐
- The film team ☐
- On the way to the cave ☐

b) Pictures can help you to understand new words. Colour the things from the list below in the pictures. Then look at the text to find the English words for the following German words.

German	English
1 Schürze	____________________
2 Messer	____________________
3 Decke	____________________

c) Sometimes English words are like German words. Do you understand the following words? Write down the German words.

English	German
1 panic	____________________
2 microphone	____________________
3 police	____________________

d) Sometimes you know parts of the English word and you can guess the meaning. Write down the German words.

English	German
1 sunny	____________________
2 rocky	____________________
3 hurried	____________________

Ich kann eine Geschichte auch verstehen, wenn ich nicht alle Wörter kenne. Ich benutze dazu Bilder oder ein Wörterbuch oder suche nach Ähnlichkeiten mit deutschen oder anderen englischen Wörtern. Ich kann eine Geschichte so genau lesen, dass ich Satzanfänge und Satzenden einander zuordnen kann.

At Cawsand

a) Read the text. Choose titles for the parts. Be careful: There is one more title than you need.

- A film scene ☐
- The kids' roles ☐
- Silly games ☐
- On the ferry to Cawsand ☐
- What a great day! ☐
- The film team ☐
- On the way to the cave ☐

b) The text has a few words that you haven't learned yet. But there are many ways to find out what they mean. Look at the table and tick the way that helps you to understand the word. Then write down the German word.

English word	Picture helps	German word helps	I know a similar word in English	German word
rocky				
microphone				
side				
sunny				
panic				
blanket				
police				
knife				
apron				
hurried				
thanked				
torch				

Ich kann eine Geschichte auch verstehen, wenn ich nicht alle Wörter kenne. Ich benutze dazu Bilder oder ein Wörterbuch oder suche nach Ähnlichkeiten mit deutschen oder anderen englischen Wörtern. Ich kann eine Geschichte so genau lesen, dass ich Satzanfänge und Satzenden einander zuordnen kann.

At Cawsand

a) Read the text and find titles for the parts.

A ____________________

B ____________________

C ____________________

D ____________________

E ____________________

F ____________________

b) The text has a few words that you haven't learned yet. But there are many ways to find out what they mean. Look at the table and tick the way that helps you to understand the English word. Then write down the German word.

English word	Picture helps	German word helps	I know a similar word in English	German word
rocky				
microphone				
side				
sunny				
panic				
blanket				
police				
knife				
apron				
hurried				
thanked				
torch				
camerawoman				

c) Sometimes the text can help you to understand new words too. Find the words in the text and guess their meaning.

1 climbed ____________________

2 cliffs ____________________

3 pub ____________________

4 understood ____________________

5 gave ____________________

Unit 5

By the sea

Meine Lernlandkarte für Unit 5

Name: ______________________ Klasse: __________

Wie gut bist du in den Lernfeldern der Unit 5?
Schätze dich darin ein und male die entsprechende Anzahl an Kreisen auf der Ampel aus.
So findest du dein Übungsblatt.

Das lief nicht gut, ich muss mehr üben.	Das war OK, aber ich könnte besser werden.	Das habe ich gut geschafft.
●○○	●●○	●●●

Setze ein Häkchen, wenn du fertig bist. ✓

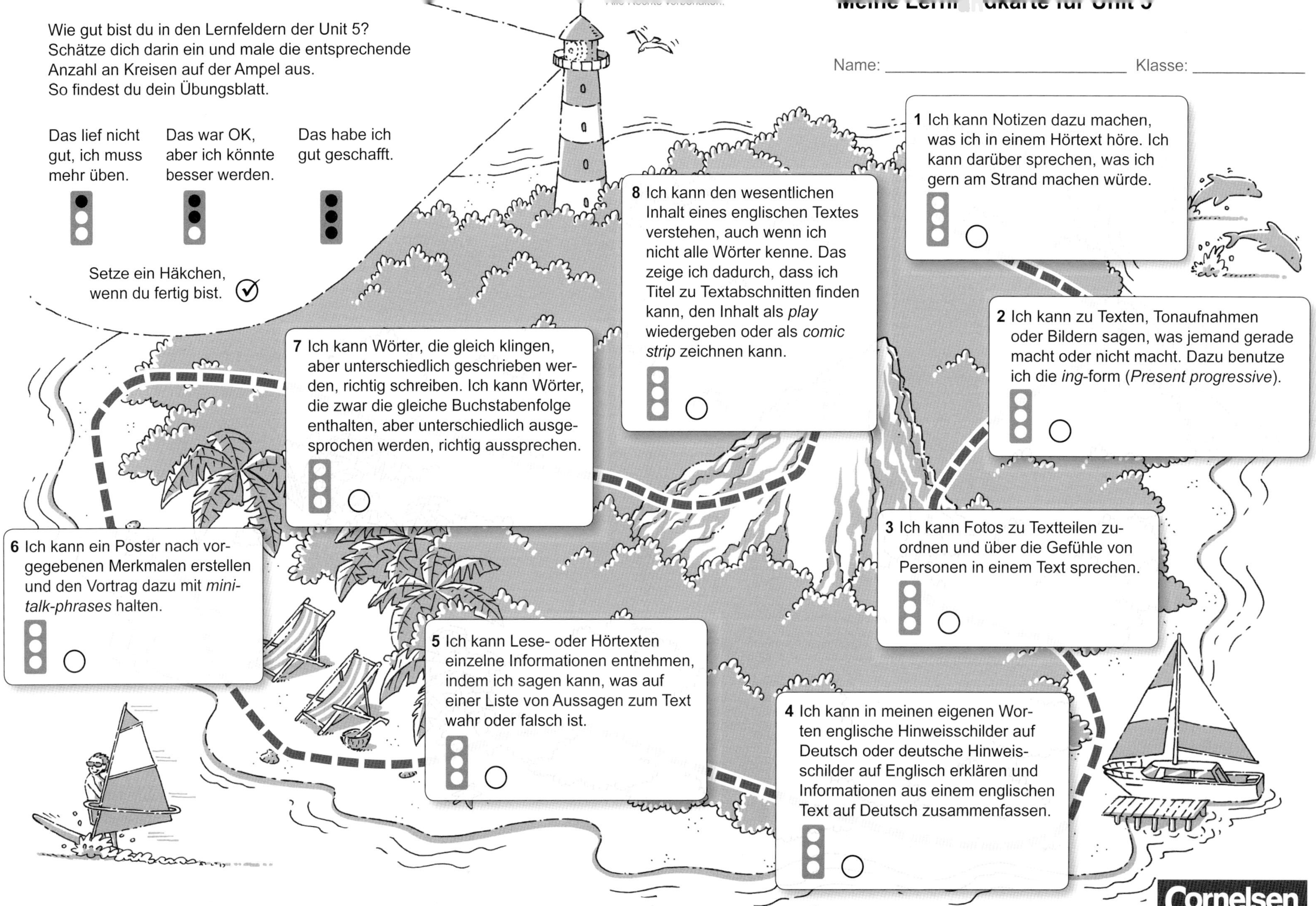

1 Ich kann Notizen dazu machen, was ich in einem Hörtext höre. Ich kann darüber sprechen, was ich gern am Strand machen würde. ○○○ ○

2 Ich kann zu Texten, Tonaufnahmen oder Bildern sagen, was jemand gerade macht oder nicht macht. Dazu benutze ich die *ing*-form (*Present progressive*). ○○○ ○

3 Ich kann Fotos zu Textteilen zuordnen und über die Gefühle von Personen in einem Text sprechen. ○○○ ○

4 Ich kann in meinen eigenen Worten englische Hinweisschilder auf Deutsch oder deutsche Hinweisschilder auf Englisch erklären und Informationen aus einem englischen Text auf Deutsch zusammenfassen. ○○○ ○

5 Ich kann Lese- oder Hörtexten einzelne Informationen entnehmen, indem ich sagen kann, was auf einer Liste von Aussagen zum Text wahr oder falsch ist. ○○○ ○

6 Ich kann ein Poster nach vorgegebenen Merkmalen erstellen und den Vortrag dazu mit *mini-talk-phrases* halten. ○○○ ○

7 Ich kann Wörter, die gleich klingen, aber unterschiedlich geschrieben werden, richtig schreiben. Ich kann Wörter, die zwar die gleiche Buchstabenfolge enthalten, aber unterschiedlich ausgesprochen werden, richtig aussprechen. ○○○ ○

8 Ich kann den wesentlichen Inhalt eines englischen Textes verstehen, auch wenn ich nicht alle Wörter kenne. Das zeige ich dadurch, dass ich Titel zu Textabschnitten finden kann, den Inhalt als *play* wiedergeben oder als *comic strip* zeichnen kann. ○○○ ○

Cornelsen

Ich kann Notizen dazu machen, was ich in einem Hörtext höre. Ich kann darüber sprechen, was ich gern am Strand machen würde.

1 WORDS Fishing for words

Be a fisherman and fish for words. Find the words in your net and circle them (→↓↘).

T	P	W	T	B	O	N	K	E	F	S	U	D	R	G
A	P	U	R	O	H	K	O	R	I	X	K	H	O	W
E	A	B	E	A	C	H	H	Y	S	O	Y	A	C	E
W	Y	A	A	T	J	C	O	S	H	I	R	T	K	N
S	A	N	D	C	A	S	T	L	E	A	T	A	S	D
U	R	T	W	E	Y	W	H	A	B	A	M	L	A	Y
N	A	C	E	A	S	I	V	I	L	W	G	B	C	D
N	I	R	P	E	D	M	C	T	P	A	P	U	K	S
Y	N	A	W	A	R	M	Z	E	L	O	W	I	L	K
I	B	B	L	N	S	E	N	M	U	O	D	D	A	L
T	U	Y	S	R	O	R	T	S	L	R	M	M	I	S
A	W	S	J	I	N	P	U	F	O	S	E	A	L	H
P	B	O	O	K	S	J	L	N	U	B	K	F	H	E
E	S	A	Z	E	W	I	C	O	L	D	T	O	M	E

- ☑ beach
- ☐ sandcastle
- ☐ sunny
- ☐ books
- ☐ fish
- ☐ rock
- ☐ warm
- ☐ cold
- ☐ seagull
- ☐ ship
- ☐ seal
- ☐ swimmer
- ☐ boat
- ☐ crab

2 At Cawsand Beach

It's 15th August and at Cawsand everyone is enjoying their summer holidays. Everyone? No, not everyone. Some people have to work so other people can enjoy their time in the sun. Martyn has an ice cream van (like a minibus) and his son Ruben has to help him on busy days.

a) FF 23 **Listen to Martyn, Ruben and the people at the ice cream van. What sounds can you hear? Tick (✓) the right boxes.**

- ☐ seagulls
- ☐ bell
- ☐ crying baby
- ☐ coins
- ☐ sea
- ☐ clock

b) FF 23 **Listen again. Circle the correct word.**

1 The first man buys two **chocolate** / **lemon** ice creams.

2 The grandmother needs to go to the **toilet** / **ferry**.

3 The little girl tells **Ruben** / **Martyn** what she wants.

4 The little girl buys one **orange** / **lemon** ice cream.

5 The second man must wait for **his wife** / **his ice cream**.

6 Martyn and Ruben have a new **orange** / **lemon** ice cream this summer.

7 Ruben wants to stop working and **play football** / **go swimming**.

8 A mother needs **some water** / **help** for her baby boy.

9 Ruben tells people that it's dangerous to feed **crabs** / **seagulls**.

3 What Ruben would really like to do

Ruben has to work in his dad's ice cream van in his summer holidays. Sometimes it's exciting and sometimes it's very boring. From the van Ruben can see what other people are doing. Ruben wants to do these things too. Find a partner and complete the dialogue. Then act out the dialogue. One partner is Ruben and the other partner is Martyn. Take turns.

Ruben: Dad, I'd like to go to the beach.

Martyn: Yes, I know. I'd like to go ______________________ ______________________ too!

Ruben: Please, can I go now? I'd like to ______________________.

Martyn: Oh, sorry, I'd like to ______________________ ______________________ too. But I really need your help now.

Ruben: But I'd really ______________________.

Martyn: I know! And I ______________________.

But we have to work now. You can do these things when your mum's back, OK? I'm sorry, Ruben.

fold here

More help

go	for a walk swimming
play	in the water in the sand
jump	into the water from a rock
take pictures	of the seagulls of the ships and boats
read	a book a magazine

Ich kann Notizen dazu machen, was ich in einem Hörtext höre. Ich kann darüber sprechen, was ich gern am Strand machen würde.

1 WORDS Fishing for beach words

Be a fisherman and fish for words. Put the letters in the box in the right order and find the correct words in the grid.

T	P	W	T	B	O	N	K	E	F	S	U	D	R	G
A	P	U	R	O	H	K	O	R	I	X	K	H	O	W
E	A	B	E	A	C	H	H	Y	S	O	Y	A	C	E
W	Y	A	A	T	J	C	O	S	H	I	R	T	K	N
S	A	N	D	C	A	S	T	L	E	A	T	A	S	D
U	R	T	W	E	Y	W	H	A	B	A	M	L	A	Y
N	A	C	E	A	S	I	V	I	L	W	G	B	C	D
N	I	R	P	E	D	M	C	T	P	A	P	U	K	S
Y	N	A	W	A	R	M	Z	E	L	O	W	I	L	K
I	B	B	L	N	S	E	N	M	U	O	D	D	A	L
T	U	Y	S	R	O	R	T	S	L	R	M	M	I	S
A	W	S	J	I	N	P	U	F	O	S	E	A	L	H
P	B	O	O	K	C	J	L	N	U	B	K	F	H	E
E	S	A	Z	E	W	I	C	O	L	D	T	O	M	E

racb • mwmiser • ales • phsi • agllesu • oldc • mraw • kroc • ifhs • kosob • nynus • lednassatc • haebc • otab

2 At Cawsand Beach

It's 15th August and at Cawsand everyone is enjoying their summer holidays. Everyone? No, not everyone. Some people have to work so other people can enjoy their time in the sun. Martyn has an ice cream van (like a minibus) and his son Ruben has to help him on busy days.

a) FF 23 Listen to Martyn, Ruben and the people at the ice cream van. What sounds can you hear? Tick the right boxes.

- ☐ seagulls
- ☐ music
- ☐ coins
- ☐ sea
- ☐ car door
- ☐ ferry
- ☐ crying baby
- ☐ bell
- ☐ dog

b) FF 23 Listen again. Finish the sentences with the correct words.

1 The first man buys two ____________________ ice creams.

2 The grandmother needs to go to the ____________________.

3 The little girl tells ____________________ what she wants.

4 The little girl wants ____________________ ice cream.

5 The second man doesn't eat ____________________.

6 The second man wants one ____________________ ice cream for his wife.

7 Martyn and Ruben have a new ____________________ ice cream this summer.

8 A mother needs ____________________ for her baby boy.

9 Ruben tells people that it's dangerous to feed ____________________.

fold here

More help chocolate • help • lemon • orange • oranges • Ruben • seagulls • toilet • vanilla

3 What Ruben would really like to do

Ruben has to work in his dad's ice cream van in his summer holidays. Sometimes it's exciting and sometimes it's very boring. From the van Ruben can see what other people are doing.
Ruben wants to do these things too. Find a partner and say what Ruben and his dad would like to do. Act out the dialogue. One partner is Ruben and the other partner is Martyn. Take turns.

Ruben: Dad, I'd like to go to the beach.

Martyn: Yes, I know. I'd ____________________
____________________ too!

Ruben: Please, can I go now? I ____________________
____________________.

Martyn: Oh, sorry, I ____________________
____________________ too. But I really need your help now.

Ruben: But I ____________________.

Martyn: I know! And ____________________.

But we have to work now. You can do these things when your mum's back, OK? I'm sorry, Ruben.

Ich kann Notizen dazu machen, was ich in einem Hörtext höre. Ich kann darüber sprechen, was ich gern am Strand machen würde.

1 WORDS Fishing for words

Be a fisherman and fish for the right letters in the box to complete the words in the mind map.

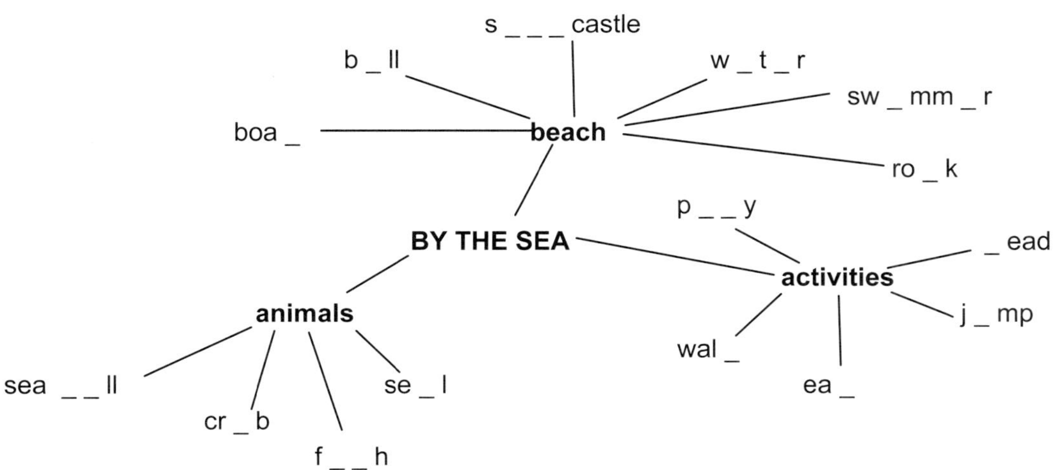

g • a • n • a • e • i • a • l • t • a • e • d • a • t • i • c • u • k • a • s • u • r

2 At Cawsand Beach

It's 15th August and at Cawsand everyone is enjoying their summer holidays. Everyone? No, not everyone. Some people have to work so other people can enjoy their time in the sun. Martyn has an ice cream van (like a minibus) and his son Ruben has to help him on busy days.

a) FF 23 **Listen to Martyn, Ruben and the people at the ice cream van. What sounds can you hear? Tick the right boxes.**

- ☐ seagulls
- ☐ ferry
- ☐ clock
- ☐ music
- ☐ crying baby
- ☐ coins
- ☐ car
- ☐ bell
- ☐ sea
- ☐ dog
- ☐ car door

b) FF 23 **Listen again and finish the sentences.**

1 The first man buys two ____________________ ice creams.
2 The grandmother needs to go to the ____________________.
3 The little girl tells ____________________ what she wants.
4 The little girl wants ____________________ ice cream.
5 The second man doesn't eat ____________________.
6 The second man wants one ____________________ ice cream for his wife.
7 Martyn and Ruben have a new ____________________ ice cream this summer.
8 A mother needs ____________________ for her baby boy.
9 Ruben tells people that it's dangerous to feed ____________________.

3 What Ruben would really like to do

a) Ruben has to work in his dad's ice cream van in his summer holidays. Sometimes it's exciting and sometimes it's very boring. From the van Ruben can see what other people are doing. Ruben wants to do these things too. Find a partner and say what Ruben and his dad would like to do. Act out the dialogue. One partner is Ruben and the other partner is Martyn.

Ruben: Dad, I'd like to go to the beach.

Martyn: Yes, I know. I'd ____________________

____________________ too!

Ruben: Please, can I go now? I ____________________

____________________.

Martyn: Oh, sorry, I ____________________

____________________ too. But I really need your help now.

Ruben: But I ____________________.

Martyn: I know! But we have to work now. You can do these things when your mum's back, OK? I'm sorry, Ruben.

b) Play a game about what you would like to do. Who remembers the most things?

Start like this:
A: I would like to play football.
B: You would like to play football and I would like to read a book.
A: I would like to play football and you would like to read a book and I would …

Ich kann zu Texten, Tonaufnahmen oder Bildern sagen, was jemand gerade macht oder nicht macht. Dazu benutze ich die *ing*-form *(Present progressive)*.

1 In Plymouth Harbour

Poppy and Mia are in Plymouth Harbour to look at all the boats. It's a warm, sunny day and people are on their boats.
FF 24 Listen. Can you find out what the people are doing? Tick (✓) the right box.

1 A man is …
a) cleaning his boat. ☐
b) making sandwiches. ☐
c) sailing out of the harbour. ☐

2 Somebody is …
a) calling a dog. ☐
b) taking photos. ☐
c) buying a boat. ☐

3 A man is …
a) eating a sandwich. ☐
b) making dinner. ☐
c) feeding his dog. ☐

4 They are …
a) lying in the sun. ☐
b) playing a game. ☐
c) having dinner. ☐

5 Children are …
a) climbing on a boat. ☐
b) playing on the beach. ☐
c) swimming in the harbour. ☐

6 Somebody is …
a) playing a game. ☐
b) reading a book. ☐
c) drinking coffee. ☐

2 GAME Trimino

Do the Trimino.
Step 1: Cut out the Trimino pieces.
Step 2: Put the Trimino together. You must always put two -ing forms from the same group together. The black dots (•) are always at the top.

TIP
Wir haben drei Gruppen von Verben für die Bildung des *Present progressive*:
Gruppe 1: read – read*ing* (→ wir hängen *-ing* an das Verb und ändern am Verb nichts)
Gruppe 2: write – writ*ing* (→ wir verlieren das stumme „e" in der Grundform)
Gruppe 3: sit – sit*ting* (→ nach einem kurzen Vokal verdoppeln wir den Konsonanten)

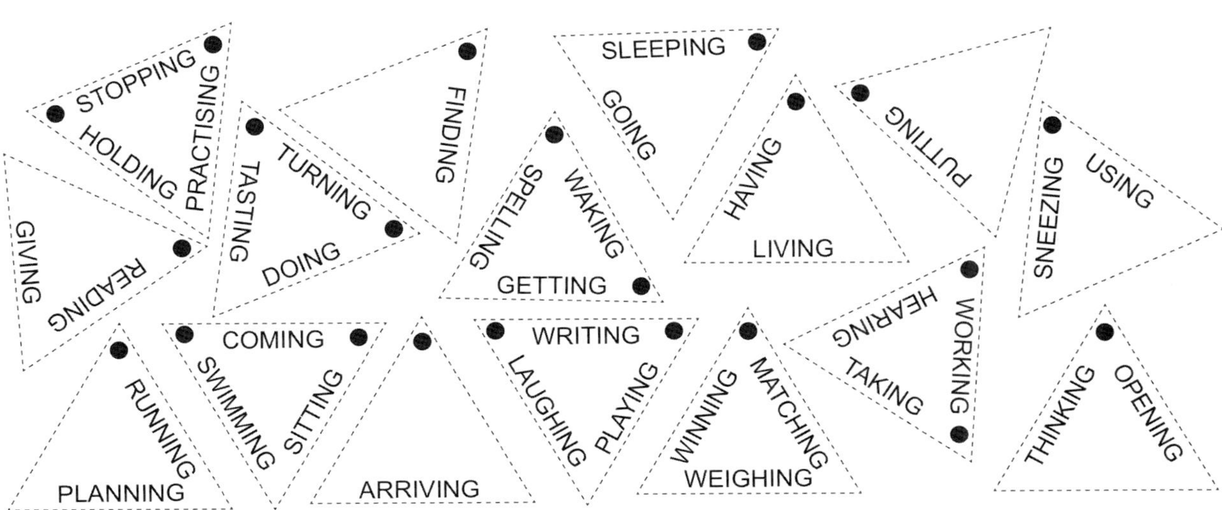

3 Poppy's sailing trip

a) Look at Poppy's photos from last summer. She is showing them to Mia. Then read Poppy's speech bubbles. Match the texts to the pictures.

A Here Bob, the skipper of the Mary Jane, is reading a sea chart. That's what you call the maps for boats.

B This is the best picture. I am looking for seals, dolphins or basking sharks. Joanna next to me is looking for other sailing boats.

C Here, Louise and I are making lunch for everyone on board.

D In this picture you can see that we are all wearing our life jackets. We have to wear them all the time.

1		2		3		4	

b) Look at the pictures again. What are the other people doing? Finish the sentences with the present progressive of the verbs in brackets.

1 In picture 1 two girls ______________________ into the sea. (jump)

2 In picture 2 a boy ______________________ a bottle. (open)

3 In picture 3 somebody ______________________ a fish. (catch)

4 In picture 4 two children ______________________ the boat. (clean)

4 LANGUAGE About Chuck

Mr Chuck Olata is the harbour master of Plymouth Harbour. Finish the sentences with the correct forms of the verbs in brackets. Use simple present or present progressive.

> **TIP**
> Things you often, usually, always do are your routines. Use the *simple present* to talk about them. *Thomas usually reads books.*
> Use the *present progressive* to talk about what somebody is doing now. *At the moment Thomas is reading a magazine.*

1 Chuck Olata came from Italy many years ago and lives in Plymouth now. He usually ______________ (speak) English. But at the moment he ______________ (speak) Italian on the phone to his mother.

2 Chuck always ______________________ (go) to work in his Aston Martin. But today he ______________________ (go) to work by bus because another car hit his car yesterday.

3 Mr Olata works in the harbour. From his window he can see the people there. In the afternoon he often ______________ (watch) tourists. But at the moment he ______________ (watch) a police officer.

4 Mr Chuck Olata likes sweets. After lunch he usually ______________ (eat) chocolate. But at the moment he ______________________ (eat) chocolate ice cream. Yummy!

5 Chuck and his friend Lemo Sorbey love computer games. On Wednesdays they usually ______________________________ (play) at Chuck's house. Today is Wednesday but at the moment they ______________________________ (not play) games. They ______________________ (watch) a kung fu film because Chuck's wife needs the computer.

Ich kann zu Texten, Tonaufnahmen oder Bildern sagen, was jemand gerade macht oder nicht macht. Dazu benutze ich die *ing*-form *(Present progressive)*.

1 In Plymouth Harbour

Poppy and Mia are in Plymouth Harbour to look at all the boats. It's a warm, sunny day and people are on their boats.
FF 24 Listen. What are the people doing? Write sentences and use the verbs from the box.

read • play • swim • eat • take pictures • clean

1 A man ______________________________.

2 Somebody ______________________________.

3 A man ______________________________.

4 They ______________________________.

5 Children ______________________________.

6 Somebody ______________________________.

2 LANGUAGE Trimino

Do the Trimino.
Step 1: Cut out the Trimino pieces.
Step 2: Put the Trimino together. You must always put two verbs from the same group together. The black dots (•) are always at the top.

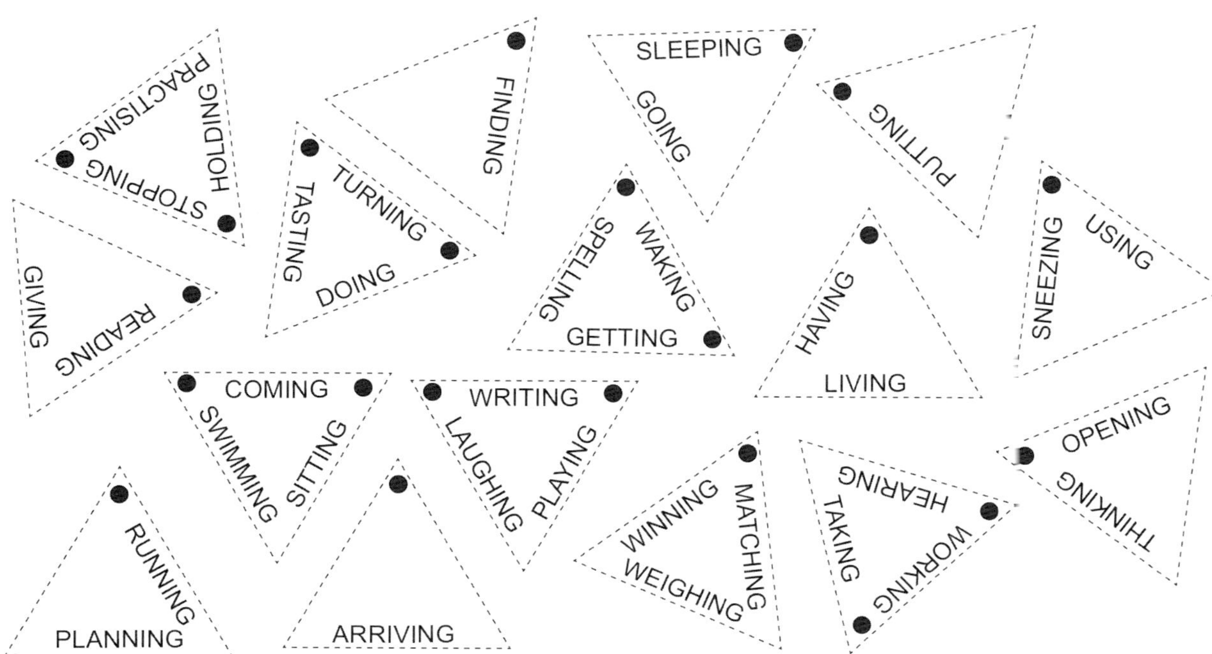

3 Poppy's sailing trip

a) Look at Poppy's photos from last summer. She is showing them to Mia. Read Poppy's speech bubbles and match the texts to the pictures.

A Here, Bob, the skipper of the Mary Jane, is reading a sea chart. That's what you call the maps for boats.

B This is the best picture. I'm looking for seals, dolphins or basking sharks. Joanna next to me is looking for other sailing boats.

C Here, Louise and I are making lunch for everyone on board.

D In this picture you can see that we are all wearing our life jackets. We have to wear them all the time.

b) Look at the pictures again. What are the other people doing? Use the words from the box and complete the sentences.

open • jump • clean • catch

1 In picture 1 two girls ______________________________ into the sea.

2 In picture 2 a boy ______________________________ a bottle.

3 In picture 3 somebody ______________________________ a fish.

4 In picture 4 two children ______________________________ the boat.

4 LANGUAGE About Chuck

Mr Chuck Olata is the harbour master of Plymouth Harbour. Finish the sentences with the correct forms of the verbs in brackets. Use *simple present* or *present progressive*.

1 Chuck Olata came from Italy many years ago and lives in Plymouth now. He almost always ________________________ (speak) English. But at the moment he ________________________ (sing) an Italian song on the phone with his mother. It was his favourite song when he was a child.

2 Chuck really likes his car. He usually ________________________ (go) to work in his Aston Martin. But today he ________________________ (not go) by car. He ________________________ (take) the bus because another car hit his car yesterday.

3 Mr Olata works in the harbour. From his window he can see the people there. In the afternoon he often ________________________ (watch) tourists. But at the moment he ________________________ (not watch) them. He ________________________ (talk) to a police officer about his car.

4 Mr Chuck Olata likes sweets. After lunch he usually ________________________ (eat) chocolate. But at the moment he ________________________ (bite) into a large piece of chocolate cake. Yummy! Mrs Olata doesn't like sweets and she thinks Chuck ________________________ (eat) sweets too often.

5 Chuck and his friend Lemo Sorbey love computer games. Every Wednesday they ________________________ (play) at Chuck's house. Today is Wednesday but they ________________________ (not play) games at the moment. They ________________________ (watch) a kung fu film because Mrs Olata needs the computer.

6 At the moment Chuck ________________________ (help) his wife in the house. He ________________________ (not help) in the house very often but tomorrow is a big day. It's their daughter's 18th birthday. Mrs Olata ________________________ (clean) the bathroom and Mr Olata ________________________ (look) at the chaos behind the sofa.

Ich kann zu Texten, Tonaufnahmen oder Bildern sagen, was jemand gerade macht oder nicht macht. Dazu benutze ich die *ing*-form *(Present progressive)*.

1 In Plymouth Harbour

Poppy and Mia are in Plymouth Harbour to look at all the boats. It's a warm, sunny day and the people are on their boats.
FF 24 Listen. What are the people doing?

1 A man ______________________________.

2 Somebody ______________________________.

3 A man ______________________________.

4 They ______________________________.

5 Children ______________________________.

6 Somebody ______________________________.

2 LANGUAGE Trimino

Do the Trimino.
Step 1: Write the -ing forms in the Trimino pieces, then cut them out.
Step 2: Put the Trimino together. You must always put two verbs from the same group together. The black dots (•) are always at the top.

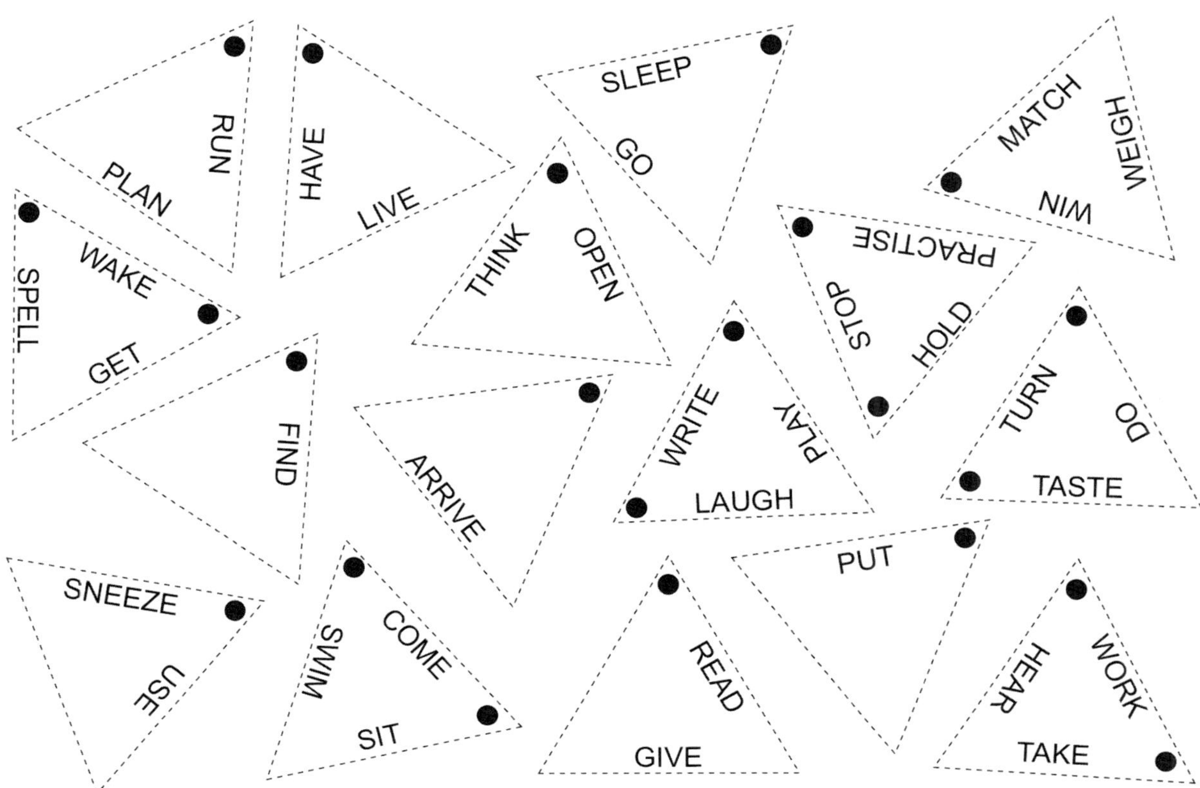

3 Poppy's sailing trip

a) Look at Poppy's photos from last summer. She is showing them to Mia. Read Poppy's speech bubbles and match the texts to the pictures.

A Here, Bob, the skipper of the Mary Jane, is reading a sea chart. That's what you call the maps for boats. I'm also looking at the map. The others aren't reading the sea chart. They're outside.

B That's me at the front of the boat. I'm looking for seals, dolphins or basking sharks. Joanna is looking for other sailing boats through binoculars. I'm not looking for other boats because a basking shark is much more exciting.

C Here you can see that we're all wearing our life jackets. We have to wear them all the time. My uncle Ian never wears a life jacket on boats. There aren't any pictures where he is wearing one.

D Here Louise and I are making lunch for everyone on board. I'm making nice cheese sandwiches. Yummy! Louise isn't making cheese sandwiches. She's putting lots of chocolate cake on a plate.

1		2		3		4	

b) Look at the pictures again. What else can you see? What are the other people doing? Use the verbs from the box.

open • jump • clean • catch

1 In picture 1 two girls ______________________ into the sea.

2 In picture 2 a boy ______________________ a bottle.

3 In picture 3 somebody ______________________ a fish.

4 In picture 4 two children ______________________ the boat.

4 GAME Now or never?

Play the game. Cut out the cards. Take one card from each category and write a sentence with the words on the cards. Use *simple present* or *present progressive*. Complete your sentence with an object.

Example: Mia usually watches the seagulls in the harbour.

Penny Pencil 	sit 	arrive 	at the moment
Busy Lizzie 	now 	take 	sometimes
Sophie 	write 	watch 	often
Barney 	Poppy 	eat 	never
Mia 	Philip 	usually	always

Ich kann Fotos zu Textteilen zuordnen und über die Gefühle von Personen in einem Text sprechen.

1 Shorty's day out

Sally, a seal mother, is swimming near the beach. She's catching fish and crabs, but she's also watching her son, Shorty. Shorty is playing with his cousins Spotty and Sandy. Shorty is hiding in the sea plants and Spotty and Sandy have to find him.

Shorty is the "baby" in the group. He's clever and he loves to find new places, and he often swims too far away.

"Don't swim near the cliff!" his mum always tells him. "The waves are very high – they can throw you against the cliff." But Shorty doesn't always listen to his mum...

When his mum and cousins aren't looking, Shorty swims away. He swims near the cliff and swims behind a big rock. "Spotty and Sandy can't find me here!" Shorty laughs. This is so much fun! (1)

Shorty wants to see where a group of fish is going, so he's swimming to the next big rock when a fast wave catches him. It takes him along the cliff. He tries to swim back, but he can't! Shorty goes up for air. The waves carry him up and down, but this isn't fun! He's far away now from where his cousins are playing. He calls out, but they can't hear him.

He can't fight against the waves anymore, he needs to rest (2). He looks for a place to get out of the water, but the waves are too high. The water is pulling him very near the land. "Oh no!" he thinks. "I'm getting too near the rocks!"

Then a big wave catches Shorty and carries him up high. "Help! Help!" he calls out. But he doesn't hit the rocks – the wave throws him into a deep rock pool[1]. Here the waves can't catch him.

Later, when it's quiet again, Shorty swims up and tries to climb out of the pool. But the rocks around the pool are too high. He can't get out! Shorty doesn't know what to do. "Mum!" he calls. "Where are you?" (3)

After a long time, Shorty hears voices – people's voices. "They're coming closer!" he thinks. "Mum always tells me to stay away from people – but I can't get away!" He swims down to the bottom of the pool. He looks up and suddenly two boys are looking down at him.

"Look! Look!" they shout. "A seal – a little seal! Mum, Dad, come here and look!"

Soon Shorty sees four faces. The boys and their parents are looking down now.

"What's he doing there?" the little boy asks. "He isn't moving. Is he sleeping?"

"No," says the big boy, "his eyes are open!"

"He can't get out of the pool!" says the boys' mother. "The poor thing!"

"Can we get him out of it?" the older boy asks.

"No, we can't touch him," his mother answers. "We have to call for help ..."

Two men arrive. "Oh no!" Shorty thinks. "More people!" The men are wearing jackets with "RSPCA" on them.

"Mum, what's R-S-P-C-A?" the little boy asks.

"It's a group that helps animals when they're in trouble," his mother answers. The men put a net into the water. They're trying to get the baby seal out of the pool.

Shorty fights, but the men catch him in the net. They pull him out of the rock pool. They give Shorty some food and check that he isn't hurt.

"I think he's OK," one of them says, "but he needs his m—"

"Hey!" the little boy shouts. "Look – there in the water! More seals!"

Shorty calls out, and three seals answer him. Shorty knows their voices – it's his mum, Spotty and Sandy! (4) Shorty hops down the rocks and dives into the water. He moves very fast. The boys, their parents and the RSPCA men are surprised. Shorty comes up again and looks back at them from the water. The people are laughing now. "Bye bye!" they call out to him. Shorty gives them a little bark, and then swims away to his mum and cousins. Shorty's mum says: "Shorty, why did you go away? I told you not to. Why don't you listen to me?" (5)

[1] rock pool [rɒk puːl] *Gezeitentümpel*

Ich kann Fotos zu Textteilen zuordnen und über die Gefühle von Personen in einem Text sprechen.

1 Shorty's day out

a) Look at the six pictures. Then underline six sentences in the text that go with the pictures.

b) In the text you can find five numbers. Which sentence (a–e) goes with which number?

a Shorty's mum is angry.
b Shorty is excited.
c Shorty is happy.
d Shorty is tired.
e Shorty is worried.

1		2		3		4		5	

2 Guess what they're doing

Cut out your seals, things and backgrounds. Use them to make pictures that your partner can't see. Find a partner and talk about your pictures. Take turns.

Partner A: Find out about your partner's picture. Ask questions with what, where, who...
Partner B: Answer the questions about your picture.
Talk like this:

What is your seal doing?

My seal is eating.

What is your seal eating?

My seal is eating a crab.

Where is your seal eating a crab?

My seal is eating a crab on the beach.

Who is eating the crab?

It's Sparky.

Ich kann Fotos zu Textteilen zuordnen und über die Gefühle von Personen in einem Text sprechen.

1 Shorty's day out

a) Look at the six pictures. Then underline six sentences in the text that go with the pictures.

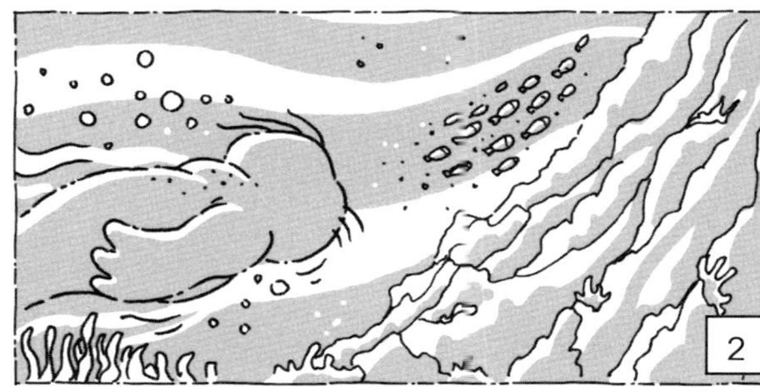

b) How does Shorty feel? Which sentence (A–E) goes with which number (1–5)? The five numbers in the text can help you.

A Shorty's mum is angry because
B Shorty is excited because
C Shorty is happy because
D Shorty is worried because
E Shorty is tired because

1 he is alone and nobody hears him.
2 he is playing with his cousins.
3 the waves are too high and he can't get out.
4 Shorty always gets into trouble.
5 he can see his mum again.

letter: ______ number: _______
letter: ______ number: _______
letter: ______ number: _______
letter: ______ number: _______
letter: ______ number: _______

2 Guess what they're doing

Cut out your seals, things and backgrounds. Use them to make pictures that your partner can't see. Find a partner and talk about your pictures. Take turns.

Partner A: Find out about your partner's picture. Ask questions with what, where, who…
Partner B: Answer the questions about your picture.

fold here

More help

What is …? • Where is …? • Who is …? • My seal is eating … • My seal is looking for …

Ich kann Fotos zu Textteilen zuordnen und über die Gefühle von Personen in einem Text sprechen.

1 Shorty's day out

a) Look at the six pictures. Then underline six sentences in the text that go with the pictures.

b) In the text you can find five numbers. For each number, use one of the following adjectives to write a sentence about Shorty or his mum and give reasons for their feelings.

angry • excited • happy • tired • worried

(1) Shorty is ______________________ because ______________________________

(2) ____

(3) ____

(4) ____

(5) ____

2 Guess what they're doing

Use a pencil to draw a line from sentence part to sentence part. Then find a partner and talk to your partner like this:

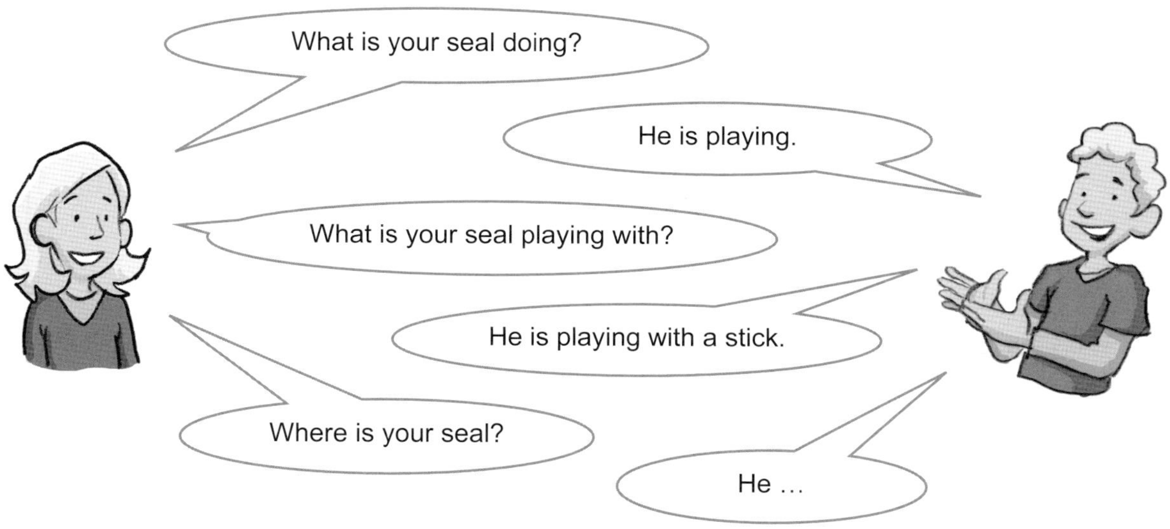

Shorty	eat	a fish	in	a rock pool
Sparky	play with	a ball	on	the beach
Sandy and Sunny	watch	a crab	under	the sea
Spotty and Softy	search for	a stone	next to	a boat
	look for	a stick		
	catch	a seagull		
		a dog		

Ich kann in meinen eigenen Worten englische Hinweisschilder auf Deutsch oder deutsche Hinweisschilder auf Englisch erklären und Informationen aus einem englischen Text auf Deutsch zusammenfassen.

1 A day at Pennywell Farm

a) Read the text on Pennywell Farm.

Pennywell Farm

Pennywell Farm has many sweet animals you can watch and play with: young ducks and chickens, giant rabbits, guinea pigs and many more which you can just take and hold.
Take your family to Pennywell Farm for a day full of family fun! We have many different things you can do every day. You can feed animals, watch sweet miniature pigs run around, find water insects in our lakes, and, and, and … We have something new every half hour!

We are also the home of the world-famous Miniature Pigs!
The pigs are very small and very friendly. Each pig is special with its own colour and spots. A piglet weighs just 250g when it is born. You can buy one at Pennywell and take it home. They cost £550 each but they make great friends!

You find us near Buckfastleigh, just 20 miles from Plymouth.
We are open from 10 am to 5 pm, 7 days a week from February to November.
Our tickets are £11.95 for adults and £9.95 for children (3–16 years).

b) You are on holiday with your family and your grandma is interested in Pennywell Farm. But her English isn't very good. Can you help her? Complete the dialogue.

Oma: Sieh dir mal die süßen Schweine an. Was steht denn da über die? So eines hätte ich ja gern!

Du: Sie wiegen ______________________________

Oma: Der Bauernhof sieht wirklich interessant aus. Ist der in der Nähe von Plymouth?

Du: Ja, Pennywell Farm ist bei ______________________________

____

Oma: Gut, das ist ja nicht so weit. Wie viel Eintritt kostet das? Muss Jonathan mit seinen zweieinhalb Jahren auch zahlen?

Du: Erwachsene kosten ______________________________

____

Oma: Das ist ja gar nicht so teuer. Wann macht der Hof denn am Abend zu?

Du: Sie haben bis ______________________________

Oma: Also mir gefällt die Idee, Pennywell Farm zu besuchen. Wir können ja mal mit Mama und Papa darüber sprechen!

2 Signs at Pennywell Farm

You are at Pennywell Farm with your family. Look at the signs and answer the questions.

1

Tractor rides
1 ride - £1
6 rides - £5

One price for children and adults.

2

Pig feeding times:
every 30 minutes

3

Stay clean at Pennywell Farm!

Touch the pigs,
touch the mice,
touch a horse,
… and wash your hands before you go home!

1 Gelten die Preise für das Traktorfahren für Kinder oder für Erwachsene?

____

2 Wann werden die Schweine gefüttert?

____

3 Wann soll man sich die Hände waschen?

____

3 A guest from England

You have a guest from England, John, and you take him to a big shopping centre. Your friend only knows some German words. He asks you about signs and posters at the shopping centre.

1

Öffnungszeiten:
Mo – Fr: 10:00 – 20:00
Sa: 10:00 – 22: 00
Sonntags geschlossen.

2

Wo ist Joey? Wir vermissen unseren Kater. Joey ist schwarz-weiß und trägt ein braunes Halsband. Bitte melden bei Familie Keller: 555-3412

3

In diesem Geschäft gilt:

– keine offenen Getränke
– kein Eis
– keine Hunde

1 **John:** I can read the times but what does the rest say?

You: The sign tells us when ______________________________

2 **John:** What's a "Kater"? And why is there a telephone number on this poster?

You: A "Kater" is a cat. The Kellers don't know ______________________________

______________________________. If you see it, you can ______________________________

3 **John:** What do I have to do here?

You: You don't have to do anything here. The sign says that you can't ______________________________

____

Ich kann in meinen eigenen Worten englische Hinweisschilder auf Deutsch oder deutsche Hinweisschilder auf Englisch erklären und Informationen aus einem englischen Text auf Deutsch zusammenfassen.

1 A day at Pennywell Farm

a) Read the text on Pennywell Farm.

Pennywell Farm and Wildlife Centre

Take your family to Pennywell Farm for a day full of family fun! There's something new every half hour – not a boring minute during the day! You don't have to pay extra for most activities – you only need your day ticket.

We have many different things you can do every day. You can feed animals, watch theatre shows, find water insects in our lakes, watch bird shows, and, and, and…

Pennywell Farm is also the home of the world-famous Pennywell miniature pigs. The pigs are very small and very friendly. Each pig is special, with its own colour and spots. A piglet weighs just 250 g when it is born. Do you love our miniature pigs? You can buy one at Pennywell and take it home. They cost £550 each but they make great friends!

Pennywell is just off the A38 near Buckfastleigh, just 30 km from Plymouth and Exeter.
It is open from 10 am to 5 pm, 7 days a week from February to November.
Our tickets are £11.95 for adults and £9.95 for children (3–16 years).

b) Your grandma is on holiday with you and your family and she's interested in Pennywell Farm. Her English isn't very good. Can you help her? Complete the dialogue.

Oma: Dieser Bauernhof sieht interessant aus. Aber ist das überhaupt in der Nähe von Plymouth?

Du: ____

Oma: Das geht ja. Was kosten die Karten? Muss Jonathan mit seinen zweieinhalb Jahre auch was zahlen?

Du: ____

____

Oma: Das ist ja für einen ganzen Tag nicht so teuer. Kommen da noch zusätzliche Kosten hinzu?

Du: ____

Oma: Wie lange hat die Farm denn geöffnet?

Du: ____

Oma: Was steht da eigentlich über diese kleinen Schweinchen? Die sind ja süß!

Du: ____

____

Oma: Hört sich gut an, vielleicht können wir ja hinfahren!

2 Signs at Pennywell Farm

You are at Pennywell Farm with your family. Your grandma doesn't understand the signs at the farm. Tell her what the signs say.

1

Tractor rides
1 ride - £1
6 rides - £5

One price for children and adults.

2

Pig feeding times: every 30 minutes

3

Stay clean at Pennywell Farm!

Touch the pigs,
touch the mice,
touch a horse,
… and wash your hands before you go home!

1 ______________________________

____

2 ______________________________

____

3 ______________________________

____

3 A guest from England

You have a guest from England, John, and you take him to a big shopping centre. Your friend only knows some German words. He asks you about signs and posters at the shopping centre. What do you tell him?

1

Öffnungszeiten:
Mo – Fr: 10:00 – 20:00
Sa: 10:00 – 22: 00
Sonntags geschlossen.

2

Wo ist Joey? Wir vermissen unseren Kater.
Joey ist schwarz-weiß und trägt ein braunes Halsband.
Bitte melden bei Familie Keller: 555-3412

3

In diesem Geschäft gilt:

– keine offenen Getränke
– kein Eis
– keine Hunde

1 **John:** I can read the times, but what does the rest say?

You: The sign tells us when ______________________________

2 **John:** What's a "Kater"? And why is there a telephone number on this poster?

You: ______________________________

____

3 **John:** What do I have to do here?

You: ______________________________

____

Ich kann in meinen eigenen Worten englische Hinweisschilder auf Deutsch oder deutsche Hinweisschilder auf Englisch erklären und Informationen aus einem englischen Text auf Deutsch zusammenfassen.

1 A day at Pennywell Farm

a) Read the text on Pennywell Farm.

Pennywell Farm and Wildlife Centre

Take your family to Pennywell Farm for a day full of family fun! There's something new every half hour – not a boring minute during the day! There are 20 hands-on activities and shows every day. You don't have to pay extra for most activities – you only need your day ticket.
Pennywell Farm is just off the A38 near Buckfastleigh, just 30 kilometres from Plymouth and Exeter. It is open from 10 am to 5 pm, 7 days a week from February to November.

At Pennywell Farm you can feed animals and watch animals like miniature pigs run around. You can also watch theatre shows or go on a pony ride. At our lakes you can discover water insects and feed fish. There are great indoor and outdoor play areas. We have something interesting for everyone. Pennywell Farm has many different animals, like young ducks and chickens, giant rabbits, guinea pigs, hedgehogs – and our famous miniature pigs.
The pigs are very small and very friendly. Each pig is special, with its own colour and spots. A piglet weighs just 250g when it is born. Do you love our miniature pigs? You can buy one at Pennywell Farm and take it home. They cost £550 each but they make great friends!
But please remember when you visit Pennywell Farm: animals aren't toys!

Day Admission Ticket Prices

ticket type	price
adult	£11.95
child (3–16 years)	£9.95

b) Your parents and your 2 ½-year-old brother Jonathan want to visit you in England. You want to do something special with them and you found information on Pennywell Farm on the internet.
Write an email to your parents and explain what Pennywell Farm is. Write about what you can do and see there, how much it costs, where it is and when you can go there.

You can start like this:

Hallo Mama, hallo Papa,
Ich habe einen tollen Bauernhof gefunden, auf dem wir ganz viel machen können!
Wir können dort …

2 Signs at Pennywell Farm

You are at Pennywell Farm with your family. Your brother doesn't understand the signs at the farm. Tell him what the signs say.

1

Tractor rides
1 ride - £1
6 rides - £5

One price for children and adults.

2

Pig feeding times: every 30 minutes

3

Stay clean at Pennywell Farm!

Touch the pigs,
touch the mice,
touch a horse,
… and wash your hands before you go home!

1 ____

2 ____

3 ____

3 What does it mean?

Draw/Write four signs in German. Give them to your partner. He/She must tell you what they mean in English.

Ich kann Lese- oder Hörtexten einzelne Informationen entnehmen, indem ich sagen kann, was auf einer Liste von Aussagen zum Text wahr oder falsch ist.

1 At Dartmoor Zoo

You are at Dartmoor Zoo. A man, Jonathan, is taking you and a group of children and their parents around the zoo.
FF 25 Listen to Jonathan. While you are listening, tick (✓) the correct sentences. There are two correct sentences for each animal.

1 The bears …	a) are grizzlies from Canada.	
	b) are called Sidney and Quentin.	
	c) like lying in the warm sun.	

2 The parrot …	a) is called Polly.	
	b) is two years old.	
	c) likes Dartmoor Zoo.	

3 The tigers …	a) eat 20 kilogrammes of meat in a day.	
	b) are difficult to see at the zoo.	
	c) come when they hear their names.	

4 The monkeys …	a) are from Africa.	
	b) are a group of seven girl-gorillas.	
	c) are very big monkeys.	

2 A quiz at the zoo

a) Dartmoor Zoo has a quiz for visitors. Read the zoo's information on the boards about the animals.

Do you know what animal this is? A leopard? A house cat? Guess again – it's a **jaguar**!

Most jaguars have orange-brown fur and black spots. They're one of the world's biggest and strongest cats. They live in South and Central America, in countries like Brazil and Mexico. They can live in places without water, but they love living in the rainforest, with trees to climb, bushes to hide in, and water. Jaguars are good swimmers.
Jaguars live alone. When they want to catch an animal, they walk slowly and listen. When they hear it, they hide, wait and jump on it. They eat all kinds of animals: snakes, monkeys, cows – even horses!

Does this animal live near you?

Foxes can be brown, silver, white ... or red! The **red fox** lives all over Europe, Asia and North America – from Alaska to Florida, from Spain to Siberia. It lives in all kinds of places, even in cities. It has thick fur and a long, bushy tail[1]. It's a fast runner and a good swimmer.
The red fox mostly eats small animals, like a mouse, for example. But it eats lots of other things too, like fruit. When it hunts, it jumps high in the air and lands on the animal it wants to eat. Red foxes live in groups, and they make many sounds to "talk" together.

This bandit is no teddy bear!

When you think of **raccoons**, you often think of their black "mask" around the eyes and their ringed tail. They come from North America, where they live all over the continent, in the country or in cities. But they need trees or other tall things to climb when they're in danger. Raccoons are active mostly at night. They eat hundreds of different kinds of food.
Raccoons are very clever. They remember what they learn. Their front paws are like hands, and they often take food from gardens and get into old food people throw away. They also like to sleep under the roofs of houses, or in garages. And they aren't friendly!

[1] tail [teɪl] *Schwanz*

b) Now read the quiz. The underlined words are wrong information. Find the correct information in the text and correct the mistakes.

Jaguars have black (1) stripes and are very strong. They live (2) in groups in the rainforest. There they climb on trees and hide in the (3) water. When they are hungry they walk slowly and listen.
When they hear an animal, they hide, wait and jump on it. Jaguars eat small and big animals.

The red fox lives (4) only in Europe. It lives in all kinds of places, even in (5) rivers. The red fox eats small animals and berries. It is very fast. When it hunts, it jumps and lands on the animal it wants to eat.

The raccoon comes from North America. In its face you can see a black (6) ring. When it is in danger it climbs on trees. It eats different kinds of food and sleeps in the day. At night, racoons come to houses to take food from the (7) kitchens and garages. Be careful, they can bite!

wrong word	correction
(1) stripes	spots
(2) in groups	______
(3) water	______
(4) Europe	______
(5) rivers	______
(6) ring	______
(7) kitchens and garages	______

3 LANGUAGE The monkey tree

Write the simple past forms correctly and match the monkeys to the correct infinitives.

1) wnek ______
2) chatug ______
3) koeps ______
4) ader ______
5) sten ______
6) sruodedont ______
7) coesh ______

Ich kann Lese- oder Hörtexten einzelne Informationen entnehmen, indem ich sagen kann, was auf einer Liste von Aussagen zum Text wahr oder falsch ist.

1 At Dartmoor Zoo

You are at Dartmoor Zoo. A man, Jonathan, is taking you and a group of children and their parents around the zoo.

a) FF 25 Listen to him. What information do you get from him? Tick (✓) the correct boxes.

	Where do they come from?	What do they eat?	What are their names?	How old are they?
bears				
parrot				
tigers				
gorillas				

b) Check your answers in a). Then listen again and write down key words to answer the questions.

bears: ______________________

____

parrot: ______________________

____

tigers: ______________________

____

gorillas: ______________________

____

2 A quiz at the zoo

a) Dartmoor Zoo has a quiz for visitors. Read the zoo's information boards.

Do you know what animal this is? A leopard? A house cat? Guess again – it's a **jaguar**!

Most jaguars have orange-brown fur and black spots. They're one of the world's biggest and strongest cats. They live in South and Central America, in countries like Brazil and Mexico. They can live in places without water, but they love living in the rainforest, with trees to climb, bushes to hide in, and water. Jaguars are good swimmers.
Jaguars live alone. When they want to catch an animal, they walk slowly and listen. When they hear it, they hide, wait and jump on it. They eat all kinds of animals: snakes, monkeys, cows – even horses!

A **meerkat** is very different from the jaguar: it isn't big and powerful, it wants to live in groups … and it isn't even a cat! Meerkats are small animals that don't need much water and can live in the deserts of southern Africa. They live together in groups of about 20 to 30 meerkats and have many tunnels to hide from the sun and other animals.
Meerkats are great diggers[1], with long claws[2] and ears that close when they dig. They dig their "homes", but they also dig to find food. They eat insects and sometimes snakes, scorpions and other small animals.
When the group looks for food, they work together and bark to tell the others when an animal is coming. Meerkats also sit up straight to warm their bodies in the morning sun!

Does this animal live near you?

Foxes can be brown, silver-grey, white or … red! The **red fox** lives all over Europe, Asia and North America – from Alaska to Florida, from Spain to Siberia. It lives in all kinds of places. It can live well near people – often even in cities. It has thick fur and a long, bushy tail. It's a fast runner and a good swimmer.
The red fox mostly eats small animals, like a mouse, for example, and hamsters. But it eats lots of other things too, like berries and fruit. When it hunts, it jumps high in the air and lands on the animal it wants to eat! Red foxes live in groups, and they use their ears, bodies and many sounds to "talk" to each other.

[1]digger [dɪɡə] *Gräber*
[2]claw [klɔː] *Klaue*

b) Read the sentences about animals at the zoo. Look at the text again: Which sentences are right and which have wrong information? Underline the wrong information and correct it.

sentence	right	wrong	correction
1) Most jaguars have orange-brown fur and black stripes.			
2) Jaguars can live in areas without water, but also in the rainforest.			
3) When jaguars want to eat, they walk around and listen. When they hear an animal, they hide, wait and then jump on it.			
4) Meerkats aren't cats – they are small animals that live in the deserts of southern Africa.			
5) Meerkats are great diggers, with long teeth.			
6) Meerkats dig to find food: insects, but also snakes, scorpions and other small animals.			
7) The red fox lives only in Europe.			
8) The red fox is a fast runner and a good swimmer.			
9) Red foxes use their ears, bodies and many sounds to "talk" to each other.			

3 LANGUAGE The monkey tree

Complete the simple past forms with the vowels from the floor and match the monkeys to the correct infinitives.

kn ___ w

c ___ ght

sp ___ ke

r ___ d

s ___ nt

underst ___ d

ch ___ se

Ich kann Lese- oder Hörtexten einzelne Informationen entnehmen, indem ich sagen kann, was auf einer Liste von Aussagen zum Text wahr oder falsch ist.

1 At Dartmoor Zoo

You are at Dartmoor Zoo. A man, Jonathan, is taking you and a group of children and their parents around the zoo.

a) FF 25 Listen to him. What information do you get from him? Tick (✓) the right boxes.

	Where do they come from?	What do they eat?	What are their names?	How old are they?
bears				
parrot				
tigers				
gorillas				

b) Check your answers in a). Then listen again and write answers to the questions.

bears: ______________________________

____

parrot: ______________________________

____

tigers: ______________________________

____

gorillas: ______________________________

____

2 A quiz at the zoo

a) Read the following information boards from Dartmoor Zoo.

Most **jaguars** have orange-brown fur and black spots, like this one, but some are all black. They live in South and Central America, in countries like Brazil and Mexico. They can live in places without water, but they love living in the rainforest, with trees to climb, bushes to hide in, and water – because jaguars are good swimmers.
Jaguars don't live in groups but alone, and they need a large area. When they look for animals to eat, they walk slowly and quietly and listen. When they hear another animal, they hide, wait... and jump on it without a sound. They eat all kinds of big and small animals: fish, snakes, monkeys, cows – even horses!

The **meerkat** is very different from the jaguar: it isn't big and powerful, it wants to live in groups … and it isn't even a cat! Meerkats are small animals with long, thin bodies. They don't need much water and can live in the deserts of southern Africa. They live together in a group of about 20 to 30 meerkats and have many tunnels to hide from the sun and from other animals.
Meerkats are great diggers, with long claws and ears that close when they dig. They dig their "homes", but they also dig to find food. They eat mostly insects, but also snakes, scorpions and other small animals.
The family does everything together. Babies come out of their "homes" when they're three weeks old. The whole clan comes to see – and to help babysit! When the group looks for food, they work together. One meerkeet barks when it sees another animal coming and the others run into their tunnels. But meerkats also sit up straight to warm their bodies in the morning sun!

The **ostrich** is the world's largest bird, with a big body, long legs and a long neck – but it can't fly! It can grow to 2.8 m tall and weigh up to 150 kg. It has a small head with large eyes, and it can see and hear very well. It uses its wings to give shade to its chicks. Ostrich eggs are the largest in the world. The mother sits on the eggs in the daytime, and the father at night.
Ostriches live in African deserts and savannahs. They move in groups of five to 50. They mostly eat plants – grass, bushes, seeds, fruit and flowers – but they also eat some insects. They can run faster than any other bird – up to 70 km/h! So when they're in danger, they run away. But they can also kill other animals with a hard kick!

b) Now Dartmoor Zoo has got a quiz for you: Look at the sentences about their animals. Find and correct the mistakes. Only look at the information boards again if you have to.

1 Some jaguars are black but most have orange-brown fur and black stripes.

____

2 When jaguars see another animal, they hide, wait and jump on it without a sound.

____

3 Meerkats live in groups and live together in tunnels.

____

4 Meerkats come to babysit when the babies come out of their "homes" after three months.

____

5 Ostriches have small eyes but can see very well.

____

6 Ostriches live in big groups.

____

3 LANGUAGE The monkey tree

Match the monkeys to the infinitives and write down the correct simple past forms.

1) ______________________

2) ______________________

3) ______________________

4) ______________________

5) ______________________

6) ______________________

7) ______________________

Ich kann ein Poster nach vorgegebenen Merkmalen vorbereiten und den Vortrag dazu mit *mini-talk-phrases* halten.

1 STUDY SKILLS Preparing a mini-talk with a poster

You want to give a mini-talk about your favourite sports personality: the Paralympic[1] swimmer Ellie Simmonds. Your first step is to prepare the mini-talk with a poster. Use a separate paper for the poster.

a) Read the information and prepare notes for the talk. You don't have to use all the information.

- her real name is Eleanor
- her birthday is 11/11/1994
- she swims for the Paralympic Games because she's very small (1,23 m)
- she started swimming when she was 5 years old
- in 2006 (at the age of 12) she was the youngest member of a British swimming team in the world championships
- she was poster girl for the 2012 London Paralympic Games – very famous athlete in Great Britain
- she won 4 medals, broke 2 world records
- she likes: history, watching TV all night, dancing, riding, gymnastics
- she doesn't like: Maths
- her day: she doesn't go to school – a teacher teaches her at home, she has training every morning from 6 to 8 (up to 18 hours per week)

b) Give your poster a title.

c) Find pictures and captions for them.

d) Design your poster. Put the title, texts, pictures and captions on your poster.

[1]Paralympics [ˌpærəˈlɪmpɪks] *Olympische Spiele für Sportler mit Behinderung, die immer drei Wochen nach den Olympischen Sommerspielen stattfinden.*

fold here

More help

Captions: With a gold medal in London 2012 • In the pool • A happy winner • On a poster for the Paralympics • Ellie with the Olympic torch at the closing ceremony in London 2012

2 Giving a mini-talk

a) You are partner A. Find a partner B and give your mini-talk about Elli Simmonds. Use your poster for your mini-talk.

TIP
When you give a talk remember to
- look at your partner
- speak slowly and clearly

b) Now partner B gives his/her mini-talk. Listen to your partner's talk. What do you think about his/her talk? Use smileys in the table to make notes.

	☺ 😐 ☹
poster – easy to read?	
used the poster for the talk?	
looked at me?	
loud enough?	
interesting?	
easy to understand?	

c) Say what you liked about the mini-talk and what your partner can do better next time. Then listen to your partner's feedback.

fold here

More help You can use these phrases in your talk:
My presentation is about… • My favourite sports person is … • I like her because … • She is very interesting because … • On my poster you can see a photo of … • That's the end of my presentation. • Do you have any questions? • Thank you very much.

Ich kann ein Poster nach vorgegebenen Merkmalen vorbereiten und den Vortrag dazu mit *mini-talk-phrases* halten.

1 STUDY SKILLS Preparing a mini-talk with a poster

You have to give a mini-talk on a place in Plymouth. You want to give your mini-talk about the lighthouse Smeaton's Tower. Your first step is to prepare the mini-talk with a poster. Use a separate paper for the poster.

a) Read the information and prepare notes for the talk. You don't have to use all the information.

- John Smeaton: designer of the lighthouse
- original position on Eddystone Reef, a group of rocks under the water near Plymouth
- history: first day in October 1759 (24 candles gave light)
- in 1877: problem with the lighthouse, the sea began to break it
- in 1882: people took the top part to the Hoe in Plymouth, today it's still on Plymouth Hoe
- Plymouth opened it for visitors in 1884
- 93 steps to go up
- from the top you can see Plymouth Sound and the city
- tickets adults £2.60, children (3–16) £1.30, students £1.60

b) Give your poster a title.

c) Find pictures and write captions for them.

d) Remember the rules to make a good poster and design your poster. Put the title, texts, pictures and captions on your poster.

fold here

More help

Eddystone Rock today • Smeaton's Tower • The view from the tower • Climbing up to the top

2 Giving a mini-talk

a) You are partner B. Find a partner A and listen to his/her talk. What do you think about his/her talk? Use smileys in the table to make notes.

	☺ 😐 ☹
poster – easy to read?	
used the poster for the talk?	
looked at me?	
loud enough?	
interesting?	
easy to understand?	

b) Now you give your mini-talk about Smeaton's Tower. Use your poster for your mini-talk.

c) Listen to your partner's feedback. Then say what you liked about your partner's mini-talk and what your partner can do better next time.

Ich kann ein Poster nach vorgegebenen Merkmalen vorbereiten und den Vortrag dazu mit *mini-talk-phrases* halten.

1 STUDY SKILLS Preparing a mini-talk with a poster

You have to give a mini-talk on a place in Plymouth. You want to give your mini-talk about the lighthouse Smeaton's Tower. Your first step is to prepare the mini-talk with a poster. Use a separate paper for the poster.

a) Read the information and prepare notes for the talk. You don't have to use all the information.

- John Smeaton: designer of the lighthouse
- original position on Eddystone Reef, a group of rocks under the water near Plymouth, 3rd lighthouse on the rocks, the others broke
- history: opened in October 1759 (24 candles gave light)
- in 1877: problem with the lighthouse, the sea began to break it
- in 1882: people took the top part to the Hoe in Plymouth, today it's still on Plymouth Hoe
- Plymouth opened it for visitors in 1884
- 93 steps to go up
- from the top you can see Plymouth Sound and the city
- on a clear day, you can still see the rest of the old lighthouse next to the new one
- tickets: adults £2.60, children (3-16) £1.30, students £1.60

b) Give your poster a title.

c) Find pictures and write captions for them.

d) Remember the rules to make a good poster and design your poster. Put the title, texts, pictures and captions on your poster.

2 Giving a mini-talk

a) You are partner B. Find a partner A and listen to his/her talk. What do you think about his/her talk? Use smileys in the table to make notes.

	☺ 😐 ☹
poster – easy to read?	
used the poster for the talk?	
looked at me?	
loud enough?	
interesting?	
easy to understand?	

b) Now you give your mini-talk about Smeaton's Tower. Use your poster for your mini-talk.

c) Listen to your partner's feedback. Then say what you liked about your partner's mini-talk and what your partner can do better next time.

Ich kann Wörter, die gleich klingen, aber unterschiedlich geschrieben werden, richtig schreiben. Ich kann Wörter, die zwar die gleiche Buchstabenfolge enthalten, aber unterschiedlich ausgesprochen werden, richtig aussprechen.

1 LANGUAGE Find the odd ones out

Say all the words. In each group there is one word that sounds different. Circle the word.

1 cat • park • can • bad
2 bright • night • city • hide
3 ghost • bottle • note • chose
4 bread • dead • learn • head
5 idea • bear • ear • clear
6 tourist • soup • through • thought
7 hungry • summer • turn • lunch
8 outside • found • enough • sound
9 boring • forty • work • morning
10 clock • won • clothes • hot
11 touch • mouth • trouble • enough

2 I know a man and his wife …

a) Write a story about a man and his wife. Use *their*, *there* or *they're*.

TIP

Write about …
them: very old • from Spain • my neighbours • tired • …
what they have: clock is green • house is big • car is in their garage • …
what's in their house: a bed • two chairs • a dog • …

You can start like this:
I know a man and his wife. They're very old …

b) Now read your text to your partner. Can your partner point to the correct pictures when you say "they're", "their" or "there"?

Ich kann Wörter, die gleich klingen, aber unterschiedlich geschrieben werden, richtig schreiben. Ich kann Wörter, die zwar die gleiche Buchstabenfolge enthalten, aber unterschiedlich ausgesprochen werden, richtig aussprechen.

1 LANGUAGE Find the odd ones out

Say all the words. In each group there is one word that sounds different. Circle the word.

1 cat • park • can • bad • snack
2 bright • night • city • hide • Friday
3 ghost • bottle • note • chose • told
4 bread • dead • learn • head • ready
5 idea • bear • ear • clear • year
6 tourist • soup • through • thought • group
7 hungry • summer • turn • lunch • butterfly
8 outside • found • enough • sound • around
9 boring • forty • work • morning • before
10 clock • won • clothes • hot • box
11 touch • mouth • trouble • enough • cousin

2 I know a man and his wife …

a) Write a story about a man and his wife. Use *their*, *there* or *they're*.

TIP

Write about …
them: very old • from Spain • my neighbours • tired • …
what they have: clock is green • house is big • …
what's in their house: a bed • a dog • …

You can start like this:
I know a man and his wife. They're very old …

b) Now read your text to your partner. Can your partner point to the correct pictures when you say "they're", "their" or "there"?

Ich kann Wörter, die gleich klingen, aber unterschiedlich geschrieben werden, richtig schreiben. Ich kann Wörter, die zwar die gleiche Buchstabenfolge enthalten, aber unterschiedlich ausgesprochen werden, richtig aussprechen.

1 LANGUAGE Find the odd ones out

Say all the words. In each group there is one word that sounds different. Circle the word.

1 cat • park • can • bad • snack
2 bright • night • city • hide • Friday
3 ghost • bottle • note • chose • told
4 bread • dead • learn • head • ready
5 idea • bear • ear • clear • year
6 tourist • soup • through • thought • group
7 hungry • summer • turn • lunch • butterfly
8 outside • found • enough • sound • around
9 boring • forty • before • morning • work
10 clock • won • clothes • hot • box
11 touch • mouth • trouble • enough • cousin

2 I know a man and his wife …

a) Write a story about a man and his wife. Use *their*, *there* or *they're*.

TIP

Write about …
them: very old • from Spain • ...
what they have: clock is green • house is big • ...
what's in their house: a bed • two chairs •...

You can start like this:
I know a man and his wife. They're very old ...

b) Now read your text to your partner. Can your partner point to the correct pictures when you say "they're", "their" or "there"?

Ich kann den wesentlichen Inhalt eines englischen Textes verstehen, auch wenn ich nicht alle Wörter kenne. Das zeige ich dadurch, dass ich Titel zu Textabschnitten finden kann, den Inhalt als *play* wiedergeben oder als *comic strip* zeichnen kann.

1 A trip to the beach

Scene 1: *The kids are pushing their bikes away from the ferry.*
Julian: Great idea to take the ferry to Cawsand.
Kathy: Hey, look – there's an ice cream van here. I'd like an ice cream before we cycle to Freathy Beach.
Julian *(smiling)*: Oh, you don't have any in your huge rucksack? It's so heavy. I'm sure you have rocks in there too …
Kathy: Don't be stupid! You always like my sandwiches and tea! I've got hot water with me.
Julian: You have hot water to make tea? That's for grandmas!
Harry: Hey, stop it. I want to enjoy the day. Let's get some ice cream.
Julian: OK, Harry – let's get some ice cream to make you happy.

Scene 2: *The kids are cycling along the road to Freathy Beach.*
Kathy: That was nice. It was my first Marula ice cream. And that nice boy said it was called Elephant Fruit too.
Julian: UHH. That NICE boy. You didn't only like the ice cream!
Kathy *(blushing)*: Oh, errr … *(turns around)* Hey, Harry! What are you looking at?
Harry: Sorry, but there's a lifeboat from the RNLI out there. I'm not sure – are they helping someone or are they training?
Kathy: Let's stop and watch for a while!

Scene 3: *The kids are unpacking their rucksacks.*
Julian: Hey, Harry, what do you think about Kathy's new boyfriend?
Kathy: You are SO stupid.
Julian: Hey – it's just a joke. *(Looking at his smart phone)*: This is the RNLI website. It tells you about all boats that are out helping people. And at the moment nobody is out.
Harry: Let me have a look. I love the sea and I love boats. It's sad that I live so far away from the sea.
Hey, look, there's a woman with a yellow surfboard – how cool. That must be the lifeguard's rescue board!

Scene 4: *Many people are listening to the lifeguard.*
Jane: Who knows about the flags on the beach? Hands up! … OK then. What do the red and yellow flag mean?
Little girl: That's where you go swimming.
Jane: That's right. That's where we lifeguards watch out and help people. And what about the orange sock?
Kathy: I know! It shows strong winds.
Jane: Great! Well done!

Scene 5: *The kids are eating their lunch.*
Julian: The sandwiches are nice. Thanks, Kathy.
Kathy *(smiles)*: That's okay.
Harry: 449 people! The lifeguard said that in 2012 the RNLI saved 449 people's lives.
Julian: That's a lot. The RNLI is great.
(They hear shouts from a boy in the water.)
Boy: OUCH! OUCH!!! That's terrible.
Julian: Look, the lifeguard is running to the boy.
Boy: OUCH!!!!!!
Jane *(carries the boy out of the water)*: Help! We need hot water and a bucket, quickly!
Kathy *(shouts)*: I've got hot water!
Jane: Put all the hot water in a bucket, please. *(Kathy does that. Jane tests the temperature.)* OK, slowly put your foot in the water. Be careful, it's hot. But hot water will help you! You stood on a weever fish in the water. It's a bit like a wasp or a bee. It can hurt a lot.
Boy: Oh, yes, it does. It's terrible. But thanks for the hot water. My foot is a bit better now.
Kathy: No problem! *(turning to Julian)*: See – tea is great – and not just for old people!
Julian: OK, but my favourite drink is still lemonade.
Harry *(with Julian's smart phone)*: Hey, look, in 2012 the RNLI lifeguards helped 4,752 people after a sting by a weever fish!
Julian: Oh, Harry, you DO like numbers!

Ich kann den wesentlichen Inhalt eines englischen Textes verstehen, auch wenn ich nicht alle Wörter kenne. Das zeige ich dadurch, dass ich Titel zu Textabschnitten finden kann, den Inhalt als *play* wiedergeben oder als *comic strip* zeichnen kann.

A trip to the beach

a) Read the play. Tick (✓) a good title for the following scenes:

Scene 1

Sandwiches and ice cream	
Tea at the beach	
To Cawsand by ferry	

Scene 3

The kids have a quiet afternoon	
The kids arrive at Freathy Beach	
The kids watch surfers	

Scene 5

Hot water helps	
Hot water for Julian's tea	
Hot water from the lifeguard	

b) Now write titles for scenes 2 and 4:

Scene 2: ____________________

Scene 4: ____________________

c) You choose

Draw a comic strip for the play in your exercise book.

> **TIP**
> Think about how many pictures you need for a scene.
> You can have speech bubbles (what people say), thought bubbles (what people think) and captions.
> But the bubbles are small: You can only use short sentences!

or:

You are Kathy. Write your diary entry for the day at Freathy Beach.

> **TIP**
> Write in the first person singular and in the past (I went …).
> Write about your feelings. What did you think?
> You can use some of these words: shout • happy • dangerous • smile • hungry • funny • joke • sad • silly • friendly • angry • surprised

Ich kann den wesentlichen Inhalt eines englischen Textes verstehen, auch wenn ich nicht alle Wörter kenne. Das zeige ich dadurch, dass ich Titel zu Textabschnitten finden kann, den Inhalt als *play* wiedergeben oder als *comic strip* zeichnen kann.

A trip to the beach

a) Read the play. Tick (✓) a good title for the following scenes:

Scene 1

By ferry to Cawsand	
Harry's huge rucksack	
Julian helps Kathy	

Scene 3

On the way to Freathy Beach	
The kids arrive at Freathy Beach	
No lifeguards at Freathy Beach	

Scene 5

Hot water helps	
Hot water for Julian	
Hot water hurts	

b) Now write titles for scenes 2 and 4:

Scene 2: ____________________________

Scene 4: ____________________________

c) You choose

Draw a comic strip for the play.

TIP
Think about how many pictures you need for a scene.
You can have speech bubbles (what people say), thought bubbles (what people think) and captions.
But the bubbles are small: You can only use short sentences!

or:

You are Kathy. Write your diary entry for the day at Freathy Beach.

TIP
Write in the first person singular and in the past (I went …).
Write about your feelings. What did you think?
Maybe these words are useful: shout • happy • dangerous • smile • hungry • funny • joke • sad • silly • friendly • angry • surprised

Ich kann den wesentlichen Inhalt eines englischen Textes verstehen, auch wenn ich nicht alle Wörter kenne. Das zeige ich dadurch, dass ich Titel zu Textabschnitten finden kann, den Inhalt als *play* wiedergeben oder als *comic strip* zeichnen kann.

A trip to the beach

a) Read the play. Tick (✓) a good title for the scenes.

Scene 1

An ice cream at the café	
Kids from Plymouth at Cawsand	
The kids arrive at Cawsand	

Scene 3

Lunch at the beach	
The kids arrive at Freathy Beach	
The lifeguard goes surfing	

Scene 5

The boy and the weever fish	
The lifeguard finds a weever fish	
Julian and the weever fish	

b) Write a multiple choice task for your partner: Think about three different titles for scenes 2 and 4. But make sure that only one title is correct. Now give your multiple choice task to your partner and you answer his or her multiple choice task.

Scene 1

Scene 3

c) You choose **Draw a comic strip for the play or write Kathy's diary entry for the day at Freathy Beach.**

Lösungen, mögliche Lösungen zu offenen Aufgaben und Transkripte zur Audio-CD

Lösungen Here we go!

HWG.1

1a) / b) Hörtext, Track 2

Philip: Hi Mia!
Mia: Hello Philip. This is my new friend.
Philip: Hello, I'm Philip. What's your (1) name?
Sophie: Hi, my name is Sophie.
Philip: Where are you (2) from?
Sophie: I'm from London.
Philip: Really? I'm from Plymouth. How old (3) are you, Sophie?
Sophie: I'm eleven years old. What about you?
Philip: I'm twelve. What's your favourite animal?
Sophie: My favourite animal is a (4) cat.
Mia: Oh, it's late. Don't you have football training, Philip?
Philip: Uh, that's true. I have to run. Bye!

2 Mögliche Lösung

Poppy: Hello! My name is Poppy. What's your name?
You: (1) Hello! My name is Alex.
Poppy: I'm ten years old. How old are you?
You: (2) I'm eleven years old.
Poppy: I come from Plymouth. Where do you come from?
You: (3) I come from Hamburg.
Poppy: My favourite animal is a rabbit. But I like horses too. What's your favourite animal?
You: (4) My favourite animal is a spider.

3 Mögliche Lösung
Hello! My name is Olivia and I'm ten years old. I'm from Rosenheim. My favourite animal is a giraffe. I don't like snakes.

HWG.1

1a) / b) Hörtext, Track 2

Philip: Hi Mia!
Mia: Hello Philip. This is my new friend.
Philip: Hello, I'm Philip. What's (1) your name?
Sophie: Hi, my name is Sophie.
Philip: Where are (2) you from?
Sophie: I'm from London.
Philip: Really? I'm from Plymouth. How old (3) are you, Sophie?
Sophie: I'm eleven years old. What about you?
Philip: I'm (4) twelve. What's your favourite animal?

Lösungen Here we go!

Sophie: My favourite (5) animal is a cat.
Mia: Oh, it's late. Don't you have football training, Philip?
Philip: Uh, that's true. I have to run. Bye!

2a)

You: Hello! (1) What's your name?
Poppy: Hello! My name is Poppy.
You: (2) How old are you?
Poppy: I'm ten years old.
You: (3) Where are you from?
Poppy: I come from Plymouth.
You: (4) What's your favourite animal?
Poppy: My favourite animal is a rabbit. But I love horses too. What about you? What's your name and where do you come from? What's your favourite animal?
You: (5) My name is Alex. I come from Hamburg. My favourite animal is a horse.

b) Individuelle Lösungen

3 Mögliche Lösung
Hello! My name is Olivia and I'm ten years old. I'm from Rosenheim. My favourite animal is a giraffe. I like snakes too.

HWG.1

1a) / b) Hörtext, Track 2

Philip: Hi Mia!
Mia: Hello Philip. This is my new friend.
Philip: Hello, I'm Philip. (1) What's your name?
Sophie: Hi, my name is Sophie.
Philip: (2) Where are you from?
Sophie: I'm from London.
Philip: Really? I'm from Plymouth. (3) How old are you, Sophie?
Sophie: I'm eleven years old. What about you?
Philip: I'm twelve. (4) What's your favourite animal?
Sophie: My favourite (5) animal is a cat.
Mia: Oh, it's late. Don't you have football training, Philip?
Philip: Uh, that's true. I have to run. Bye!

2 Lösung siehe

3 Lösung siehe

Lösungen Here we go!

HWG.2

Hörtext, Track 3

Philip: Hi, Mia.
Mia: Hi, Philip!
Philip: The weather is great today. Let's go to the zoo together. I want to see the elephants, and there's a new black snake too.
Mia: Hm … well, I need to go shopping. I need a new exercise book and a pencil. Let's go to the Barbican. We can go to the Big Wheel too.
Philip: Oh, no, I don't want to go shopping. We can go to the beach, to Plymouth Sound and eat some ice cream.
Mia: But what about my exercise book and my pencil?
Philip: Don't worry. That's okay. We can go tomorrow when it's raining. So … Plymouth Sound and ice cream?
Mia: Good idea. But what about the Aquarium? They have a new baby seal there. It's called Lucy.
Philip: Oh, you want to see a baby animal? Well, let's go to the zoo, then. There's a baby zebra and a baby giraffe. They're really sweet. You have to see them!
Mia: That sounds great! Let's go to the zoo. But I want to see the monkeys too. They're so funny.

a) 1: monkey; 2: giraffe; 3: Plymouth Sound; 4: Big Wheel; 5: elephant; 6: ice cream; 7: clock; 8: Aquarium; 9: zebra; 10: Barbican; 11: boat

b) Philip and Mia talk about: elephants, Barbican, Big Wheel, Plymouth Sound, ice cream, Aquarium, zebra, giraffe, monkeys

c) elephants, Barbican, Big Wheel, Plymouth Sound, ice cream, Aquarium, zebra, giraffe, monkeys

HWG.2

a) / b) Hörtext, Track 3 und **Lösung** siehe

c)

Mia	Philip	Mia and Philip
Barbican, Big Wheel, Aquarium	zoo, Plymouth Sound	zoo

Lösungen Here we go!

HWG.3

						B		
	P				H	I	L	L
B	O	A	T			G		
	O		O			•		
	L		W			W		
			E			H		
			R	I	V	E	R	
						E		
		C	A	S	T	L	E	
				E				
				A				

HWG.3

1a) Lösung siehe

b) Individuelle Lösung

HWG.4

1 1: Saturday; 2: Thursday; 3: Sunday; 4: Friday; 5: Tuesday; 6: Monday; 7: Wednesday

2a) Monday, Tuesday, Wednesday, Thursday, Friday, Saturday, Sunday

b) / c) Individuelle Lösungen

HWG.4

1 1: Tuesday; 2: Saturday; 3: Sunday; 4: Friday; 5: Thursday; 6: Wednesday; 7: Monday

2a) Monday, Tuesday, Wednesday, Thursday, Friday, Saturday, Sunday

b) / c) Individuelle Lösungen

Lösungen Here we go!

HWG.4

1a) Mögliche Lösung

														S			
														u			
														n			
												F		d			
								S	a	t	u	r	d	a	y		
												i		y			
					T							d					
					u							a					
				W	e	d	n	e	s	d	a	y					
					s												
T	h	u	r	s	d	a	y										
					a												
M	o	n	d	a	y												

b) Individuelle Lösungen

2a) / b) Individuelle Lösungen

HWG.5

1 Mögliche Lösung

ant, bear, bird, butterfly, cat, dog, elephant, frog, giraffe, guinea pig, horse, lion, monkey, pig, rabbit, rat, snake, whale

2 Hörtext, Track 4

Mia: Look, Philip. This is our map. We're here at the entrance. Let's go to number 1, where the monkeys are.
Philip: Okay, let's go. I like monkeys. They're funny. Oh, look, the zookeeper is there too. He has bananas and apples. Listen to the monkeys. They're hungry and they're happy to see him.
Mia: They're really loud. Let's go to the baby giraffe.
Philip: Hm … that's number 5 on the map. Let's go to number 3 first. The seals have a baby seal too.
Mia: OK, let's go to the seals. Oh look! They have a red ball in the water. Wow, the big seal can push it with his nose.
Philip: Look, there's the baby seal.
Mia: Oh, that's so sweet! It's so small.
Philip: Well, let's go on. I don't like the smell of fish!
Mia: What about the lions? That's number 6. Let's go there!
Philip: OK. Let's go to the lions.
Wow, listen. They're hungry too. Do lions eat fish too?
Mia: Um … I don't know. But they eat meat.
But now, let's go to number 5. I want to see the baby giraffe.
Philip: Good, let's go to number 5 to see the baby giraffe. Look, the baby giraffe is over there.
Mia: Giraffes are my favourite animals.
Philip: Let's go to see my favourite animal too.
Mia: What is your favourite animal?

Lösungen Here we go!

Philip: My favourite animal is a frog. That's number 7 on our map. That frog is special. It's green, but it has red eyes.
Mia: Uh, wait. I don't want to go there. There are snakes there too. I don't like snakes. Let's go to number 2, to the elephants.
Philip: Hm, OK. Let's go to number 2. Hey, look! One of the elephants is in the pool.
Can elephants swim?
Mia: Yes, they can swim. That's so great! Look, the elephant is having fun in the water.
Philip: That's so funny!
I want some ice cream. What about you?
Mia: Oh yes, that's a great idea! Let's go back to the entrance. We can buy ice cream there.
Philip: Mm … I like vanilla. What about you?

a) / b)

c)

1 The monkeys are funny.
2 The seals have a red ball.
3 The lions are number six.
4 There's a baby giraffe.
5 Philip likes frogs.
6 The elephant is in the water.

3 Individuelle Lösungen

HWG.5

1 Mögliche Lösung siehe

Lösungen Here we go!

2 Hörtext, Track 4 siehe

a) / b) Lösung siehe

b)

[X] The monkeys are funny.	[X] The seals have a red ball.	[X] The lions are number six.
[ ] The monkeys are red.	[X] There's a baby seal.	[ ] The lion is six years old.

[X] There's a baby giraffe.	[ ] Mia loves snakes.	[X] The elephant has a pool.
[ ] The giraffes are number nine.	[X] Philip's favourite animal is a green frog with red eyes.	[X] The elephant has fun in the water.

3 Individuelle Lösungen

HWG.5

1 Mögliche Lösung siehe

2 Hörtext, Track 4 siehe

a) / b) Lösung siehe

c) 1a) • 2a), c) • 3b) • 4a) • 5b) • 6a), c)

3 Individuelle Lösungen

HWG.6

1a) Mögliche Lösung

animal	colour	sentence
Storch	*black + white*	*It's a black and white animal.*
Tiger	black + orange	It's a black and orange animal.
Schwein	pink	It's a pink animal.
Frosch	green	It's a green animal.
Affe	brown	It's a brown animal.
Pony	brown	It's a brown animal.

Lösungen Here we go!

b) Mögliche Lösung
blue whale, green and yellow butterfly, yellow and black giraffe

2

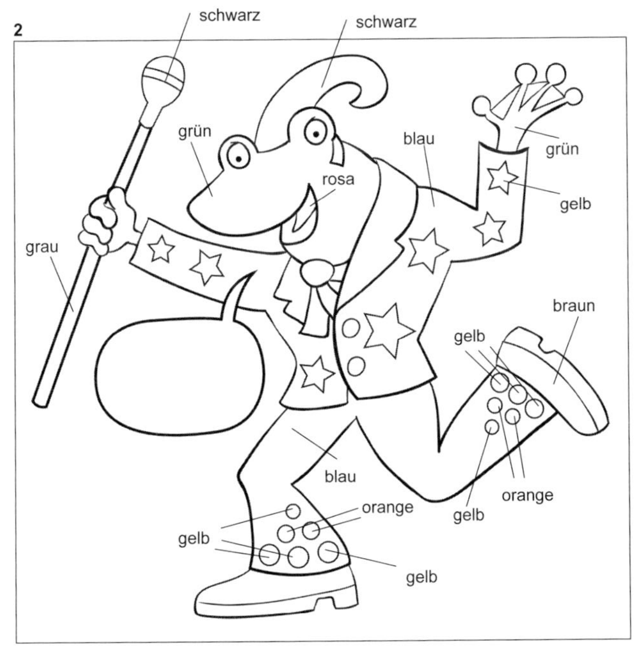

HWG.6

1 a) Lösung siehe

b) Mögliche Lösung
white polar bear, yellow snake, blue whale

Lösungen Here we go!

HWG.9

1a) 1: twenty-three • 2: seventy-six • 3: eighty-one • 4: thirty-three • 5: fifty-three • 6: nine • 7: forty-four • 8: fifteen • 9: thirty-four • 10: forty-eight

b) Mögliche Lösung
eleven + three = ____________
ninety-two – fifteen = ____________
seventy-four + nineteen = ____________

c) Mögliche Lösung
fourteen, seventy-seven, ninety-three

2a) 479320611

b) Individuelle Lösung

3 Individuelle Lösung

Lösungen Unit 1

1.1

1a)
I'm a seal. You are a boy. We are children. • I'm happy! Seals are great!
It is Sunday. Jeremy and his mum are at Plymouth Aquarium. There are many seals. Jeremy is happy. Seals are Jeremy's favourite animals. The little seal is happy too.

b)
Dad: Is the aquarium big?
Jeremy: Yes, it is.
Dad: Are you happy?
Jeremy: Yes, I am.

Dad: Are seals great?
Jeremy: Yes, they are.
Dad: Are you and the seals friends now?
Jeremy: No, we aren't, dad. You are silly!

2 Hörtext, Track 6
Sharon: Hi, everyone! Please be quiet now. Welcome to Plymouth Aquarium. It's great to have you all here. I'm Sharon and I work at the aquarium. There are lots of new kids here today. Let's sit down for a moment and listen to them so we all know everyone in our group. The girl with the red shoes, can you start, please?
Jenny: Hi, er … my name is Jenny. Jenny Davis. I'm from Dudley, a town near Birmingham. Maybe you know Dudley Castle. It's very old. I'm here in Plymouth with my grandparents this weekend.
Sharon: Great, Jenny! Welcome! How old are you?
Jenny: I'm twelve. I have a sister, Jessica. She's thirteen. But she isn't here today. She's in London with her best friend.
Sharon: Aha, thank you, Jenny! Now, let's have a boy next. The boy over there with the big rucksack. Can you tell us about yourself, please?
Phil: I'm from Plymouth and I go to Coombe Dean. I often come here at the weekend. I'm eleven and my hobby is fishing. I love fish.
Sharon: OK. But you can't eat the fish in the aquarium. You can only look at them. We still don't know your name. Who are you?
Phil: My name is Phil. My mum and dad like fishing too. We have a boat. Its name is Telly and we often go sailing in …
Sharon: OK, thank you, Phil. We have plenty more time to hear about your family later. Maybe the girl with …

a) The girl talks about her hometown. • The boy talks about his family.

b) 1a) • 2c) • 3a) • 4a)

1.1

1a) / b) Lösung siehe

2 Hörtext, Track 6 siehe

2a) 1c), d) • 2a), c)

b) 1b) • 2d) • 3b) • 4a)

Lösungen Unit 1

1.1

1a) Mögliche Lösung
It's Sunday. Jeremy and his mum are at Plymouth Aquarium. There are many fish. Jeremy is happy. Fish are Jeremy's favourite animals. The little fish are happy too.
I'm a seal. You're a boy. We're children.
I'm happy! Seals are great!

b)
Dad: Is the aquarium big?
Jeremy: Yes, it is.
Dad: Are you happy?
Jeremy: Yes, I am.

Dad: Are seals great?
Jeremy: Yes, they are.
Dad: Are you and the seals friends now?
Jeremy: No, we aren't, dad. You are silly!

2 Hörtext, Track 6 siehe

2a) 1c), d) • 2a), e)

b) (2) sister • (3) Jessica • (4) thirteen • (5) fishing • (6) boat • (7) sailing

1.2

1
(2) I'm • (3) You're • (4) He's • (5) It's • (6) I'm • (7) They're • (8) She's • (9) We're • (10) It's

2b)
(1) Susan • (2) Gary • (3) Sophie • (4) Lorcan • (5) Susan

3 Mögliche Lösung
a) / b) age 10, mum works in a shop, likes animals, friends Chris and Ewan

c) Mögliche Lösung Alice

d) Mögliche Lösung
A: Hi, my name is Alice. What's your name?
B: Oh, hello! My name is Katy. I have a pet. It's a dog. What about you?
A: I like animals. I have a hamster and two rabbits.
B: My mum is from Turkey. What about your mum?
A: My mum is from Hamburg in Germany. She works in a shop. I'm from Berlin. What about you?
B: I'm from Karlsruhe.

e) Mögliche Lösung
My name is Alice. I'm from Berlin in Germany. I like animals. I have a hamster and two rabbits. My hobby is reading. My mum is from Hamburg. She works in a shop. My friends are Chris and Ewan.

Lösungen Unit 1

1.2

1a) Lösung siehe

2b) Lösung siehe

3 Mögliche Lösung
a) / b) age 10, mum works in a shop, likes animals, friends Chris and Ewan, doesn't like pink, hobby football.

c) Mögliche Lösung Alice

d) Mögliche Lösung
A: Hi, my name is Alice. What's your name?
B: Oh, hello! My name is Katy. I have a pet. It's a dog. What about you?
A: I like animals. I have a hamster and two rabbits.
B: My mum is from Turkey. What about your mum?
A: My mum is from Hamburg in Germany. She works in a shop. I'm from Berlin. What about you?
B: I'm from Karlsruhe. What's your favourite colour?
A: I like all colours, but I don't like pink. Do you play football? I play football with my friends Chris and Ewan.
B: Yes, I like football. Let's go!

e) Mögliche Lösung
My name is Alice. I'm from Berlin in Germany but my mum is from Hamburg. She works in a shop. I like animals and I have a hamster and two rabbits. My hobby is football. I play football with my friends Chris and Ewan.

1.2

1 (1) We're • (2) I'm • (3) You're • (4) He's • (5) It's • (6) I'm • (7) They're • (8) She's • (9) We're • (10) It's

2b) (1) Susan • (2) Gary • (3) Lorcan • (4) Sophie • (5) Susan

3b) Mögliche Lösung
age 10, mum works in a shop, dad in the Navy, pets rabbits, hobby football, likes animals, doesn't like pink, hometown Manchester, friends Chris and Ewan

c) Mögliche Lösung Alice

d) Mögliche Lösung
A: Hi, my name is Alice. What's your name?
B: Oh, hello! My name is Katy. I have a pet. It's a dog. What about you?
A: I like animals. I have rabbits.
B: My mum is from Turkey. What about your mum?
A: My mum is from Hamburg in Germany, but I'm from Manchester. She works in a shop. My dad is in the Navy. What about your dad?

Lösungen Unit 1

B: My dad works in a museum. What's your favourite colour?
A: I like all colours, but I don't like pink. Do you play football? I play football with my friends Chris and Ewan.
B: Yes, I like football. Let's go!

e) Mögliche Lösung
My name is Alice, I'm 10 years old. I'm from Manchester. My mum is from Hamburg. She works in a shop. My dad is in the Navy. I like animals and I have two rabbits. My hobby is football. I play football with my friends Chris and Ewan. But our T-shirts aren't pink, I don't like pink!

1.3

1 Hörtext, Track 7

a)
1 Let's go to the cinema and see a film.
2 Okay, good idea. Let's see Harry Potter. At what time does it start?
1 It starts at quarter past eight.

b)
Dr. Smith: Doctor Smith speaking.
Patient: Hello, Doctor Smith, can I see you at half past two today?
Dr. Smith: 2:30 ... yes, that's fine.

c)
Dear visitors, it's time to go home. It's 7:45 and all our animals must sleep now.
Please go to the exit.

d)
At 6:20 tonight you can listen to the football game between Manchester United and Arsenal on BBC Radio 4.

e)
Dear passengers, we'll be arriving at London Heathrow Airport shortly. Local time is 11:25.
Thank you for travelling with British Airways. Goodbye and have a nice day.

f)
The train from Bristol is 40 minutes late. The new arrival time is 4:30. The train from Bristol is 40 minutes late. The new arrival time is 4:30.

g)
1 John says his party starts at 5 o'clock. Can we go together?
2 I must do my homework first. What about quarter to six?
1 Okay, fine. Let's go at quarter to six.

h)
Customer announcement. Today we have a guest in our sports department. David Beckham will be with us for one hour and you can talk to him. Come to our sports department to talk to David Beckham at ten to three.

Lösung: a) 8:15 • b) 2:30 • c) 7:45 • d) 6:20 • e) 11:25 • f) 4:30 • g) 5:45 • h) 2:50

Lösungen Unit 1

2 Mögliche Lösung
B: What time is it, please?
A: It's eleven twenty.
B: Thank you!
A: What time is it, please?
B: It's a quarter to nine.
A: Thank you!

Auswertung
A: This is correct.
B: Sorry, this is wrong, I said a quarter to nine. Let me help you … look.

1.3

1 Hörtext, Track 7 und **Lösung** siehe

2 Methodisch-didaktischer Hinweis:
Die S schneiden das Uhr-Raster und zwei Papierstreifen zurecht und kleben die Streifen zusammen. Zielbild: Im Stil einer *Fruit machine* drehen sich Räder, auf denen links Stunden und rechts Minuten angezeigt werden. Es gibt eine Uhr pro S-Paar.

Mögliche Lösung
A: What time is it, please?
B: It's a quarter to ten.
A: Yes, that's right.
B: Can you tell me the time, please?
A: …

1.4

1a)
Philip's classroom
There are six tables and six chairs / three schoolbags / two posters / no windows / two students / six books in Philip's classroom.
There is one desk (and one chair) / one board / one door / one teacher / Philip / one timetable / no clock / one dog / one shelf in Philip's classroom.

Mia's classroom
There are seven tables and six chairs / four schoolbags / three posters / two doors / four students / two birds / three books in Mia's classroom.
There is one desk (and one chair) / one board / one teacher / Mia / no timetable / a clock / one shelf / a window in Mia's classroom.

Lösungen Unit 1

b) (six things)

There are …	
Philip	**Mia**
six tables, six chairs	seven tables, six chairs
three schoolbags	four schoolbags
two posters	three posters
no windows	windows
two students	four students
no birds	two birds
six books	three books
There is …	
Philip	**Mia**
Philip	Mia
one timetable	no timetable
no clock	a clock
one dog	no dog
one door	two doors

2
Lesson 1 on Monday is Biology. • At Woodpark High there are six lessons every day. • The first lesson is at half past eight. • There's a (short) break at twenty past ten. It's 20 minutes long. • The lessons are 55 minutes long. • It's time to go home at 3 o'clock.

1.4

1a) / b)
Philip's classroom
There are six tables and six chairs / three schoolbags / two posters / two students / six books in Philip's classroom.
There is one desk (and one chair) / one board / one door / one teacher / Philip / one timetable / one dog / one shelf in Philip's classroom.
There isn't a clock / … . There aren't any birds / windows … .

Mia's classroom
There are seven tables / four schoolbags / three posters / two doors / four students / two birds / three books in Mia's classroom.
There is one desk / one board / one teacher / Mia / a clock / one shelf / a window in Mia's classroom.
There isn't a timetable / a dog … .

2 Mögliche Lösung
A: Royal Grammar School, Manchester
Lesson 1 on Monday is Biology. • At Royal Grammar School there are five lessons every day. • The first lesson is at nine o'clock. • There's a (short) break at eleven o'clock. It's 20 minutes long. • The lessons are one hour long. • It's time to go home at 2.55.

Lösungen Unit 1

B: Woodpark High, Liverpool
Lesson 1 on Monday is Biology. • At Woodpark High there are six lessons every day. • The first lesson is at half past eight. • There's a (short) break at twenty past ten. It's 20 minutes long. • The lessons are 55 minutes long. • It's time to go home at 3 o'clock.

1.4

1a) / b)
Philip's classroom
Is/Are there any students / windows / schoolbags / … in your classroom? – Yes, there is / are.
There are six tables and six chairs / three schoolbags / two posters / two students / six books in Philip's classroom.
There is one desk (and one chair) / one board / one door / one teacher / Philip / one timetable / one dog / one shelf in Philip's classroom.
There isn't a clock / … . There aren't any birds/windows … .

Mia's classroom
There are seven tables / four schoolbags / three posters / two doors / four students / two birds / three books in Mia's classroom.
There is one desk / one board / one teacher / Mia / a clock / one shelf / a window in Mia's classroom.
There isn't a timetable / a dog … .

2 Mögliche Lösung
A: At Royal Grammar School there are five lessons every day. On Thursday and Friday there are four lessons. Are there four lessons at your school on Thursdays and Fridays?
B: No, there are five lessons on Monday. But on Friday there are four lessons too. What about Friday?
A: The lessons at my school are one hour long. What about your school?
B: The lessons are 55 minutes long.
A: On Friday it's time to go home at 1:20. What about your school?
B: It's time to go home at 12:30. I can come to Manchester.
A: Good. Let's meet in Manchester.

1.5

1

M								N		
A	U	G	U	S	T			O		
Y				E				V		
				P				E		
	M			T		F		M		
	A		D	E	C	E	M	B	E	R
	R			M		B		E		
O	C	T	O	B	E	R		R		J
	H			E		U				U
				R		A	P	R	I	L
						R				Y
J	A	N	U	A	R	Y				

Missing month: June

Lösungen Unit 1

2a) Mögliche Lösung
ninth, eleventh, fourth, sixth, fifth, first, third, seventh, twelfth, second, eighth

2b) Mögliche Lösung
A: Are the frogs your first pair?
B: No, they aren't, the elephants are my first pair.
A: Are the frogs your second pair?
B: Yes, they are.

3a) Hörtext, Track 8
Teacher: Now, I want you to talk with your classmates. Tell a classmate your name and your birthday. Then talk to another classmate, and another. Find out: Who has the first birthday in the class? And the second? And the third? So, March birthdays come before April birthdays. And the 10th of April comes before the 20th of April, and so on. I want the kid with the first birthday to stand here, then the one with the second birthday, then the third birthday, and so on – from the 1st of January to the 31st of December!

Lösung: birthdays

b) Hörtext, Track 9
Teacher: Okay, let's go.
Tim: Hello. My name is Tim. What's your name?
Anna: My name is Anna.
Tim: When's your birthday, Anna?
Anna: My birthday is on the 16th of November. When's your birthday, Tim?
Tim: My birthday is on the 12th of March.

Mary: Hi. My name is Mary. What's your name?
Harry: My name is Harry.
Mary: When's your birthday, Harry?
Harry: It's on the 31st of July. When's your birthday?
Mary: It's on the 3rd of May.

Ben: Hello. My name is Ben.
Indira: Hi. My name is Indira. When's your birthday, Ben?
Ben: My birthday is on the 2nd of March. When's your birthday?
Indira: My birthday is on the 20th of January.

Teacher: Okay, class. Now I want you all to tell us when your birthday is. Let's start with Tim. When's your birthday, Tim?
Tim: My birthday is on the 12th of March.
Teacher: Very good. And Anna, when's your birthday?
Anna: My birthday is on the 16th of November.
Teacher: Excellent. What about you, Mary? When's your birthday?
Mary: My birthday is on the 3rd of May. (…)
Indira: My birthday is on the 20th of January. (…)

Lösungen Unit 1

Lösung
Anna: 16th November • Tim: 12th March • Harry: 31st July • Mary: 3rd May • Ben: 2nd March • Indira: 20th January

4 Mögliche Lösung
My best friend's birthday is the 28th of August.
My mother's birthday is the 17th of August. My grandfather's birthday is the 25th of January. My aunt's birthday is the 4th of March. My brother's birthday is the 24th of June. My sister's birthday is the 19th of March. My birthday is the 25th of September.

5 an …
appointment • answer • animal • ant • elephant • English song • MP3 player • hour • Art lesson • ICT teacher • orange rubber • exercise book • open window

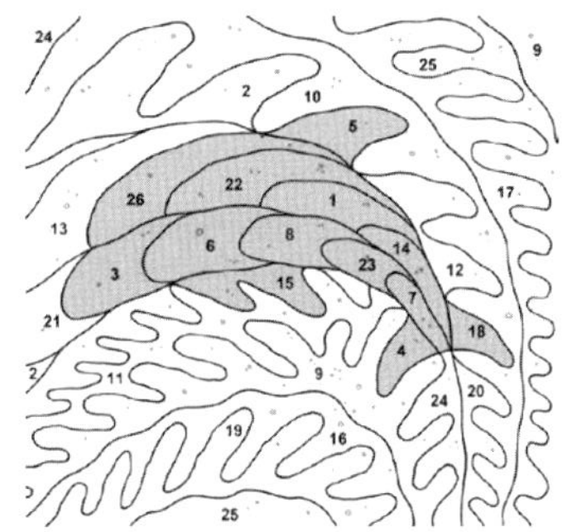

1.5

1

					J			N		
A	U	G	U	S	T	U		O		
				E			N	V		
				P				E		
M	M			T		F		M		
	A		D	E	C	E	M	B	E	R
	R	Y		M		B		E		
O	C	T	O	B	E	R		R		J
	H			E		U				U
				R		A	P	R	I	L
						R				Y
J	A	N	U	A	R	Y				

2a) / b) Lösung siehe

3a) Hörtext, Track 8 und **Lösung** siehe

Lösungen Unit 1

3b) Hörtext, Track 9 und **Lösung** siehe

4 Lösung siehe

5 Lösung siehe

1.5

1

J					J	J	U	N	E	
A	U	G	U	S	T	U		O		
		L		E			N	V		
			Y	P				E		A
M	M	A	Y	T		F		M		P
	A		D	E	C	E	M	B	E	R
	R	Y		M		B		E		I
O	C	T	O	B	E	R		R		L
	H			E		U				
				R		A	P	R	I	L
				M	A	R	C	H		
J	A	N	U	A	R	Y				

2a) Mögliche Lösung siehe

2b) Mögliche Lösung
A: Are the frogs your first pair?
B: No, they aren't, the elephants are my first pair.
B: Are the frogs your second pair?
A: Yes, they are.
(…)
B: Are the bears your twentieth pair?
A: No, they aren't, the bears are my seventy-ninth pair.

3a) Hörtext, Track 8 und **Lösung** siehe

3b) Hörtext, Track 9 und **Lösung** siehe

4 Lösung siehe Aufg. 5

Lösungen Unit 1

1.6

1b) Mögliche Lösung
A: I like Maths. – **B:** I like Maths too.
A: I like dogs! – **B:** I like animals and I like dogs too. – **A:** I like dogs too but I don't like all animals.
A: We like Maths and dogs.

2 Hörtext, Track 10

1
Speaker 1: Don't touch that! That's my new skateboard! ... Hey, come back here! That's mine! …

2
Friend 1: Did you win your football game this morning?
Friend 2: No …
Friend 1: Uh-oh – was it bad?
Friend 2: Yeah …
Friend 1: Mmh … How bad was it?
Friend 2: Six to one.
Friend 1: Oh, no. That is bad. … Well, hey, the sun is out. Do you want to go to the beach with us after lunch?
Friend 2: No, not today …

3
Friend 3: Hey, we're going to the zoo on Saturday. Do you want to come?
Friend 4: Yeah, I'd love to!
Friend 3: Great! Let's meet there at three.
Friend 4: Okay! Thanks! See you on Saturday!

4
Friend 5: Oh, no!
Friend 6: What's the matter? Did you forget something?
Friend 5: Yeah, it's my mum's birthday and I don't have a present for her!

5
Mum: Here, John, this is for you.
John: Uh … for me?
Mum: Yeah!
John: Really? What is it?
Mum: Go on, open it and see!
John: A new MP3 player! I can't believe it!
Mum: Do you like it?
John: Yeah, it's great! But why … I mean, why now? It isn't my birthday or anything.
Mum: I know, dear, but your marks are so good this term, I just wanted to give you something nice.
John: Wow! Thanks a lot, Mum!

Lösung
1 angry • 2 sad • 3 happy • 4 sorry • 5 surprised

Lösungen Unit 1

3b) Mögliche Lösung
(1) Hi! • (2) What's your name? • (3) Hello! • (4) My name is Fred. • (5) Nice to meet you. • (7) Let me show you. (8) • That's cool! • (9) What about you? • (10) I like books about cars • (11) Here's the canteen, OK? • (12) Goodbye. • (13) Goodbye! • (14) Thank you.

1.6

1b) Mögliche Lösung siehe

2) Hörtext, Track 10 und **Lösung** siehe

3b) Mögliche Lösung siehe

1.6

1b) Mögliche Lösung siehe

2 Hörtext, Track 10 und **Lösung** siehe

3b) Mögliche Lösung
Charlie Rud: Hi! I'm new here. My name is Charlie. What's your name?
Fred Snap: Oh. Hello! Nice to meet you. My name is Fred.
Charlie Rud: Can you help me, please? Where is the canteen?
Fred Snap: It's near the library. Let me show you.
Charlie Rud: The library? Hm. That's cool. I like books. What about you?
Fred Snap: Oh. I like books about cars. Here's the canteen, OK?
Charlie Rud: Thank you! Goodbye!
Fred Snap: Goodbye!

1.7

1 (1) at • (2) in • (3) from • (4) at • (5) to • (6) at • (7) on • (8) at • (9) to • (10) at • (11) to • (12) with • (13) on

2a) Mögliche Lösung
On the last day of school we only have two lessons. Our lessons are 45 minutes long. We watch a film in our classroom or the library. Then there's a short break at 9.35. It's 10 minutes long. We go out and play. Then we all sing songs in front of the school and our parents come and sing too. I like the films we watch. I don't like the songs. It's time to go home at 10:30 am.

Lösungen Unit 1

b) Mögliche Lösung
What? Come to my last-day-of-school-party!
Where? It's in Oxford at 47 Linton Road.
When? Wednesday, 24th July, at 6 pm.

1.7

1 Lösung siehe

2a) Mögliche Lösung
Come to my summer party.
Let's have lots of fun in the sun.
I live at 37 Church Lane.
On Saturday, 15th July.
At 4 o'clock.
Please wear trainers. The party is in the garden.
See you!

2b) Mögliche Lösung
Come to my last-day-of-school-party.
Don't wear your school uniform!
Let's have lots of fun and eat lots of cake.
It's in Oxford at 47 Linton Road.
On Monday, 24th July.
At 6 pm.

1.8

1
1 Can I open the window, please? • 2 Sorry, I'm late. • 3 What's for homework? • 4 Can you speak louder, please? • 5 Sorry, I don't know. • 6 Can I have a pen, please? • 7 Can you spell "boat", please? • 8 Sorry, I haven't finished. • 9 Can I go to the toilet, please? • 10 What's "Klassenkamerad" in English?

2
2 Have a break here. • 3 Don't talk. • 4 Win a teddy bear. • 5 Don't open the window. • 6 Like me.

1.9

1 Hörtext, Track 11
Announcer: Flight AA 6178 to Washington is late.
Announcer: Flight IB 7447 to Madrid is now boarding.
Announcer: Flight AC 6551 to Dublin has been changed to gate 8.
Announcer: Passenger Nolan Cameron, booked on flight LH 907 to Frankfurt, please go to gate D12.
Announcer: Passenger Adrian Connolly, booked on flight GF 4381 to Boston, please go to luggage inspection.

Lösung: 1: AA 6178 • 2: IB 7447 • 3: AC 6551 • 4: LH 907 • 5: GF 4381

Lösungen Unit 1

2 Mögliche Lösung
A: Is code MAD5F on your list?
B: Yes, it is. What about code ARP5N? Is it on your list?
A: Sorry, say it again, please!
B: Is code ARP5N on your list?
A: No, it isn't. Can I write it down, please? What about …

1.9

1 Hörtext, Track 11 und **Lösung** siehe

2 Mögliche Lösung
A: Is code YARP5N on your list?
B: Yes, it is. What about code GMAD5F? Is it on your list?
A: Sorry, say it again, please!
B: Is code GMAD5F on your list?
A: No, it isn't. Can I write it down, please? What about …

1.10

Methodisch-didaktischer Hinweis:
Die Kärtchen sind in der richtigen Reihenfolge auf der KV angeordnet. Das Domino sollte daher vorab von L oder nicht mitspielenden S zerschnitten werden. Zur Selbstkontrolle der S kann L eine unzerschnittene Kopie des Domino-Spiels als Lösungsschablone zur Verfügung stellen.

Lösungen Unit 2

2.1

Methodisch-didaktischer Hinweis:

Dieses Aufgabenblatt kann nach der Methode Lerntempoduett (auch *Bus Stop*, HRU-Seite 208) durchgeführt werden. Dazu können Sie vorab das Foto links viermal vergrößern, kopieren und die Kreise nummerieren. Zu den Aufgaben mit dem Partnerarbeitssymbol treffen sich die S jeweils an im Klassenraum als *Bus Stop* markierten Punkten (z. B. in den Zimmerecken) und werten ihre Ergebnisse kommunikativ aus. Differenzierungsart: Offene Aufgaben, die Ergebnisse unterschiedlichster Qualität und Quantität zulassen. In der Auswertungsphase können leistungsstärkere S ihre Mit-S unterstützen bzw. lernschnellere S bereits gemeinsam weiterarbeiten.

a) Lösungen: Aus Unit 2: bedroom, bathroom, dining room, kitchen, living room, (1) cupboard • (2) clock • (3) desk • (4) photo • (5) shelf • (6) poster • (7) picture • (8) toilet • (9) table • (10) lamp • (11) sofa • (12) window • (13) TV • (14) chair • (15) toy • (16) door • (17) armchair • (18) book • (19) bed. Weitere Begriffe sind möglich.

b) Mögliche Lösung
What's this? – This is a shelf. – Yes, that's right. What's this? – This is a sofa. No, it isn't. It's an armchair. What do you think? Can you help me with the spelling? – a-r-m-c-h-a-i-r …

c) Individuelle Lösungen

d) Look, this is my bedroom. There is a desk and there are my books. This is my bed and here's my iPod. …

e) Individuelle Lösungen

f) Mögliche Lösung
A: Look, my lamp in the bedroom is green. What colour is your lamp?
B: My lamp is pink. What about the sofa in your living room? My sofa is yellow.
A: My sofa in the living room is brown. What colour is your …?

g) Mögliche Lösung
My dream house
My dream house is very big. It's an old house. It's made of stone. The house has colourful walls: red, orange, green and yellow. My bedroom is very big too. In my bedroom there is a computer, a CD player

and a big bed. I have an ice cream machine in my bedroom. On the walls there are posters of my favourite pop stars. I love my bedroom! In the kitchen I can eat pizza, cookies and pancakes all day. There are lots of flowers in the house. In the garden there is a swimming-pool. My friends often come and swim in the pool with me. That's lots of fun. Come and visit me!

h) Mögliche Lösung

In your dream house the walls have many colours. The house is very big. Your bedroom is big too. You have a computer and an ice cream machine there. In the kitchen you can eat pizza, cookies and pancakes all day. There are lots of flowers in your house and there's a swimming pool in the garden. You can swim there with your friends.

2.2

Methodisch-didaktischer Hinweis

Die Übung eignet sich für den Einsatz im Unterricht mit der Methode *Think-Pair-Share* (HRU-Seite 209). L sollte die Würdigung einzelner Beiträge aus **d)** in einer anschließenden *Share*-Plenumsphase einplanen.

a) / b)

	Me	Mia	Partner 1: Ayse	Partner 2: Lisa
On Mondays	I wake up at seven o'clock.	wakes up at quarter past six.	wakes up at quarter to seven.	wakes up at half past seven.
On Tuesdays	I have breakfast in the kitchen.	has breakfast in her bedroom/alone.	has breakfast with her family.	has breakfast at 7 o'clock.
On Wednesdays	I play with my dog.	plays computer games.	plays in her bedroom.	plays alone.
On Thursdays	I meet my best friend Timo.	meets her friend/Poppy.	meets her cousin.	meets her aunt and uncle.
On Fridays	I often have spaghetti for lunch.	often has pancakes for lunch.	often has fish for lunch.	often has a sandwich for lunch.
On Saturdays	I fall asleep late.	falls asleep at ten o'clock.	falls asleep at half past nine.	falls asleep at midnight.
On Sundays	I watch a game show on TV.	watches a film on TV.	watches the news on TV.	watches a thriller on TV.

b) Mögliche Lösung

You: On Mondays I wake up at 7.00 am. What about you?
Your partner: I wake up at 6.45. On Tuesdays I have breakfast with my family. What about you?
You: I have breakfast in the kitchen. On Wednesdays I play with my dog. What about you?
Your partner: I play in my bedroom. On Thursdays I meet my cousin. What about you?
You: I meet my best friend Timo. On Fridays I often have spaghetti for lunch. What about you?
Your partner: I often have fish for lunch. On Saturdays I falls asleep at half past nine. What about you?
You: I fall asleep late. On Sundays I watch a game show on TV. What about you?
Your partner: I watch the news on TV.

c) / d) Mögliche Lösung

On Mondays Ava wakes up at 6.45. On Tuesdays she has breakfast with her family. On Wednesdays she plays in her bedroom. On Thursdays she meets her cousin. On Fridays she often has fish for lunch. On Saturdays she falls asleep at half past nine. On Sundays she watches the news on TV.

2.2

a) – c) Lösung siehe

d) Mögliche Lösung

My mum's typical week

On Mondays my mum always gets up at 6.30 am. On Tuesdays she has breakfast with us, her family. On Wednesdays she does yoga. On Thursdays she works late. On Fridays she often has fish for lunch. On Saturdays she goes out with friends or with my dad. On Sundays she watches the news and *Tatort* on TV. What a week!

2.3

1 Methodisch-didaktischer Hinweis: Es handelt sich um ein selbstdifferenzierendes Aufgabenblatt mit individuellen Lösungen. Für einige der Aufgaben finden Sie unten mögliche Lösungen. Wichtig ist die Besprechung offener Fragen sowie die Würdigung einzelner Beiträge in einer Plenumsphase.

Mögliche Lösungen

a)

Hinweis: Die S kennen zu diesem Zeitpunkt der Wortschatzprogression aus *English G Access* folgende *family words* noch nicht: daughter, grandchild/-daughter/-son, husband, niece, nephew, son, wife. Es gibt nicht zu jedem Buchstaben ein *family word*.

Family Words		
English Spelling	**German Meaning**	**Example Sentence**
aunt	Tante	I like my aunt very much.
brother	Bruder	My brother is ten years old.
cousin	Cousine, Cousin	I have five cousins.
divorced	geschieden	My parents are divorced.
father	Vater	My father is a teacher.
grandmother/grandfather	Großmutter/Großvater	I love my grandmother's pancakes.
grandparents	Großeltern	My grandparents live in Berlin.
married	verheiratet	My sister is married.
mother	Mutter	My mother has black hair.
parents	Eltern	My parents are divorced.
single	ledig	My uncle Henry is single.
sister	Schwester	My sister is younger than me.
twins	Zwillinge	Luke and Leia are twins.
twin-sister/twin-brother	Zwillingsschwester/Zwillingsbruder	Luke is Leia's twin-brother and Leia is Luke's twin-sister.
uncle	Onkel	My uncle doesn't eat pizza.

b)

In my family there are five people: my mum Olga, my dad Alexander, my brother Dima, my grandmother and me. My name is Xenia. My grandmother lives in our house. She is seventy years old. My grandfather is dead. My brother is younger than me. He goes to kindergarten in the morning. Dima's

Lösungen Unit 2

favourite food is spaghetti. He likes ice-cream too. My mum is a teacher. She loves to sing. My dad's favourite pop band is AC/DC. He can't sing but he plays football at the weekend. We don't have a pet, but I love cats.

c) Individuelle Lösungen

d)

A: Do you know the Potter family?
B: Yes, I know all the books. The Potters are a very famous magical family.
A: Harry Potter is a famous wizard. He doesn't have any brothers or sisters. He's an only-child. Is that correct?
B: Yes, but his parents are dead. He's an orphan.
A: He lives in his aunt and uncle's house, right?
B: Yes, together with his cousin Dudley. They are all Muggles. He doesn't like them. He leaves them and goes to Hogwarts.
A: What do you know about Harry's parents?
B: His mum Lily was muggle-born, and his father James was a pure-blood wizard. So their son Harry is a half-blood wizard.
A: Does Harry have children in the end?
B: Yes, he has two sons and one daughter with his wife Ginny.
A: I think I will read the books too. They sound interesting.
B: Good idea.
A: See you. Bye.
B: Bye-bye.

e)

I like my grandmother. Her name is Elfi and she is sixty-one years old. She lives in a flat in the city centre. My grandmother and grandfather are divorced. My grandfather is nice too but I don't see him very often. He has a new wife. My grandmother has two cats and two budgies. She loves her pets!
I see my grandmother every week. We often play *Mensch ärgere Dich nicht* and *Mau-Mau* together. Sometimes I go to her flat after school and she makes lunch for me. My grandmother's soup is yummy. I always eat lots of soup when I visit her.

f) Individuelle Lösungen

g)

In my dream family, my parents don't work. They are always at home. They have lots of time for my sisters and me. We have lots of money and live in a big house. My grandparents live in our house too. My favourite aunt comes to our house every day and plays with us. We have a cook and everybody can eat what he or she likes. Sometimes the whole family goes on a holiday. We visit Disneyland together. We always have a lot of fun.

h) Individuelle Lösungen

Lösungen Unit 2

2.3

2 Methodisch-didaktischer Hinweis: Individualisierende Herangehensweise innerhalb des Kooperativen Lernens. Besprechung offener Fragen und Würdigung einzelner Beiträge in einer *Share*-Plenumsphase. Absicherung/Festigung durch das *Grammar file*.

3 Lösung

1 Barney likes cats. • 2 Barney doesn't eat carrots. • 3 Barney plays with other dogs. • 4 Barney sleeps in a basket. • 5 Barney doesn't like swimming. • 6 Barney jumps when he is happy.

4 Mögliche Lösung

A: Really? You like football?
B: That's right.
A: Really? You play the guitar?
B: That's not right. I play the violine.

2.3

2–3 Lösungen siehe

4 a) Mögliche Lösung

A: I like football. I normally go to football training on Mondays. What about you?
B: I don't like football, but I like playing the guitar. I have guitar lessons on Thursdays.
A: Do you like pizza? We normally have pizza on Fridays.
B: Yes, I like pizza! But my sister doesn't like it.
A: You can eat pizza at our house on Friday.
B: Thank you!

b) Mögliche Lösung

What I like and what I don't like at school
I like school! I like my friends here, and I like my teachers. I normally play with my friends in the breaks. What I don't like about school is our small school yard. We like football, but the school yard is too small. So we can't play football in the breaks.
I like all subjects, but I don't like Maths. We normally have Maths on Mondays, Tuesdays, Thursdays and Fridays. At home, I like my room. I always read there or play with my Nintendo after school. But I don't like homework!

2.3

2–3 Lösungen siehe

4a) – c) Individuelle Lösungen

Lösungen Unit 2

2.4

Hörtext, Track 12

Mia: Good morning.
Dad: Good morning, Mia.
Mum: Hi, love, how are you this morning?
Mia: Tired.
Dad: Do you have any tests at school today?
Mia: No. But I have a violin lesson in the afternoon.
Dad: A violin lesson? That sounds nice. I have a meeting at work – not so nice!
Mia: Do you have to go to work now too, Mum?
Mum: No, the library opens later today, so I'm free this morning.
Mia: That's nice … for you.
Dad: Mia, can you pass the cornflakes, please?
Mia: Here you are.
Dad: Thank you. And the milk too, please.
Mia: Oh, right.
Dad: Thanks.
Mum: Would you like some tea, Mia?
Mia: Yes, please.
Mum: And what would you like to eat?
Mia: Nothing, thanks. Just tea for me.
Mum: What? Only tea? You need food to learn, Mia.
Dad: Have some cornflakes.
Mia: Cornflakes are for little kids.
Dad: For little kids? Really?
Mia: That's right.
Dad: Hmm …
Mum: You only have five minutes, Mia. What would you like to eat?
Mia: I'm really not hungry, Mum.
Mum: But you have to eat something.
Mia: Are there any scones?
Mum: No, I'm sorry, there aren't any more. Can I give you some toast and jam?
Mia: Hmm … no, thanks
Mum: Some yoghurt, then?
Mia: You know I don't like yoghurt, Mum.
Mum: Oh, of course.
Mia: Can I have some fruit salad?
Mum: Sorry, love, we don't have any fruit salad.
Mia: All right, just some fruit then.
Mum: Would you like a banana or an apple?
Mia: Oh, I don't know … a banana.
Mum: Here you are.
Mia: Thanks.
Mum: Would you like a sandwich for school?
Mia: No, that's too big.
Mum: Then just take a slice of bread with cheese.
Mia: Oh, all right.

Lösungen Unit 2

Mum: You can take some biscuits too.
Dad: What's for dinner this evening?
Mum: Well, what would you like: meat or fish?
Mia: I'd like spaghetti.
Mum: Not again! But I can make yummy roast beef with potatoes. What do you think?
Mia: Not so yummy.
Mum: Or a nice vegetable soup and a green salad?
Dad: Not today, thanks. Let's have pizza.
Mum: Okay, then you can make it!
Mia: Or go to the pizzeria …
Dad: Good idea!
Mum: I think I have two kids here!
Dad: That's right! More cornflakes, please!
Mum: So, no roast beef and potatoes for you – you want *fast* food!
Dad: Mmm, yes! And cake and ice cream for dessert.
Mia: Uh-oh, I'm late! Bye!
Dad: Bye, Mia. Have a nice day at school!
Mum: Bye-bye, love. Now wait, Mia, your banana! It's here on the table …

1
1a) • 2b) • 3b) • 4c) • 5c) • 6c)

2
(1) (vegetable) pizza • (2) (peanut butter & jam) sandwich • (3) (chocolate-banana) milkshake

2.4

1 Hörtext, Track 12 siehe
(1) tired • (2) violin lesson • (3) tea • (4) scones • (5) pizza • (6) banana

2 Lösung siehe

2.4

1a) Hörtext, Track 12 siehe

Mögliche Lösung
We can hear Mia and her parents. They talk. The family has breakfast together. They talk about food and what they have for breakfast and dinner. In the end Mia leaves for school and forgets her banana on the breakfast table.

b) Mögliche Lösung
Mia doesn't want anything for breakfast. She just wants some tea.
But her mother thinks Mia needs food to learn.

Lösungen Unit 2

c) Mögliche Lösung
Mia's mother says that because Mia and her father both want fast food/pizza for dinner.

d) Mögliche Lösung
I (don't) think this is a realistic conversation because there's so much food on the table / there's lots of healthy food / Mia's mum wants Mia to eat / Mia's mother is not angry / the family has lots of time in the morning / Mia's father wants pizza / Mia can say what she wants for dinner / the whole family is together / nobody is in a hurry / healthy food is important / there is no *Schwarzbrot* on the table … .

2a) / b)
Pizza
Use ready-made dough and put some tomato sauce on it.
Put mixed vegetables on the sauce.
Top with cheese.
Bake at 225 degrees for 20 to 25 minutes.

Sandwich
Take one piece of bread and put peanut butter on it.
Put jam on the other piece of bread.
Put the pieces of bread together.

Milkshake
Cut two bananas into pieces and put them into a blender.
Add two spoons of chocolate spread and one cup of cold milk.
Now add two scoops of vanilla ice-cream.
Blend until the drink is frothy.

2.4

3 Methodisch-didaktischer Hinweis: Lösungen auf dem Arbeitsblatt; Partnerkontrolle. Schwerpunktmäßige Verwendung des Vokabulars aus der Unit; Differenzierung durch Einbeziehen bzw. Außerachtlassen von More help.

2.5

1 Methodisch-didaktischer Hinweis: Die S aller Levels erhalten denselben Text, gekennzeichnet durch das ▯-Symbol. Die Aufgabenblätter sind jedoch auf drei Levels konzipiert. An die das Textverständnis sichernden Aufgaben **1–3** schließt sich der selbstdifferenzierende Aufgabenbereich **4** an, aus dem die S nach Neigung drei bis fünf Transferaufgaben auswählen. Die möglichen Lösungen unten dienen hier nur zur Orientierung, es sind gemäß des Leistungsstandes der S unterschiedliche Ergebnisse möglich.

Einige der Aufgaben in **4** wurden für Level ▮ angepasst, mögliche Lösungen siehe 2.5 ▮.

Lösungen Unit 2

2.5

2

Right	Wrong
Little Al is unhappy because Pirate Sid is late.	
(one ship)	Before the sun goes down, Al sees two ships.
Al makes a bonfire and goes home.	
The next morning Al's father's pirate ship is not there.	
(The captain and his men help her.)	For three days Al is alone when she makes a bonfire.
(a chest of gold)	Pirate Sid and Captain Cooper fight for a bag of gold.
Pirate Sid and Captain Cooper make friends and shake hands.	
(for Al's father, his men and little Al)	There is a party, but only for Al's father and his men.
With the gold coins they build a lighthouse in Plymouth.	
The story isn't real, or maybe it is … ☺	

3
1 Father is late • 2 A big ship • 3 The fight • 4 New friends • 5 A present

4 Mögliche Lösungen
a) Pirates and friends • A lighthouse for Plymouth • A good pirate story

b) unhappy, beach, pirate, sky, cloudy, (to) hope, bonfire, (to) get dark, storm, (to) be excited, beautiful, (to) save sb., gold coins, (to) be afraid, (to) be in trouble, loud sounds, together, a chest of gold, (to) go between, (to) understand, (to) attack, (to) sail, (to) shake hands, (to) smile from ear to ear, everyone, ready, in front of, (to) build, lighthouse, very, (to) dance, (to) leave

c) unhappy, (to) hope, (to) be excited, (to) be afraid, (to) be in trouble, surprised, happy

d)

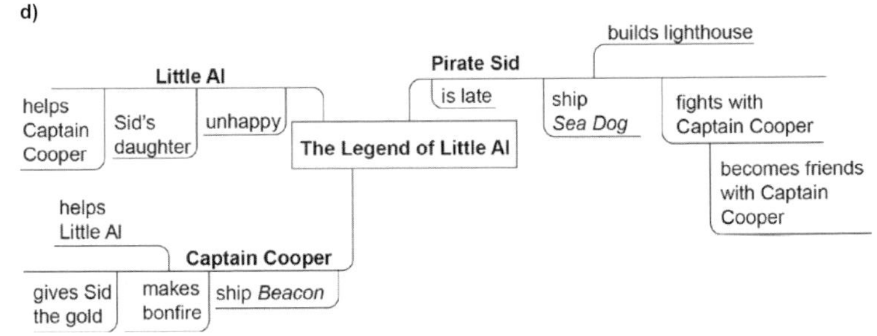

e) / g) Individuelle Lösungen

f)
Little Al: Sid's daughter, unhappy, helps Captain Cooper, makes bonfires, stops the pirates' fight, gives the chest of gold to the captain, …

h)
The next day, Little Al says, she doesn't want to sail to London with Pirate Sid and Captain Cooper: "I say good-bye, Captain! I don't like sailing ships. I can stay here with my friends and make plans for the lighthouse." The captain is very sorry, but he says: "OK, my little friend! I can sail with your father. Please send me a postcard of the lighthouse!"

2.5

2

Right	Wrong
Little Al is sad because her father is late.	
(before the sun goes down)	When it gets dark Al sees a ship.
(the bonfire burns into the night)	The storm blows out the bonfire.
Cooper is the captain of the *Beacon*.	
(Sid and his pirates take a chest of gold from the *Beacon*)	Captain Cooper steals a chest of gold from Sid and his pirates.
The *Sea Dog's* captain wants to help Captain Cooper on their way to London.	
There's a party.	
The lighthouse can make Plymouth rich.	
(in front of the Beacon)	The *Sea Dog* is behind the *Beacon*.
The story isn't real. Or maybe it is … ☺	

3 Lösung siehe

4 Mögliche Lösung siehe

2.5

2

Right	Wrong	Not in the text
Little Al is worried because she can't see her father's ship.		
When Al sees a ship, she thinks it's her father's and she tries to give him a sign that shows him where Plymouth is.		
(He thanks her.)	The *Beacon's* captain doesn't know that it was Al's bonfire.	
		The *Sea Dog* isn't in Plymouth because of the storm.

	Al's father is very surprised that his daughter and the *Beacon's* captain are friends.	
		London is the *Beacon*'s home harbour.
(for Captain Cooper and his men)	Sid wants to give a party because he is so proud (stolz) of his little daughter.	
They build a lighthouse because it helps the ships to find Plymouth, like the bonfires.		
		Captain Cooper wants to come back to Plymouth.
The story isn't real. Or maybe it is … ☺		

3 Mögliche Lösung
The fight • A present • New friends • A big ship • Father is late

4

a) Lösung siehe

b) Mögliche Lösung
Mögliche Sätze: The bonfire burns into the night. / Its sails are torn from the storm. / You saved us from the storm. / I'm afraid he's in trouble. / Al goes out to the ships. / Al's boat goes between the two ships. / I want to help you now. What can I do? / Can you sail to London with us? / This is a present for you.

c) / d) Lösung siehe

e) Individuelle Lösungen

f) Mögliche Lösung

Little Al	Pirate Sid
unhappy, worried (father is late)	
excited (sees ship)	
surprised (about the gold coins)	
afraid, sad (father is still at sea)	
worried (Sid and Cooper fight)	surprised (Al is angry at the fight)
angry (Sid has Captain Cooper's gold)	
happy (to have her father back)	sorry (wrong to fight Cooper)
	happy (to sail with Cooper to London and help against other pirates)
	excited (about the party)
	happy (about the gold for the lighthouse)

Lösungen Unit 2

g) Mögliche Lösung

Al: Let's have lots of good food at the party! And drinks!
Sid: Yes, and cake! Lots of cake! Ah! Here are Captain Cooper and his men. Wow, they have a big chest!
Captain Cooper: This is a present for you.
Al opens the chest with the gold coins. Al and Sid are surprised.
Sid: Thank you! But this gold is not only for Al and me. It's for all of Plymouth! Let's build a great lighthouse so ships at sea can find our good harbour. Let's bring lots of ships here and make Plymouth a great city!
Captain Cooper: That's a great idea! Very good!
Everybody looks happy.
Al: Let's eat!
Sid: Yes, let's eat, my friends!

h) Mögliche Lösung siehe

2.6

a) Hörtexttranskripte 13 und 14 siehe Arbeitsblatt 2.6

b) Silky the Seal

Snake sounds [s]	Bee sounds [z]	Special bee sounds [ɪz]
wakes, jumps, tricks, counts, boats, lots (2x), eats, makes	does, whales, swims, seagulls, finds, friends, plays, has, crabs, sees, goes (2x), dives, comes	watches, chases, catches,

A riddle

Snake sounds [s]	Bee sounds [z]	Special bee sounds [ɪz]
rocks, thinks (2x), docks, waits, puts, across, tastes	runs, he's (2x), his (2x), goes, wears, shows, claws, says, gives	dances, catches

c) – f) Individuelle Lösungen

2.7

Hörtext, Track 15

1 you – soup – <u>book</u> – shoe
2 glue – zoo – food – <u>go</u>
3 pool – group – <u>double</u> – who
4 fruit – <u>touch</u> – Lucy – do
5 <u>look</u> – two (too) – Tuesday – blue
6 school – <u>door</u> – room – new
7 uniform – student – afternoon – <u>but</u>

b) / c) Individuelle Lösungen

Lösungen Unit 2

2.8

a) Hörtext, Track 16

Here is Lucy's cupboard. Here is Lucy's bed. Here is the dog's basket. Here is mum's paper. Here are Jack's trophies. Here is the Bakers' TV. Here is the Bakers' toilet. Here is Jack's uniform. Here is the Bakers' dining room. Here is Jack's bedroom. Here is Lucy's clock. Here are mum's books. Here is the Bakers' bathroom. Here is dad's watch. Here is Jack's desk. Here is the Bakers' kitchen. Here is the dog's ball. Here is the Bakers' garden.

b)

(1) Lucy's • (2) Lucy's • (3) the dog's • (4) mum's • (5) Jack's (6) the Bakers' • (7) the Bakers' • (8) Jack's • (9) the Bakers' • (10) Jack's • (11) Lucy's • (12) mum's • (13) the Bakers' • (14) dad's • (15) Jack's • (16) the Bakers' • (17) the dog's • (18) the Bakers'

2.8

a) / b) Hörtext , Track 16 und **Lösung** siehe

c) Mögliche Lösung

This is Lucy's brother. This is Jack's sister. These are Mr and Mrs Baker's children. This is Lucy's/Jack's/Mr and Mrs Baker's bedroom. …

2.8

a) Hörtext, Track 16 siehe

b) Lösung siehe **c)**

c) siehe TIP auf dem Arbeitsblatt

2.9

1 (1) animals • (2) people • (3) food • (4) adjectives • (5) classroom phrases • (6) around the year • (7) Plymouth

2 Individuelle Lösungen

Lösungen Unit 3

3.1

1 Hörtext, Track 17

Philip: Hi, Mia!
Mia: Hi, Philip! How are you?
Philip: I'm fine, thanks. What about you? Do you want to choose a new club?
Mia: I'm fine, but … yes, I really want to join a new club, but I don't know which one. I'm in a music club and the book club. But I want to join a sport club too. Do you know a good one?
Philip: We have great sport clubs at school. What about our hockey club? I love hockey and I usually go on Wednesdays. It's outside and the other kids are nice. There are nice girls in our team too.
Mia: Hockey … mh … I don't know, hockey isn't really my cup of tea.
Philip: Oh, come on. It's great! The players are fun and you can run a lot.
Mia: But the hockey club meets on Wednesdays right after lunchtime, doesn't it?
Philip: Yeah, it does. It starts at 2 pm.
Mia: Well, I often can't run after lunch. Sorry.
Philip: Okay, what about cricket? Emma goes to the cricket club too.
Mia: That sounds good, but the cricket club meets on Mondays. On Mondays I play the violin in the orchestra. Music club, you know.
Philip: Ah, right! That's a nice club. Mh … What about judo then?
Mia: I know Chen, who goes to the judo club on Tuesdays. He says it's a great club, but I want to choose a club that meets outside.
Philip: Well, do you like football? You could join the girls' team. They usually play on Thursdays, I think.
Mia: Yeah, that sounds good. I'm free on Thursdays and I like football a lot. But … well …
Philip: What's the problem?
Mia: You know … I have two left feet.
Philip: Well, how are your hands? I mean, it's never bad to have another goalkeeper in the team.
Mia: Right, that's me – the new star goalkeeper!
Philip: Exactly! Just try it! I know some girls in that club. They're all really nice and you can always make new friends.
Mia: Does Poppy play in that team, too? I know she plays football.
Philip: Yeah, Poppy is in the club too.
Mia: OK, it's football on Thursdays for me then! Thanks, Philip. You're always a great help.
Philip: No problem! That's what friends are for, right?

a) / b) Lösung

cricket club	hockey club	football club	judo club	music club
2	1	5	4	3

c) 1: right • 2: right • 3: wrong • 4: wrong • 5: right • 6: right
d) b) und c) sind richtig

Lösungen Unit 3

2
1a) • 2b) • 3c) • 4b) • 5c) • 6a) • 7c)

3a) Mögliche Lösung

Penny Pencil: Does Poppy go to the hockey club?
You: No, she doesn't. But she goes to the football club.
Penny Pencil: And does she go to the music club?
You: Yes, she does.
Penny Pencil: Does Chen go to the book club?
You: No, he doesn't. But he goes to the hockey club.
Penny Pencil: Does he go to the judo club?
You: Yes, he does.

b) Mögliche Lösung
We have a volleyball club at our school. They play volleyball in teams. They meet on Wednesday in the gym. We have a music club too. They learn songs and they play instruments. The club meets on Tuesday in the music room.

4 Mögliche Lösung
A: Do you like football?
B: Yes, I do. Do you play tennis?
A: No, I don't. Do you play the piano?
B: Yes, I do. Do you go sailing?
A: Yes, I do. Do you do kung fu?
B: No, I don't.

3.1

1a) Hörtext, Track 17 und **Lösung** siehe

b) Mögliche Lösung
(1) Mia plays the violin in the music club. (2) Philip goes to the hockey club. (3) Emma goes to the cricket club. (4) Chen goes to the judo club. (5) Poppy goes to the football club.

c) 1 Mia • 2 Wednesday • 3 Monday • 4 music club • 5 judo club

d) Mia wants to join the girls' football club because Poppy is in the girls' team too.

2
1a) • 2b) • 3c) • 4b) • 5c) • 6a) • 7c) • 8c)

3a) / b) Mögliche Lösung siehe

Lösungen Unit 3

4 Mögliche Lösung
A: Do you like football?
B: Yes, I do. I play football every Monday. Do you play tennis?
A: No, I don't. I never play tennis. Do you play the piano?
B: Yes, I do. I play the piano on Thursday. Do you go sailing?
A: Yes, I do. I go sailing on Saturday. Do you do kung fu?
B: No, I don't. I never do kung fu. Do you like chess?
A: Yes, I do. I play chess with my grandfather. Do you like chess?
B: No, I don't like chess.

3.1

1 Hörtext, Track 17 siehe

a) 2: Philip • 3: Emma • 4: Mia • 5: Chen • 6: Poppy

b) 1: right • 2: wrong • 3: right • 4: wrong • 5: right • 6: wrong
corrections: 2: He usually plays on Wednesday. • 4: The hockey club starts Wednesday at 2 pm. • 6: Poppy plays football in the girls' team too.

c) Mia wants to join the football club because Poppy is in the team too.

2 1c) • 2a) • 3b) • 4c) • 5b) • 6a)

3 Mögliche Lösung siehe

4 Mögliche Lösung
A: Do you like football?
B: Yes, I do. I play football every Monday. Do you play the violin?
A: No, I don't. I never play the violin. Do you read Harry Potter?
B: Yes, I do. I like Harry Potter. Do you like apples?
A: Yes, I like apples. Do you have a dog?
B: No, I don't have a dog. I don't like dogs.

3.2

1a)
Chen and Philip have to do their homework. • Poppy and Mia have to go shopping on Thursday. • Sophie has to clean her room. • Poppy has to go for a walk with her dog, Barney. • Sophie has to visit her grandparents on Sunday.

Lösungen Unit 3

b) Mögliche Lösung
I have to visit my aunt and uncle on Saturday. I have to go shopping on Tuesday. I have to clean my room on Friday.

2
Dear fairy,
Thank you for your email.
I want to go dancing with you but I can't go on Tuesday because I have to clean the child's room.
I don't have time on Thursday because I have to clean all the windows.
I can't go dancing on Friday because I have to make dinner for my family.
But what about Sunday?
Do you have time on Sunday?
Love,
your friend, the house elf

3.2

1 Mögliche Lösung
(1) … we have to clean the car.
(2) … we have to feed the frogs.
(3) … he has to work in the garden.

2 Mögliche Lösung siehe

3.2

1 Mögliche Lösung siehe

2 Mögliche Lösung siehe

3.3

Mögliche Lösung
A: I never go swimming. What about you?
B: I sometimes go swimming. But I never play football.
A: I often play football. What about you?
B: I always listen to music.
A: I always listen to music too and I usually do my homework. What about you?
B: I always do my homework.
A: I always read comics. What about you?
B: I sometimes read comics.

Lösungen Unit 3

3.3

Mögliche Lösung

A: I never go swimming. What about you?
B: I sometimes go swimming. But I never play football.
A: I often play football and I usually do my homework. What about you?
B: I always do my homework.
A: I always read comics. What about you?
B: I sometimes read comics and I often eat pizza.
A: I often eat pizza too.

3.3

Mögliche Lösung

A: I never go swimming. What about you?
B: I sometimes go swimming. But I never play football.
A: I often play football and I often listen to music. What about you?
B: I often listen to music too.
A: I always read comics. What about you?
B: I sometimes read comics and I often eat pizza.
A: I often eat pizza too.
B: I often do my homework. What about you?
A: I always do my homework and I usually play hockey on Wednesday. What about you?
B: I never play hockey.

3.4

1a) Hörtext, Track 18

Golo: Welcome back to Radio PLYM, the radio station for Plymstock and beyond. I'm Golo Gadget and here with me are Anne Parker and Dave Brubeck to tell us about their favourite clubs at Plymstock School.
Anne, Dave, welcome to the show. This summer you joined a new club. Tell us about it.
Anne: Hi, everyone, I'm Anne. I'm here to tell you about the Book Club. I love reading good books, and in the Book Club you can meet other people who love books too.
Dave: Yeah, I'm also in the Book Club and I'm in two sport clubs too, but reading books is a good way to relax. When you read a book, you can hop right into the story. You're in a new time and place, you meet animals that can talk, and you can have great adventures. It's really great! In the book club we read, talk about new books and have extra activities around books too. Oh, and I'm Dave by the way.

Lösung: Club B, the book club

b) Hörtext, Track 19

Golo: The Book Club sounds interesting. Tell me more about it.
Anne: Well, we have a special room for the Book Club with sofas. You can drink tea and eat biscuits and fruit there any time. It's a really nice room – a great place to enjoy reading.
Dave: You usually read on your own, but we often have a book talk where we talk about the books we read. There are always books that sound interesting and sometimes there are boring books too. For example, I don't like romantic stories.
Anne: Well, but I do! There are usually four or five people and everyone talks about the book they read. So we talk about adventure stories, crime stories, animal stories, and … yes … sometimes romantic stories.
Dave: You usually get good ideas about what to read next. And what you don't have to read …

Lösung: 1c) • 2b) • 3a) • 4c)

c) Hörtext, Track 20

Golo: You do extra activities around books too. What do you do?
Dave: That's always fun! We choose children's books we like and go to the kindergarten. We usually read to the kindergarten children for one hour and they love it. They're always so happy. And they're funny too.
Anne: Yeah, they often have funny questions about the book. They want to know where the bear lives and why the elephant can fly in the story.
Dave: We also have book nights that lots of pupils always come to. We usually meet at the Book Club at school, or sometimes somewhere outside the school, and read to the people from really funny or scary books. That's really great and people love it.
Golo: So I hope that lots of students want to join your club now to find good new books. I love reading too. When I read a good book, I often forget where I am and what time it is. So, tell us: When do you meet?
Anne: We almost always meet on Fridays from 2 to 4 pm at the Book Club.
Dave: … or in the school garden when it's sunny and warm.
Golo: That sounds so good. Too bad I'm on air every Friday afternoon.
Anne: Well, the club is for students anyway.
Golo: I know, but can you say no to a good book? I have books at home that say READ ME AGAIN AND AGAIN!!! But I need new ideas too. A book club is perfect!
Dave: Yeah, it really is. But we don't always read new books. We sometimes read older ones too …

	Right	Wrong
We usually read to the kindergarten children.	X	
They sometimes have funny questions about the book.		X
We also have book nights where lots of pupils always come to.	X	
We usually meet every Friday from 2 to 4 pm in the book club …	X	
… or in Anne's garden when it's sunny and warm.		X

2a) 1B • 2C • 3D • 4A

b)
name: Walli
age: 87 years
best in: tennis
favourite sport: football
sport I like: table tennis and judo
sport I don't like: swimming

Lösungen Unit 3

3.4

1a) Hörtext, Track 18 siehe
Lösung: 1 ~~photo~~, book • 2 ~~three~~, two • 3 ~~aliens~~, animals • 4 ~~boats~~, books

b) Hörtext, Track 19 siehe
Lösung: 1b) • 2a) • 3c) • 4a) • 5c)

c) Hörtext, Track 20 siehe
Lösung: 2

2a) 1 ears • 2 basketball • 3 Go • play
1B • 2C • 3D • 4A

b)
name: Walli
age: 87 years
best in: tennis
favourite sport: football
sport I like: table tennis and judo
sport I don't like: swimming, dancing

3.4

a) Hörtext, Track 18 siehe
Lösung: Golo: 1, 3 • Anne: 5 • Dave: 4, 2

b) Hörtext, Track 19 siehe
Lösung: 1 ~~bananas~~, biscuits • 2 ~~never~~, often • 3 ~~watch~~, like • 4 ~~three~~, four • 5 ~~eat~~, read

c) Hörtext, Track 20 siehe
Lösung: 1 • 3

2a)
1 Train your ears with Joe.
2 Play basketball with Oscar.
3 Go swimming with Mando.
4 Try to win against Ivy: Play hockey in the sand.
1B • 2C • 3D • 4A

Lösungen Unit 3

b)
name: Walli
age: 87 years
best in: tennis, basketball
favourite sport: football
sport I like: table tennis, kung fu and judo
sport I don't like: swimming, dancing

3.5

1
(2) What • (3) What • (4) Do • (5) Do • (6) Why • (7) Where • (8) when • (9) Do • (10) What • (11) What

2 Mögliche Lösung
Why does the frog go for a walk with the dog?
Does she do gymnastics?
When do we go dancing?
Where do I do judo?
Does Mr Donald make breakfast?
Where does your friend go for a walk with the dog?
Why do you do gardening?
When does Walli help in the kitchen?

3.5

1
(1) What sport do you like?
(2) What about you?
(3) Do you play tennis in a club?
(4) Do you like dancing, Lizzie?
(5) Why do you like dancing?
(6) Are you in a dancing club?
(7) Where is the dancing club?
(8) When does it meet?
(9) Do you have other hobbies too?
(10) What are your other hobbies?
(11) What do you usually read?

2 Mögliche Lösung
A: Does the frog go sailing?
B: No, he doesn't. He helps in the kitchen. When do we go surfing?
A: We go surfing on Saturday. Why do you play the guitar?
B: I play the guitar because I like music. Where does Walli do gymnastics?
A: He does gymnastics in the gym. Why does Mr Donald make breakfast?
B: He makes breakfast because he likes breakfast. When does he listen to music?
A: He listens to music in the evening. Does your friend play the guitar?
B: No, she doesn't. She plays the piano.

3.5

1a) Mögliche Lösung

Questions	Answers
What's your favourite colour?	My favourite colour is yellow.
Do you like pink?	No, I **hate** pink!
Where do you live?	I live in Bonn.
When do you go to sleep?	I usually go to sleep at nine o'clock.
What do you do at the weekend?	I often play football at the weekend.
Why do you read books?	I read books because I like ghost stories.
Where do you go to school?	I go to school in Mannheim.
When do you go home?	I usually go home at four o'clock.
Why do you have to go shopping?	I have to go shopping because I need a new ruler.
When do you get angry?	I often get angry when I can't sleep.

b) Mögliche Lösung

Question	Answer
Why do you go to school?	
Where do you have your lunch?	
What are your favourite animals?	
	Yes, I like music.
	Silky is a seal.
	My birthday is in June.

2 Mögliche Lösung

A: Does Walli clean Pfiffi's room?
B: No, he doesn't. He does judo. Why does the house elves go sailing?
A: He goes sailing because he wants to join a sport club. Why do you play the guitar?
B: I play the guitar because I like music. Where does the frog do gymnastics?
A: He does gymnastics in the gym. Why does Mr Donald make breakfast?
B: He makes breakfast because he likes breakfast. When does he do gardening?
A: He does gardening in the evening. Does your friend go for a walk with the dog?
B: No, she doesn't. She plays the piano.

3.6

a) Mögliche Lösung

(1) I often sit on a tree.
(2) I never eat with my fingers.
(3) I always drink water.
(4) I never sleep at seven o'clock in the evening.
(5) I sometimes eat ice cream.
(6) I usually go to school by bike.

b) Mögliche Lösung

Lisa never flies to the moon on Sundays. She often sits on a tree. She never eats with her fingers. Lisa always drinks water. She never sleeps at seven o'clock in the evening. She sometimes eats ice cream. Lisa usually goes to school by bike.

3.6

a) Mögliche Lösung

(1) I often sit on a tree.
(2) I never eat with my fingers.
(3) I always drink water.
(4) I never do my homework at four o'clock in the morning.
(5) I never go to bed at seven o'clock in the evening.
(6) I often eat roast beef, I never eat scones but I always eat cake.
(7) I often eat ice cream.
(8) I sometimes play basketball and I never do gymnastics.
(9) I sometimes do sport at school.
(10) I usually go to school by bike.

b) Mögliche Lösung

Lisa never flies to the moon on Sunday. She often sits on a tree. She never eats with her fingers. Lisa always drinks water. She never does her homework at four o'clock in the morning. She never goes to bed at seven o'clock in the evening. Lisa often eats roast beef, never eats scones but she always eats cake. She often eats ice cream. She sometimes plays basketball and never does gymnastics. She sometimes does sport at school. Lisa usually goes to school by bike.

3.6

a) / b) Mögliche Lösung siehe

3.7

a)

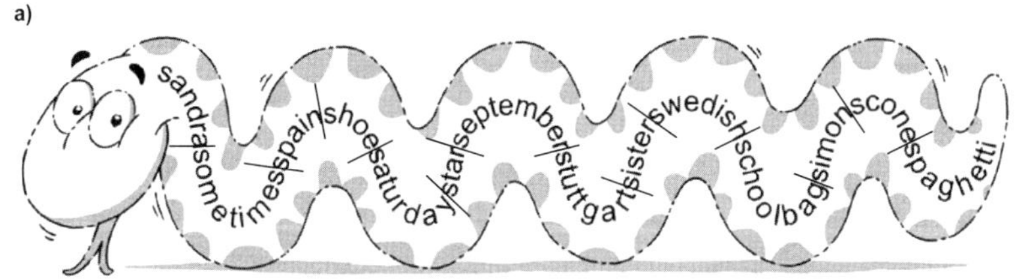

Lösungen Unit 3

b)

small letter	CAPITAL LETTER	Why do you use a capital letter?
	Sandra	name
sometimes		
	Spain	country
shoes		
	Saturday	day
stars		
	September	month
	Stuttgart	city
sister		
	Swedish	city adjective
schoolbag		
	Simon	name
scone		
spaghetti		

3.7

a) 1 England • 2 Saturday • 3 Penny Pencil • 4 a funny monkey • 5 American hamburger • 6 Sophie • 7 Smeaton's Tower • 8 a great castle

b)

	Which word do you write with a capital letter?	Why do you write a capital letter?
englaNd	England	country
saTuRDaY	Saturday	day
peNNy penCil	Penny Pencil	name
amErIcan hAMburgeR	American	country adjective
sMeatOn's toWer	Smeaton's Tower	name
sOPhIe	Sophie	name

3.7

a) Lösung siehe

b) Lösung siehe

c) Individuelle Lösungen

Lösungen Unit 3

3.8

1

wall	for
your	sport
door	small
four	horse

2 1 mouse • 2 hour • 3 shower • 4 sometimes

3 1 talk • 2 ball • 3 door

3.8

1 Lösung siehe

2a) Lösung siehe

b) Mögliche Lösung
small • water • room

3 Lösung siehe

3.8

1 Lösung siehe

2a) Lösung siehe

b) Mögliche Lösung
small • water • room
sport • talk • soup

3 Lösung
1 walk – talk
2 tall – ball – fall
3 floor – door – four – more

3.9

1 Mögliche Lösung
Opa: Worum geht es denn bei der Ausstellung?
Du: Es geht um die Geschichte von Plymouth Harbour.

Lösungen Unit 3

Opa: Was macht denn Plymouth Harbour so besonders?
Du: Von hier aus sind wichtige Seereisen gestartet, die Pilgrim Fathers sind z. B. im Jahre 1620 nach Amerika gesegelt.
Oma: Ist die Ausstellung das ganze Jahr geöffnet?
Du: Ja, aber von April bis Oktober haben sie montags bis samstags geöffnet, von November bis März nur von montags bis freitags.
Opa: Wir haben ja unsere kleine Carla dabei. Gibt es so etwas wie ein Familienticket?
Du: Ja, zwei Erwachsene und bis zu drei Kindern kosten £5.

2a) Mögliche Lösung
Mia: Hi, Poppy. Good to see you. How are you?
Poppy: Hi, Mia. Good, thanks. What do we want to do this afternoon?
Mia: I have no idea. But, hey, wait a minute. Look at that flyer from the Plymouth Mayflower Exhibition. Maybe we can go there?
Poppy: What is the exhibition about?
Mia: It's about the history of the harbour. I know that many ships started their tours around the world from the harbour. The Mayflower with the Pilgrim Fathers for example.
Poppy: How much is it?
Mia: It's two pounds.
Poppy: OK, sounds good. When can we go there?
Mia: We can go there now! Oh no, sorry we can't. It's half past four already. Let's go there tomorrow.

3.9

1 Mögliche Lösung
Opa: Worum geht es denn bei der Ausstellung?
Du: Es geht um die Geschichte von Plymouth Harbour.
Opa: Was macht denn Plymouth Harbour so besonders?
Du: Von hier aus sind wichtige Seereisen gestartet, z. B. sind die Pilgrim Fathers von hier aus nach Amerika gesegelt.
Oma: Und was können wir in der Ausstellung tun?
Du: Wir können Geschichten über einige reiche Familie aus Plymouth lesen; es gibt Informationen über die Fischindustrie und den Militärhafen, und es werden Geschichten, Fotos und Dokumente gezeigt.
Opa: Ist die Ausstellung das ganze Jahr geöffnet?
Du: Ja, aber von April bis Oktober haben sie montags bis samstags geöffnet, von November bis März nur von montags bis freitags.
Opa: Wir haben ja Carla dabei. Gibt es so etwas wie ein Familienticket?
Du: Ja, zwei Erwachsene und bis zu drei Kindern kosten £5.

2a) Mögliche Lösung
Mia: Hi, Poppy. Good to see you. How are you?
Poppy: Hi, Mia. Good, thanks. What do we want to do this afternoon?
Mia: I have no idea. But, hey, wait a minute. Look at that flyer from the Plymouth Mayflower Exhibition. Maybe we can go there?
Poppy: What is the exhibition about?
Mia: It's about the history of the harbour.

Lösungen Unit 3

Poppy: Why is it special?
Mia: Plymouth Harbour is special because from here, many ships started their trips. The Pilgrim Fathers went on their way to America from here.
Poppy: I don't have much money. How much is a ticket?
Mia: It's one pound.
Poppy: OK, that sounds good. It's half past four now. Can we go there now?
Mia: No, we can't go there now. They close at five.
Poppy: OK, then let's go there tomorrow. Maybe we can go and meet the others at the Barbican now.
Mia: OK, good idea.

3.9

1 Lösung siehe

2a) Mögliche Lösung siehe

3.10

a) table

activity	basketball	piano class	art class
day	Tuesday	Wednesday	Friday afternoon
place	in the gym	at home	at school
what Penny needs	ball	piano	pens

activity	dancing class	singing class	reading club
day	Monday	every day	Saturday
place	school	music school	library
what Lizzie needs	dancing shoes	voice	books

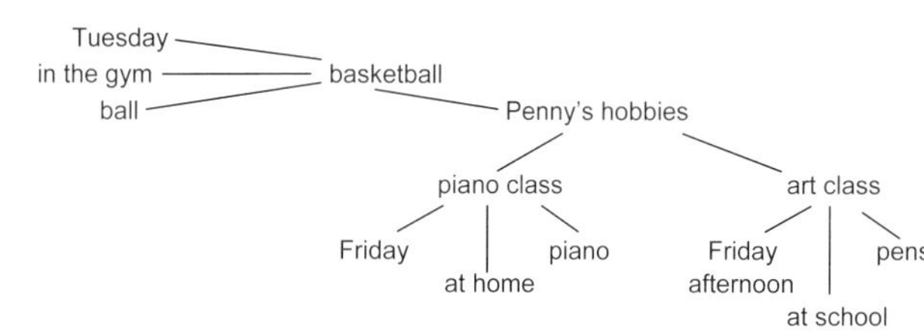

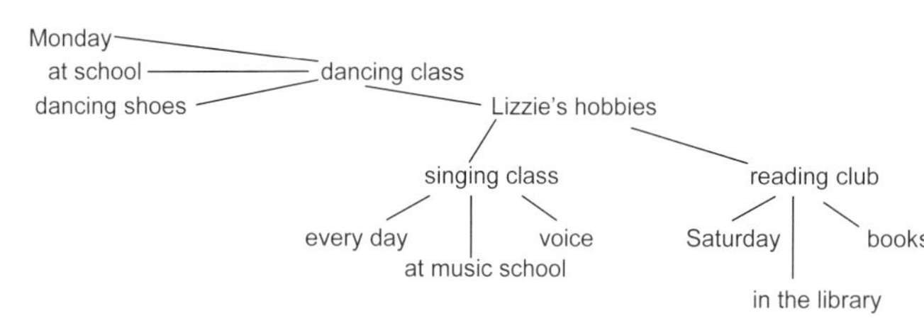

Lösungen Unit 3

b) Mögliche Lösung

Penny Pencil:

Hi there, I'm Penny Pencil. Let me tell you about my favourite hobbies. I play basketball on Tuesday in the gym. I need a ball. I have my piano class on Wednesday at home. I need a piano, of course. I have my art class on Friday afternoon at school. I need my pens.

Busy Lizzie:

Hi there, I'm Busy Lizzie. Let me tell you about my favourite hobbies. I go to dancing class at school on Monday. I need my dancing shoes. Every day I have my singing class at our music school. I need my voice, of course. And I go to the reading club in the library every Saturday. I need books for this club.

Lösungen Unit 4

4.1

1b) Bild 1: Ella's mum • Bild 2: Ella's grandpa • Bild 3: Ella's grandma • Bild 4: Ella's dad • Bild 5: Ella

2) Hörtext, Track 21

Ella: Hi, Jenny, nice to see you today. What did you do at the weekend? Where were you on Saturday?
Jenny: Hi Ella. I was at the cinema. But this time my two brothers weren't there. They were sad and I was happy.
Ella: Why weren't they there?
Jenny: They were ill. But they are OK now.
Ella: Was the film good?
Jenny: Yes, it was. It was really scary. My favourite actor was the ghost in the film. Where were you on Saturday, Ella? Were you at the shopping mall?
Ella: No, I wasn't. I was at home in my bedroom!
Jenny: Oh. Wasn't that boring?
Ella: No, it wasn't. My dad was in the garage working on the car. He is always in the garage at the weekend. My mum was in the garden. She likes trees and flowers.
Jenny: And your granny and grandpa, where were they?
Ella: My granny and grandpa were in the attic with their old books, my sister was at a museum for her school project and me, I was happy! Nobody was in the house. They were all away and I could do what I wanted!
Jenny: That's exciting. What did you do?
Ella: I was on Skype for six hours and then I checked the kitchen for some food. There was some cake in the fridge!
Jenny: Oh, Ella.

Lösung: 1a) • 2b) • 3c) • 4a) • 5c) • 6b)

3a) Mögliche Lösung

Sophie: Were you at the beach on Sunday?
Philip: No, I wasn't. Were you at the beach in Sunday?
Sophie: Yes, I was. Were you at the cinema on Sunday?
Philip: Yes, I was. Were you at the cinema on Saturday?
Sophie: No, I wasn't. Were you at the cinema on Saturday?
Philip: No, I wasn't. Were you in the park on Sunday?
Sophie: No, I wasn't. Were you in the park on Saturday?
Philip: Yes, I was. Were you at the beach on Saturday?
Sophie: No, I wasn't. Were you at the beach on Saturday?
Philip: Yes, I was. Oh no, you're the winner. You found all my places.

b) Mögliche Lösung

1st pair:

A: In our team, Philip was at the cinema on Sunday. He was in the park on Saturday. On Saturday, he was at the beach too.
B: In our team, Sophie was at the beach on Sunday.

Lösungen Unit 4

2nd pair…
A: In our team, Philip was in London on Saturday. He was in a café on Saturday too. Philip was at the zoo on Sunday.
B: In our team, Sophie was in London on Sunday. She was in a café on Saturday. Sophie was at the zoo on Saturday.

4.1

1b) 1: Ella's grandpa • 2: Ella's dad • 3: Ella

2 Hörtext, Track 21 und **Lösung** siehe

3a) Mögliche Lösung

Sophie: Were you at the cinema on Wednesday?
Philip: No, I wasn't. Were you at the cinema on Monday?
Sophie: Yes, I was. Were you at the cinema on Thursday?
Philip: Yes, I was. Were you at the zoo on Friday?
Sophie: No, I wasn't. Were you at the zoo on Saturday?
Philip: Yes, I was. Were you at the zoo on Wednesday?
Sophie: Yes, I was. Were you in the park on Monday?
Philip: No, I wasn't. Were you in the park on Monday?
Sophie: Yes, I was.
Philip: I'm the winner!

b)
1st pair:
A: In our team, Philip wasn't at the cinema on Wednesday. He was at the cinema on Thursday. He wasn't in the park on Tuesday. He was in the park on Monday. He wasn't at the zoo on Sunday. He was at the zoo on Saturday.
B: In our team, Sophie wasn't in the park on Sunday. She was in the park on Monday. She wasn't at the cinema on Friday. She was at the cinema on Thursday. She wasn't at the zoo on Tuesday. She was at the zoo on Wednesday.
2nd pair:
A: Philip wasn't at the café on Friday. He was at the café on Tuesday. He wasn't in London on Saturday. He was in London on Wednesday. He wasn't in town on Monday. He was in town on Friday.
B: In our team, Sophie wasn't at the café on Tuesday. She was at the café on Monday. She wasn't in London on Wednesday. She was in London on Sunday. She wasn't in town on Tuesday. She was in town on Thursday.

4.1

1b)
1: Ella's grandpa • 2: Ella's dad
Mögliche Lösung
3 On the day of the jump, this person wasn't at a lake, this person wasn't at a party, this person wasn't on a train and this person wasn't at home. (Ella's grandma)

Lösungen Unit 4

4 On the day of the jump, this person wasn't at a lake, this person wasn't on a train, this person wasn't at a party and this person wasn't on a bus. (Ella)
5 On the day of the jump, this person wasn't at home, this person wasn't at a party, this person wasn't on a bus and this person wasn't at a lake. (Ella's mum)

2 Hörtext, Track 21 siehe
1 Jenny was at the cinema.
2 Ella's father was in the garage.
3 Ella's mother was in the garden.
4 Ella's grandparents were in the attic.
5 Ella's sister was at a museum.
6 Ella was in her bedroom.

3a) Mögliche Lösung siehe

b) Mögliche Lösung siehe

4.2

1a)

b)
[d]: lived, stayed, spelled
[t]: looked, walked, helped
[ɪd]: counted, waited, wanted, tasted

c) Aussprache der past tense-Formen: siehe **b)**

2 Hörtext, Track 22
Last summer I had a holiday in southern England. I travelled from my hometown – Glasgow, Scotland – to London by train. It was my first time in London. What a great city! There's so much you can do there – too much for just two days! On my first day there, I visited Westminster Abbey, the great old church. I went on a tour of the church. I learned that it's over seven hundred years old! In the afternoon, I went to see Big Ben, the big clock tower. I listened to the bells. On the second day, I went for a walk along the River Thames and over Tower Bridge. When I was on the bridge, I went up to the high walkway and looked down onto the river and the busy streets. That was exciting! So many boats, people, cars, the black taxis, the red buses …

After two days in the big city, I was ready for my next stop: Dartmoor National Park. From London, it was over five hours on the bus! When I arrived there, I went to my hotel, where I ate a nice meal. In the evening, I watched TV. I got up very early the next morning, took some food with me and went out

Lösungen Unit 4

for a long day in the Park. I walked up and down the hills for hours. Along the way, I saw lots of Dartmoor ponies. I took a break to watch them. I tried to give them some food, but they ran away from me. Then I had a picnic lunch on a very high hill. It was so nice there that I stayed for over two hours.

On the way back to my hotel in the afternoon, I stopped and played football with a group of kids – and their dog! It was really funny, because the dog always tried to bite the ball – or my foot! We all had a lot of fun. Back at the hotel, I was so hungry and tired ... I ate a big dinner and had a nice, warm bath. Then I went to bed and slept like a baby.

At the weekend, I really wanted to have some time at the sea. I got the bus to Plymouth, the last stop on my holiday. I loved the beach. I saw a lot of crabs on the beach, and I saw seals in the harbour. One seal had a big crab in its mouth. That was a very happy seal! It was great to be at the sea. I enjoyed the sunny weather and I went swimming in the warm water. But the best thing was an ice cream shop I found. The ice cream was fantastic! I went back three more times before I left for Glasgow!

It was a great holiday. I'd like to do it again next summer!

a) 1a) • 2c) • 3b) • 4b) • 5a) • 6a)

b) Mögliche Lösung
When Tony was in London, he visited Westminster Abbey and Big Ben. On the second day he walked along the River Thames and he saw Tower Bridge. Then he took the bus to Dartmoor National Park and saw Dartmoor ponies. At the weekend he took the bus to Plymouth and went to the beach.

c) Mögliche Lösung
Dear Glenda,
How are you? I am fine. Last week I was on holiday in London and Dartmoor. I travelled to London by train. On the first day, I visited Westminster Abbey. In the afternoon, I looked at Big Ben. On the next day I walked along the River Thames and saw Tower Bridge. That was great!
On the next day I took the bus to Dartmoor National Park. I stayed in a hotel. I really liked the dinner. The next morning I went for a long walk in the Park. I saw lots of Dartmoor ponies and I had a nice picnic. Then I played football with a group of kids.
At the weekend, I took the bus to Plymouth. The ice cream at the beach was fantastic!
I want to go back next summer!
Lots of love from
Tony

4.2

1a)

win – won • have – had • come – came • go – went • see – saw

Lösungen Unit 4

b)

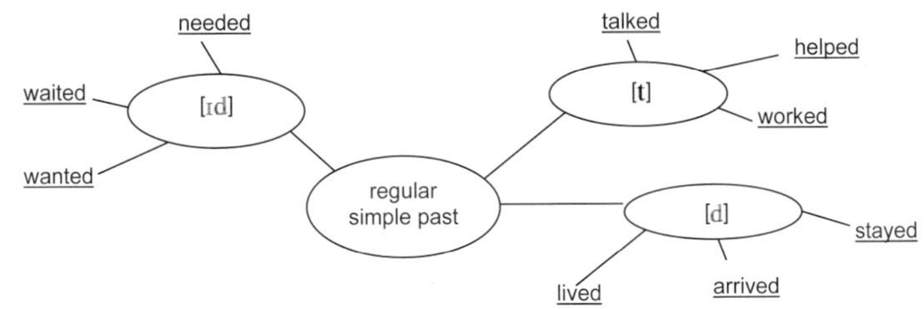

c)

A:	B:
1 Daniel called [d] his dog.	5 Sally liked [t] her new dress.
2 Bob counted [ɪd] all his pencils.	6 Claire looked [t] at the tiger.
3 Dilara spelled [d] a new word.	7 Felix waited [ɪd] for a friend.
4 Tobi walked [t] to the beach.	8 The sandwich tasted [ɪd] great.

2 Hörtext, Track 22 siehe

a) 1a) • 2b) • 3c) • 4b) • 5b) • 6a) • 7c)

b) Mögliche Lösung siehe

c) Mögliche Lösung siehe

4.2

1a) Lösung siehe

b) Lösung siehe

c) Mögliche Lösung

A:	B:
1 He counted [ɪd] from 1 to 10.	5 They wanted [ɪd] to play a game.
2 Sally walked [t] to the shop.	6 Dennis spelled [d] the word "think".
3 We liked [t] the food.	7 Sophie looked [t] into the box.
4 The sandwiches tasted [ɪd] great.	8 My parents called [d] your parents.

2a) Hörtext, Track 22 siehe
1a) • 2a) • 3c) • 4b) • 5b) • 6a) • 7a) • 8a)

Lösungen Unit 4

b) Mögliche Lösung siehe

c) Mögliche Lösung siehe

4.3

1b) 1a) • 2b) • 3a) • 4b)

2 Mögliche Lösung
A: Last Monday I didn't go to school.
B: Last Monday you didn't go to school and I didn't play volleyball.
A: Last Monday I didn't go to school, and you didn't play volleyball and last week I didn't watch TV.
B: Last Monday you didn't go to school, and I didn't play volleyball, and last week you didn't watch TV and I didn't meet Marleen.
A: Last Monday I didn't go to school, you didn't play volleyball, last week I didn't watch TV and you didn't meet Marleen, and last summer I didn't go on holiday….
B: Last Monday you didn't go to school, and I didn't play volleyball, and last week you didn't watch TV, I didn't meet Marleen, you didn't go on holiday and I ….

4.3

1b) 1c) • 2a) • 3c) • 4a)

2 Mögliche Lösung siehe

4.3

1a)
(1) No, I didn't.
(2) I can never remember names.
(3) Yes, I did.
(4) So we're going there today.
(5) I don't want to be there the whole afternoon.
(6) I know that whales are too big for this aquarium.

1b)

	Right	Wrong	Not given
1 On Saturday Lauren didn't go to the aquarium.	x		
2 On Sunday Mr Newman didn't have his computer.			x
3 On the bus, Chen didn't make a joke.		x	
4 Lauren didn't listen to Mr Newman.	x		

Lösungen Unit 4

2 Mögliche Lösung siehe

4.4

1 One half – <u>two halves</u> • one problem – <u>two problems</u> • one box – <u>three boxes</u> • one child – <u>five children</u> • one diary – <u>three diaries</u>

4.4

1 Lösung siehe

4.4

1 Mögliche Lösung
four boxes • fifteen books • fourteen parties • seven cars • nine shelves • twenty-three cakes • four children

4.5

1a)
Bild 1: The three friends ate their sandwiches and watched the Dartmoor ponies on the next hill. (ll. 15–17)
Bild 2: He took the leg of Poppy's jeans in his mouth and pulled. (ll. 22/23)
Bild 3: They saw that it had blood on its legs. (ll. 37)
Bild 4: Five minutes later, Poppy's mobile rang. (ll. 41/42)
Bild 5: The ranger and her helpers put the pony in a horse trailer. (ll. 62/63)
Bild 6: They shook hands with the kids and with Poppy's dad, and they shook Barney's paw. (ll. 63/64)

b)

1 The kids had a snack on the rocks on Rippon Tor.	line 15–17
2 The pony couldn't move and looked at the kids.	line 30
3 Poppy's dad called the ranger station.	lines 41/42
4 The ranger came with three helpers.	lines 46/47
5 The ranger had food for the pony.	lines 49/50

2b) Mögliche Lösung
A: Hi Lisa, did you have a good weekend?
B: Yes, I did. I went to the park with two friends. We had a lot of fun.
A: What did you do there?
B: We played table tennis. Where were you on Saturday?
A: On Saturday I played computer with my friend.
B: And what did you do on Sunday?
A: On Sunday we went for a walk. That was boring. In the afternoon I went swimming with my parents.

Lösungen Unit 4

4.5

1a)

Bild 1: The three friends ate their sandwiches and watched the Dartmoor ponies on the next hill. (ll. 15–17)
Bild 2: He took the leg of Poppy's jeans in his mouth and pulled. (ll. 22/23)
Bild 3: They saw that it had blood on its legs. (l. 37)
Bild 4: Five minutes later, Poppy's mobile rang. (ll. 46/47)
Bild 5: The ranger and her helpers put the pony in a horse trailer. (ll. 62/63)
Bild 6: They shook hands with the kids and with Poppy's dad, and they shook Barney's paw. (ll. 63/64)

b)

1 The kids had a snack on the rocks on Rippon Tor.	line 15–17
2 The pony couldn't move and looked at the kids.	line 30
3 The pony was small.	line 34
4 Poppy's dad called the ranger station.	lines 41/42
5 The ranger had food for the pony.	line 49
6 The kids went home in the evening.	lines 67/68

2b) Lösung siehe

4.5

1a)

Bild 1: The ranger and her helpers put the pony in a horse trailer. (ll. 62/63)
Bild 2: The three friends ate their sandwiches and watched the Dartmoor ponies on the next hill. (ll. 15–17)
Bild 3: Five minutes later, Poppy's mobile rang. (ll. 46/47)
Bild 4: They shook hands with the kids and with Poppy's dad, and they shook Barney's paw. (ll. 63/64)
Bild 5: He took the leg of Poppy's jeans in his mouth and pulled. (ll. 22/23)
Bild 6: They saw that it had blood on its legs. (l. 37)

b)

1 What did the pony do when it saw the kids?	line 30
2 Who called the ranger station for help?	line 41
3 Was the pony small?	line 34
4 Where did the kids eat their snacks?	lines 6/7
5 What did the ranger give the pony?	lines 49/50
6 How many helpers arrived with the ranger?	line 47

2b) Lösung siehe

4.6

1a)

1c) ll. 4/5 • 2b)/c) ll. 8/9 • 3c) ll. 6/7

Lösungen Unit 4

b) Mögliche Lösung

A: What do basking sharks look like?
B: They're very big. Their colour is dark and light grey.
A: What do they eat?
B: They eat very small animals from the water.
A: What can they do?
B: They can filter a lot of water.
A: Where do basking sharks live?
B: They live near the coast in Cornwall and Devon.
A: And they live there between May and October. What about their babies? Do you know how big they are?
B: Yes, I know that. They're about 1.5 metres long.
A: Thank you very much for the interview.

2

Wann findet das Shark Summer Event statt?	Am letzten Wochenende im August
Wo findet das Shark Summer Event statt?	Am North Sands Beach in Salcombe
Was kann man beim Shark Summer Event machen? Gib zwei Beispiele an.	1. Riesenhaie aus Sand bauen 2. Spiele spielen
Was kann man beim Shark Summer Event lernen? Finde eine Regel für Schwimmer, wie man sich verhalten soll, wenn man auf einen Riesenhai trifft.	Schwimmer in Gruppen sollten zusammenbleiben

4.6

1a)

1c) ll. 6/7 • 2a) ll. 10/11 • 3c) ll. 7/8 • 4a) ll. 3/4

b) Mögliche Lösung siehe

2 Mögliche Lösung

1 Am letzten Wochenende im August, am North Sands Beach in Salcombe
2 Riesenhaie aus Sand bauen, Informationen über Riesenhaie und andere Fische erhalten
3 Schwimmer in Gruppen sollten beieinander bleiben und die Haie nicht anfassen

4.6

1a)

1c) ll. 5/6 • 2b) ll. 12/13 • 3d) ll. 8/9 • 4a) ll. 3/4

b) Mögliche Lösung siehe

2 Mögliche Lösung

1. Am letzten Wochenende im August, am North Sands Beach in Salcombe
2. Riesenhaie aus Sand bauen, Informationen über Riesenhaie und andere Fische bekommen, Spiele spielen
3. Schwimmer in Gruppen sollten beieinander bleiben und die Haie nicht anfassen, beim Fotografieren keinen Blitz verwenden

Lösungen Unit 4

4.7

a)

[2] He made two journeys to Antarctica. The first one was from 1901 to 1904 on a ship called Discovery. He travelled very far south with his team and when he came back to Britain he was a hero. He wanted to go to the South Pole again and he collected money so he could go.
The second journey started in June 1910. They used ponies and dogs to pull their things, but the ponies weren't happy in the cold weather and in the end the people had to pull all the things. Only Scott and four friends walked all the way to the South Pole. When they arrived, they found out that they weren't the first people there. People from Norway had been there before! On the way back to the ship Scott and his friends died because they had no food and because of the bad weather. That's sad because they had only 20 km more to walk.

[3] Scott's dead body is still in Antarctica today. He wasn't the only man who died, but most people only remember him today.

[1] Robert Falcon Scott was a navy officer and an explorer who wanted to be the first to reach the South Pole. He was born on 6 June 1868 in Devonport, the naval part of Plymouth. He had 5 brothers and sisters.

b) – d) Individuelle Lösungen

4.7

a)

[2] He was born on 6 June 1868 in Devonport, the naval part of Plymouth. He had five brothers and sisters.

[4] The second journey started in June 1910 and they used ponies and dogs to pull their things, but the ponies weren't happy in the cold weather and in the end the people had to pull all the things. Only Scott and four friends walked all the way to the South Pole. When they arrived, they found out that they weren't the first people there. People from Norway had been there before! On the way back to the ship, Scott and his friends died because they had no food and because of the bad weather. That's sad because they had only 20 km more to walk.

[3] He made two journeys to Antarctica. The first one was from 1901 to 1904 with a ship called Discovery. He travelled very far south with his team and when he came back to Britain he was a hero. He wanted to go to the South Pole again and he collected money so he could go.

[5] Scott's dead body is still in Antarctica today. He wasn't the only man who died, but most people only remember him today.

[1] Robert Falcon Scott was a navy officer and an explorer who wanted to be the first to reach the South Pole.

b) – d) Individuelle Lösungen

Lösungen Unit 4

4.7

a)

[2] He was born on 6 June 1868 in Devonport, the naval part of Plymouth. He had five brothers and sisters.

[x] Many great sea captains came from Great Britain, and one of the most famous ones even came from the small town of Tavistock near Plymouth. Sir Francis Drake was born in 1540 and was the 12th son of his parents. People remember him today for being a pirate, a sailor and an English hero.

[4] The second journey started in June 1910. They used ponies and dogs to pull their things, but the ponies weren't happy in the cold weather and in the end the people had to pull all the things. Only Scott and four friends walked all the way to the South Pole. Wenn they arrived, they found out that they weren't the first people there. People from Norway had been there before! On the way back to the ship, Scott and his friends died because they had no food and because of the bad weather. That's sad because they had only 20 km more to walk.

[3] He made two journeys to Antarctica. The first one was from 1901 to 1904 with a ship called Discovery. He travelled very far south with his team and when he came back to Britain he was a hero. He wanted to go to the South Pole again and he collected money so he could go.

[5] Scott's dead body is still in Antarctica today. He wasn't the only man who died, but most people only remember him today.

[x] He died on board his ship, the Defiance, in 1596. He was ill and sad because his last journey was not successful. The people in South America now knew that he wanted their gold, and it was more difficult to get it. When he died, his body was thrown into the sea in Panama in a heavy box. So this famous British sailor never came home again.

[1] Robert Falcon Scott was a navy officer and an explorer who wanted to be the first to reach the South Pole.

b) – d) Individuelle Lösungen

4.8

a) A: On the ferry to Cawsand • B: A film scene • C: On the way to the cave • D: The kids' roles • E: Silly games • F: What a great day!
b) 1 apron • 2 knife • 3 blanket
c) 1 Panik • 2 Mikrofon • 3 Polizei
d) 1 sonnig • 2 felsig • 3 beeilte

4.8

a) Mögliche Lösung siehe

Lösungen Unit 4

b)

English word	Picture helps	German word helps	I know a similar word in English	German word
rocky			x	felsig
microphone		x		Mikrofon
side		x		Seite
sunny			x	sonnig
panic		x		Panik
blanket	x			Decke
police		x		Polizei
knife	x			Messer
apron	x			Schürze
hurried			x	beeilte
thanked			x	dankte
torch	x			Taschenlampe

4.8

a) **Mögliche Lösung** siehe

b)

English word	Picture helps	German word helps	I know a similar word in English	German word
rocky			x	felsig
microphone		x		Mikrofon
side		x		Seite
sunny			x	sonnig
panic		x		Panik
blanket	x			Decke
police		x		Polizei
knife	x			Messer
apron	x			Schürze
hurried			x	beeilte
thanked			x	dankte
torch	x			Taschenlampe
camerawoman			x	Kamerafrau

c) 1: kletterten • 2: Klippen • 3: Kneipe • 4: verstand • 5: gab

Lösungen Unit 5

5.1

				B					F				R	
				O					I				O	
		B	E	A	C	H			S				C	
				T				S	H				K	
S	A	N	D	C	A	S	T	L	E					
U						W	H			A				
N		C				I		I			G			
N		R		E		M			P			U		
Y		A	W	A	R	M							L	
		B		T		E								L
						R								
										S	E	A	L	
	B	O	O	K	S									
							C	O	L	D				

2 Hörtext, Track 23

Martin: Hello there. How can I help you?
1st man: Er, hi. Er … two double chocolate ice creams, please.
Martin: Anything else?
1st man: No, thank you. That's all!
Martin: That's three pounds, please.
1st man: Here's one pound … two pounds, and … hm, where's the rest of my money? Ah, there's another 50 p.
Old woman: Sorry, but... I'm looking for the toilet.
Martin: The toilet? It's at the village centre.
Old woman: And how do I get there?
Martin: Just walk along this street. It's only two minutes' walk.
Old woman: Thank you very much.
1st man: Here's the rest of the money.
Martin: Thank you, goodbye! Next please!
Emma: Hi, I, I …
Martin: Would you like to buy some ice cream?
Emma: Yes, please.
Martin: OK. What kind of ice cream would you like?
Emma: Em...
Ruben: Let me do that, Dad! Hi, I'm Ruben. What's your name?
Emma: I'm Emma.
Ruben: Hi, Emma, and you want some ice cream, don't you?
Emma: Yes … lemon, please.
Ruben: Here you are. Be careful, it's very soft.
Emma: Thank you!
Martin: Well done, Ruben!
2nd man: Oh, dear, we don't have all day! We have to catch the ferry back home to Plymouth in an hour! I don't like all this waiting! I have to get home soon.
Martin: What can I do for you?

Lösungen Unit 5

2nd man: One vanilla ice cream for my wife... and for me? Hm. Do you have apple ice cream?
Ruben: Daad …
Martin: No, sorry. We don't have apple ice cream. But we have orange ice cream. It's new this year.
2nd man: No, I don't like oranges. I can't eat them.
Martin: OK …
Ruben: Daaaad …
2nd man: Give me two vanilla ice creams, then.
Martin: That's two pounds 50. … Some people…
Ruben: Daad …
Martin: What is it, son?
Ruben: Please, Dad, can I go and play football with the others on the beach? They're playing out there in the sun and I have to work, work, work in here …
Martin: Sorry. You can't go now. I need your help. Please get me a new box of chocolate sticks.
Ruben: OK, Dad.
Young mother: Help! A crab just bit my baby's hand! He's over there. See? Right over there – his dad is holding him! Please, can you –
Martin: Don't panic! Here's some ice to cool his hand!
Young mother: Oh, thank you! Thank you very much!
Ruben: Look, Dad! Those people over there are feeding the seagulls!
Martin: Well, that isn't a good idea, is it? They shouldn't do that! Can't they see the signs? Ruben, can you go and speak to them, please?
Ruben: All right, Dad!
Martin: Who's next? What can I do for you?
Old man: Good afternoon, Martin!
Martin: Hello, George! How are you today?
Old man: Not too bad, thank you.
Martin: A small strawberry ice cream like every day?
Old man: Yes, like every day! Where is that young son of yours? Is he not working today?
Martin: Oh, yes he is. He's coming back any minute.
Old man: Poor boy. Work, work, work. And in his summer holidays ...
Martin: Don't go on like that, George! I need his help.
Ruben: Phew! Silly people! Everyone knows you shouldn't feed seagulls!
Old man: Some people feed seagulls and other people leave their dogs in hot cars. There are silly people everywhere!
Ruben: But they make the days interesting!

a) seagulls, sea

b) 1 chocolate • 2 toilet • 3 Ruben • 4 lemon • 5 his ice cream • 6 orange • 7 play football • 8 help • 9 seagulls

3 Mögliche Lösung
Ruben: Dad, I'd like to go to the beach.
Martyn: Yes, I know. I'd like to go to the beach too!
Ruben: Please, can I go now? I'd like to go swimming.
Martyn: Oh, sorry, I'd like to go swimming too. But I really need your help now.
Ruben: But I'd really like to jump into the water.

Lösungen Unit 5

Martyn: I know! And I'd like to read a book. But we have to work now. You can do these things when your mum's back, OK? I'm sorry, Ruben.

5.1

1 Lösung siehe

2a) Hörtext, Track 23 und **Lösung** siehe

b) 1 chocolate • 2 toilet • 3 Ruben • 4 lemon • 5 oranges • 6 vanilla • 7 orange • 8 help • 9 seagulls

3 Lösung siehe

5.1

1

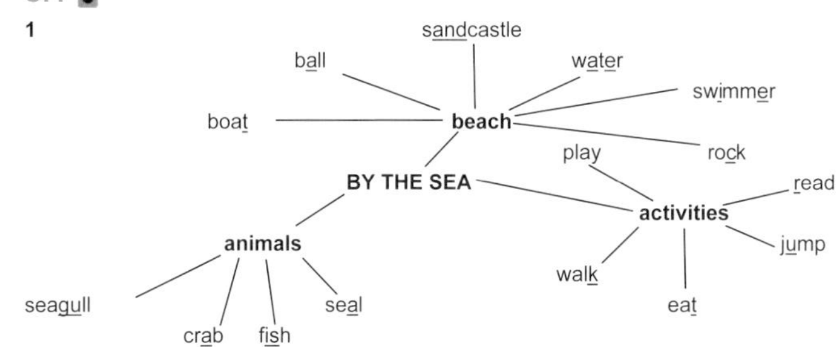

2 a) Hörtext, Track 23 und **Lösung** siehe

b) Lösung siehe

3a) Lösung siehe

b) Mögliche Lösung
A: I would like to play football.
B: You would like to play football and I would really like to read a book.
A: I would like to play football and you would like to read a book and I would like to go to the cinema.
B: You would like to play football and I would like to read a book. You would like to go to the cinema and I would like to eat a sandwich.
A: I would like to play football and you would like to read a book and I would like to go to the cinema and you would like to eat a sandwich and I would like to play hockey. …

Lösungen Unit 5

5.2

1 Hörtext, Track 24

1
Voice: … so much work … this is so dirty …

2
Voice 1: Look at that one!
Voice 2: That's a great boat!
Voice 3: Oh, I like this one!

3
Voice: Mmmm … nice … I love cheese …

4
Voice: One, two, three, four.

5
Voice: Come on, let's swim around this boat …

6
Voice: *(lacht leise in sich hinein, Buchrascheln)*

1a) • 2b) • 3a) • 4b) • 5c) • 6b)

2

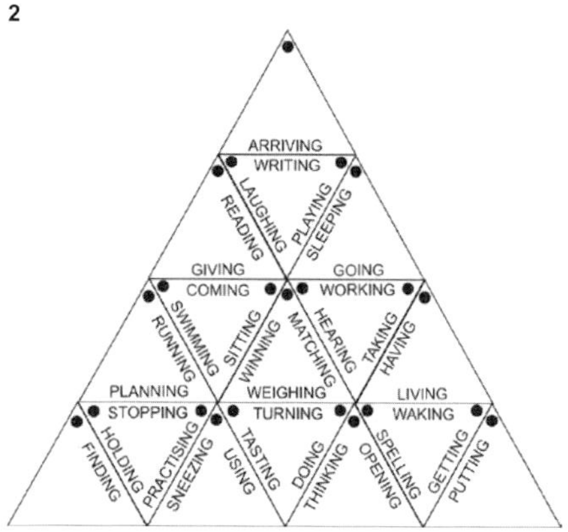

3a) 1D • 2C • 3A • 4B

b) 1 are jumping • 2 is opening • 3 is catching • 4 are cleaning

4
1 speaks, is speaking • 2 goes, is going • 3 watches, is watching • 4 eats, is eating • 5 play, aren't playing, are watching

Lösungen Unit 5

5.2

1 Hörtext, Track 24 siehe

Mögliche Lösung
1 A man is cleaning a boat. • 2 Somebody is taking pictures. • 3 A man is eating a sandwich. • 4 They are playing a game. • 5 Children are swimming in the harbour. • 6 Somebody is reading a book.

2 Lösung siehe

3a) / b) **Lösung** siehe

4
1 speaks, is singing • 2 goes, isn't going, is taking • 3 watches, isn't watching, is talking • 4 eats, is biting, eats • 5 play, aren't playing, are watching • 6 is helping, doesn't help, is cleaning, is looking

5.2

1 Hörtext, Track 24 und **mögliche Lösung** siehe

2

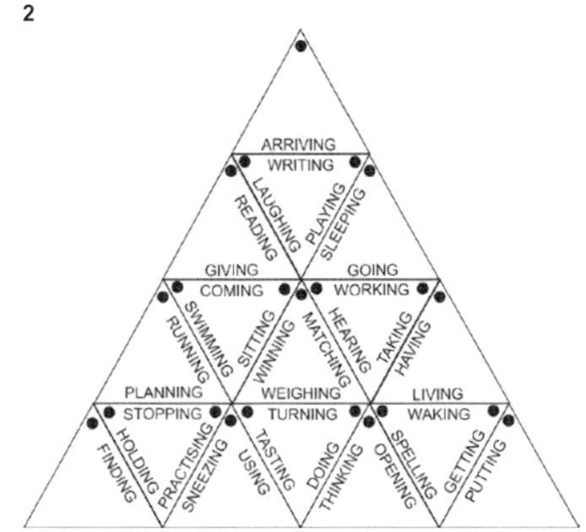

3a) / b) **Lösung** siehe

4 Mögliche Lösung
Penny Pencil is sitting in a café now. • Busy Lizzie usually eats ice cream in the morning. • Philip never watches TV in the morning. • Sophie is eating a sandwich at the moment.

Lösungen Unit 5

5.3

1a)
1 Shorty is hiding in the sea plants and Sunny and Sandy have to find him. (ll. 4–6)
2 Shorty wants to see where a group of fish is going, so he's swimming to the next big rock when a fast wave catches him. (ll. 19–21)
3 Later, when it's quiet again, Shorty swims up and tries to climb out of the pool. (ll. 36/37)
4 He looks up and suddenly two boys are looking down at him. (ll. 45/46)
5 Shorty fights, but the men catch him in the net. (l. 67)
6 Shorty gives them a little bark, and then swims away to his mum and cousins. (ll. 81–83)

b)

1	b	2	d	3	e	4	c	5	a

2 Individuelle Lösungen

5.3

1a)
1 Later, when it's quiet again, Shorty swims up and tries to climb out of the pool. (ll. 36/37)
2 Shorty wants to see where a group of fish is going, so he's swimming to the next big rock when a fast wave catches him. (ll. 19–21)
3 Shorty gives them a little bark, and then swims away to his mum and cousins. (ll. 81–83)
4 Shorty is hiding in the sea plants and Sunny and Sandy have to find him. (ll. 4–6)
5 He looks up and suddenly two boys are looking down at him. (ll. 45/46)
6 Shorty fights, but the men catch him in the net. (l. 67)

b)
letter: A number: 4 (sentence 5 in the text)
letter: B number: 2 (sentence 1 in the text)
letter: C number: 5 (sentence 4 in the text)
letter: D number: 1 (sentence 3 in the text)
letter: E number: 3 (sentence 2 in the text)

2 Individuelle Lösungen

5.3

1a) Lösung siehe

b) Mögliche Lösung
1 Shorty is excited because he is playing with his cousins.
2 Shorty is tired because the waves are too high and he can't get out of the pool.
3 Shorty is worried because he is alone and nobody hears him.
4 Shorty is happy because he can see his mum again.
5 Shorty's mum is angry because Shorty always gets into trouble.

Lösungen Unit 5

2 Individuelle Lösungen

5.4

1b)
Oma: Sieh' dir mal die süßen Schweine an. Was steht denn da über die? So eines hätte ich ja gern!
Du: Sie wiegen nur 250g, wenn sie zur Welt kommen. Wenn du möchtest, kannst du dort eins kaufen, aber es kostet £ 550!
Oma: Der Bauernhof sieht wirklich interessant aus. Ist der in der Nähe von Plymouth?
Du: Ja, Pennywell Farm ist bei Buckfastleigh. Das ist nur 30 Kilometer von Plymouth entfernt.
Oma: Gut, das ist ja nicht so weit. Wie viel Eintritt kostet das? Muss Jonathan mit seinen zweieinhalb Jahren auch zahlen?
Du: Erwachsene kosten £11,95, Kinder £9,95. Jonathan ist frei.
Oma: Das ist ja gar nicht so teuer. Wann macht der Hof denn am Abend zu?
Du: Sie haben bis 17.00 Uhr geöffnet.
Oma: Also mir gefällt die Idee, Pennywell zu besuchen. Wir können ja mal mit Mama und Papa darüber sprechen!

2 Mögliche Lösung
1 Der Preis gilt für alle.
2 Alle 30 Minuten.
3 Immer, wenn man nach Hause geht.

3 Mögliche Lösung
1 The signs tells us when they open the shop.
2 A "Kater" is a cat. The Kellers don't know where their cat is. If you see it, you can call them.
3 You don't have to do anything here. The signs says that you can't have drinks, ice cream or dogs in this shop.

5.4

1b)
Oma: Dieser Bauernhof sieht interessant aus. Aber ist das überhaupt in der Nähe von Plymouth?
Du: Pennywell Farm ist bei Buckfastleigh. Das ist nur 30 Kilometer von Plymouth entfernt.
Oma: Das geht ja. Was kosten die Karten? Muss Jonathan mit seinen zweieinhalb Jahre auch was zahlen?
Du: Erwachsene kosten £11,95, Kinder £9,95. Jonathan ist frei.
Oma: Das ist ja für einen ganzen Tag nicht so teuer. Kommen da noch zusätzliche Kosten hinzu?
Du: Die meisten Dinge, die man machen kann, sind im Eintrittspreis enthalten.
Oma: Wie lange hat die Farm denn geöffnet?
Du: Sie haben bis 17.00 Uhr geöffnet.
Oma: Was steht denn da eigentlich über diese kleinen Schweinchen? Die sind ja süß!
Du: Sie wiegen nur 250g, wenn sie zur Welt kommen. Wenn du möchtest, kannst du dort eins kaufen, aber es kostet £550!
Oma: Hört sich gut an, vielleicht können wir ja hinfahren!

Lösungen Unit 5

2 Mögliche Lösung
1 Eine Traktorfahrt kostet £1, 6 Fahrten kosten £5. Der Preis gilt für alle.
2 Die Schweine werden hier alle 30 Minuten gefüttert.
3 Man soll sich die Hände waschen, wenn man Tiere gestreichelt hat.

3 Mögliche Lösung siehe

5.4

1 b) Mögliche Lösung
… viele verschiedene Tiere ansehen und füttern oder auf ihnen reiten. Und es gibt noch etwas ganz Besonderes dort: Mini-Schweine, die bei Geburt nur 250g wiegen! Die kann man dort sogar kaufen, aber sie kosten £550. Pennywell Farm ist gar nicht so weit, von Plymouth sind es nur 30 Kilometer. Für Erwachsene kostet es £11,95 und für mich nur £9,95. Für Jonathan ist es sogar kostenlos! Und im Eintrittspreis ist dann fast alles enthalten, man muss also nicht noch mehr Geld ausgeben und kann den ganzen Tag dort bleiben. Geöffnet ist von 10:00 Uhr morgens bis 17:00 Uhr.
Ich freu mich auf euch!

2 Lösung siehe

3 Individuelle Lösungen

5.5

1 Hörtext, Track 25

Jonathan: Hello children, hello mums and dads… good morning and… oh, I'm sorry, hello grandmas, of course… good morning and welcome to Dartmoor Zoo! My name is Jonathan and I can tell you everything about our animals here. Do you like animals? … Good! Come with me. Let's begin right over there with our bears.

Jonathan: So these are our two bears. They are very big and dangerous, so you can't touch them! The one on the left is Sidney, and the smaller one is Quentin. They eat meat, fish, and also insects, worms and honey. When they aren't eating, they like to lie around in the sun. But sometimes, when it's not too hot, they can be very funny. They have big balls in their cage and they play football with them … well, not real football, but they kick the balls around. … OK, let's move on.

Jonathan: OK, children, look at this cage… can you see the big bird up there? Can you tell me what it is? Yes, you …
Child 1: It's a parrot.
Jonathan: Yes, it is, very good. This is Polly and she's from Australia. She came here as a baby when she was two years old. Now she is 21 years old and I think she likes Dartmoor Zoo.
Child 2: But she's always in a cage!
Jonathan: Yes, I know, but it's a very big cage, isn't it? And, wait a second … Listen to this … Hello, Polly, how are you?

Lösungen Unit 5

Polly: Polly, Polly, Polly. Hello, children, how are you, how are you, how are you?;
Jonathan: See … she likes it here! Come on, let's go.

Jonathan: OK, stop. Be very quiet. It's very difficult to see these animals. Let me have a look… yes… look over there, under that tree. Can you see the rocks? Behind the small rock on the right there are two ears … can you see them? … Now, watch this … and there he is … Ravi! … Shush … and here he comes. Ravi is 17 years old. For a tiger, that's very old! There are three more tigers in here, but we can't see them today. They're hiding. But I can tell you their names. There are two more boy-tigers, Khan and Sunny. They're both eight years old. And there is one girl-tiger, Sushma. She's four. They're all from India and together they eat about 20 kilograms of meat every day! So, how much meat does one tiger need for one day?
Child 3: Five kilos!
Jonathan: Correct! That's why you can't have a tiger at home – it's too expensive!

Jonathan: And here are the monkeys. A lot of people say that the monkeys are their favourite animals. Are they your favourite animals? (Yes!) Well, let me tell you a little bit about them. The monkeys you can see here are gorillas. They're very big monkeys and come from Africa. At the moment we have seven gorillas: one boy-gorilla – he's the boss – and six girl-gorillas. Sometimes we have baby gorillas here at Dartmoor Zoo. The girl-babies can stay here, but the boy-babies have to go to other zoos. There can always be only one boy-gorilla in a group.

1 Lösung 1b), c) • 2a), c) • 3a), b) • 4a), c)

2b) 2 alone • 3 bushes • 4 all over Europe, Asia and North America • 5 cities • 6 mask • 7 gardens

3
1) know, knew – e
2) catch, caught – au
3) speak, spoke – o
4) read, read – ea
5) send, sent – e
6) understand, understood – oo
7) choose, chose – o

5.5

1 Hörtext, Track 25 siehe

a)

	Where do they come from?	What do they eat?	What are their names?	How old are they?
bears		✓	✓	
parrot	✓		✓	✓
tigers	✓	✓	✓	✓
gorillas	✓			

Lösungen Unit 5

b)
bears: meat, fish, insects • Sidney and Quentin
parrot: Australia • Polly • 21 years
tigers: India • meat • Ravi, Khan, Sunny, Sushma • 17, 8 and 4 years
gorillas: Africa

2b) 2 spots • 3 right • 4 right • 5 wrong, correction: claws • 6 right • 7 wrong, correction: in North America, Europe and Asia • 8 right • 9 right

3 Lösung siehe

5.5

1 Hörtext, Track 25 siehe

a) / **b) Lösung** siehe

2b) 1 ~~stripes~~ – spots • 2 right • 3 right • 4 ~~months~~ – weeks • 5 ~~small~~ – large • 6 right

3 Lösung siehe

5.6

1a) – d) Individuelle Lösungen

2a) Mögliche Lösung
My favourite sports personality is Ellie Simmonds. She is a very small English Paralympic swimmer.
Her real name is Eleanor and her birthday is in November 1994.
I like her because she is a very good swimmer. She started swimming when she was 5 years old. When she was twelve, she went to the world championships. In 2012 she was a poster girl for the Paralympics in London and won four medals there.
She likes history, watching TV all night, dancing, riding and gymnastics.
Ellie doesn't like Maths.
It's interesting that she doesn't go to school. A teacher teaches her at home because she does a lot of swimming. She swims up to 18 hours per week. That's the end of my presentation. Do you have any questions?

b) / c) Individuelle Lösungen

5.6

1a) – d) Individuelle Lösungen

Lösungen Unit 5

2a) Mögliche Lösung
My mini-talk is about the lighthouse, Smeaton's Tower in Plymouth. It's called Smeaton's Tower because John Smeaton was the designer of this lighthouse.
I like Smeaton's Tower because it's interesting and because you get a great view from the top.

It's interesting because the original position of the lighthouse was on Eddystone Reef, a group of rocks in the sea under the water near Plymouth. But now it's on the Hoe in Plymouth.

The first day of Smeaton's Tower as a lighthouse was in October 1759. In 1877 there was a problem with the lighthouse because the sea began to break it.
In 1882 people took the top part of the tower to the Hoe in Plymouth. The city opened Smeaton's Tower for visitors on the Hoe in 1884.
You have to climb 93 steps to go up. From the top you can see Plymouth Sound and the city. That's why I like it.
Tickets are £2.60 and £1.30 for children (3–16). Thank you very much. Do you have any questions?

b) / c) Individuelle Lösungen

5.6

1a) – d) Individuelle Lösungen

2a) Mögliche Lösung
My mini-talk is about the lighthouse, Smeaton's Tower in Plymouth. It's called Smeaton's Tower because John Smeaton was the designer of this lighthouse.
I like Smeaton's Tower because it's interesting and because you get a great view from the top.

It's interesting because the original position of the lighthouse was on Eddystone Reef, a group of rocks in the sea under the water near Plymouth. But now it's on the Hoe in Plymouth.

Smeaton's Tower wasn't the first lighthouse on Eddystone Reef. It was the third. Number one and two broke. The first day of Smeaton's Tower as a lighthouse was in October 1759. 24 candles gave light. In 1877 there was a problem with the lighthouse because the sea began to break it.
In 1882 people took the top part to the Hoe in Plymouth.
The city opened Smeaton's Tower for visitors on the Hoe in 1884.
You have to climb 93 steps to go up. From the top you can see Plymouth Sound and the city. On a clear day, you can still see the rest of the old lighthouse next to the new one on Eddystone Reef.
That's why I like it.
Tickets are £2.60 and £1.30 for children (3–16). Tickets for students cost £1.60. That's the end of my mini talk. Do you have any questions?

b) / c) Individuelle Lösungen

5.7

1 1 park • 2 city • 3 bottle • 4 learn • 5 bear • 6 thought • 7 turn • 8 enough • 9 work • 10 clothes • 11 mouth

Lösungen Unit 5

2a) Mögliche Lösung
I know a man and his wife. They're very old. They're my neighbours and they're from Italy. Their children live in Mannheim. They're called Paolo and Anna. Their house is big, their car is red and their garden is small. There are many plants in the garden. Their dog always plays in the garden. There are always friends in their house because they're nice people.

b) Individuelle Lösungen

5.8

a) Scene 1: To Cawsand by ferry • Scene 3: The kids arrive at Freathy Beach • Scene 5: Hot water helps

b) Mögliche Lösung
Scene 2: Kathy and the ice cream boy • Scene 4: The lifeguard talks to people

c)
comic strip: **Individuelle Lösungen**
diary entry: **Mögliche Lösung**
Today was an interesting day! Julian, Harry and I took our bikes on the ferry to Cawsand because we wanted to go to Freathy Beach. Julian made jokes about my huge rucksack. That wasn't funny! I was a bit sad because I always carry things for him too!
Then we had an ice cream. I had my first Marula ice cream. It tasted great. On the way to Cawsand we watched a lifeboat from the RNLI. It was interesting and Harry checked the RNLI website about it later. He uses his mobile all the time!

On the beach we saw a lifeguard. She was very friendly and told us about animals and the flags on the beach. Then suddenly a boy in the water started to shout. He stood on a weever fish and the lifeguard needed hot water because that helps. I smiled and was very happy when I could help the boy with the hot water from my rucksack. No tea for us, but a happy boy in the end!

5.8

a) Scene 1: By ferry to Cawsand • Scene 3: The kids arrive at Freathy Beach • Scene 5: Hot water helps

b) / c) Mögliche Lösung siehe

5.8

a) Scene 1: The kids arrive at Cawsand • Scene 3: The kids arrive at Freathy Beach • Scene 5: The boy and the weever fish

b) Mögliche Lösung
Scene 2

RNLI training	
Kathy and the ice cream boy	✓
Eating ice cream	

Lösungen Unit 5

Scene 4

The lifeguard talks to people	✓
Asking the lifeguard questions	
Flags say: No swimming!	

c) Mögliche Lösung siehe